CHILTON'S GUIDE TO
ENGINE REPAIR and REBUILDING

Senior Vice President	Ronald A. Hoxter
Publisher and Editor-In-Chief	Kerry A. Freeman, S.A.E.
Executive Editors	Dean F. Morgantini, S.A.E., W. Calvin Settle, Jr., S.A.E.
Managing Editor	Nick D'Andrea
Special Products Manager	Ken Grabowski, A.S.E., S.A.E.
Senior Editors	Jacques Gordon, Michael L. Grady, Debra McCall, Kevin M. G. Maher, Richard J. Rivele, S.A.E., Richard T. Smith, Jim Taylor, Ron Webb
Project Managers	Martin J. Gunther, Will Kessler, A.S.E., Richard Schwartz
Production Manager	Andrea Steiger
Product Systems Manager	Robert Maxey
Director of Manufacturing	Mike D'Imperio

CHILTON BOOK COMPANY

Manufactured in USA
©1985 Chilton Book Company
ISBN 0-8019-7643-X

Tenth Printing, October 1996

ACKNOWLEDGEMENTS

Chilton Book Company acknowledges the cooperation and assistance of all those companies that supplied information and technical assistance in the preparation of this manual.

Champion Spark Plug Company,
Toledo, Ohio

Oldsmobile Division,
General Motors Corporation,
Lansing, Michigan

RADAR Corporation,
Havertown, Pennsylvania

Toyo Kogyo Ltd. (Mazda),
Hiroshima, Japan

TRW Replacement Division,
TRW Inc.,
Cleveland, Ohio

Volkswagen of America, Inc.,
Englewood Cliffs, New Jersey

Woodhill Permatex,
Cleveland, Ohio

CONTENTS

1 THEORY OF ENGINE OPERATION 1

Engine Design and Construction 1
Component Design and Construction 3
The Four Stroke Cycle 13
Air Cooled Engines 15
Diesel Engines 15
The Wankel Engine 15
The Two Stroke Engine 18

2 ENGINE DIAGNOSIS 19

Is the Engine Worth Rebuilding? 19
Does the Engine Need Rebuilding? 19
Isolating Engine Problems and
    Determining Their Severity 19
Engine Noises 20
Using Test Instruments to Determine
    Engine Condition 25
Professional Methods of Determining
    Engine Condition 31

3 TOOLS AND SUPPLIES 33

Fasteners 33
Necessary Engine Rebuilding Tools and
    How To Use Them 37
Measuring Tools 41
Other Tools and Equipment 44
Supplies 44
Servicing Your Car Safely 44

4 ENGINE REMOVAL/DISASSEMBLY/CLEANING 47

In-Car Services 47
Engine Removal—Rear Wheel Drive
    Cars 50
Engine Removal—Front Wheel Drive
    Cars 52
Engine Disassembly 53
Cleaning 56

5 CYLINDER HEAD 57

Disassembly 57
Cleaning 59
Inspection 61
Crack Repair 61
Machine Shop 62
Reconditioning 62
Cam Bearings—OHC Engines 68
Valve Train Components 68
Assembly 73

6 BLOCK INSPECTION AND RECONDITIONING 74

Cylinder Walls 74
Main Bearing Alignment 78
Deck Flatness 78
Crankshaft 78
Camshaft 80
Pistons and Connecting Rods 84
Engine Bearings 87
Oil Pump 87

7 COMPONENT INSPECTION AND REPAIR 91

Cooling System 91
Battery/Charging System 93
Starting System 95
Carburetor 103
Distributor 106

8 ENGINE ASSEMBLY 108

Gasket Sets 108
Gasket Sealers 108
Freeze Plug Installation 108
Cylinder Head Assembly 109
Engine Assembly 109

9 ENGINE INSTALLATION AND TUNE-UP 118

Installation 118
Tune-Up 119
Break In 121

10 REBUILDING VOLKSWAGEN AND PORSCHE ENGINES 122

General Information 122
Cylinder Head 122
Engine Block and Crankcase 129

11 REBUILDING DIESEL ENGINES 135

General Information 135
Troubleshooting Diesel Engine
  Performance 138
Turbochargers 139
Audi 4000/5000 142
Mercedes-Benz 156
Peugeot 165
Volvo 176
Volkswagen 187
General Motors 194

12 ROTARY ENGINE OVERHAUL 213

Disassembly 1975 and Later 213
Assembly 1975 and Later 220

INDEX 225

SAFETY NOTICE

Proper service and repair procedures are vital to the safe, reliable operation of all motor vehicles, as well as the personal safety of those performing repairs. This manual outlines procedures for servicing and repairing vehicles using safe effective methods. The procedures contain many NOTES, CAUTIONS and WARNINGS which should be followed along with standard safety procedures to eliminate the possibility of personal injury or improper service which could damage the vehicle or compromise its safety.

It is important to note that repair procedures and techniques, tools and parts for servicing motor vehicles, as well as the skill and experience of the individual performing the work vary widely. It is not possible to anticipate all of the conceivable ways or conditions under which vehicles may be serviced, or to provide cautions as to all of the possible hazards that may result. Standard and accepted safety precautions and equipment should be used when handling toxic or flammable fluids, and safety goggles or other protection should be used during cutting, grinding, chiseling, prying, or any other process that can cause material removal or projectiles.

Some procedures require the use of tools specially designed for a specific purpose. Before substituting another tool or procedure, you must be completely satisfied that neither your personal safety, nor the performance of the vehicle will be endangered.

PART NUMBERS

Part numbers listed in this book are not recommendations by Chilton for any product by brand name. They are references that can be used with interchange manuals and aftermarket supplier catalogs to locate each brand supplier's discrete part number.

THEORY OF ENGINE OPERATION

It has been said that an automobile engine is nothing more than a large heat pump, and, essentially, this is true. The basic operating principles of the modern automobile engine are fairly straightforward. The first part of this book discusses the theory and design of a typical automobile engine, followed by the design and function of the various components of the engine. The exceptions are the external engine components, such as fuel and ignition systems, which will be discussed in Chapter Seven.

ENGINE DESIGN AND CONSTRUCTION

The automobile engine is a metal block containing a series of chambers or holes. The volume of these holes varies in relation to the position of a rotating shaft. There is a port for each chamber that provides for the admission of the combustible mixture and another port for the expulsion of burned gases. The volume of the combustion chambers must be variable in order for the engine to make use of the expansion of the burning gases. This ability also enables the chamber to compress the gases before combustion and to purge itself of the burned material and refill itself with a fresh combustible charge after combustion has taken place.

The upper end of the engine block is usually an iron or aluminum alloy casting, consisting of outer walls that form hollow water jackets around the cylinder walls. The lower part of the engine block is used to provide a number of rigid mounting points (usually four, five or

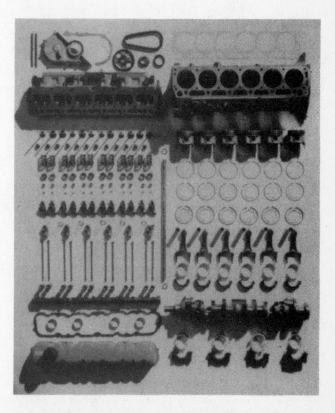

Exploded view of a typical in-line, OHV engine

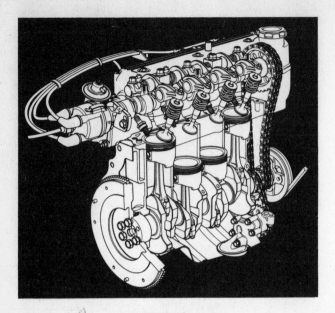

Cutaway view of a 4-cylinder OHC engine

ally, the water and oil pumps are mounted directly to the block.

The crankshaft is a long iron or steel fabrication made up of bearing points called journals. These journals turn on their own axes, allowing for the rotating motion that is necessary for engine operation. The crankshaft is also equipped with counterweighted crank throws, or crankpins, which are located several inches away from the center of the shaft, and which, of course, turn in a circle as the crankshaft turns. The crank throws are centered under the cylinders that are machined into the upper block. Pistons equipped with sealing rings are located in the cylinders and are linked to the crankpins with steel connecting rods. The rods are connected to the pistons with piston pins and bushings, and are connected to the crank throws at the lower end with insert bearings.

When the crankshaft turns, the pistons move up and down within the cylinders, and the connecting rods convert their reciprocating motion into the rotary motion of the crankshaft. A flywheel at the rear of the crankshaft provides a large, stable mass for smoothing out the rotation.

The cylinder heads form tight covers for the tops of the cylinders and contain machined chambers into which the contents of the cylinder (the fuel/air mixture) are forced as the pistons reach the upper limit of their travel. Two valves in each cylinder are opened and

seven) for the bearings that hold the crankshaft in place, and is known as the crankcase. The hollow jackets of the upper block add rigidity to the entire structure and contain the liquid coolant that carries the heat away from the cylinders and the other parts of the block.

The block also provides rigid mounts for the engine's camshaft and its drive gears or chains. Studs are installed in the top of the block to provide for the rigid mounting of the cylinder heads to the top of the block itself or the cylinder heads are held on with bolts. Usu-

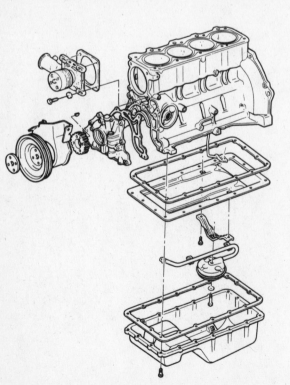

In-line engine block, oil pan and front end components

Typical piston, connecting rod, piston-rings and bearing cap (© Volkswagen of America, Inc.)

Typical OHV V-6 or V-8 engine showing camshaft, hydraulic lifters, pushrod, rocker arm and valve

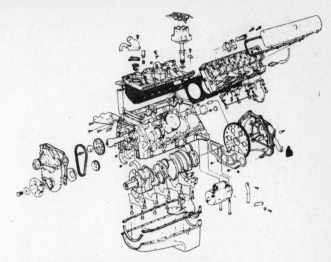

Exploded view of typical V-8, OHV engine

closed by the action of the camshaft and related valve train. The camshaft is connected to the crankshaft by a gear or a chain and is driven at one-half crankshaft speed. In other words, for every complete circle the crankshaft makes, the camshaft makes a half-circle. The camshaft may be mounted in the engine block itself, or on or in the cylinder head. It can operate the valves remotely through pushrods and rocker arms (if it is located in the engine block or in the cylinder head), or it may act on the valves in a more direct manner (if it is located on top of the cylinder head). The cylinder heads also have threaded holes for the spark plugs that screw right into the heads so that their tips protrude into the combustion chambers.

Lubricating oil for the engine is normally stored in a pan at the bottom of the engine and is force-fed to almost all parts of the engine by a gear pump.

DESIGN AND CONSTRUCTION FEATURES OF MAJOR ENGINE COMPONENTS

CYLINDER BLOCK

The block is the foundation upon which the entire engine is built. All other components are either attached to the block or located inside the block. Generally, blocks are constructed of cast iron, although there are some that are constructed of aluminum alloy. Aluminum blocks are naturally lighter than cast iron blocks, but their chief drawback is their susceptibility to overheating and warpage. Also, aluminum blocks cannot be cleaned in a hot tank because the caustic solution used will literally eat away the aluminum.

The block contains the cylinders and, in water-cooled engines, also contains the coolant passages. Cam-in-block, or overhead valve (OHV), engines mount the camshaft in the engine block itself, while overhead camshaft (OHC) engines run the camshaft in the cylinder

head. Overhead valve engines used to be the prevailing type, but the current trend is toward OHC engines.

One of the main concerns in overhauling an engine is the cylinder wall condition. Properly finished cylinder walls are probably one of the most important factors in oil control. In other words, if you rebuild an engine because it is burning oil, and it still burns oil after you finish the job, the rings are failing to seat against the cylinder walls. What constitutes a good cylinder wall finish is discussed in Chapter Eight.

CRANKSHAFT

The main function of a crankshaft is to convert the pumping or reciprocating motion of the pistons into rotary motion. The crankshaft is constructed of either cast iron or a steel alloy and is held in place by main bearing caps that contain bearing inserts, commonly called bearings. The crankshaft is equipped with a series of counterweights to provide balance and to dampen out vibration.

Cylinder block showing water jackets surrounding cylinders

FLYWHEEL

The flywheel is attached to the rear end of the crank-shaft. The function of the flywheel is twofold: it operates in conjunction with the starter motor to spin the crankshaft when the engine is started, and it acts as a large stable mass to smooth out the power impulses generated by the four-stroke cycle.

PISTONS AND CONNECTING RODS

Pistons are nothing more than large metal plugs that move up and down in the cylinders to provide the pumping motion necessary for engine operation. In order for the piston to move up and down in the cylinder, there must be a slight amount of clearance between the piston and the cylinder wall. This clearance varies, but is generally held to less than 0.004 in. (0.10mm).

Because pistons, like any other metal, will expand when they are heated, some method must be found to prevent the piston from expanding so much that it seizes in the cylinder bore. The method normally used is to build the piston in an oval instead of a round shape. As the piston heats up, the expansion of the piston skirt (the lower part of the piston) causes the piston to assume a round shape. This type of piston is called a cam-ground piston, because the machine used to manufacture the piston utilizes a cam.

The connecting rod is the device used to attach the piston to the crankshaft. The end of the connecting rod is attached to the piston is often called the rod "small end," while the end that attaches to the crank-shaft is called the rod "big end."

Connecting rods are made of steel. The rod big end is

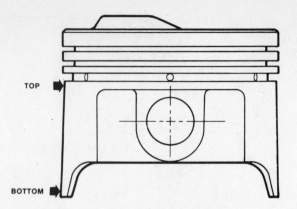

The piston skirt is actually wider at the bottom

fastened to the crank by means of a rod cap held with nuts and bolts. There are bearings in the rod cap similar to the crankshaft's main bearings, although slightly smaller. As with the main bearings, the bearing halves and the crank throw to which they are mounted receive oil through oil holes drilled in the crankshaft.

Piston pins are always used to attach the connecting rod to the piston itself. There are, however, several methods of attaching the pin to the piston. The most common is the press fit method. As the name implies, the pin is simply pressed into place and rides on bushings in the piston itself. Needless to say, the amount of pressure needed to press fit a piston pin is considerable.

Another method is to use a free-floating pin held in place with lock-rings that ride in grooves cut in the piston. With this method, the pin is not locked to either the piston or the rod and is free to turn in either part.

PISTON RINGS

Usually a piston is equipped with three piston rings that are divided into two groups: compression rings and oil control rings. The top two rings are compression rings and the bottom ring is the oil control ring.

Piston showing ring grooves and compression dome

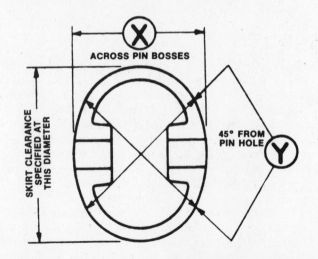

Pistons are also cam-ground in an elliptic shape

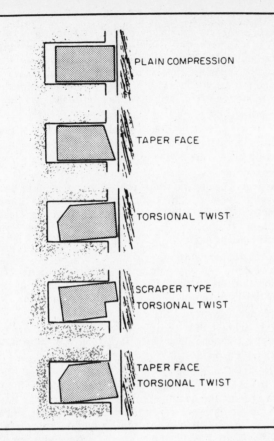

Types of piston rings

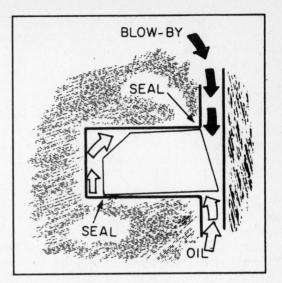

Twisting (torsional) action of certain types of piston rings

Compression Rings

The primary purpose of compression rings is to provide a seal between the piston itself and the cylinder wall. The piston must have some slight clearance in the cylinder bore in order to move up and down. Without piston rings, the fuel/air mixture would simply blow past the piston when the charge was ignited. In fact, blow-by is the term used to describe the condition that exists when rings wear out and can no longer provide an effective seal. The burned gases are blown down into the crankcase instead of exerting force on the top of the piston.

Compression rings are normally made of cast iron, with a coating of chrome plate or molybdenum (moly). Before the advent of high-compression engines, compression rings were simple plain-faced rings that made full contact with the cylinder wall along their entire width. While there are still some plain compression rings in use, the trend has been to taper face or torsional twist rings as shown. The reason for this is that it was found that a moderate taper or twist on the face of the ring improved performance by reducing contact between the ring and the cylinder wall. Instead of a relatively wide area riding on the cylinder wall, tapered ring contact is a thin line. The reasons for this relate to ring inertia.

Ring inertia is the tendency for the piston ring to keep going in the direction it is heading. As a piston reaches either top dead center (TDC) or bottom dead center (BDC) and changes direction, the rings have a tendency to keep going. They cannot, of course, but in the process of reversing direction, they exert a fair amount of force on the ring grooves. Naturally, the wider and heavier the ring, the greater the force exerted. It is easy to see why engineers prefer to reduce ring mass and ring con-

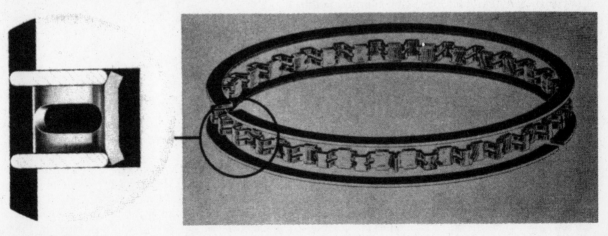

Typical oil control ring

tact area. The narrow line contact also improves ring seating and provides a better scraping action on the cylinder wall.

Oil Control Rings

An oil control ring's primary function is to control the amount of oil that remains on the cylinder walls. More than enough oil is splashed or thrown onto the cylinder walls, and most of it must be scraped off by the oil control ring.

Oil control rings are made up of three separate pieces. The two outside pieces are thin rings called rails. The inner section of the ring is called the expander ring. In the illustration, notice how the expander ring fits behind the two outer rails. The outer rails are pushed upward and outward by this action and thereby do the work of scraping the oil off the cylinder walls.

ENGINE BEARINGS

All engine bearings, no matter where they are located in an engine, perform the same functions. The primary function is to reduce friction between a moving part and a stationary part. A secondary function is to support the moving or rotating part. Bearings are made of a softer metal than the part they support and will thus wear out more quickly. However, bearings are *designed* to wear out. Obviously, when one piece of metal rubs against another piece of metal, one or both of them will wear out. It makes more sense to design a less expensive part to protect the more expensive part.

A bearing reduces friction partly because of the fact that dissimilar materials will slide against each other with somewhat less friction than similar materials. Because automotive bearings are almost always used to support a steel surface, they are generally made of materials such as lead, copper, or tin.

An engine bearing can reduce some friction by itself, but its performance is greatly improved by the presence of a lubricating agent between the bearing surface and the part it is supporting. Because of this, one of the major design considerations for engine bearings is the establishment and maintenance of an oil film between the two mating surfaces.

Engine Bearing Requirements

An engine bearing must meet a number of requirements in order to perform its job adequately, including the following.

1. Fatigue Strength or Load Strength.
   A bearing must be constructed of a material that is sufficiently strong to withstand the constant pounding of the rotating part. This is particularly true in the case of main bearings (the bearings in the block that support the crankshaft). All of the bearing materials currently in use have varying capacities to withstand these loads without self-destructing.

2. Conformability.
   A bearing must be constructed of a material sufficiently flexible to allow it to conform to the inevitable irregularities that occur between the rotating shaft and the bearing. No surface, no matter how finely finished, is perfectly smooth. Bearing material must be soft enough to conform to these minute imperfections.

3. Surface Action.
   A bearing must be able to resist seizure in the event that the bearing and the rotating part make contact while the engine is operating.

4. Embeddability.
   A bearing must be able to absorb any minute particles in the oil film that might otherwise harm the surface of the rotating part. Embeddability is closely related to conformability in that they both require a soft bearing surface.

5. Corrosion Resistance.
   A bearing must be able to resist any chemical corrosion that might occur. This corrosion can be caused by the acids that are formed during combustion.

6. Temperature Strength.
   A bearing must be able to carry its load at high engine temperatures without distorting or deteriorating under the strain.

7. Thermal Conductivity.
   A bearing must be able to absorb heat and conduct it away from the bearing surface into the bearing housing. Bearings perform better at cooler temperatures. Much of the heat generated by engine operation is removed by the oil, but a good deal remains for the bearing to cope with.

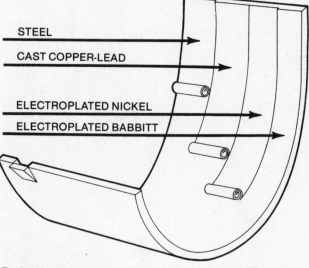

STEEL

CAST COPPER-LEAD

ELECTROPLATED NICKEL

ELECTROPLATED BABBITT

Typical bearing construction

Bearing Materials

Modern automotive bearings are generally of the multiple layer type. Some known as bimetal bearings, are constructed of two layers. The first layer is a steel backing, and the second is the bearing material. There are also trimetal bearings which, in addition to the first two layers, incorporate an overlay on the bearing material.

The most commonly used bearing surface material is babbit metal, a soft alloy composed of lead, antimony, tin, and arsenic. Babbit is widely considered an almost ideal bearing surface material.

Babbitt bearings are generally divided into two categories: conventional babbitt, and microbabbitt. They are available in either lead or tin base material. The difference is that conventional babbitt bearings have a thicker bearing surface than microbabbitt.

Conventional babbitt bearings exhibit excellent conformability, embaddability, surface action, and corrosion resistance. However, they exhibit poor fatigue strength, making them unsuitable for heavy-duty operation.

On the other hand, microbabbitt has excellent fatigue strength and corrosion resistance, but poor conformability and embeddability because of its harder bearing surface.

Another commonly used type of bearing is the sintered copper-lead bearing. A copper-lead powder is applied to a strip of steel and then heated to produce the bearing.

Cast copper-lead bearings differ in their manufacturing process, but both cast and sintered copper-lead bearings are considered heavy-duty bearings. Trimetal cast copper-lead bearings have a babbit overlay of lead, tin and copper and are especially suited for severe service applications.

The last type is the aluminum bearing. Solid aluminum bearings have been in use for a number of years. They are not actually pure aluminum, but an amalgam of 1 percent copper, 6 percent tin, and 1 percent nickel, with the balance being aluminum. Generally, this type of bearing does not have a steel back, and in most cases, a flash coating of tin is applied to the finished bearing to assist in break-in. Because solid aluminum bearings are made with fairly heavy walls, they cannot be used in engines where crankshaft diameter and housing bore diameter make the use of a thin-wall bearing mandatory.

In addition to solid aluminum bearings, there are a number of bimetal and trimetal aluminum bearings in use today. These are generally of thin-wall design. The bimetal designs are considered medium-duty bearings, while the trimetal bearings are suitable for heavy-duty operation.

Bearing Design Factors

Almost all bearings today are *insert* bearings. In other words, the bearing is manufactured as a separate piece and then inserted into the bearing housing. Very early automotive practice called for the bearing surface to be cast directly on the bearing support surface and then machined to fit. However, this type of bearing has not been in use for many years.

There are two types of insert bearings: precision bearings and resizeable, or semi-finished, bearings. The precision bearing is used to meet most automotive needs. It is manufactured to exact tolerances at the factory and is simply inserted into the bearing housing.

Resizeable bearings are manufactured with extra bearing material on the inside diameter and can be machined to the desired size at the time of assembly. This type of bearing is rarely used in normal automotive work.

There are two different configurations for normal insert bearings: full round and split. Split bearings are used when the bearing must be assembled *around* the part to be supported. Connecting rod bearings, for example, are split bearings. So are almost all main bearings. Full round bearings are used when it is possible to slide the bearing journal into place on the bearing surface. In the average automotive engine, the only full round bearings are the camshaft bearings.

In addition to straight shell insert bearings, there are thrust, or flanged bearings. As the name implies, these bearings are equipped with side flanges to control any horizontal movement in the shaft being supported. Generally, thrust bearings are used to control fore-and-aft movement, or end play, in the crankshaft. In some applications, thrust bearings are made in three pieces, with the outside pieces being known as thrust washers.

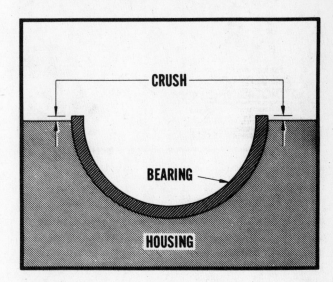

Bearing crush

BEARING CRUSH

All split bearings are designed with what is known as a *crush* factor. This simply means that each half of the bearing is slightly larger than an exact semicircle. If you snap a bearing half into the housing, you will see a slight protrusion at each end of the bearing. The parting faces extend just slightly beyond the housing seat. This slight protrusion is the crush. When both halves of the bearing are in place and the housing cap is tightened, this crush effect forces the bearing halves tightly into the housing bore. A tight fit is vital to thermal conductivity.

BEARING SPREAD

Almost all rod and main bearings are manufactured so that they are slightly greater in diameter than the diameter of the housing bore. This means that the bearing half has to be forced into place. It does not require much force, but the light pressure needed ensures that the bearing half will remain in place. Bearing spread also ensured total contact between the back of the bearing half and the housing bore.

BEARING LOCATING DEVICES

All engine bearings have some means of ensuring that they will not shift or move in the housing bore once they are installed. Most bearings utilize a bearing lug, which is simply a small projection that fits into a recess in the housing bore. Some bearings use a locating dowel in the housing bore with a mating hole in the bearing insert.

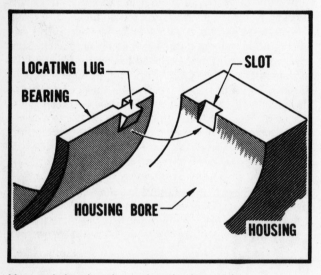

Most main bearings have a locating lug or tab

OIL HOLES

In order to function for any length of time, bearings must receive oil. Most bearings receive their oil supply through holes drilled in the crankshaft. Naturally, this means that there must be a matching hole in the bearing.

OIL GROOVES

Sometimes, a simple oil hole in the bearing insert is inadequate. In these instances, an oil groove is used. Oil grooves provide a greater flow of oil to the bearing surface than oil holes.

CAMSHAFTS

Function

The primary function of an engine camshaft is to control the entry and exit of the fuel/air mixture in relation to the position of the piston in the cylinder. In addition, it is also connected to the engine's distributor in such a way as to coordinate ignition of the compressed fuel/air charge in relationship to valve and piston position.

For each valve in the engine, there is a cam (or cam lobe) on the camshaft. The shape of the cam lobe determines the rate at which a valve opens (rate of lift) and closes, the length of time it stays open or closed (duration), and the actual distance it opens (lift). The actual shape of the cam lobes is called the cam profile. The design of cam profiles, particularly for late model emission-controlled engines, is a very complex matter and is determined by a computer.

Design Features

Camshafts are normally made of steel, either cast or forged. Until recently, camshafts were always supported by a series of insert bearings riding in bearing housings, but some cars now support the camshaft directly in the housing without using an insert bearing.

The faces of all automotive cams are ground to a specific taper. This taper is what moves the tappet or the rocker arm. In almost all cases, a gear is cut in the camshaft to drive the distributor and the oil pump. The camshaft will often have an additional lobe to drive the fuel pump, if the engine is equipped with a mechanical fuel pump.

As stated before, camshafts are geared to the crankshaft and turn at one-half crankshaft speed. The camshaft may be turned by a gear, a timing chain, or a toothed belt.

LIFTERS

Lifters are also called tappets. They are the first link in the chain that converts the camshaft's rotary motion into reciprocating motion at the valve. Not all engines use lifters. However, all overhead valve engines use them, as well as some OHC engines. Lifters can be either mechanical (solid) or hydraulic. Mechanical lifters are usually made of cast iron, and the part that contacts the cam is usually hardened. Although solid lifters have no moving parts, it is possible for them to wear out, especially if they are not kept in correct adjustment.

The major operational difference between mechanical and hydraulic lifters is that hydraulic lifters do not require periodic adjustment. They also operate with no lifter-to-rocker arm clearance and are much quieter in operation.

PUSHRODS

Pushrods are probably the simplest of all engine components. A pushrod is nothing more than a piece of tubular steel placed between the lifter and the rocker arm. Unless they are made of defective material or subjected to extreme abuse, pushrods are practically trouble-free. Like any other mechanical device, they can wear out, but it takes a lot of miles.

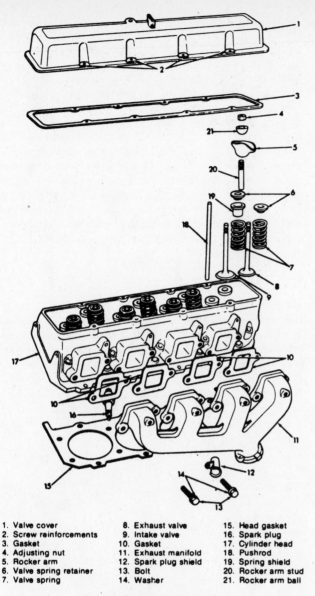

1. Valve cover
2. Screw reinforcements
3. Gasket
4. Adjusting nut
5. Rocker arm
6. Valve spring retainer
7. Valve spring
8. Exhaust valve
9. Intake valve
10. Gasket
11. Exhaust manifold
12. Spark plug shield
13. Bolt
14. Washer
15. Head gasket
16. Spark plug
17. Cylinder head
18. Pushrod
19. Spring shield
20. Rocker arm stud
21. Rocker arm ball

Typical OHV cylinder head

actuates the valves in a much more direct manner because it is located in the cylinder head (hence the name) rather than in the block. This means that a substantial portion of the valve gear (the lifters, pushrods, and, in some cases, the rocker arms) can be eliminated. (Valve gear, incidentally, is simply the term used to describe all the components between the camshaft and the valves.) The OHC design is a much simpler method of valve actuation.

Beneath the camshaft are rocker arms or lifters. In some OHC designs, the cam lobes act directly on the valves, but the rocker arm arrangement is more common. The rocker arms are generally pedestal-mounted, with their centers slightly offset from the camshaft. As the camshaft turns, the cam lobes actuate the rockers. The other end of the rocker arm bears on the tip of the valve stem, thereby moving the valve on and off its seat. This sort of direct valve actuation allows much lighter valve train reciprocating weight and, consequently, higher engine speed and greater engine efficiency. However, due mainly to reasons of cost, the design is really only practical for mass production use in in-line engines because V-type engines require a camshaft in each cylinder head. Not only are production costs much higher, but valve adjustment is twice as complex, and there are twice as many parts to wear out. For in-line engines, though, the OHC design is the simplest and most efficient. The only component that routinely wears out is the cam chain or belt. Most chains have a useful life of anywhere from 75,000 to 100,000 miles. Belts have a much shorter life but are quieter in operation and less expensive to manufacture.

CYLINDER HEADS

Cylinder heads are complex devices made up of a number of components that require some study. As mentioned earlier, the cylinder head performs two basic functions: it forms a tight cover for the top of the engine, and it controls (by means of the valves and camshaft) the admission of the fuel/air mixture. It also carries water passages for cooling.

Currently, there are two types of cylinder heads: the overhead valve (OHV) cylinder head, and the overhead camshaft (OHC) cylinder head. The primary difference between the two lies in the method of valve actuation. Overhead valve engines carry the camshaft in the engine block itself and initiate valve action by the use of pushrods and lifters. In an OHC engine, the camshaft

Typical OHC cylinder head

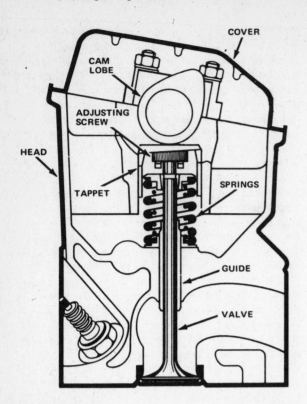

OHC valve actuation

der head via the valve seats. Because coolant circulates through the cylinder heads constantly, the heat is effectively removed. If, however, contact between the valve face and the valve seat is poor, much less heat will be transferred to the seat, and, consequently, the valve will run hotter, resulting in deterioration. To combat this problem, sodium-filled valves were introduced. Sodium is a metal at normal temperatures, but it melts at 208°F (97.7°C). The hollow stem of the valve is filled with sodium. At the high engine operating temperatures, the sodium melts. As the valve moves up and down, the sodium is constantly moving from the valve head to the valve stem. Because the lower part of the stem is enclosed in the valve guide, heat is absorbed and dissipated here. Metallurgical advances have made sodium-filled valves extremely rare, except on racing engines.

VALVE SEATS

Valve seats are a part of the cylinder head. There are two types of valve seats: the integral, in which the seat is machined into the surface of the cylinder head itself, and the insert, in which a seat insert, made of a special heat-resistant metal, is pressed into the cylinder head.

VALVES AND RELATED COMPONENTS

Automotive engine valves are the devices that ultimately control the entrance and exit of the fuel/air mixture from the cylinder. In terms of construction, they seem simple; in terms of metallurgy, they are fairly complex. Each cylinder must have at least one intake valve and one exhaust valve. It is possible to use three or four valves per cylinder (or even eight!), but generally this is only done in motorcycle or racing engines.

The relationship between the valve and the valve seat in the cylinder head is extremely important. The face of the valve must match the cylinder head seat as closely as possible. There are two reasons for this. First, combustion pressure created by ignition of the fuel/air mixture must be contained in the cylinder, and second, heat must be conducted away from the head of the valve.

Two major components control the containment of the ignited fuel/air mixture in the cylinder: the piston/ring combination and the valve. If the valve does not form a tight seal against the cylinder head seat, there will be a resultant and obvious loss of combustion chamber pressure. Without adequate pressure in the combustion chamber, an engine will function very poorly, if at all, because the gases must be contained if they are to force the piston downward.

Heat conduction is the valve's other major function. While the engine is in operation, the valves get quite hot. It is not uncommon for exhaust valve temperatures to exceed 1000°F. (538°C). Most of the accumulated heat in the head of the valve is dissipated into the cylin-

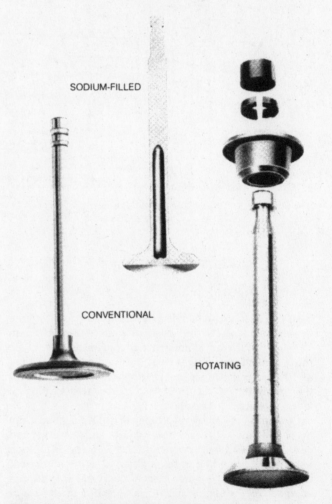

Different types of valves used in modern engines

VALVE SPRINGS

Valve springs are used to hold the valve tightly against the seat in the absence of cylinder pressure and to pull the valve back against the seat after it has been opened. Valve spring pressure also holds the retainer locks or keepers in position. In some engines, only one spring per valve is used; in others, two springs are used per valve. In this case one spring is inside the other.

VALVE SPRING RETAINERS

Valve spring retainers are also called valve spring locks, or keepers. They are used to hold the valve spring onto the end of the valve stem. The retainer is usually a large washer, and the lock is a small piece of steel that fits onto the valve stem. The valve stem is grooved to accept the lock.

VALVE SEALS

Valve seals or valve stem seals are installed on the stem of the valve to prevent oil from running down the stem and into the combustion chamber. Excessive oil in the combustion chamber will foul spark plugs and piston rings. The seals are made of either rubber or hard plastic.

Different types of valve seals. Left to right: ring, umbrella and positive. (Courtesy TRW, Inc.)

ROCKER ARMS

Rocker arms transmit the eccentric motion of the cam lobes into the vertical motion of the valve. One end of the rocker arm bears on the tip of the valve stem and the other end bears on the pushrod (in OHV engines). In some engines, the rocker arms are individually mounted on studs or pedestals, and on others, the rockers are mounted on a rail.

VALVE ROTATORS

Some engines are equipped with devices called valve rotators. Every time the valve opens or closes, the rotator turns the valve slightly to prevent valve sticking or burning.

Timing Chains, Gears, and Belts

There must be some method of driving the camshaft from the crankshaft. Depending on the engine, the camshaft may be connected to the crankshaft by gears, a timing chain, or a timing belt. Because the camshaft *always* turns at one-half crankshaft speed, the gear on

Camshaft gear (top), crankshaft gear (bottom) and timing chain used on typical V-8, OHV engine

the cam will always be twice as large as the gear on the crank. The illustrations show chains, gears, or belts. Proper alignment of the timing marks on the camshaft and crankshaft is critical to correct engine operation, and will be examined in greater detail in subsequent chapters.

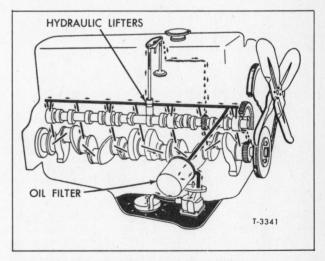

Typical engine lubrication on an in-line OHV engine

ENGINE LUBRICATION SYSTEMS

The primary purpose of an engine lubrication system is to distribute oil to all the moving parts in the engine.

Basically, the system operates in the following manner. Oil is stored in the oil pan at the bottom of the engine (it is possible to store oil in a remote location, but this is almost never done on production engines) and is picked up from the pan by the oil pump and distributed throughout the engine through passageways. The crankshaft, the camshaft, and the valve train all need oil to function.

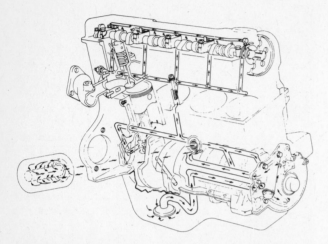

Typical engine lubrication on an in-line OHC engine

Oil Pumps

There are two common types of oil pumps on automotive engines: the gear type and the rotor type. They differ in their internal makeup, but both are usually driven by the camshaft. A look at the illustrations will reveal the essential differences. Most oil pumps are mounted in the oil pan, but some pumps are mounted away from the pan.

ENGINE-COOLING SYSTEMS

Although an engine needs a certain amount of heat to operate, an excessive amount of heat can destroy an engine. Conversely, an engine that runs too cool will run poorly. It is the job of the cooling system to regulate the dissipation of heat from the engine. The major components of the cooling system are the radiator, thermostat, water pump, fan belt, and radiator hoses. The function of some of these components is obvious, but the function of others requires explanation.

Radiators

Usually, radiators consist of a body, called a core, and two tanks. The size (capacity) of radiators is designed in conjunction with the cooling requirements of a given engine, but apart from size, tank placement, and flow of coolant, all radiators are basically alike. The tanks may be mounted on the sides of the core, or on the top and bottom.

Typical gear and rotor type oil pumps

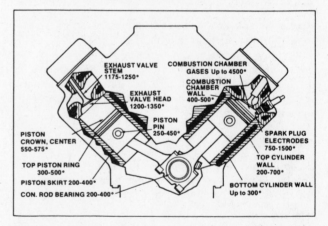

Typical operating temperatures of various internal engine parts

Thermostats

Thermostats are designed to regulate the amount of water that flows through the engine and the speed at

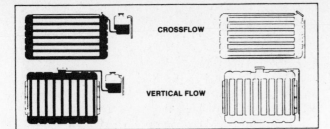

Cross-flow and vertical flow radiators

areas of the engine block—cylinders, combustion chambers, spark plugs, and valves. After circulating throughout the engine, the coolant flows into the hot side of the radiator, and then through tubes attached to cooling fins back to the cool side of the radiator. It should be noted that the "cool" side of the radiator is not particularly cool.

which it flows. Faulty thermostats are a frequent cause of engine overheating. If you are in doubt about a thermostat's performance, drop it in a pan of water, measure the temperature of the water, and watch the opening point of the thermostat as the water is heated to boiling. The temperature at which a thermostat should open fully is almost always stamped on the thermostat.

Water Pumps

Clearly, the radiator cannot cool the engine unless there is some method of transferring the coolant to and from the radiator. The water pump performs this function. Usually, the water pump and the engine cooling fan are mounted on the same shaft at the front of the engine and driven by a belt running off the crankshaft pulley, but many late model engines use an electrically operated fan, either to reduce the power drain on the engine, or because of transverse (across the car) mounting of the engine which makes fan placement at the front of the engine impractical. Pumps are generally of an impeller type. Coolant is drawn from the cool side of the radiator and circulated through passages surrounding the hot

THE FOUR-STROKE CYCLE

As noted previously, an engine is basically a large heat pump. By means of a continuous pumping action, heat is converted into energy. The heat results from the controlled burning of the compressed fuel/air mixture which expands as it burns. The pumping action results from each piston being forced down in turn in response or in reaction to the controlled explosion in each cylinder. This pumping action (reciprocating movement) is converted into rotary motion by the crankshaft. Four strokes of a single piston are required to complete one cycle of events necessary for the conversion of reciprocating motion to rotary motion. Hence, the term four-stroke cycle. The four strokes, in order of occurrence, are the intake stroke, the compression stroke, the power stroke, and the exhaust stroke.

THE INTAKE STROKE

Because the engine depends upon a combustible (burnable) mixture to provide the impetus for the pumping action of the pistons, there must be a way for this fuel to enter (and exit) the cylinder. The initial stroke of the

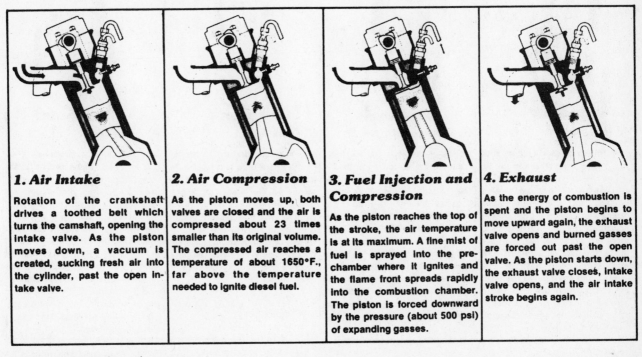

1. Air Intake

Rotation of the crankshaft drives a toothed belt which turns the camshaft, opening the intake valve. As the piston moves down, a vacuum is created, sucking fresh air into the cylinder, past the open intake valve.

2. Air Compression

As the piston moves up, both valves are closed and the air is compressed about 23 times smaller than its original volume. The compressed air reaches a temperature of about 1650°F., far above the temperature needed to ignite diesel fuel.

3. Fuel Injection and Compression

As the piston reaches the top of the stroke, the air temperature is at its maximum. A fine mist of fuel is sprayed into the prechamber where it ignites and the flame front spreads rapidly into the combustion chamber. The piston is forced downward by the pressure (about 500 psi) of expanding gasses.

4. Exhaust

As the energy of combustion is spent and the piston begins to move upward again, the exhaust valve opens and burned gasses are forced out past the open valve. As the piston starts down, the exhaust valve closes, intake valve opens, and the air intake stroke begins again.

Diesel engine 4-stroke cycle

four-stroke cycle is called the intake stroke, and it is on this stroke that the fuel/air mixture *enters* the cylinder.

The intake stroke begins with the piston near the top of its travel, the exhaust valve nearly closed and the intake valve opening rapidly. As the piston reaches the top of its travel (top dead center) and begins its descent, the exhaust valve closes fully, the intake valve reaches a fully open position, and the volume of the cylinder begins to increase as the piston moves down, creating a vacuum. As the piston descends, the fuel/air mixture is drawn from the carburetor into the cylinder via the intake manifold. (The intake manifold is simply a series of tubes that connect each cylinder with the fuel system.) The intake stroke ends with the piston having reached the bottom of its travel (bottom dead center or BDC). The cylinder is now filled with the fuel/air mixture.

THE COMPRESSION STROKE

As the piston begins to move upward, the intake valve closes and the fuel/air mixture is forced into the small chamber machined into the cylinder head. This is called the combustion chamber. Because both valves are fully closed, the fuel/air mixture has nowhere else to go and the piston compresses the mixture until it occupies roughly $1/8$ to $1/11$ the volume that it did at the time the piston began its ascent. This compression raises the temperature and pressure of the mixture, vastly increasing the force generated by the expansion of gases during the upcoming power stroke.

THE POWER STROKE

The fuel/air mixture is ignited by the spark plug just before the piston reaches the top of its stroke. Exactly how long before top dead center (TDC) the fuel/air mixture is ignited is a function of ignition timing and varies considerably with individual engines. In fact, some late model emission-controlled engines actually ignite the fuel/air mixture *after* top dead center. While this practice lowers emission levels, needless to say it does little for performance. In any event, the fuel/air mixture is ignited and burns fiercely, forcing the piston downward. Note that the mixture does *not* explode. If the mixture explodes, the result is detonation. Detonation is familiar to all as that pinging or rattling noise occasionally heard on acceleration. Detonation is extremely harmful to the engine, because it can seriously damage pistons and bearings.

In theory, all of the fuel/air mixture will have burned by the time the piston begins descending again. In reality, the best that can be hoped for is that a large portion of the fuel/air mixture is burned. Obviously, the more mixture that is burned, the greater the force exerted on the piston. The combustion process is a complex one and involves such variables as ignition timing, compression ratio, camshaft timing and cylinder head design.

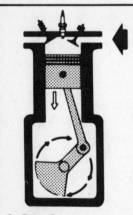

1. Intake

The intake stroke begins with the piston near the top of its travel. As the piston begins its descent, the exhaust valve closes fully, the intake valve opens and the volume of the combustion chamber begins to increase, creating a vacuum. As the piston descends, an air/fuel mixture is drawn from the carburetor into the cylinder through the intake manifold. The intake stroke ends with the intake valve closed just after the piston has begun its upstroke.

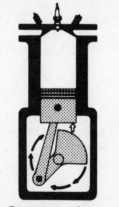

2. Compression

As the piston ascends, the fuel/air mixture is forced into the small chamber machined into the cylinder head. This compresses the mixture until it occupies ⅛th to 1/11th of the volume that it did at the time the piston began its ascent. This compression raises the temperature of the mixture and increases its pressure, increasing the force generated by the expansion of gases during the power stroke.

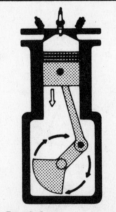

3. Ignition

The fuel/air mixture is ignited by the spark plug just before the piston reaches the top if its stroke so that a very large portion of the fuel will have burned by the time the piston begins descending again. The heat produced by combustion increases the pressure in the cylinder, forcing the piston down with great force.

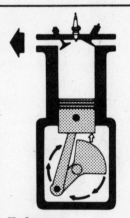

4. Exhaust

As the piston approaches the bottom of its stroke, the exhaust valve begins opening and the pressure in the cylinder begins to force the gases out around the valve. The ascent of the piston then forces nearly all the rest of the unburned gases from the cylinder. The cycle begins again as the exhaust valve closes, the intake valve opens and the piston begins descending and bringing a fresh charge of fuel and air into the combustion chamber.

4-stroke cycle (gasoline engine)

THE EXHAUST STROKE

Now that the fuel/air mixture (or most of it) is burned and the piston has been forced downward in the cylinder on the power-producing stroke, all the burned and unburned gases must be expelled from the cylinder. As the piston approaches the bottom of the power stroke, the exhaust valve begins to open, and the pressure in the cylinder begins to force the gases out around the valve. The ascent of the piston then forces all or nearly all of the rest of the gases from the cylinder. The cycle of events is now complete and begins over again immediately as the exhaust valve closes, the intake valve opens, and the piston begins descending and bringing a fresh charge of fuel and air into the combustion chamber.

AIR-COOLED ENGINES

Air-cooled engines are just that—engines cooled by the passage of air around the engine rather than by the circulation of coolant through the engine.

DIESEL ENGINES

Diesels, like gasoline-powered engines, have a crankshaft, pistons, a camshaft, valves, oil and water pumps, and so on. Also, four-stroke diesels require the same four strokes for the complete combustion cycle as a gasoline engine. The primary difference lies in how the fuel is ignited. A diesel engine does not rely on a conventional spark-type ignition to ignite the fuel mixture for the power stroke. Instead, it relies on the heat produced by compressing air in the combustion chamber to ignite the fuel and produce a power stroke. This is known as a

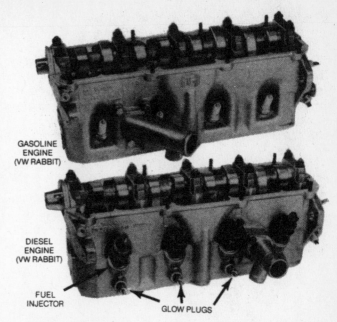

GASOLINE ENGINE (VW RABBIT)

DIESEL ENGINE (VW RABBIT)

FUEL INJECTOR

GLOW PLUGS

VW Rabbit gasoline engine cylinder head (top) and diesel engine cylinder head (bottom). Note the fuel injectors and glow plugs on the diesel engine version in place of spark plugs on the gasoline version

compression-ignition engine. No fuel enters the cylinder on the intake stroke, only air. Because only air is present, only air is compressed on the compression stroke. At the end of the compression stroke, fuel is sprayed into the combustion chamber and the mixture ignites. The fuel/air mixture ignites because of the very high combustion chamber temperatures generated by the extraordinarily high compression ratios used in diesel engines. Typically, the compression ratio used in automotive diesels run anywhere from 16:1 to 23:1. A typical spark-ignition engine has a ratio of about 8:1. (Incidentally, a spark-ignition engine that continues to run after the ignition is shut off is said to be "dieseling." It is running on combustion chamber heat alone.)

Designing an engine to ignite on its own combustion chamber heat poses certain problems. For instance, although a diesel engine has no need for a conventional ignition system, it does need what are known as "glow plugs." These superficially resemble spark plugs, but are used only to warm the combustion chamber when the engine is cold. Without these plugs, cold starting would be impossible because not even the enormously high compression ratios could warm the air sufficiently to cause ignition. Also, because fuel timing, rather than ignition timing, is critical to a diesel's operation, all diesel engines are fuel-injected rather than carbureted; the precise fuel metering necessary is not possible with a carburetor.

THE WANKEL ENGINE

Like a conventional piston engine, the Wankel engine is an internal combustion engine and operates on the four-stroke cycle. Also, it runs on gasoline and the spark is

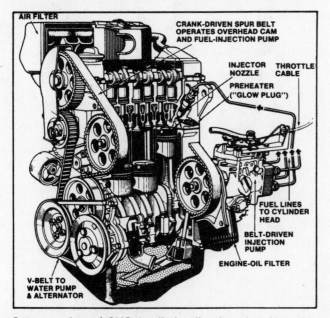

AIR FILTER

CRANK-DRIVEN SPUR BELT OPERATES OVERHEAD CAM AND FUEL-INJECTION PUMP

INJECTOR NOZZLE

THROTTLE CABLE

PREHEATER ("GLOW PLUG")

FUEL LINES TO CYLINDER HEAD

BELT-DRIVEN INJECTION PUMP

ENGINE-OIL FILTER

V-BELT TO WATER PUMP & ALTERNATOR

Cut-away view of OHC 4 cylinder diesel engine. Note the similarity in design to a comparable gasoline engine

generated by a conventional distributor-coil ignition system. However, the similarities end there.

In a Wankel engine, the cylinders are replaced by chambers, and the pistons are replaced by rotors. The chambers are not circular in section, but have a curved circumference that is identified as an *epitrochoid*. An epitrochoid is the curve described by a given point on a circle as the circle rolls around the periphery of another circle of twice the radius of the generating circle.

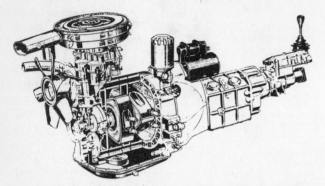

Cut-away view of Mazda's rotary engine. Note the trailing (top) and leading (bottom) spark plug for each rotor

The rotor is three-cornered, with curved sides. All three corners are in permanent contact with the epitrochoidal surface as the rotor moves around the chamber. This motion is both orbital and rotational, as the rotor is mounted off center. The crankshaft of a piston engine is replaced by a rotor shaft, and crank throws are replaced by eccentrics. Each rotor is carried on an eccentric. Any number of rotors is possible, but most engines have one or two rotors. The valves of the piston engine are replaced by ports in the Wankel engine housing. They are opened and closed by rotor motion.

One of the key differences between the Wankel rotary engine and the piston engine is in the operational cycle. In the piston engine, all the events take place at the top end of the cylinder (intake, compression, expansion, and exhaust). The events are spaced out in time only. The Wankel engine is the opposite. The events are spaced out geographically, and are taking place concurrently and continuously around the epitrochoidal surface.

The intake phase takes place in the area following the intake port and overlaps with the area used for compression. Expansion takes place in the area opposite the ports, and the exhaust phase takes place in the area preceding the exhaust port, overlapping with the latter part of the expansion phase. All three rotor faces are engaged in one of the four phases at all times.

In other words, one rotor gives three working spaces, all of which are permanently in action. As one rotor apex sweeps past the intake port, it ends the intake phase in the leading space, and starts it in the trailing space. The third space is then engaged in its expansion phase. As rotor motion continues, the leading space will approach the point of maximum compression and ignition, while the trailing space will enter the compression phase as the following apex closes it off from the intake port.

The trochoidal shape of the chamber, combined with the orbital motion of the rotor, produces large variations in displacement in the three spaces. Displacement is at its minimum on one rotor face when its opposite apex is centered on the minor axis. The minor axis is the line across the chamber where it is narrowest, and the major axis is the line across the chamber where it is widest. The major and minor axes intersect perpendicularly in the center of the chamber. Displacement is at its maximum on one rotor face when its opposite apex is

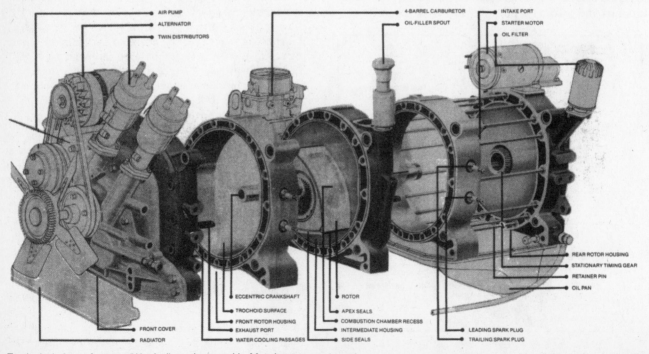

Exploded view of rotary (Wankel) engine used in Mazda cars and trucks

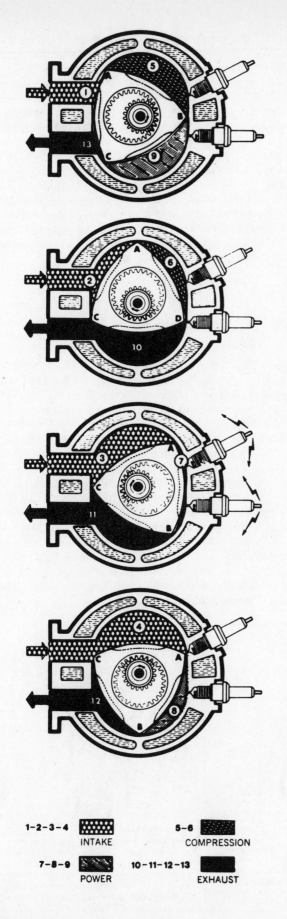

centered on the major axis. These differences in displacement produce the pumping action required for operation as an engine.

How does rotor motion turn the rotor shaft? By exerting pressure on the eccentric. Gas pressure on the rotor face during the expansion phase produces rotor motion. That means rotation. But the rotor is not free to spin—it is mounted on its eccentric, and has to follow an eccentric path. The rotor transfers the gas pressure to the eccentric. That moves the eccentric, which is part of the rotor shaft, and as the eccentric moves, it causes the shaft to rotate.

The relationship between the eccentric and the position of the rotor apices is quite intricate. Each apex is always in contact with the epitrochoidal surface, and to avoid jamming the rotor at some point, its position relative to the eccentric's position must be closely controlled. This phasing is controlled by a stationary reaction gear that meshes with an internal ring gear in the rotor. It is important to note that this gearing has nothing to do with power flow or torque transmission. It is simply a phasing gear to assure smooth rotation of the eccentric and its rotor.

The stationary reaction gear is carried by a sleeve fixed to the end cover. The gear ratio is 3:2. If the reaction gear has 36 teeth, the rotor ring gear must have 54 teeth. A corresponding 3:1 ratio exists between the rotor and the rotor shaft (eccentric bearing). When the rotor makes one revolution, the shaft makes three revolutions.

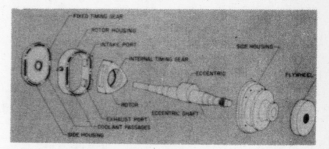

Major parts of Mazda's rotary engine

When the rotor advances 30°, the eccentric advances 90°. For each time a rotor apex passes the intake port, the main shaft starts another complete revolution. There is a power impulse for each one-third turn of each rotor. That gives one expansion (or power) phase for each main shaft revolution.

In passenger car Wankel engines, the housing is water-cooled and the rotor is oil-cooled. The coolant passages in most engines run axially, and the passages are dimensioned to provide the most cooling in the area around the spark plug(s).

The oil supply can be carried in the sump or in a separate reservoir. It is fed in through the rotor shaft, circulates inside the rotor, and returns to the reservoir (often via a heat exchanger cooled by water). The same oil that cools the rotor also lubricates the eccentric bearing.

| 1-2-3-4 | INTAKE | 5-6 | COMPRESSION |
| 7-8-9 | POWER | 10-11-12-13 | EXHAUST |

Rotary (Wankel) engine power cycle

Time-lapse photo showing the eccentric path of the rotor in a rotary engine

It is not exactly true that the rotor touches the epitrochoidal surface. The rotor comes close but is never in direct contact with the surface or the end covers. To seal the spaces for gas leaks, there is a complex seal system. Its duties are similar to those of piston rings in conventional engines.

A radial slot in each apex has a seal strip that rubs against the chamber surface. It is spring-loaded, and designed to make use of gas pressure to increase its sealing effectiveness. The rotor flanks have a seal grid intersecting with the trunnions that provide the mounting base for the apex seals. To fulfill their sealing duties, the seals must be lubricated. This oil is, of course, burned. The amounts needed are minute, and oil consumption is on a par with modern V-8 engines. The oil for the seals can be mixed with the gasoline (for instance, in the carburetor float bowl) or injected separately by a metering pump.

There are two types of intake ports: peripheral ports and side ports. Side ports produce a gas flow that tends to give higher low-range torque, while peripheral ports produce a gas flow that tends to give higher peak power. All Wankel engines have peripheral exhaust ports.

In the air-cooled Fichtel & Sachs and Outboard Marine engines, the rotor is also air-cooled. The incoming charge is led through the rotor, and thereby undergoes a preheating process. This type of engine is not considered suitable for automotive purposes.

THE TWO-STROKE CYCLE

Several cars that have been imported into the United States use two-stroke cycle engines. These operate with only a compression stroke and a power stroke. Intake of fuel/air mixture and purging of exhaust gases takes place between the power and compression strokes while the piston is near the bottom of its travel. Ports in the cylinder walls replace poppet valves located in the cylinder heads on four-stroke cycle engines. The crankcase is kept dry of oil, and the entire engine is lubricated by mixing the oil with the fuel so that a fine mist of oil covers all moving parts. The ports are designed so the fuel and air are trapped in the engine's crankcase during most of the downstroke of the piston, thus making the crankcase a compression chamber that force-feeds the combustion chambers after the ports are uncovered. The pistons serve as the valves, covering ports whenever they should be closed.

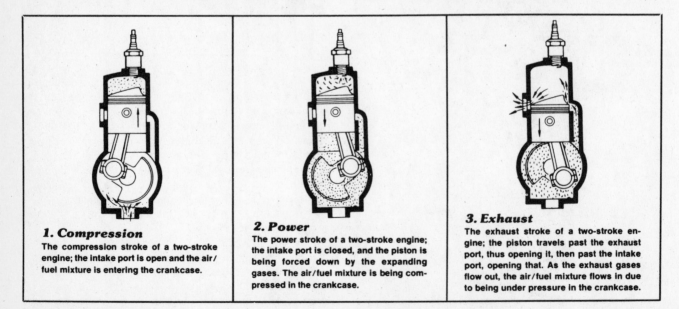

1. Compression
The compression stroke of a two-stroke engine; the intake port is open and the air/fuel mixture is entering the crankcase.

2. Power
The power stroke of a two-stroke engine; the intake port is closed, and the piston is being forced down by the expanding gases. The air/fuel mixture is being compressed in the crankcase.

3. Exhaust
The exhaust stroke of a two-stroke engine; the piston travels past the exhaust port, thus opening it, then past the intake port, opening that. As the exhaust gases flow out, the air/fuel mixture flows in due to being under pressure in the crankcase.

2 stroke engine power cycle

2

ENGINE DIAGNOSIS

IS THE ENGINE WORTH REBUILDING?

The question of whether or not an engine is worth rebuilding is largely a subjective matter and one of personal worth. Is the engine a popular one, or is it an obsolete model? Are parts available? Will it get acceptable gas mileage once it is rebuilt? Is the car it's being put into worth keeping? Would it be less expensive to buy a new engine or a used engine from a junkyard? Or would it be simpler and less expensive to buy another car? If you have considered all these matters and more and have still decided to rebuild the engine, then it is time to decide if you *need* to rebuild it.

DOES THE ENGINE NEED REBUILDING?

The usual yardstick for determining whether or not an engine needs rebuilding is mileage. As a very rough guideline, this is a useful method. Most engine rebuilders would consider 100,000 miles as the maximum mileage an average engine can go without a rebuild. The significant word here is *average*. There is absolutely no reason why a carefully maintained engine cannot easily exceed 100,000 miles and still provide excellent service. Conversely, a poorly maintained or abused engine will never get to 100,000 miles without help. This book, will omit discussion of the mileage factor and concentrate on the symptoms of an engine in trouble.

ISOLATING ENGINE PROBLEMS AND DETERMINING THEIR SEVERITY

OIL CONSUMPTION PROBLEMS

An engine's oil consumption is probably the single best indicator of the engine's internal condition. An engine's internal parts are tightly fitted, and an inevitable amount of wear occurs as the engine accumulates mileage. Because oil is used as the lubricating agent between the moving parts, excessive wear will invariably result in excessive oil consumption. The consequent question is, what constitutes excessive oil consumption? Any engine, no matter how new or how carefully built, will consume a certain amount of oil. Most rebuilders agree that an engine that uses no more than one quart of oil every 1000 miles is in good condition. This is essentially an optimum figure. An engine can use far more oil than this and still function on a daily basis. Just because the engine continues to run, however, does not mean that it does not need attention.

There are two ways an engine can lose oil. It can be leaking large amounts of oil due to a faulty gasket or external seal, or it can be losing oil "out of the tailpipe." The first condition is easy to spot. Simply park the car over a clean, dry area and let it idle for a short time. If any oil accumulates on the floor, the engine is leaking.

Once you have fixed the leak, you can look for other causes of oil consumption.

Major internal oil consumption problems are generally caused by either worn or broken piston rings or severely worn valve guides. If oil can get past the oil control ring, it will enter the combustion chamber and be burned along with the fuel/air mixture. It can also be blown right past the rings into the crankcase, creating a condition called blow-by. Before the advent of emission controls, blow-by was vented from the crankcase into the atmosphere by means of a road draft tube or a crankcase vent. Emission-controlled engines have sealed crankcase ventilation systems, and vent excessive blow-by through the PCV valve, into the air cleaner, and eventually back into the combustion chamber. Oil that is at least partially burned in the combustion chamber along with the fuel/air mixture is responsible for the blue smoke that comes from the tailpipe of an engine that needs an overhaul. When you see this kind of "death smoke" coming from an engine, you know it is time for an overhaul. Ways to isolate and determine piston ring condition will be discussed later in this chapter.

Severely worn valve guides are the other major internal cause of excessive oil consumption. A worn valve guide will allow oil to get past the valve stem and into the combustion chamber or into the exhaust port. In either case, excessive amounts of oil will be lost. Generally speaking, by the time valve guides wear to this extent, the piston rings will be badly worn as well. In fact, rings frequently wear out before valve guides, depending on how often the oil is changed. But do not mistake worn valve stem seals for worn valve guides. Worn seals will create exactly the same conditions as worn guides. So always check the seals before worrying about the guides, especially if the engine has less than 75,000 miles on it. Ways to spot worn guides and seals will be discussed later in this chapter.

Whether it is caused by worn rings, worn valve guides, or anything else, the bottom line on oil consumption is this: if the engine is using a quart or more of oil every 500 miles, it needs some very careful attention. If you discover that the cause of the oil consumption is an internal problem, it is time for a rebuild.

ENGINE NOISES AND THEIR POSSIBLE CAUSES

One of the most common reasons for rebuilding an engine is unusual or excessive engine noise. It is, however, extremely difficult to diagnose engine condition from noises alone. Engine noises *are* a useful indicator of engine condition, provided other factors, such as oil consumption, test instrument results, and performance loss problems are taken into account. This section will help you to determine which engine noises indicate serious trouble and which do not.

Accessory Noises

If the engine begins to make an unusual noise, the *very* first things to check are the engine accessories. Water pumps, alternators, air pumps, and air-conditioning compressors can all make noises that are easily mistaken for more serious engine noises. There is only one sure way to check possible accessory noises, and that is to remove the belt that drives that particular accessory. Of course, most belts drive more than one accessory, but at least you will have narrowed the field. Worn bushings or bearings in any of these accessories will often make a knocking noise that easily can be mistaken for a more serious knock. If you have removed all the belts and the noises remain, the noise is not in the accessories.

Crankshaft or Bottom End Noises

Crankshaft noises are generally much heavier in volume and tone than other engine noises. They will also occur at engine speed; that is, the noise will rise and fall in perfect synchronization with engine speed. Worn crankshaft bearings will produce an audible knock when the engine is idling, especially if the idle is uneven. If you suspect a bottom end noise, disconnect each spark plug lead one at a time and listen for changes in the noise. If the noise decreases or goes away with a particular plug disconnected, you have located the cylinder and/or bearing with the noise.

Piston Noises or Piston Slap

Piston slap is caused by excessive clearance between the piston skirt and the cylinder wall. Generally, piston slap decreases as the engine warms up and the piston expands, so listen for it when the engine is cold. As a general rule, piston slap will create a hollow dull sound, much lower in intensity than a crankshaft noise. A more accurate test of piston slap is to accelerate the engine from low speed under a load; that is, apply a lot of throttle, but do not shift to a lower gear. If the noise increases in intensity, you have located the problem.

You can also check for piston slap by disconnecting each spark plug in turn, or by retarding the spark. If all of the pistons have excessive clearance, retarding the spark should reduce the noise by reducing the load on the pistons. Disconnecting the spark plug leads will do the same thing for each individual piston. Keep in mind, however, that other engine noises are also affected by these operations.

It is sometimes possible to temporarily eliminate piston and ring noises by pouring a small amount of very heavy oil into the cylinder (through the spark plug holes). Crank the engine over (coil wire disconnected) until the oil works past the rings. Start the engine. If the noise has gone away, piston slap is the probable diagnosis.

PISTON PIN NOISES

Excessive piston pin clearance will frequently create a sharp metallic noise or clatter that is usually most audible when the engine is idling. You can check for excessive pin clearance in the same manner as you do for piston slap. Retard the spark and listen for any reduction in the noise. Generally, retarding the spark will reduce the intensity of the knock. Then short out each spark plug in turn. If the piston pin is worn, the sharp metallic knock should become *more*, not less, pronounced in that particular cylinder. Remember that the same problem exists here that exists with all other internal engine noises: if one component is worn out, other components are probably worn out and making noise as well. So keep in mind that the engine is likely making more than one noise, especially if it has well over 100,000 miles on it.

Valve Train Noises

Because the camshaft and all related valve train components operate at one-half crankshaft speed, any noise coming from the valve train will occur at one-half the frequency of other noises. If the engine is equipped with hydraulic valve lifters, a sharp rapping or clicking noise probably indicates a worn or collapsed lifter. A somewhat lighter noise may indicate excessive clearance between the rocker arm and the valve stem. Sometimes this clearance is adjustable, and sometimes it is not. (This is only the case with hydraulic lifters; solid lifter valve trains are always adjustable.) Engines equipped with solid lifters will inevitably make a certain amount of noise. It is simply a question of experience and familiarity with a particular engine that will enable you to determine whether or not the noise is excessive.

It is much easier to detect valve train noises with a mechanic's stethoscope or a large, long screwdriver. Place the tip of the screwdriver or stethoscope against the valve cover. Any valve train noises will be greatly amplified. Place the stethoscope against the valve cover at regular intervals along its length, and you may be able to isolate the noise.

If you definitely suspect a valve train noise, and have an engine that is equipped with adjustable rockers, the next step is to remove the valve cover or camshaft cover

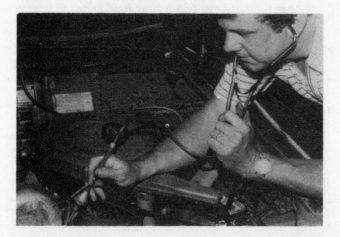

A mechanic's stethoscope is often helpful in diagnosing and pinpointing noises

and check the valve clearance. The valve clearance should be checked as a normal part of a good tune-up anyway. If you find that the valve clearances are correct and you still hear excessive valve train noises, the engine may have severely worn lifters or a worn camshaft. If you cannot adjust the excessive clearance out of the valve train, the engine's rocker arms are probably worn out. And remember that worn rockers usually mean worn valve stems or lifters as well.

Connecting Rod Bearing Noises

Connecting rod bearing noises are similar to main bearing noises in that they occur in exact synchronization with engine speed. However, they are much lighter in intensity than main bearing noises. In terms of noise intensity, they fall somewhere between valve train noises and main bearing noises. Check for rod bearing noises by shorting out each cylinder in turn and listening for a reduction in the noise. Remember, you may not be able to eliminate the noise entirely, but you will be able to reduce it considerably. A stethoscope or long screwdriver held against the block is a big help, provided you can reach it.

Detonation and Preignition

Detonation and preignition are *not* the same thing, but both can create the same symptoms, and both can severely damage an engine's performance. In addition, both can create a rapid metallic rattle, generally called "ping" or "spark knock." Preignition occurs when the combustion process is initiated by any source other than the spark plug. In other words, preignition is caused by the presence of any hot spot in the combustion chamber. A piece of glowing carbon, the sharp edge of a valve, a hot spot on the piston crown—any of these can cause premature ignition of the fuel/air mixture. As a result, the fuel/air mixture ignites while the piston is on the way up in the cylinder on the compression stroke. The resultant pressure attempts to force the piston back down while it is still trying to come up. This places a tremendous load on the piston, connecting rod, and the bearings, as well as resulting in a sharp knocking sound.

To understand detonation, you must remember that the ignition of the fuel/air mixture is *not* an explosion, but a very rapid, controlled burning process. The spark plug ignites the fuel/air mixture, which spreads very rapidly out in a specific pattern. This is what occurs during normal ignition of the fuel/air charge. Detonation occurs when part of the charge autoignites from excessive combustion chamber heat and pressure. This explosion spreads out and meets the oncoming flame front created by normal ignition. The resultant collision creates extremely high combustion chamber pressures, places great strain on the piston, connecting rod and bearings, eats away metal where it occurs, and causes a sharp knocking sound.

A number of things can cause preignition or detona-

ENGINE NOISES

Possible Cause	Correction

NOISY VALVES

Constant loud clacking, light clicking or intermittent noise indicates faulty hydraulic valve lifters (tappets), or mal-adjusted mechanical tappets.

Possible Cause	Correction
1. High or low oil level in crankcase.	Check for correct oil level.
2. Low oil pressure.	Check engine oil level.
3. Dirt in tappets.	Clean tappets.
4. Bend push rods.	Install new push rods.
5. Worn rocker arms.	Inspect oil supply to rockers.
6. Worn tappets.	Install new tappets.
7. Worn valve guides.	Replace guides if removable or ream and install new valves.
8. Excessive run-out of valve seats or valve faces.	Grind valve seats and valves.
9. Incorrect tappet lash.	Adjust to specifications.

CONNECTING ROD NOISE

A metallic knock when idling or retarding engine speed, which disappears under load indicates worn or loose connecting rod bearings. The bearing at fault can be found by shorting out the spark plugs one at a time. The noise will disappear when the cylinder with the faulty bearing is shorted out.

Possible Cause	Correction
1. Insufficient oil supply	Check engine oil level.
2. Low oil pressure.	Check engine oil level.
3. Thin or diluted oil.	Change oil to correct viscosity.
4. Excessive bearing clearance.	Measure bearings for correct clearance or failures.
5. Connecting rod journals out-of-round.	Remove crankshaft and regrind journals.
6. Misaligned connecting rods.	Remove bent connecting rods.

MAIN BEARING NOISE

A main bearing knock is more of a bump than a knock, and it can be located by shorting out the plugs near it. The noise is loudest when the engine is "lugging" (pulling hard at slow speed). The sound is heavier and more dull than a connecting rod knock.

Possible Cause	Correction
1. Insufficient oil supply.	Check engine oil level. Inspect oil pump relief valve damper and spring.
2. Low oil pressure.	Check engine oil level.
3. Thin or diluted oil.	Change the oil to correct viscosity.
4. Excessive bearing clearance.	Check the bearings for correct clearances or failures.
5. Excessive end-play.	Check thrust main bearing for wear on flanges.
6. Crankshaft journals out-of-round or worn.	Remove crankshaft and regrind journals.
7. Loose flywheel.	Tighten correctly.

OTHER ENGINE NOISES

Possible Cause	Correction
1. A sharp rap at idle speed indicates a loose piston pin. The pin at fault can be found by shorting out the spark plugs one at a time. The noise will disappear when the cylinder with the faulty pin is shorted out.	Replace piston pin.
2. A flat slap, when advancing engine speed under load, indicates a loose piston.	Replace piston and rebore cylinder block if necessary.

tion, including excessive carbon deposits or poor quality fuel. For the purposes of this book, it should be noted that excessively high combustion chamber temperatures or pressures can be detected by a careful spark plug analysis. If the engine is pinging or rattling, and you suspect it might be preignition or detonation, the first thing to do is to analyze the spark plugs and give the car a good tune-up. Pay particular attention to correct ignition timing and spark plug heat range. In the end, you may find that the car is pinging and rattling simply because of poor quality gas, a common problem today.

If you find that the car is in a good state of tune, and you have switched to high octane gas but still have rattling noises coming from the engine, the problem may be excessive carbon deposits on the valves or on the tops of the pistons. There are gasoline additives on the market that will loosen carbon deposits. It is not uncommon, however, for these additives to work all too well, loosening the carbon from the piston crown and the valves and

allowing it to bounce around in the combustion chamber. The point to remember is that carbon is a symptom of a problem rather than the problem itself. This does not mean that carbon buildup cannot cause problems, only that simply getting rid of the carbon does not necessarily solve the problem. Frequently, carbon deposits are caused by vehicle usage: if you do a lot of low-speed driving and stop-and-go driving, you stand a good chance of developing carbon deposits in the engine.

Carbon deposits can also be caused by worn piston rings or valve stems, allowing oil to get into the combustion chamber where a certain amount of it will be glazed onto the valves or the piston crown by combustion chamber heat. Carbon deposits can cause knocks that easily may be mistaken for more serious noises. The only positive way to determine whether or not the engine has developed excessive carbon deposits is to remove the cylinder heads, but that is going far beyond simple diagnosis.

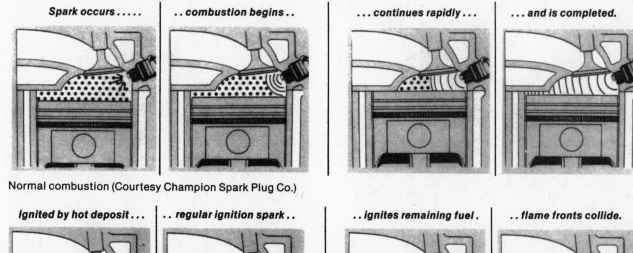

Spark occurs . . . . .   *. . combustion begins . .*   *. . . continues rapidly . . .*   *. . . and is completed.*

Normal combustion (Courtesy Champion Spark Plug Co.)

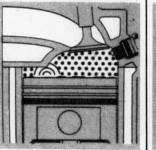  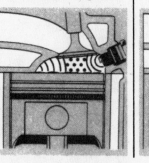 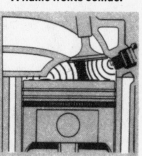

Ignited by hot deposit . . .   *. . regular ignition spark . .*   *. . ignites remaining fuel .*   *. . flame fronts collide.*

Preignition (Courtesy Champion Spark Plug Co.)

 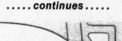  

Spark occurs . . . . .   *. . . . . continues . . . . .*   *. . . . . . detonation.*

Detonation (Courtesy Champion Spark Plug Co.)

TYPES OF PISTON DAMAGE

Damaged pistons, after thorough examination, can many times be attributed to some form of abnormal combustion.

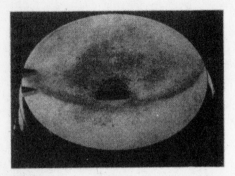

Preignition

Detonation

Severe Detonation

Scuffing (extremely high temperatures from abnormal combustion)

Mechanical damage (due to severe detonation)

Mechanical damage (possibly due to the top land contacting the cylinder). Thermal expansions from prolonged abnormally high temperatures could cause this.

PERFORMANCE LOSS PROBLEMS AND POSSIBLE CAUSES

The possible causes of poor performance are almost limitless, but this book will discuss only serious internal engine problems that will directly and obviously affect engine performance. If, for instance, the engine is using a lot more gas and showing serious power losses, it could have a blown head gasket or a warped cylinder head. If the engine is using coolant but there is no leak, that may also indicate a blown head gasket or warped head. Check for the presence of water in the oil or oil in the water. If coolant is getting into the oil supply, oil on the dipstick will be whitish and foamy. The presence of oil in the cooling system will be immediately obvious because there will be an oily scum apparent when the radiator cap is removed. Use a pressure tester to locate any coolant leaks.

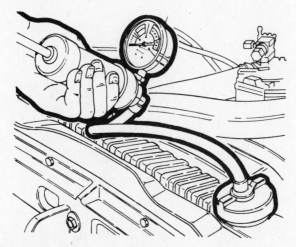
Pressure testing the cooling system

Burned valves will definitely affect an engine's performance. Keep in mind, however, that larger, more powerful engines show less effect from a burned valve than a small engine. In other words, a burned valve on a four-cylinder car is immediately apparent, but you may not notice the power loss on a large V–8. A compression test will reveal a burned valve. Vacuum gauge readings will also detect burned valves, assuming that the engine is in a good state of tune to begin with.

A worn timing chain or a worn camshaft can also drastically affect performance, yet not be noticeable when the engine is idling. Unfortunately, it is almost impossible to detect this problem with external diagnosis. A badly worn timing chain may give a late valve timing reading on the vacuum gauge, but it is entirely possible that it may not.

USING TEST INSTRUMENTS TO DETERMINE ENGINE CONDITION

Test instruments are the most reliable and accurate way to determine an engine's condition. There are three very important tests that you must perform on any engine before you decide to rebuild it. They are the vacuum gauge readings, compression test results, and spark plug analysis.

VACUUM GAUGE READINGS

A vacuum gauge simply measures how well the engine is pumping air. To use it, locate a vacuum gauge fitting on the intake manifold and connect the vacuum gauge to the fitting. Variations in atmospheric pressure will affect vacuum gauge readings, so remember that the action of the needle is more important than the actual reading.

Vacuum gauge is one of the best diagnostic tools to determine internal engine condition

COMPRESSION TESTING

A compression gauge measures the pressure within the cylinder in pounds per square inch (psi). Along with

A compression check should always be made as part of the diagnostic process

VACUUM DIAGNOSIS CHART
WHITE POINTER INDICATES STEADY HAND. BLACK POINTER INDICATES FLUCTUATING HAND.

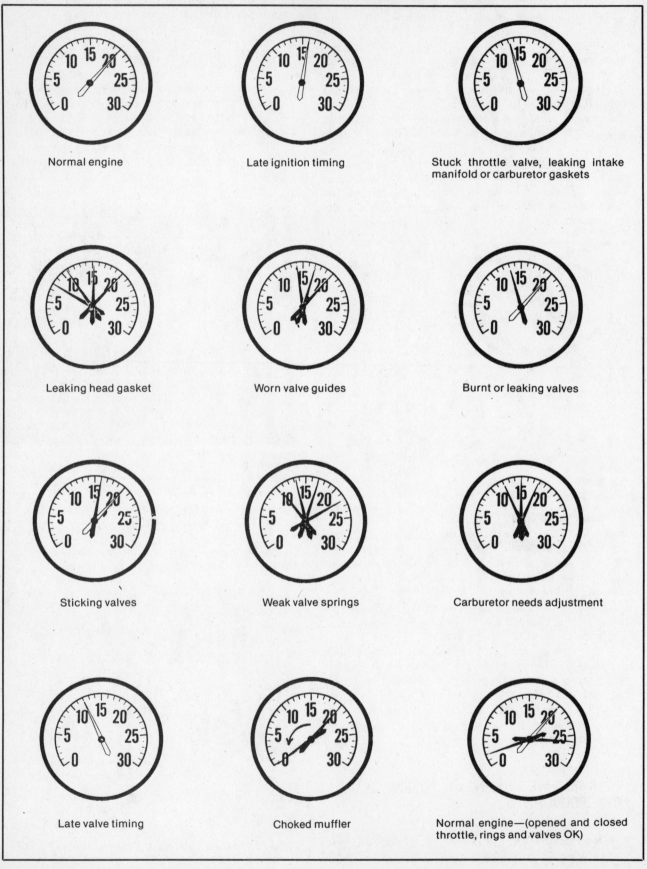

Normal engine

Late ignition timing

Stuck throttle valve, leaking intake manifold or carburetor gaskets

Leaking head gasket

Worn valve guides

Burnt or leaking valves

Sticking valves

Weak valve springs

Carburetor needs adjustment

Late valve timing

Choked muffler

Normal engine—(opened and closed throttle, rings and valves OK)

vacuum gauge readings and spark plug condition, compression test results are extremely valuable indicators of internal engine condition. Most professional mechanics will automatically check an engine's compression as the first step in a comprehensive tune-up.

There are two types of compression gauges: hand-held and screw-in. The hand-held gauge is less expensive, but more difficult to obtain an accurate reading with, because the accuracy of the reading depends on how tightly you hold the gauge in the spark plug hole. The screw-in gauge is more expensive and considerably more tedious to use, but it provides a much more accurate reading.

Gasoline Engines

1. Run the engine until it reaches operating temperature (a few minutes after the upper radiator gets hot). If the car is equipped with a temperature gauge instead of an idiot light, check the gauge before you test compression.
2. Note the position of the spark plug wires and remove the plug wires from the plugs.
3. Clean all dirt and foreign material from around the spark plugs and remove all of the plugs.
4. Block the throttle wide open.
5. Have an assistant crank the engine over while you hold the gauge. The engine should be cranked over for at least one full revolution and until you obtain the highest reading.
6. Check each cylinder in the same manner, making sure that you crank the engine an equal number of times for each cylinder.
7. Observe and write down the maximum reading for each cylinder.

VACUUM GAUGE READINGS

Diesel Engines

The procedure for testing compression on a diesel engine is essentially the same as that for a gasoline engine. However, compression must be tested with a gauge that registers at least 500 to 600 psi. A normal automotive gauge will not do the job because it will not register high enough. The diesel gauge is inserted into the glow plug hole after the glow plug is removed. Some glow plugs may require a special tool to remove them.

Rotary Engines

Because of the unique design of the rotary engine, special equipment is necessary to measure the rotary engine's compression.

Checking the Results

Now that you have all your compression readings, it is time to decide what they mean. Depending on the engine, you may observe readings anywhere from 80 to 200 or even 250 psi. Specific readings, however, are not as important as the spread between cylinders. In other words, no one cylinder should be appreciably lower than any other. All cylinder readings should be within a range of 25 percent. If, for example, the highest reading is 100 psi and the lowest is 75 psi, the compression readings are within tolerance.

If the compression readings do not fall within this range, the first thing to do is to perform a "wet test." Squirt a teaspoonful or two of heavy oil into the cylinder and give it a couple of minutes to seep down around the rings. Then recheck the compression. If the readings improve appreciably, the piston rings (at least) are worn out. You may also have worn pistons and cylinder bores.

If you discover two adjacent cylinders with low compression, chances are that there is a blown head gasket or a warped cylinder head—probably a blown gasket—between the two cylinders. Keep in mind that there should be other indications of a blown head gasket, such as water in the oil or oil in the water. It is also possible for a blown head gasket to affect only one cylinder. Run the engine to operating temperature and then carefully remove the radiator cap. If you see a lot of bubbles, that is another indication of a blown gasket.

If compression buildup is erratic on any of the cylinders, the problem could be sticky valves. Check for this condition by removing the valve or camshaft cover and connecting a timing light to the spark plug lead of the suspect cylinder. Aim the timing light at the valves of the cylinder in question. Loosen the distributor and vary the timing gradually in order to observe the motion of the valve or valves. If the valve appears to be operating erratically, it could *possibly* be sticking. Keep in mind that it is a tricky test (not to mention a messy one), and it takes a lot of experience to detect a sticky valve.

CHECKING SPARK PLUGS

The single most accurate indicator of the engine's condition is the firing end of the spark plugs. Although the spark plug has no moving parts. It is exposed to more stress than any other engine part.

It is required to deliver a high-voltage spark thousands of times a minute, at precisely timed intervals, under widely varying conditions. Because it is inside the combustion chamber, it is exposed to the corrosive effects from chemical additives in fuel and oil and to extremes of temperature and pressure. The terminal end may be as cold as ice, but the firing tip will be exposed to flame temperatures in excess of 3000°F (1650°C).

Normal

APPEARANCE

This plug is typical of one operating normally. The insulator nose varies from a light tan to grayish color with slight electrode wear. The presence of slight deposits is normal on used plugs and will have no adverse effect on engine performance. The spark plug heat range is correct for the engine and the engine is running correctly.

CAUSE

Properly running engine.

RECOMMENDATION

Before reinstalling this plug, the electrodes should be cleaned and filed square. Set the gap to specifications. If the plug has been in service for more than 10,000 to 12,000 miles, the entire set should probably be replaced with a fresh set of the same heat range.

Incorrect Heat Range

APPEARANCE

The effects of high temperature on a spark plug are indicated by a clean, white, often blistered insulator. This can also be accompanied by excessive wear of the electrode and the absence of deposits.

CAUSE

Check for the correct spark plug heat range. A plug that

is too hot for the engine can result in overheating. A car operated mostly at high speeds can require a colder plug. Also check ignition timing, cooling system level, fuel mixture and the intake manifold seal.

RECOMMENDATION

If all ignition and engine adjustments are known to be correct, and no other malfunction exists, install spark plugs one heat range colder.

Oil Deposits

APPEARANCE

The firing end of the plug is covered with a wet, oily coating.

CAUSE

The problem is poor oil control. On high-mileage engines, oil is leaking past the rings or valve guides into the combustion chamber. A common cause also is a plugged PCV valve, and a ruptured fuel pump diaphragm also can cause this condition. Oil-fouled plugs such as these are often found in new or recently overhauled engines, before normal oil control is achieved, and can be cleaned and reinstalled.

RECOMMENDATION

A hotter spark plug may temporarily relieve the problem, but the engine is probably in need of repair.

Carbon Deposits

APPEARANCE

Carbon fouling is easily identified by the presence of dry, soft, black, sooty deposits.

CAUSE

Changing the heat range can often lead to carbon fouling, as can prolonged slow, stop-and-start driving. If the heat range is correct, carbon fouling can be attributed to a rich fuel mixture, sticking choke, clogged air cleaner, worn breaker points, retarded timing, or low compression. If only one or two plugs are carbon-fouled, check for corroded or cracked wires on the affected plugs. Also look for cracks in the distributor cap between the towers of affected cylinders.

RECOMMENDATION

After the problem is corrected, these plugs can be cleaned and reinstalled if not worn severely.

Ash Deposits

APPEARANCE

Ash deposits are characterized by light brown or white colored deposits crusted on the side or center electrodes. In some cases the plug may have a rusty appearance.

CAUSE

Ash deposits are usually derived from oil or fuel additives burned during normal combustion. In this case, they are harmless, although excessive amounts can cause misfiring. If deposits are excessive in short mileage, the valve guides or seals may be worn.

Reddish or rusty deposits are caused by manganese, an anti-knock compound in unleaded gas. No engine malfunction is indicated.

RECOMMENDATION

Ash-fouled plugs can be cleaned, gapped, and reinstalled.

Splash Deposits

APPEARANCE

Splash deposits occur in varying degrees as spotty deposits on the insulator.

CAUSE

By-products of combustion have accumulated on pistons and valves because of a delayed tune-up. Following tune-up or during hard acceleration, the deposits loosen and are thrown against the hot surface of the plug. If sufficient deposits accumulate, misfiring can occur.

RECOMMENDATION

These plugs can be cleaned, gapped, and reinstalled.

High Speed Glazing

APPEARANCE

Glazing appears as a shiny coating on the plug, either yellow or tan in color.

CAUSE

During hard, fast acceleration, plug temperatures rise suddenly. Deposits from normal combustion have no chance to burn off; instead, they melt on the insulator forming an electrically conductive coating that causes misfiring.

RECOMMENDATION

Glazed plugs are not easily cleaned. They should be replaced with a fresh set of plugs of the correct heat range. If the condition recurs, using plugs with a heat range one step colder may cure the problem.

Detonation

APPEARANCE

Detonation is usually characterized by a broken plug insulator.

CAUSE

A portion of the fuel charge will begin to burn spontaneously from the increased heat following ignition. The explosion that results applies extreme pressure to engine components, frequently damaging spark plugs and pistons.

Detonation can result from overadvanced ignition timing, inferior gasoline (low octane), lean fuel/air mixture, poor carburetion, engine lugging, or an increase in compression ratio due to combustion chamber deposits or engine modification.

RECOMMENDATION

Replace the plugs after correcting the problem.

READING SPARK PLUGS

A close examination of spark plugs will provide many clues to the condition of an engine. Keeping the plugs in order according to cylinder location will make the diagnosis even more effective and accurate. The following diagrams illustrate some of the conditions that spark plugs will reveal.

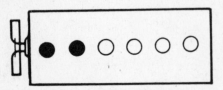

Two adjacent plugs are fouled in a 6-cylinder engine, 4-cylinder engine or either bank of a V-8. This is probably due to a blown head gasket between the two cylinders.

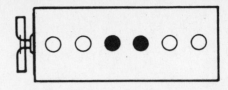

The two center plugs in a 6-cylinder engine are fouled. Raw fuel may be "boiled" out of the carburetor into the intake manifold after the engine is shut-off. Stop-start driving can also foul the center plugs, due to overly rich mixture. Proper float level, a good needle and seat or use of an insulating spacer may help this problem.

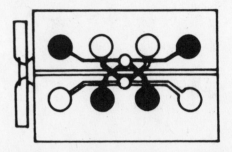

An unbalanced carburetor is indicated. Following the fuel flow on this particular design shows that the cylinders fed by the right-hand barrel are fouled from overly rich mixture, while the cylinders fed by the left-hand barrel are normal.

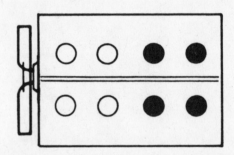

If the four rear plugs are overheated, a cooling system problem is suggested. A thorough cleaning of the cooling system may restore coolant circulation and cure the problem.

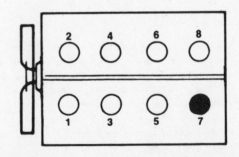

Finding one plug overheated may indicate an intake manifold leak near the affected cylinder. If the overheated plug is the second of two adjacent, consecutively firing plugs, it could be the result of ignition cross-firing. Separating the leads to these 2 plugs will eliminate cross-fire.

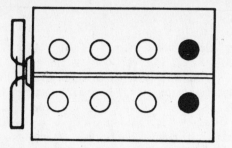

Occasionally, the 2 rear plugs in large, lightly used V-8's will become oil fouled. High oil consumption and smoky exhaust may also be noticed. It is probably due to plugged oil drain holes in the rear of the cylinder head, causing oil to be sucked in around the valve stems. This usually occurs in rear cylinders first, because the engine slants that way.

PROFESSIONAL METHODS OF DETERMINING ENGINE CONDITION

There are certain diagnostic tools that no amateur, no matter how talented, is likely to have at his disposal. Very few have a chassis dynamometer or oscilloscope. It is also unlikely that he would have a leak-down tester or a power balance tester. If you are contemplating an engine rebuild, it is money well spent to have your car checked on a professional analyzer.

An oscilloscope is usually part of a good engine performance tester and is one of the best ways to diagnose problems.

LEAK-DOWN TESTING

A leak-down tester is actually a more sophisticated type of compression tester. Instead of cranking the engine over to test its sealing capabilities, the leak-down tester is connected to the cylinder in question and pressure is applied. The tester will then monitor the cylinder's pressure. This method eliminates such variables as camshaft timing and engine cranking speed. Leak-down

Cars connected to our engine performance tester

testers are an integral part of most modern diagnostic consoles. Generally speaking, an engine that leaks 20 percent or more of its test pressure is in need of attention.

CHASSIS DYNAMOMETER

A chassis dyno is a device for measuring a car's rear wheel horsepower. Serious power losses can be easily detected by running a car on the dyno and then checking the horsepower against the advertised rear wheel horsepower. In addition, the engine's operation at various road speeds can be monitored and analyzed.

The dynamometer uses rollers to roll the car wheels

A dynamometer allows the engine to operate at speed while measuring power output.

POWER BALANCE TESTING

In power balance testing, each cylinder is shorted out in turn, and the resultant rpm drop is monitored. If any one cylinder shows a less significant drop than the others, there is a strong possibility that the particular cylinder was not contributing as much power as the others. As a general rule, all the cylinders should stay within about 40 rpm of each other. If you discover a cylinder or cylinders with little or no rpm drop, it is time to take a closer look at that cylinder.

3

TOOLS AND SUPPLIES

There is no greater mistake an engine rebuilder can make than to attempt to tackle the job without the proper tools and supplies. No amount of technical information and expertise is going to do you much good if you don't have the tools to do the job. Besides the basic hand tools an engine rebuilder must have a number of specialized tools. This chapter will discuss all the necessary (and not so necessary) tools. First will give some information about the fasteners on which these tools are used.

FASTENERS

There are a tremendous variety of fasteners used to hold the car and the engine together, but basically they fall into three categories: bolts and screws, nuts, and studs.

BOLTS AND SCREWS

Technically speaking, bolts are hexagon head or cap screws. For the purposes of this book, however, cap screws will be called bolts because that is the common terminology for them. Both bolts and screws are turned into drilled or threaded holes to fasten two parts together. Frequently, bolts require a nut on the other end, but this is not always the case. Screws seldom, if ever, require a nut on the other end.

Screws are supplied with slotted or Phillips heads. For obvious reasons, screws are not generally used where a great deal of torque is required. Most of the screws you will encounter will be used to retain components, such as the camshaft cover or other components, where strength is not a factor. Screw sizes are designated as 8–32, 10–32, or 1/4–32. The first number indicates the minor diameter, and the second number indicates the number of threads per inch.

NUTS

Nuts have only one use: they simply hold the other end of the bolt and, thereby, hold the two parts together. There are a variety of nuts used on cars, but a standard hexagon head (six-sided) nut is the most common. Castellated and slotted nuts are designed for use with a cotter pin and are usually used when it is extremely important that the nuts do not work loose (in wheel bearings, for example). Other nuts are self-locking nuts that have a slot cut in the side. When the nut is tightened, the separated sections pull together and lock the nut onto the bolt. Interference nuts have a collar of soft metal or fiber. The bolt cuts threads in the soft material which then jams in the threads and prevents the nut and bolt from working loose. A jam nut is a second hexagon nut that is used to hold the first nut in place. They are usually found where some type of adjustment is needed, valve trains, for instance. Palnuts are single-

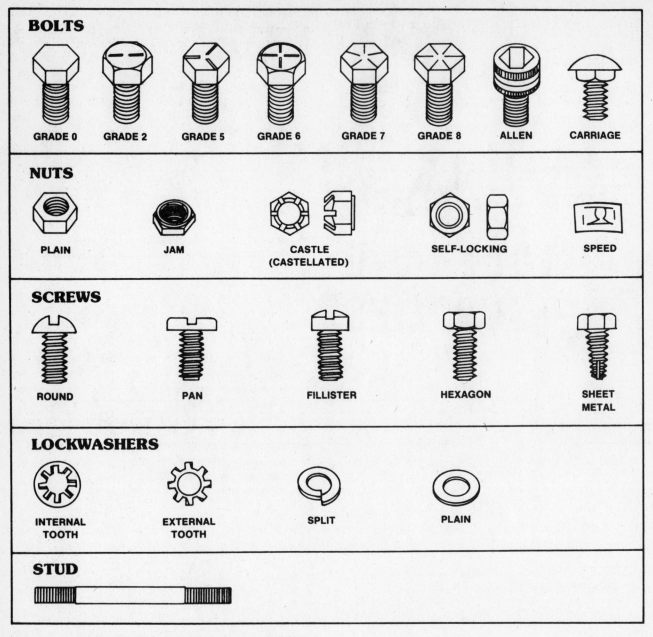

Various types of fasteners found in automotive applications

thread nuts that provide some locking action when they have been turned down on the nut. Speed nuts are simply rectangular bits of sheet metal that are pushed down over a bolt, screw, or stud to provide locking action.

STUDS

Studs are simply pieces of threaded rod. They are similar to bolts and screws in their thread configuration, but they have no heads. One end is turned into a threaded hole and the other end is generally secured by same type of nut. Unless the nut is self-locking, a lockwasher or jam nut is generally used underneath it.

LOCKWASHERS

Lockwashers are a form of washer. They may be either split or toothed, and they are always installed between a nut or screwhead and the actual part being held. The split washer is crushed flat and locks the nut in place by spring tension. The toothed washer provides many edges to improve the locking effect and is usually used on smaller bolts and screws.

SCREW AND BOLT TERMINOLOGY

Bolts and screws are identified by type, major diameter,

minor diameter, pitch or threads per inch, class, length, thread length, and the size of the wrench required.

Major Diameter

This is the widest diameter of the bolt as measured from the top of the threads on one side to the top of the threads on the other side.

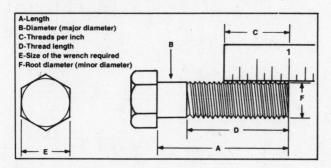

A-Length
B-Diameter (major diameter)
C-Threads per inch
D-Thread length
E-Size of the wrench required
F-Root diameter (minor diameter)

Major fastener dimensions

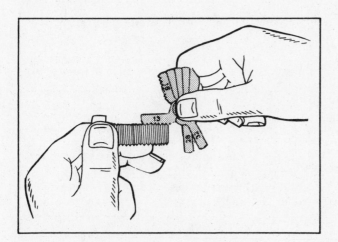

A thread gauge will quickly identify the thread size

Minor Diameter

This is the diameter obtained by measuring from the bottom of the threads on one side of the bolt to the bottom of the threads on the other side. In other words, it is the diameter of the bolt if it does not have any threads.

Pitch or Threads per Inch

Thread pitch is the distance between the top of one thread to the top of the next. It is simply the distance between one thread and the next. There are two types of threads in general use today. Unified National Coarse thread, and Unified National Fine. These are usually known simply as either fine or coarse thread. Anyone who has been working on cars for any length of time can tell the difference between the two simply by looking at the screw, bolt, or nut. The only truly accurate

way to determine thread pitch is to use a thread pitch gauge. There are some general rules to remember, however. Coarse thread screws and bolts are used frequently when they are being threaded into aluminum or cast iron because the finer threads tend to strip more easily in these materials. Also, as a bolt or screw's diameter increases, thread pitch becomes greater.

Thread Class

Thread class is a measure of the operating clearance between the internal nut threads and the external threads of the bolt. There are three classes of fit, 1, 2, or 3. In addition, there are letter designations to designate either internal (class A) or external (class B) threads.

Class 1 threads are a relatively loose fit and are used when ease of assembly and disassembly are of paramount importance. Class 2 bolts are most commonly encountered in automotive applications and give an accurate, but not an overly tight, fit. Class 3 threads are used when utmost accuracy is needed. You might find a class 3 bolt and nut combination on an airplane, but you won't encounter them very often on a car.

Length and Thread Length

Screw length is the length of the bolt or screw from the bottom of the head to the bottom of the bolt or screw. Thread length is exactly that, the length of the threads. The illustrations show this in greater detail.

Types or Grades of Bolts and Screws

The tensile strength of bolts and screws varies widely. Standards for these fasteners have been established by the Society of Automotive Engineers (SAE). Distinctive markings on the head of the bolt will identify its tensile strength. These outward radiating lines are normally called points. A bolt with no points on the head is a grade 1 or a grade 2 bolt. This type of bolt is suitable for applications in which only a low-strength bolt is necessary. On the other hand, a grade 5 bolt is found in a number of automotive applications and has double the

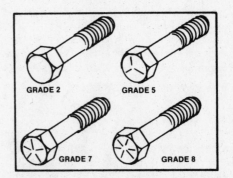

GRADE 2   GRADE 5

GRADE 7   GRADE 8

Markings on SAE bolts indicate the relative strength of the bolt tensile strength of a grade 2 bolt. A grade 5 bolt will have three embossed lines or points on the head. Grade 8 bolts are the best and are frequently called aircraft grade bolts. Grade 8 bolts have six points on the head.

METRIC BOLTS

While metric bolts may seem to be the same as their SAE counterparts, they definitely are not. The pitch on a metric bolt is different from that of an SAE bolt. It is entirely possible to start a metric bolt into a hole with SAE threads and run it down a few turns. Then it is going to bind. Recognizing the problem at this point is not going to do much good. It is also possible to run a metric nut down on an SAE bolt and find that it is too loose to provide sufficient strength.

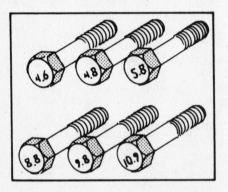

Metric bolts are marked with numbers that indicate the relative strength of the bolt. These numbers have nothing to do with the size of the bolt.

Metric bolts are marked in a manner different from that of SAE bolts. Most metric bolts have a number stamped on the head. This metric grade marking won't be an even number, but something like 4.6 or 10.9. The number indicates the relative strength of the bolt. The higher the number, the greater the strength of the bolt. Some metric bolts are also marked with a single-digit number to indicate the bolt strength. Metric bolt sizes are also identified in a manner different from that of SAE fasteners. If, for example, a metric bolt were designated 14 × 2, that would mean that the major diameter is 14 mm (.56 in.), and that the thread pitch is 2 mm (.08 in.). More important, metric bolts are not classified by number of threads per inch, but by the distance between the threads, and the distance between threads does not quite correspond to number of threads per inch. For example, 2 mm between threads is about 12.7 threads per inch.

Whitworth Bolts

Unless you own an earlier British automobile, you won't have to worry about Whitworth nuts and bolts. The British used the Whitworth thread on automobiles and motorcycles for years (until about the mid-60s) before switching to the metric system.

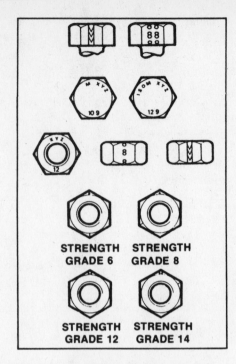

ISO markings indicate the relative strength of nuts

REPAIRING DAMAGED THREADS

Several methods of repairing damaged threads are available. Heli-Coil® (shown here), Keenserts® and Microdot® are among the most widely used. All involve the same principle—drilling out stripped threads, tapping the hole, and installing a prewound insert—making welding, plugging, and oversize fasteners unnecessary.

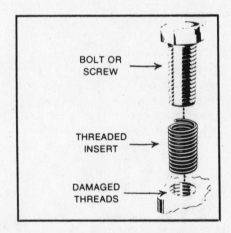

Damaged bolt holes can be repaired with thread repair inserts

Two types of thread repair inserts are usually supplied: a standard type for most Inch Coarse, Inch Fine, Metric Coarse, and Metric Fine thread sizes and a spark plug type to fit most spark plug port sizes. Consult

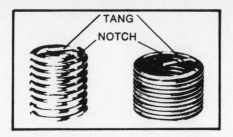

Standard thread repair insert (left) and spark plug thread insert (right)

the individual manufacturer's catalog to determine exact applications. Typical thread repair kits will contain a selection of prewound threaded inserts, a tap (corresponding to the outside diameter threads of the insert), and an installation tool. Spark plug inserts usually differ because they require a tap equipped with pilot threads and a combined reamer—tap section. Most manufacturers also supply blister-packed thread repair inserts separately, in addition to a master kit containing a variety of taps and inserts plus installation tools.

Before effecting a repair to a threaded hole, remove any snapped, broken, or damaged bolts or studs. Penetrating oil can be used to free frozen threads; the offending item can be removed with locking pliers or with a screw or stud extractor. After the hole is clear, the thread can be repaired, as follows:

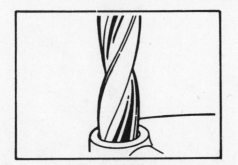

Drill out the damaged threads with specified drill. Drill completely through the hole or to the bottom of a blind hole.

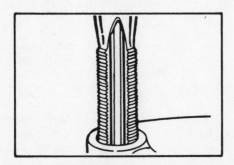

With the tap supplied, tap the hole to receive the thread insert. Keep the tap well oiled and back it out frequently to avoid clogging the threads.

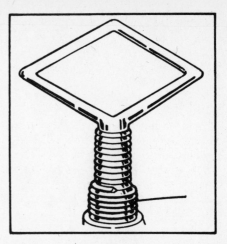

Screw the threaded insert onto the installation tool until the tang engages the slot. Screw the insert into the tapped hole until it is ¼ – ½ turn below the top surface. After installation break off the tang with a hammer and punch.

NECESSARY ENGINE REBUILDING TOOLS AND HOW TO USE THEM

HAND TOOLS

Anyone who is contemplating rebuilding an engine probably already has a fairly complete collection of hand tools, but a brief review of them is still in order. The first thing to remember is that nobody ever did a good job safely using improper tools. There are a large number of quality manufacturers. Stick to them because with hand tools, you get what you pay for. Manufacturers like Snap-On, Craftsman, Mac, Proto, and many others make top quality tools that will last a lifetime. Most brand name tools are sold with a "no questions asked" guarantee. If a tool breaks, return it and it will be replaced. Before you buy anything, check whether you need metric or SAE tools. Today many American cars are put together with metric fasteners, and quite a few more are put together with a combination of metric and SAE fasteners. A shop manual is a great help in this case.

While there are some points of interchange between metric and SAE fasteners, it is not a good idea to use metric wrenches on SAE fasteners and vice versa. In an emergency, you can use anything that will fit, but prolonged use will only ruin the fastener (and your knuckles).

Wrenches

Wrenches come in several varietes, in open-end and box-end types. Box-end wrenches are usually twelve-point and apply force to all six corners of the nut or bolt at once. The drawback is that they cannot be used for some jobs simply because of space limitations. Open-end wrenches exert force against only two sides of the

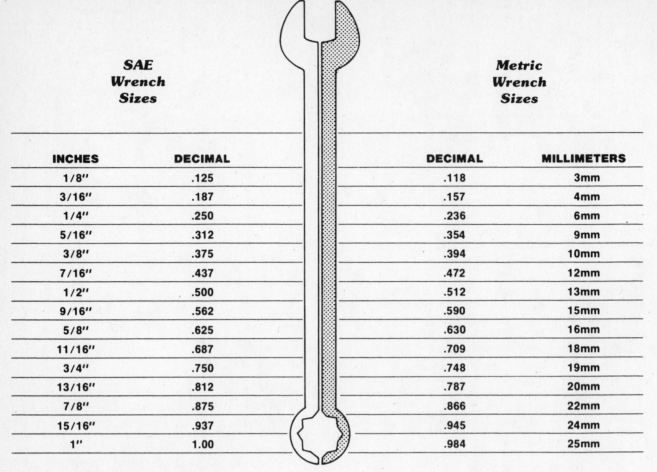

SAE Wrench Sizes		Metric Wrench Sizes	
INCHES	**DECIMAL**	**DECIMAL**	**MILLIMETERS**
1/8"	.125	.118	3mm
3/16"	.187	.157	4mm
1/4"	.250	.236	6mm
5/16"	.312	.354	9mm
3/8"	.375	.394	10mm
7/16"	.437	.472	12mm
1/2"	.500	.512	13mm
9/16"	.562	.590	15mm
5/8"	.625	.630	16mm
11/16"	.687	.709	18mm
3/4"	.750	.748	19mm
13/16"	.812	.787	20mm
7/8"	.875	.866	22mm
15/16"	.937	.945	24mm
1"	1.00	.984	25mm

Comparison of SAE and Metric wrench sizes

fastener at once and, consequently, are not quite as effective as box-end wrenches. Many tool manufacturers offer combination wrenches that consist of a box-end wrench on one end and an open-end wrench on the other. Box-end wrenches are also available in ratcheting models that can come in quite handy. There is also a special type of wrench known as a line wrench that is used for fuel and brake line work. It is really nothing more than a box-end wrench with one of the flats cut out so that it can be slipped over the fuel or brake line. Adjustable open-end wrenches are useful, but make sure you buy a good one because the inexpensive ones won't hold their setting.

Sockets and Ratchets

Ratchet and socket sets come in a number of sizes, ranging from 1/4 to 3/4-in. drive models. Most automotive work requires the 1/2-in. and the 3/8-in. drive models. The 1/4-in. model is only useful for very small jobs and the 3/4-in. models are of use only if you plan to work on large trucks. Drive simply refers to the size of the connection between the handle and the. socket or extension. Obviously, the larger the handle, the more torque the wrench can apply. Handles come in a variety of sizes and are

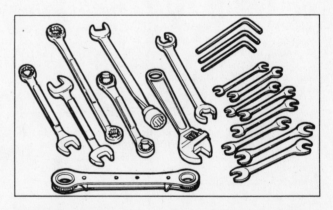

A sampling of the variety of wrench styles. The ratchet (bottom), adjustable (center) and combination open/box end (left) are the most useful.

available with a number of accessories. Engine rebuilding work requires a swivel head ratchet in either 3/8 or 1/2-in. drive. Actually, it would be best to have one of each. Because many tool manufacturers sell their ratchets and sockets in sets, it is not hard to figure out what sockets will be needed. Sockets are available in six- and twelve-point faces and in standard and deep

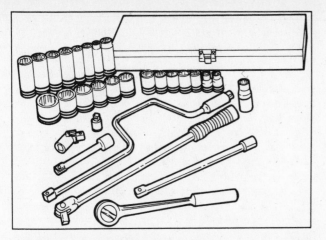

A ratchet, extension, breaker bar and a selection of normal and deep sockets will handle most jobs.

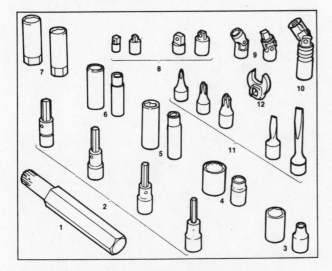

Some of the socket bits available for ratchet sets.
1. Star, serrated or Torx bit
2. Allen wrenches
3. ¼″ drive 6-point sockets
4. ¼″ drive 12-point sockets
5. ½″ or ⅜″ drive 6-point sockets
6. ½″ or ⅜″ drive 12-point sockets
7. ⅝″ (right) and ¹³/₁₆″ (left) spark plug sockets
8. Ratchet drive adaptors
9. Universal joints
10. Universal joint with socket wrench
11. Screwdriver socket bits

sizes. If you are interested enough in cars to attempt rebuilding an engine, you probably already have every socket you will ever need.

Screwdrivers

There are two general types of screwdrivers: Phillips head and slot head. You will need several sizes of each. The slot in any screw has definite dimensions and just because you have a Phillips head screw and a Phillips screwdriver does not mean that the two are compatible. Once again, screwdrivers are often sold in sets, which makes it easier for you because the sets will contain the most popular sizes. Magnetic screwdrivers with interchangeable heads or bits are very handy.

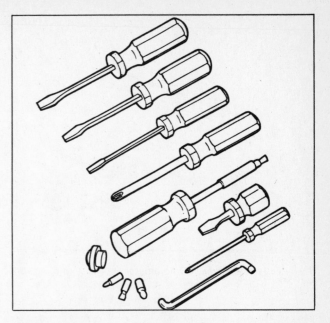

Screwdrivers come in all shapes and sizes for many different applications

Pliers

Pliers come in a bewildering array of shapes and sizes, and no mechanic's tool kit is complete without at least four or five pairs. The ones you will need are slip joint pliers, needle nose pliers, the type commonly known as water pump pliers, locking pliers (Vise Grips), cutting pliers, and spark plug pliers.

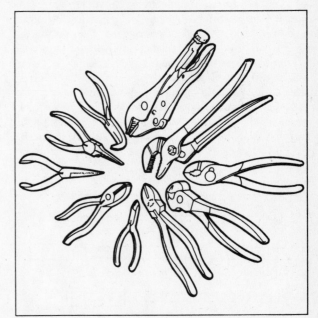

A variety of pliers are necessary for specialized jobs

Hammers

Some people say that a really good mechanic does **not**

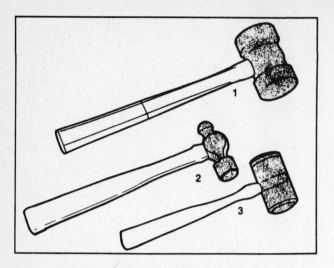

Three common types of hammers: 1-rubber mallet, 2-machinists or ball peen and 3-plastic (soft-faced)

need hammers, but don't believe them. They are probably the same people who say that they can calculate torque without a torque wrench, or look at a crankshaft and tell if it's out-of-round. Granted, hammers should not be used indiscriminately, but there are times when you will need them. *At least* one good ball peen hammer plus a soft-faced hammer are absolute necessities. There are plastic-faced hammers, brass hammers, rawhide-faced hammers, and rubber hammers.

Torque Wrenches

Every fastener on an automobile has a specific limit to which it can be safely stretched. Torque is the force required to produce the desired degree of strain and a torque wrench is the tool used to deliver and monitor this degree of stretch. Torque is calculated by using a fundamental law of physics regarding leverage: force times distance equals torque around a particular pivot point. For example, if 10 lbs. (4.5 kg) of force are exerted around a bolt or nut at a distance of 1 ft. (30.5 km) from that bolt or nut, then the torque is 10 ft. lbs. If the distance is measured in inches, then the torque is read in in. lbs.

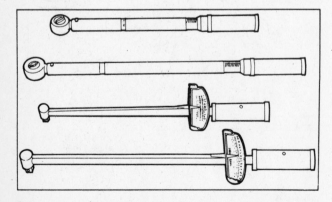

Various types of torque wrenches. Top to bottom—"click" type (in. lbs. and ft. lbs.), beam type (in. lbs. and ft. lbs.).

There are four different types of torque wrenches, direct reading, or pointer types, utilize a calibrated scale on the handle and a pointer rod attached to the head of the wrench. They are quite durable, but not as accurate as the others. Dial torque wrenches operate on the same principle, but have a calibrated dial that is a little easier to read accurately. Clutch torque wrenches can be present to a specific torque and the drive will slip or disengage when the correct torque is reached. Click torque wrenches will produce an audible clicking noise when the preset torque is reached.

No matter which torque wrench you use, remember that any extension of the handle will alter the force applied (linear extension, of course). Occasionally, adapters are needed to reach a particular spot, and torque wrench manufacturers do publish correction formulas.

Pullers

There are a variety of pullers, and you will probably need at least one to do engine rebuilding. They come in two types: screw-actuated pullers and impact pullers. You will need screw-actuated pullers to remove such parts as the crankshaft pulley or the timing gear.

Power-Driven Tools

Power-driven tools or impact wrenches are very useful for tearing down an engine, but only if you have an air compressor (although there are some electric impact wrenches on the market today). As a general rule, the cost of impact wrenches restricts their use to the professional level. These tools are simply too expensive for the amateur.

SPECIAL ENGINE TOOLS

While the tools discussed previously can be used for other automotive applications, the following are specialized tools that you will need to rebuild engines. Some of them are fairly expensive but well worth the investment.

Gasket Scraper

You don't have to be an engine rebuilder to need a gasket scraper, but you do need a gasket scraper to rebuild engines. They are a very simple tool, but absolutely invaluable.

Ring Groove Cleaner

Some engine rebuilders will say that a ring groove cleaner is not necessary, that an old piece of broken piston ring will work just as well. While a broken piston ring will accomplish the same thing, it will take three times as long, and you will wear your hands out. Buy the ring groove cleaner.

Piston Ring Compressor

There are two basic types of ring compressor. The most common utilizes an allen wrench to activate the compression process. The other uses a pliers. This tool is indispensible. There is simply no way to get a ringed piston into the cylinder without a compressor. It's use will be discussed further in Chapter Eight.

Clockwise from top—2 kinds of piston ring compressors, a piston ring groove cleaner and piston ring expander.

Piston Ring Expander

Unlike piston ring compressors, a piston ring installer is not absolutely necessary. But if you are a little doubtful of your ability, you should get one. They are not that expensive (certainly not as much as a new set of rings), and they will add immeasurably to your peace of mind.

Cylinder Hone or Glaze Breaker

There are two types of cylinder hones: those that follow the existing bore (spring-loaded or ball-type hones) and those that remain rigid and cut their own path. Rigid hones are used to hone cylinders that have a pronounced amount of wear and out-of-roundness. Spring-loaded or ball-type hones are used for cylinders that are not as badly worn or to get a good cross-hatch pattern on a recently rebored cylinder. Ball-type hones are generally acknowledged to give a better result, but they are not as versatile as the spring-loaded type because each particular ball-type hone will only fit a certain range of bore sizes.

Ridge Reamer

A ridge reamer is the sort of tool you will not know you are going to need until you get the cylinder heads off the engine. Engines with well over 100,000 miles on them sometimes won't have a ridge, and some with 50,000 miles on them will. A cylinder ridge is a combination of

Cylinder hone (top) and glaze breaker (bottom)

unworn cylinder bore and some carbon buildup. Because the top piston ring cannot get all the way to the top of the cylinder, there will always be a slight (or not so slight) amount of unworn bore here. It has to be removed before you can remove the pistons from the engine. A ridge reamer is essentially a cutting tool designed to do this particular job. The cutter can be expanded to fit a variety of bore sizes.

MEASURING TOOLS

There are a number of measuring tools that you will need to correctly reassemble the engine, including

Cylinder ridge reamer

inside and outside micrometers, dial indicators, calipers, telescope gauges, and depth gauges. Plastigage is also necessary.

MICROMETERS

Outside Micrometers

Outside micrometers are used to check the diameters of such components as the pistons and crankshaft. The most common type of micrometer reads in $1/1000$ of an inch. Micrometers that use a vernier scale can estimate to $1/10$ of an inch. The illustrations show the various part names.

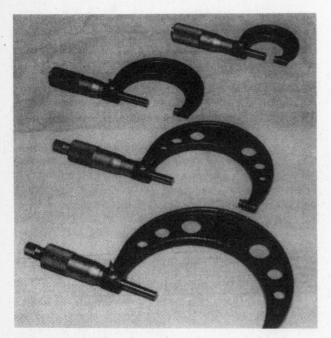

Micrometers in various sizes

One complete revolution of the outside handle of a mike moves the spindle 0.025 in. The sleeve is marked with a series of lines, each of which represents 0.025. Every fourth line is marked 1, 2, 3, 4, on up to 9. These sleeve numbers indicate 0.100, 0.200, 0.300, and so on. So all this means is that a 1-in. micrometer will read from zero to 1 in. or from 0.000 to 1.000. Ideally, you should purchase a complete set of mikes ranging from 1-in. to 12-in. sizes. Because this could be expensive, it might be easier to buy one multiple-range micrometer with interchangeable anvils.

Reading the Micrometer

As noted earlier, one complete turn of the outside handle of the mike will move the spindle 0.025 in. The tapered end of the thimble is marked into 25 parts, so that moving from one of these lines to the next moves the spindle in or out $1/25$ of 0.025 or 0.001 in. To read the

mike, multiply the number of vertical divisions on the stationary handle and add the number of divisions on the tapered part of the movable handle. For example, if a full 3 is visible on the stationary handle or sleeve plus two small lines, the total is 0.350. If the sleeve long line is lined up with the 0 on the beveled part of the thimble, the reading is 0.300 + 0.050 + 0 = 0.350. If there were ten small lines on the beveled part of the thimble in line with the sleeve long line, the reading would be 0.300 + 0.50 + 0.010 = 0.360. If this were a 2- to 3- in. mike, the actual reading would be 2 in. plus 0.360 or 2.360 in.

Inside Micrometers

Inside micrometers are used to measure the distance between two parallel surfaces. In engine rebuilding work, the inside mike measures cylinder bore wear, connecting rod big end wear, and block main bearing bore sizes. Inside mikes are graduated the same way as

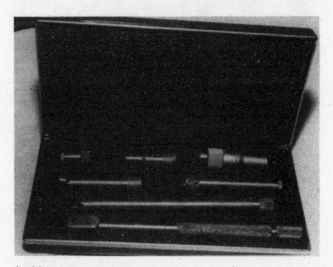

Inside micrometer set

outside mikes and are read the same way as well. Remember that an inside mike must be absolutely perpendicular to the work being measured. When you measure with an inside mike, rock the mike gently from side to side and tip it back and forth slightly so that you find the widest part of the bore. Just to be on the safe side, take several readings. It takes a certain amount of experience to work any mike with confidence.

Metric Micrometers

Metric micrometers are read in the same way as inch micrometers, except that the measurements are in millimeters. Each line on the main scale equals 1 mm. Each fifth line is stamped 5, 10, 15, and so on. Each line on the thimble scale equals 0.01 mm. It will take a little practice, but if you can read an inch mike, you can read a metric mike.

DIAL INDICATORS

A dial indicator is a gauge that utilizes a dial face and a needle to register measurements. There is a movable contact arm on the dial indicator. When the arms moves, the needle rotates on the dial. Dial indicators are calibrated to show readings in thousandths of an inch and typically, are used to measure end play and runout on camshafts, crankshafts, gears, and so on. Dial indicators are quite easy to use, although they are relatively expensive. A variety of mounting devices are available so that the indicator can be used in a number of situations. Make certain that the contact arm is always parallel to the movement of the work being measured.

Main bearing micrometer

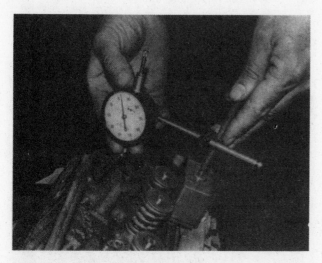

Dial indicator with magnetic base stand

Dial indicators for special purposes (measuring inside cylinder bore)

INSIDE AND OUTSIDE CALIPERS

Inside and outside calipers are useful devices to have if you need to measure something quickly and precise measurement is not necessary. Simply take the reading and then hold the calipers on an accurate steel rule.

TELESCOPING GAUGES

A telescope gauge is used to measure the inside of bores, connecting rod big ends, and so on. They can take the place of an inside mike for some of these jobs. Simply insert the gauge in the hole to be measured and lock the plungers after they have contacted the walls. Remove the tool and measure across the plungers with an outside micrometer.

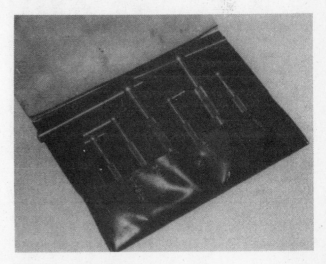

Set of telescope gauges in various sizes

FEELER GAUGES

Feeler gauges are a necessity for anyone contemplating rebuilding an engine. They can be used for measuring crankshaft thrust play, piston-to-bore clearance, valve lash, rod side play, and so on.

STEEL RULE AND STEEL STRAIGHTEDGE

It is imperative to have an accurate straightedge long enough to measure across the length of a block or a cyl-

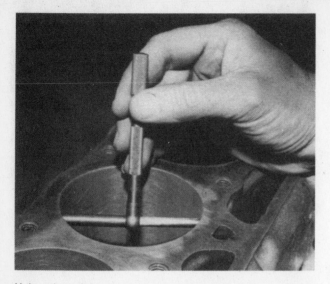

Using the telescope gauge to gauge the size of cylinder bore

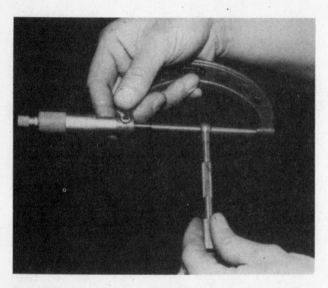

The telescope gauge can be accurately measured with a micrometer

inder head in order to check them for warpage. A good quality steel rule is also a handy thing to have.

PLASTIGAGE

Plastigage is a sort of soft plastic that will flatten out to predetermined widths when subjected to torquing. These widths will equal a specific clearance. Plastigage is normally used to check main and rod-bearing clearance. It is sold in a paper sleeve that also doubles as the scale upon which it is measured. The scale reads out in thousandths of an inch. The most common type is green Plastigage which is used to measure clearances from 0.001 to 0.003 in. It is often called "one-to-three" Plastigage. Its use will be discussed further in Chapter Eight.

OTHER TOOLS & EQUIPMENT

Unless you work in a garage or have a relative or friend who does, there are going to be a certain number of tools you will need for an overhaul that it simply would not be feasible to buy. Few amateur mechanics have a valve-grinding machine or a boring bar. Not many have an arbor press either. About the only one of these large tools you can rent is an engine crane or a "cherry picker." They are definitely worth renting too. As far as the other tools go, you will simply have to rely on your local machinist to take care of your more elaborate rebuilding problems. However, all of the machine shop operations that comprise a complete overhaul will be discussed in the remaining chapters of this book.

A portable hoist, overhead crane or "cherry-picker" is useful for engine removal

SUPPLIES

To do an adequate job, you will need a few supplies. Make sure that you have plenty of clean shop rags on hand, as well as lots of hand cleaner. You will need rust penetrant, gasket sealers, probably an assortment of nuts, bolts, and washers, a flat pan for catching coolant and oil, a set of *good* jack stands, a couple of heavy-duty wire brushes, and a regular brush or two.

SERVICING YOUR CAR SAFELY

It is virtually impossible to anticipate all of the hazards involved with automotive maintenance and service, but care and common sense will prevent most accidents.

The rules of safety for mechanics range from "don't smoke around gasoline," to "use the proper tool for the job." The trick to avoiding injuries is to develop safe work habits and take every possible precaution.

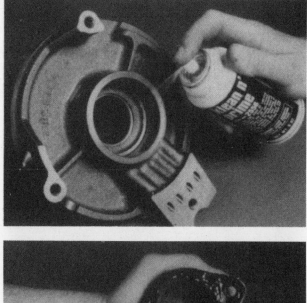

In addition to the normal automotive supplies, you'll probably also need some surface cleaner/gasket primer and a selection of sealants and self forming gasket compounds

DO'S

- DO keep a fire extinguisher and first aid kit within easy reach.
- DO wear safety glasses or goggles when cutting, drilling, grinding or prying. If you wear glasses for the sake of vision, they should be made of hardened glass that can serve also as safety glass or wear safety goggles over your regular glasses.
- DO shield your eyes whenever you work around the battery. Batteries contain sulphuric acid. In case of contact with the eyes or skin, flush the area with water or a mixture of water and baking soda and get medical attention immediately.
- DO use safety stands for any undercar service. Jacks are for raising vehicles; safety stands are for making sure the vehicle stays raised until you want it to come down. Whenever the car is raised, block the wheels remaining on the ground and set the parking brake.
- DO use adequate ventilation when working with any chemicals or hazardous materials. Follow the manufacturer's directions for usage. Brake fluid, antifreeze, solvents, paints, and so on are all deadly poisons if taken internally. Seal the containers tightly after use and store them safely, out of the reach of children.

- DO use caution when working on clutches or brakes. The asbestos used in the friction material will cause lung cancer if inhaled. Wipe the component with a damp rag to remove dust and dispose of the rag after use.
- DO disconnect the negative battery cable when working on the electrical system. The secondary ignition system can contain up to 40,000 volts.
- DO properly maintain your tools. Loose hammerheads, mushroomed punches and chisels, frayed or poorly grounded electrical cords, excessively worn screwdrivers, spread open-end wrenches, cracked sockets, slipping ratchets, or faulty droplight sockets can cause accidents.
- DO use the proper size and type of tool for the job being done.
- DO when possible, pull on a wrench handle rather than push on it, and adjust your stance to prevent a fall.
- DO be sure that adjustable wrenches are tightly closed on the nut or bolt and pulled so that the face is on the side of the fixed jaw.
- DO select a wrench or socket that fits the nut or bolt. The wrench or socket should sit straight, not cocked.
- DO strike squarely with a hammer; avoid glancing blows.
- DO set the parking brake and block the drive wheels if the work requires the engine running.

DONT'S

- DON'T run an engine in a garage or anywhere else without proper ventilation—EVER! Carbon monoxide is poisonous; it takes a long time to leave the human body and you can build up a deadly supply of it in your system by simply breathing in a little every day. You may not realize you are slowly poisoning yourself. Always use power vents, windows, fans or open the garage doors.
- DON'T work around moving parts while wearing a necktie or other loose clothing. Short sleeves are much safer than long, loose sleeves; hard-toed shoes with neoprene soles protect your toes and give a better grip on slippery surfaces. Jewelry, such as watches, fancy belt buckles, beads or body adornment of any kind is not safe. Long hair should be hidden under a hat or cap.
- DON'T use pockets for toolboxes. A fall or bump can drive a screwdriver deep into your body. Even a wiping cloth hanging from the back pocket can wrap around a spinning shaft or fan.
- DON'T smoke when working around gasoline, cleaning solvent, or other flammable material.
- DON'T smoke when working around the battery. When the battery is being charged, it gives off explosive hydrogen gas.
- DON'T use gasoline to wash your hands; there are excellent soaps available. Gasoline may contain lead, and lead can enter the body through a cut, accumulating in the body until you are very ill. Gasoline also removes all the natural oils from the skin so that bone dry hands will suck up oil and grease.

AIR-CONDITIONING EQUIPMENT

CAUTION: *The refrigerant, R 12 used in automotive air-conditioning systems is extremely cold when compressed and when released into the air will instantly freeze any surface it contacts, including your eyes. Although normally nontoxic, R 12 becomes a deadly poisonous gas when in the presence of an open flame. One good whiff of the vapors from burning refrigerant can be fatal.*

When preparing to remove a cylinder head or engine, the air-conditioning system should be discharged. Never attempt to discharge the system by merely loosening a fitting or removing the service valve caps and cracking the valves. The only **safe and proper way** to discharge the system is with a set of service gauges.

4

ENGINE REMOVAL DISASSEMBLING CLEANING

A definite series of steps is followed when removing or disassembling an automobile engine. Procedures may vary slightly, depending upon the make and model and the repairs or rebuilding to be done. If the engine only needs a valve job, only cylinder head removal is required, which can be done with the engine in the car. If the engine needs piston rings and/or rod bearings, the cylinder head and oil pan must be removed; although, in most cases, engine removal would probably make the job easier. If the engine needs reboring, or if the crankshaft is damaged and needs regrinding, the engine must be removed from the car and completely disassembled.

Before removing the cylinder head or the engine, some degreasing should be done. Check with your local car wash, service station, or radiator shop to see if they offer engine steam cleaning. If so, have the engine and as much of the underneath chassis and frame of the car cleaned as possible. If no steam cleaning services are available, get some engine degreaser in spray cans and some of the brush-on type, follow the directions on the can, and get the engine as clean as possible. It is much easier to work on a clean engine.

IN-CAR ENGINE SERVICES

CYLINDER HEAD REMOVAL

Before starting to remove the cylinder head or heads from the engine, be sure several containers are on hand to put various bolts and retainers in. Pay special attention to the size and location of the fasteners so at reassembly time there will be no questions as to where they fit. Before removing any wires or vacuum lines, tag them for location and identification.

After the engine has been steamed cleaned or degreased with solvent, park it in the work area and disconnect the negative (ground) cable from the battery. Drain the coolant into a suitable container if it is going to be reused. It will probably be easier to work on the engine with the hood of the car removed. Scribe a line around both hood hinges and remove the mounting bolts and the hood. Have a friend assist. If working clearance will be a problem, as in the case of some imported cars, the fan blades, fan shroud, and radiator may have to be removed.

Remove the air cleaner, air intake hoses, and crankcase ventilation lines. If the radiator does not require removal, disconnect the upper hose and remove it from the engine. Disconnect all of the vacuum lines, fuel lines, control switch wire harnesses, and linkage going to the carburetor or mounted on the manifold. Remove the ignition coil, spark plug wire retaining brackets, and any other lines or wires that will interfere with the removal of the valve cover(s) or cylinder head(s). Remove the valve cover(s).

On some engines, the distributor mounts through the intake manifold or will interfere with manifold removal. If so, disconnect the spark plug wires from the spark plugs, unfasten the distributor cap, and remove the cap

Align the TDC mark with the pointer

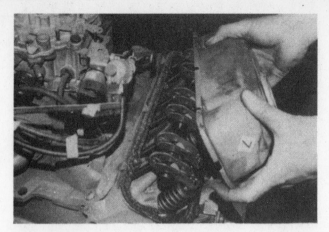

Remove the valve cover

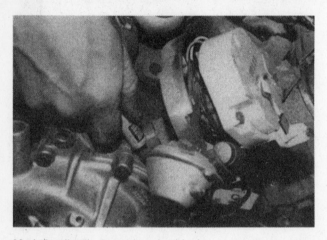

Mark the distributor and engine block

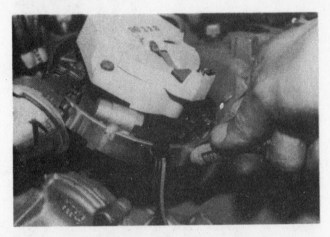

Reference mark the rotor at No. 1 firing position

and wires as a unit. Remove the spark plugs. Use a wrench or socket and ratchet and turn the engine until the No. 1 cylinder is at TDC (timing marks aligned; see Chapter Eight). Mark the distributor base and engine for reference; mark the distributor body at the point the rotor is pointing and remove the distributor. The distributor is usually retained by a bolt going through a base bracket or a clamp squeezed by a nut and bolt. Remove the bolt or loosened the nut and bolt. Remove the distributor. Remove the valve cover(s).

Remove the belts of any driven equipment mounted to the cylinder head(s), air pump, air-conditioner compressor, alternator, power steering pump, and so on. Remove any of the driven equipment that will interfere with head removal.

CAUTION: *Do not disconnect either of the lines on the air-conditioner compressor (see servicing your car safely in Chapter Three). In most cases, the air-conditioner compressor and the power-steering pump have enough slack in their lines so that they may be unmounted and placed out of the way.*

Remove the center-mounted intake manifold on V-type engines. In some cases, it may be necessary to dis-

Remove the distributor mounting bolt

connect a water bypass hose connected between the water pump and manifold. Manifold bolts should be loosen and removed from the outer edges, working toward the center, alternating sides and ends.

Disconnect the exhaust pipe(s) from the exhaust manifold(s) and remove the exhaust manifold(s) from the head, or loosen and remove the exhaust manifold(s) from the head with the exhaust pipe(s) connected. Place the manifold(s) and pipe(s) out of the way.

Remove the distributor

Lift the intake manifold from the engine

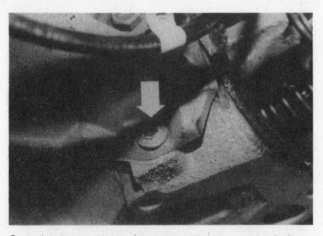

Some intake manifolds use special "Torx" mounting bolts

Typical "cookie pan" intake manifold gasket

Loosen the manifold mounting seal after all the mounting bolts are removed

Overhead camshaft engines may have some of the cylinder head bolts mounting the cam and rockers. If this style OHC engine is encountered, the cam and rockers are removed after the drive chain or belt is disconnected.

NOTE: *Set the cam at TDC on No. 1 cylinder and mark the position of the chain in relation to the cam gear.*

On belt-driven camshafts the timing cover is removed and the tensioner relaxed, allowing for belt removal. Chain-driven camshafts are disconnected, in most cases, by unbolting the cam gear and dismounting it from the camshaft.

NOTE: *If the engine is installed in the car, it will be necessary to devise a way of hanging the cam chain in place to keep the tension on the chain. Otherwise, the chain will fall off the crankshaft gear and the entire front end of the engine will have to be disassembled to put the engine back in time.*

After the camshaft and rockers are removed, the rest of the cylinder head retaining bolts are accessible and can be removed. On overhead valve engines after the valve cover(s) has (have) been removed, the rocker arm shaft and rocker arms (if shaft-equipped) are removed by taking out the mounting bolts that go through the mounting stands or shafts and into the cylinder head. If the rocker arms are stud or fulcrum-and-bolt-mounted, take out or loosen the bolt or adjusting nut until the rocker arm can be removed or swung off the pushrod and out of the way.

NOTE: *If individually mounted rocker arms are removed, keep the rocker arms, balls and/or studs together as matched sets.*

Remove the pushrods and valve lifters (if worn lifters are suspected). On some six cylinders engines, there

Remove the rocker arm shaft and rocker arms, or individual rocker assemblies

Cylinder head on "homemade" holding stands

Remove the cylinder head mounting bolts

are side covers that must be removed to service the hydraulic lifters. On most V-type engines the lifters are removed from the "valley" under the intake manifold. The pushrods and lifters should be kept in order after removal because they must be reinstalled in their original location.

Remove the remaining bolts that retain the cylinder head and remove the head. Remove the bolts in the reverse order of the tightening sequence. Never drive a tool between the cylinder head and the block to pry the head loose. Damage to the head or block gasket surfaces will occur. If you encounter resistance, try a short pry bar in an exhaust port, or between the exhaust manifold and head, and apply steady upward pressure. Make sure all of the head bolts have been removed; several heads have recessed mounting bolts that get covered with sludge and oil.

If the head still refuses to come loose, install the spark plugs, and connect the battery and crank the engine. Compression and a little "lifting" should break the head free. If the distributor has been removed it will be necessary to relocate TDC position after reinstalling the head. On OHC engines the engine should not be cranked because of the possibility of dropping the timing chain into the front cover or causing the auxiliary drives to get out of time.

PAN REMOVAL, PISTON AND CONNECTING ROD SERVICE

In some cases, it is possible to remove the oil pan and the piston and connecting rod assemblies from the engine while it is still installed in the car. However, removing the engine, in all cases, will make the job easier.

If the service must be performed while the engine is still mounted in the car, jack up the front and rear of the car evenly, and safely support it on jackstands. Remove the front tire and wheel assemblies. Drain the engine oil, remove the lower radiator hose, disconnect the transmission fluid cooler lines from the lower or side radiator cooling tank (if equipped), and move the lines out of the way. Drop the steering linkage if it interferes with the oil pan removal. Place a block of wood on a floor jack or small hydraulic jack and position the jack underneath the oil pan. Remove the bolts or cross nut and bolt attaching the front engine mounts to the engine block or two halves of the mount. Using the wood to spread the weight, slowly raise the engine and place blocks between the mounts and engine for support. Disconnect the rear engine mount, and raise and block in a similar manner if more clearance for oil pan removal is required. Remove the starter motor.

Remove the oil pan mounting bolts and lower the oil pan. In some cases it will be necessary to dismount the oil pump and/or the pickup tube and screen before enough room is gained to slide the oil pan from between the bottom of the engine and chassis cross-member.

ENGINE REMOVAL—REAR WHEEL DRIVE

Mark the location of the hood hinges by scribing a line around the hinge. Remove the hood and put it in a safe place out of the way. Place the car under the chain hoist and engine sling or in the working area accessible to the portable engine crane. Drain the coolant into a suitable container, disconnect the battery cables, and remove the battery if it will be in the way when the engine is removed.

If you have not already done so, cover the fenders with fender covers or some sort of material to protect them from dirt and scratches. Remove the condenser (air-conditioner) and radiator with the upper and lower hoses. If the radiator is equipped with a fan shroud, disconnect the shroud and position it back and over the water pump while you extract the radiator. If the car has an automatic transmission, disconnect the two transmission cooler lines connected to the radiator (at the bottom of a down-flow radiator and at the side on a cross-flow). Use a special open-end tubing wrench, if possible, to disconnect the lines; this will help protect the fittings from getting rounded off. Use a piece of rubber tubing to slide over the ends and connect the two cooler lines so the transmission fluid will not leak all over the place. The radiator may be mounted by bolts along the sides or by a bracket or brackets holding it at the top. Check clearance. On some cars it may be necessary to remove the radiator support and, possibly, the grille.

Loosen the bolts mounting the fan and spacer to the water pump, and remove the bolts, fan, and spacer.

Remove the air intake hoses to the air cleaner and the air cleaner assembly. Remove any other air hoses connecting the air cleaner or carburetor to a fender or frame-mounted unit, such as charcoal evaporative emission cannister and the power brake booster.

Label each wire, (for identification and location) harness, vacuum line, and cable before disconnecting. This will aid hookup after the engine has been reinstalled. Loosen and disconnect any bonding straps that connect the engine to the frame or fender wells. Disconnect the throttle and transmission control (automatic transmission) linkage at the carburetor. In some cases it will be necessary to remove a linkage "bell crank" that is usually mounted on the firewall end of the manifold. Disconnect and remove all heater hoses.

Loosen all belt-driven accessories and remove the drive belts. Label the belts for identification. Remove the alternator and air pump. If the car is equipped with power steering, remove the pump and mounting brackets. In some cases it will be possible to allow the power steering lines to remain connected to the pump. After the pump is dismounted from the engine, place it out of the way if the slack in the lines is sufficient.

Remove the air-conditioner compressor and mounting brackets (if necessary). *Remember, the refrigerant under high pressure in the lines leading to and from the compressor can hurt or blind you if you are careless. Wear goggles to protect your eyes when bleeding pressure from the system.* As with the power steering pump, there may be enough slack in the compressor lines so that after the compressor is dismounted, it can be secured out of the way with the lines still connected.

The water pump drive pulley should be free and can be removed after the drive belts are off. However, on some engines a two-piece crankshaft pulley might interfere and the outer pulley must be removed. If this is the case, remove the outer pulley mounting bolts. Tap the pulley lightly with a plastic or rubber hammer to loosen it.

Look around the top of the engine. Label and disconnect any wire or hose that is still connected. Remove any exhaust manifold heat shrouds; unbolt the exhaust manifold(s) from the cylinder head(s). In some cases it will not be necessary to disconnect the exhaust pipe from the manifold. After the exhaust manifold has been disconnected from the head, wire it and the exhaust pipe out of the way.

Tension the hoist and remove the engine mount bolts. On most cars the engine may be removed by itself, after being separated from the transmission. However, there are some cars that require the transmission and engine be removed as a unit. (See Engine Removal—Transmission Attached).

Engine Removal—Transmission Unattached

Remove any transmission linkage that can be reached from the top that is interfering with engine removal. Remove the upper transmission bell-housing bolts, if the car is equipped with an automatic transmission or has the bell housing cast with the transmission. If the transmission fluid filler tube is fastened to the rear of the engine with a bolt and bracket, remove the mounting bolt.

Jack up the front of the car and support it safely on jackstands. Remove the front motor mount bolts from the engine block or, if the mount is two-piece, remove the through bolt. Some jacking of the engine may be necessary to ease the weight off the mount before the bolts can be removed. Remember to put a block of wood between the engine and the jack.

From under the car, disconnect any transmission linkage still in the way. Remove the starter motor and lower bell-housing splash shield if the car is equipped with an automatic transmission. On cars with automatic transmission, remove the converter mounting nuts (turn the engine with a bar, using the flexplate teeth) from the engine flexplate. Use a flat pry bar and gently ease the converter back from the flexplate as much as possible. Take a piece of mechanics wire and run it from one side of the transmission to the other to secure the converter so that it cannot fall off the front pump of the transmission or come out with the engine. Remove the remaining bell-housing bolts.

On cars with manual transmission, the transmission can usually be disconnected from the engine by removing the mounting bolts connecting the transmission to the bell-housing. There are a few cars that have the bell-housing cast with the transmission case. The bell-housing bolts will have to be removed from the back of the engine. Take one last look to make sure that anything mounted or connected to the engine has been disconnected. Drain the engine oil. Remove and drain the oil filter.

Engine Removal—Transmission Attached

Jack up the front of the car and safely support it on jackstands. Remove the driveshaft by disconnecting the rear flange from the differential yoke. If the car has a two-piece driveshaft, disconnect the center bearing mount. Slide the driveshaft from the tail housing of the transmission. Plug the back of the transmission so the fluid will not run out when the engine and transmission are lifted from the car, or better yet, drain the transmission fluid.

Place a jack, with a block of wood on the saddle, under the point where the engine and transmission are attached. Just make contact with the piece of wood. Remove the rear motor mount bolts and loosen the cross-member mounting bolts. Take one last look to make sure that anything mounted or connected to the engine or transmission, such as the speedometer cable, neutral safety switch or backup light switch has been disconnected. Drain the engine oil. Remove and drain the oil filter.

ENGINE REMOVAL—FRONT WHEEL DRIVE

In most cases the engine and transaxle are removed as a unit.

Disconnect the battery cables (ground cable first); remove battery holddown and battery. Remove the battery tray.

Remove the air cleaner assembly. Disconnect the purge control vacuum hose from the purge valve. Remove the purge control valve mounting bracket. Remove the windshield washer reservoir, radiator tank, and carbon canister.

Drain the coolant from the radiator. Remove the radiator assembly with the electric cooling fan attached. Be sure to disconnect the fan wiring harness and the transmission cooler lines (automatic transmission).

Disconnect the following cables, hoses, and wires from the engine and transaxle: clutch, accelerator, speedometer, heater hose, fuel lines, PCV vacuum line, high-altitude compensator vacuum hose, bowl vent valve purge hose, inhibitor switch (automatic transmission), control cable (automatic transmission), starter, engine ground cable, alternator, water temperature, ignition coil, water temperature sensor, backup light (manual transmission), and oil pressure wires.

Remove the ignition coil. The next step will be to jack up the car. Before you do this, look around to make sure all wires and hoses are disconnected.

Jack up the front of the car after you block the rear wheels. Support the car on jackstands. Remove the splash shield (if equipped).

Drain the lubricant out of the transaxle and the oil from the engine.

Remove the right and left driveshafts from the transaxle and support them with wire. Plug the transaxle case holes so dirt cannot enter.

Disconnect the assist rod and the control rod from the transaxle. If the car is equipped with a range selector, disconnect the selector cable.

Remove the mounting bolt(s) from the front and rear roll control rods.

Disconnect the exhaust pipe from the engine and secure it with wire.

Loosen the engine and transaxle mounting bracket nuts.

Lower the car.

Attach a lifting device and a shop crane or chain hoist to the engine. Apply slight lifting pressure to the engine. Remove the engine and transaxle mounting nuts and bolts.

Make sure the rear roll control rod is disconnected. Lift the engine and transaxle from the car.

Make sure the transaxle does not hit the battery bracket when the engine and transaxle are lifted.

Hoisting the Engine

Jack up the car, remove the jackstands, and lower the car to the ground. Check the position of the chain hoist; reposition the car if necessary. If the transmission is to be removed with the engine, place a jack and block of wood under the transmission and raise slightly. Remove the cross-member. If the transmission is to remain in the car, support it with a jack. In either case, allow the jack to remain until the engine, or engine and transmission are removed.

Engine sling mounted to the rear of an engine

Front mounting of the engine sling

Sling centered on hoist

Front of engine angled

Fasten the engine-lifting sling to the front of the (or one) cylinder head and to the rear of the other end (or head). If lifting brackets are provided use them. If the engine and transmission are to be lifted as a unit, more weight will be at the rear; therefore, the front sling-mounting point should be a little to the rear. Make sure there is enough slack in the hoist chain so that the engine can be set on the ground after removal from the car. Connect the hook from the chain hoist at the center of the engine sling.

Raise the engine until it is clear of the front mounts. Pull it toward the front of the car. This will disengage the transmission, if it is to remain in the car. If the engine does not readily disengage from the transmission, adjust the height of the jack and pull forward on the engine; do not use force. Lower the sling, raise the jack, or use a combination of both to free it. Make sure that no wire or hose was overlooked when disconnecting. Slowly raise the hoist while pulling forward on the engine. Some tilting will be required on the front of the engine if the transmission is connected. As soon as the engine is free from the transmission and firewall, hoist it up out of the engine compartment. It will be necessary to move the car back and away from the engine/trans-

mission combination before hoisting it free of the engine compartment.

Do not allow the engine to hang on the hoist for too long a time, but before moving the car out from under, secure the transmission and remove the jack. Check for any other loose parts, such as the exhaust pipe and manifold, and secure them with wire. Move the car from under the engine or the portable crane away from the car and lower the engine or engine and transmission to the ground. Separate the transmission from the engine, raise the engine, and mount it on a rebuilding stand if one is available. If the car is equipped with an automatic transmission, mark a converter mounting stud and its mounting hole on the flexplate for reference. The same will hold true when the flywheel is removed from the crankshaft on a car with manual transmission.

The temptation to remove parts from the engine while it is still hanging from the hoist is great. Resist it. For safety's sake, mount the engine on a rebuilding stand or work on it on the floor.

ENGINE DISASSEMBLY

Remove any "bolt-on" accessory still attached. Remove the intake manifold (V-type engines) and the cylinder head(s) (see Cylinder Head Removal at the beginning of this chapter). Remove the clutch pressure plate and disc assembly (manual transmission) by evenly loosening the six mounting bolts. Remove the flywheel or flexplate. Remember to mark its relationship with the crankshaft; use a punch or paint mark.

Remove the water pump, crankshaft pulley, and timing case cover or timing case. In some instances it is necessary to remove the front oil pan bolts to remove the timing case. The crankshaft pulley or pulley hub usually requires a special puller for removal. Do not use a hammer.

Remove the timing gears, timing gears and chain or chains. The gears are generally secured by center bolts.

An engine mounting stand makes the rebuilding job easier

A special tool used to hold or turn the flywheel

Some will slide off readily; others require a puller. Never use force or the gear will be broken. In some cases, a fuel pump eccentric cam is mounted in front of the cam gear. Remove it first.

Turn the engine on its top or bell-housing end and remove the oil pan, oil pickup screen, oil pump (if "pan" mounted), and the distributor drive rod (if equipped).

Turn the engine back over so the top is facing up. If you are working on the floor, raise the engine on wooden blocks so the crankshaft turns freely.

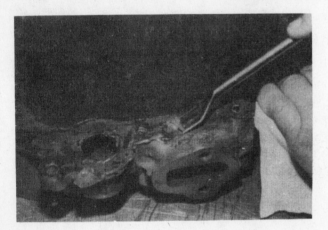

Use a scraper to remove old gaskets and sealing compounds

CYLINDER RIDGE REMOVAL

Because the top piston ring does not travel to the very top of the cylinder, a ridge is built up between the end of the travel and the top of the cylinder bore.

Pushing the piston and connecting rod assembly past the ridge is difficult, and damage to the piston ring lands could occur. If the ridge is not removed before installing a new piston, or not removed at all, piston ring breakage and piston damage will occur.

After the ridge is removed from the top of the cylinder walls the piston and connecting rod assemblies can be removed. (See Piston and Connecting Rod Removal).

As noted in Chapter Three, there are several different types of ridge reamers on the market, none of which are inexpensive. Unless a great deal of engine rebuilding is anticipated, borrow or rent a reamer.

Turn the crankshaft until the piston is at the bottom of its travel. Cover the head of the piston with a rag. Cut away the ridge, exercising extreme care to avoid cutting too deeply. Remove the ridge reamer, the rag, and as many of the cuttings as possible.

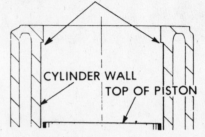

Cylinder bore ridge

Ridge Reamers

Three popular types of ridge reamers are the roller, the expanding-leg, and the flexible-blade.

ROLLER

The cutter height on the roller ridge reamer is adjustable. This allows the cutter blade to be located just under the ridge. The roller, located under the cutting blade, prevents any undercutting. By following the contour of the cylinder, the roller causes the cutter to remove the most material where the ridge is deepest. By setting the depth, stop carefully on the first cylinder, it will be impossible to cut into the ring travel area of the other cylinders because the cutter travels upward.

EXPANDING-LEG

The expanding-leg ridge reamer is held in position by three expanding legs. The legs are brought into contact with the cylinder wall by turning an adjustment screw. The cutting blade should be located 1/32 in. or less below the bottom of the ridge. A blade stop prevents cutting too deeply. Cutter tension is adjustable by a spring-loaded adjustment screw. This permits removal of uneven ridges because a stop follows the uneven portion of the cylinder wall.

FLEXIBLE-BLADE

The flexible-blade ridge reamer is extremely fast to operate because it is only necessary to expand the jaws until they fit the cylinder wall. The cutting blade is flexibly mounted so that it can follow the contour of the cylinder wall. However, there is no built-in safety factor to prevent undercutting. Exercise extreme care when using this reamer.

Matching numbers on the connecting rod and cap

Put pieces of rubber hose on the connecting rod bolts

PISTON AND CONNECTING ROD REMOVAL

Check the bottom of the connecting rod and cap for mating cylinder location numbers. If no numbers are present, mark the rod and cap, starting with the first connecting rod at the front of the engine. Stamp the numbers while the rods are still connected to the crankshaft; this will prevent any distortion. If a metal stamp is not available, use a scribe or punch. The numbers not only tell which cylinder the piston and rod came from, but also help to make sure the rod caps are assembled in the correct matching position. If the piston is separated from the rod, the numbers will ensure the correct "hand" (offset) position of the connecting rod at reassembly.

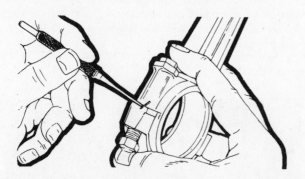

Scribe connecting rod match marks

Turn the crankshaft until the rod and piston is at its lowest position. Remove the rod nuts and cap. Install two pieces of rubber hose over the rod bolts. Push the connecting rod up into the cylinder bore about 1 in. (25mm) and remove the upper bearing insert. Take a wooden hammer handle and push the piston and connecting rod up until the rings are out of the cylinder bore. Remove the piston and rod by hand, put the upper half of the bearing insert back into the rod, install the cap with insert installed, and hand-tighten the two nuts. If the parts are kept together in this manner, they will

not get lost and you will be able to tell which bearings came from what cylinder if any problems are discovered and diagnosis is necessary. Take special care when pushing the rod up from the crankshaft because the sharp threads will score the crank journal. Make sure that special plastic caps are placed over the rod bolts, or cut two pieces of rubber vacuum hose and fit them over the bolts. Remove all the other pistons and connecting rods in this manner.

Crankshaft

Check the main bearing caps. They should be numbered and have an arrow or casting boss mark indicating the front. If the caps are not identified, mark them using a number stamp, punch, or scribe. Start at one end, either front or back, and remove a cap. Alternate to the other end. Proceed in this manner until all main bearing caps are removed. Lift the crankshaft from the engine block. Remove the main bearing inserts from each cap and block saddle, one set at a time. Use masking tape and tape them together, back to back. Number the taped halves for position identification in case the need for bearing wear diagnosis is necessary. Remount the bearing caps in position.

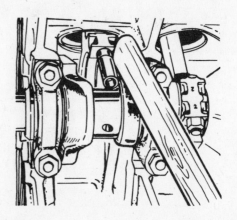

Removing the piston

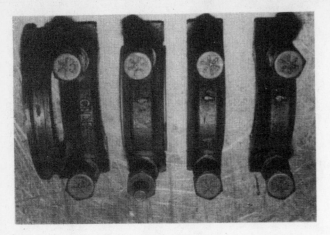

Typical main bearing "cast" markings

Use a stiff brush to help clean the block

Camshaft

If the lifters have not been removed from the block, do so at this time. Be sure to keep them in order. The camshaft is usually retained by a thrust plate that is mounted to the engine block by two cap screws. Remove these bolts.

Take a long bolt that has the same threads as the cam gear mounting bolt and screw it into the front of the camshaft. This will give you support while sliding the camshaft forward and out of the block. Be careful so the lobes do not cut or gouge the camshaft bearings (if new ones are not going to be installed).

Lowering a block into a cold tank

CLEANING

Various methods of cleaning are discussed in Chapter Five. The best way to clean the engine block is by hot tanking.

CAUTION: *if the engine block is made of aluminum, the hot tank method must not be used because the caustic solution will destroy aluminum. Hot tanking will also ruin cam bearings, so be prepared to have new ones installed.*

If the block is not "very" dirty inside, steam cleaning or hand cleaning with solvent is all that is necessary. However, for the "dirty" block, hot tanking is the method to use.

Prepare the block by removing all the core (freeze) plugs and oil galley drive-in or threaded plugs. Remove the rear cam "freeze" plug too. Have the cam bearings removed so the cleaning solution can work into the oil feed grooves and drilled passages.

Most shops will "tank" the cylinder head and crankshaft for the same price as the blocks, or for only a small additional charge. Disassemble the head, and take it and the crank along. Once again a word of caution: if the cylinder head is made of aluminum, do not have it hot tanked.

An extreme example of a dirty, sludged up engine

5

CYLINDER HEAD

The cylinder head was previously described as a tight cover for the top of the cylinders that contains machined passages through which the fuel/air mixture passes into the combustion chambers via an intake valve and exhaust gases pass out via an exhaust valve.

The valve and valve seats are subjected to great heat that is dissipated through the valve seats into the cylinder head itself and usually cooled by a liquid coolant. If the engine is air-cooled, cast fins and metal shrouds direct the air over the cylinder head and cooling occurs.

Wear in the valves, valve seats, and valve train usually occurs through high mileage, poor maintenance, or improper adjustment. As a valve or valve seat wears, the seal created by them starts to leak and a loss of combustion chamber pressure occurs. Without adequate pressure in a cylinder, the performance of the engine suffers.

If a compression check was performed as part of the engine diagnosis, you will have a pretty good idea of what to expect before you start disassembling the cylinder head: burnt valves or possibly worn valve guides. Once the cylinder head or heads are removed, an examination of the tops of the pistons and the cylinder wall above the piston can tell a lot about the engine.

An oily deposit on the top of any piston is a fairly reliable indication that too much oil has been getting into the combustion area. If, after the cylinder head has been disassembled, the underside of the intake valve head (corresponding to the piston with the oil deposit) is oily or has heavy carbon deposits, it is most likely that the valve guide is worn. When the intake valve head and port are wet with oil in two cylinders adjacent to the manifold connection of the vacuum booster pump, it is likely that the pump diaphragm is ruptured. A wet oily condition between two adjacent cylinders will result from a cylinder head blown out between the two cylinders. If any piston head is wet with oil and the intake valve head is dry, it is most likely that the oil is coming past the piston rings.

When an oiling condition is isolated in one cylinder, check the spark plug from that cylinder. If a plug is too cold, it will not burn off the normal amount of oil that passes the rings. If the spark plug is dry, the most likely causes of oil consumption are worn rings or a scored cylinder wall.

CYLINDER HEAD DISASSEMBLY

Place the cylinder head on a workbench and remove any manifolds that are still connected. Remove the rocker arm retaining devices (nuts, fulcrums, shafts, etc.) and the rocker arms. Always keep all parts from the same cylinder separated from the others. Specially divided trays are sold by some parts houses for this purpose, or muffin pans or frozen juice cans can be used. Be sure to label each container with the cylinder number so that the parts won't get mixed up.

Turn the head over and block it evenly on wooden blocks. Scrape off all of the gasket material that is stuck

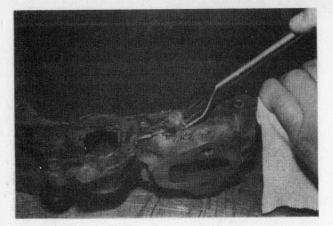

Use a scraper to remove old gaskets and sealing compounds

on the mounting surface of the head. If the cylinder head is aluminum, use a dull scraper or damage (grooves) may occur. Use a drill-driven wire carbon-removing brush to clean away all of the carbon on the valve chambers. After the carbon has been removed from the valve faces, take a marking pen and number the valves, in order, from the front of the head to the rear. If you are working on a V–6 or V–8 engine, put the number 1 on the first valve according to the No. 1 cylinder of the engine's firing order.

C clamp valve spring compressor

Block the head on its side, or install a pair of head-holding brackets that are made especially for valve removal. Take a valve spring compressor (the locking C-clamp is the easiest kind to use) and compress the valve spring. If you meet more than spring pressure resistance when trying to compress the valve spring, take a socket large enough to fit over the valve stem and keepers, place it over them, and gently hit the socket with a plastic hammer. This should break loose any varnish buildup holding the keepers and spring retaining caps in place. Remove the valve keepers, retainer, damper shield (if equipped), and valve spring. Put the removed parts in the container with the other parts removed

Typical notched valve stem

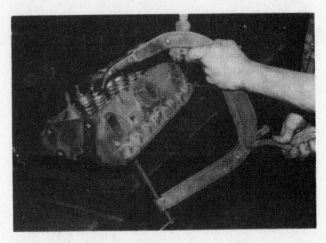

Compressing the valve spring

Remove the keepers, retainer, and spring.

Varnish buildup around the keepers and retainer

Place the valves in a valve stick or piece of cardboard in order of removal

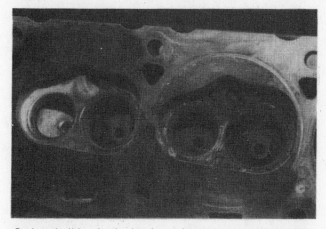

Carbon buildup in the intake, exhaust ports, and combustion chamber

from that cylinder. Remove and discard the oil seal from the valve stem or the valve guide top (use a new seal for assembly).

Remove the valves, one at a time, from the cylinder head. Place the valves, in order, through holes punched in a stiff piece of cardboard or a wooden valve stick. It

helps to number the holes in the cardboard or stick so if the numbers on the faces of the valves get wiped off, position can still be identified.

Take a ¼-in. electric drill and wire carbon-removing brush and clean the intake and exhaust ports, combustion chamber, and valve seats. In some cases, the carbon will need to be chipped away, and a blunt pointed drift will usually do the job. Use a wire guide-cleaning brush and some safe solvent to clean the valve guides.

Use a rotary wire brush to clean away the carbon

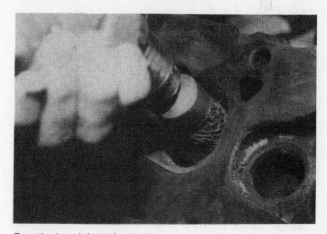

Run the brush into the ports

CLEANING

If a complete engine rebuild job is being done and the engine has been steam cleaned with the rocker arm covers off, most of the oil and dirt has already been removed from the tops of the cylinder heads. If not, now is the time to take some solvent and clean as much surface grease and dirt off as possible. Do not worry about "super" clean at this time because machine work still has to be done. After that has been completed, the time for that extra special cleaning job will be at hand. If a complete engine rebuild is necessary and the block is to be hot tanked, take the head(s) along. Hot tanking will remove grease, corrosion, and scale from the surfaces and water passages. If you are working on an OHC engine, the caustic solution may damage the cam bearings. Heads that are to be hot tanked should have the freeze plugs removed so the solution can reach as many places in the water passages as possible.

Some machine shops offer glass bead cleaning. This does a good job, and the head or part comes back looking like new.

Parts cleaning can be handled in several different ways, depending on the part and the cleaning equipment available. The five basic methods of cleaning parts are 1) hand scrubbing and scraping, 2) cold spraying, 3) hot tank immersion, 4) cold tank immersion, and 5) steam cleaning.

There are three types of deposits which cleaning chemicals are called on to remove: grease, carbon, and scale. No chemical can do all three of these jobs, but two chemicals may be mixed to remove grease and carbon. Rust and scale require a special agent.

HAND CLEANING

Many parts of the engine block and cylinder head are cleaned best by hand. Carbon deposits are usually scraped by hand scrapers or with a wire brush. Soft metal parts, such as bearings, should be washed in a cleaning solvent. Parts containing leather or impregnated material diaphragms must not be cleaned in tank solutions containing caustic alkalies. Aluminum should be cleaned by hand with a safe solvent.

Wire Brushing Carbon

A solid core brush is used to clean the cylinder heads, the top of the block, and the piston heads. A flared wire brush is used for the upper cylinder walls and the recessed valve ports. A ¼-in. electric drill is used to drive the brush. Light pressure on the brush is important when cleaning aluminum heads and the tops of pistons. A small screwdriver or blunt drift is necessary to remove carbon deposits from pocket areas where carbon buildup would form an insulator and prevent proper cooling.

Cleaning Valves

Hold each valve against a revolving wire brush. Be sure that all carbon, and especially gum and varnish deposits, are removed and not merely burnished. Heavy deposits of carbon may be removed by chopping off the carbon with a scraper or blunt drift.

Cleaning Valve Guides

Valve guides require very careful cleaning. Carbon and gum left in the guide will deflect the pilot for the seat-grinding tool and cause an inaccurate seat. Any remaining gum will cause the valve to stick in the guide, caus-

ing a burnt valve seat or valve face. Use the correct size valve guide cleaning brush or tool. Using a ¼-in. electric drill, run the cleaning tool up and down the full length of the valve guide. Use a safe solvent on the tool and in the guide to help dissolve the gum. Pay special attention to the top of the guide. If it looks out-of-round or shows an irregularity, the valve guide will have to be serviced to ensure a true valve seat.

Valve Springs and Valve Train Components

Clean the valve springs, keepers, and caps in cleaning solvent. Do not use too strong a solvent that will remove the paint or coating on the valve springs (if painted). Count the number of parts you are going to clean and make sure you have the same number when you are finished.

COLD SPRAYING

In this method, a cleaning solvent is sprayed over the part to be cleaned. The chemical softens the dirt and helps loosen the bond. The grime and grease are flushed off with water. If the grime and grease are stubborn, a heavier application of spray and some working in with a cleaning brush and strong water pressure will help remove it. Several coats of spray and some soaking time also help to remove stubborn deposits.

HOT TANK IMMERSION

A hot tank immersion is one of the most efficient and economical means of cleaning parts. The work is placed in the hot solution and agitation takes place making cleaning more efficient. The parts are rinsed off with a high-pressure water hose after cleaning. **Remember, never have aluminum parts hot tanked.** Cam bearings immersed in a hot tank will have to be replaced.

COLD TANK IMMERSION

Cold tanks are generally used for cleaning small parts; however, they are usually big enough to take a cylinder head or a disassembled engine block. Some cold tanks have a sliding tray near the top to put parts on and a pump that circulates the cleaning solvent through an adjustable nozzle to help clean and wash the parts.

STEAM CLEANING

Steam cleaners get their name from the fact that steam is used to generate pressure and is also the by-product of heating the cleaning solution. The steam itself has little cleaning power. However, the cleaning solution, when heated and under pressure, does a reasonable job of cleaning.

CYLINDER HEAD INSPECTION

The cylinder head is now completely disassembled and reasonably clean. Before any machine work is done, check it for cracks. Cracks in the cylinder head usually start around an exhaust valve seat because it is the hottest part of the combustion chamber. There are several methods of locating cracks, besides a visual inspection.

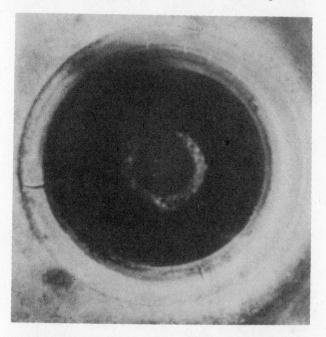

A valve seat crack. A new seat will have to be installed

MAGNETIC INSPECTION OF FERROUS PARTS

Magnaflux is a method of inspecting ferrous metal parts that can be magnetized. A magnetic field is set up on the parts under inspection, and a section of the part under examination is covered with finely divided ferromagnetic particles. Leakage fields caused by cracks attract the particles. Their pattern outlines the crack or defect and gives definite indications of the exact location of a crack and the shape of a defect, even under the surface. This method can be used only on material that can be magnetized.

Another method that uses a magnetic technique is Magnaglo. A special fluorescent paste is mixed with oil to form a suspension of fluorescent ferromagnetic particles. This solution is sprayed on the part being checked. When viewed under blacklight, a crack, if present, will appear as a streak of white against a bluish black background.

DYE PENETRANTS

One method of checking with a dye is to use a mixture of 25 percent kerosene and 75 percent light engine oil. Brush the mixture on the suspected area then wipe dry.

Immediately apply a coating of zinc oxide dissolved in wood alcohol. If cracks are present, the white coating will become discolored at the defective area. This method is effective in locating the extreme ends of visible cracks or for checking the areas where a crack is suspected.

ZYGLO

Another dye penetrant method makes use of a fluorescent penetrant that is viewed under blacklight. This inspection method can be used on practically all solid materials, both magnetic and nonmagnetic. The essentials of this method are as follows: 1) penetration of the defect by a fluorescent oil-base penetrant; 2) removal of excess penetrant from the surface by washing with hot or cold water; 3) developing the indication using wet or dry developer; and 4) inspection under blacklight. A brilliant fluorescent indication will mark the crack.

SPOT CHECK

A dark red stain against a white background will show a crack in daylight when the spot method is used. After thoroughly cleaning the part or section to be tested, the penetrant (in its own spray can) is sprayed on the surface. Excess penetrant is washed off. A developer is then sprayed over the penetrant. If a crack is present a red stain line will appear.

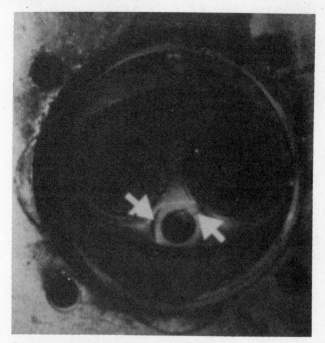

Cylinder head combustion chamber crack

CRACK REPAIR

Cracks in a cylinder head or block can usually be repaired, although it usually is less expensive, in the long run, to pick up a good used head or block and recondition it. A crack under a valve seat can be repaired by inserting a series of tapered threaded pins all along the crack and across the valve seat. The valve seat area is then machined to receive a valve seat insert.

If a crack is to be repaired on a cast iron head, the tapered threaded pin repair is not possible because of the fine thread line left. However, a repair is possible using tapered drive-in plugs that can be ground smooth. Check with your local machine shop and ask their advice.

If a crack is repaired in either the head or the engine block, always add a can of heavy-duty ceramic sealer to the cooling system.

MACHINE SHOP

As mentioned in Chapter Three, certain rebuilding operations require special tools that may be too expensive or not feasible to buy for only occasional use. The answer to these problems is the local automotive machine shop. The machine shop can usually handle any job from drilling out and replacing a broken stud to any major rebuilding.

The following sections will describe the machining operations. In some cases greater detail will be provided, while in others, just a description of the operation will be given when it is felt that the job will be handled by a machine shop.

Consult the man behind the counter of your local machine shop. Most jobs from simple to complex can be handled

CYLINDER HEAD RECONDITIONING

CHECKING THE CYLINDER HEAD FOR FLATNESS

After you have cleaned the gasket surface of the cylin-

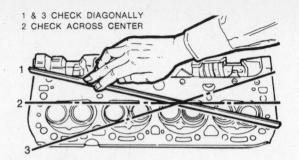

1 & 3 CHECK DIAGONALLY
2 CHECK ACROSS CENTER

Checking for cylinder head warpage

der head of any old gasket material, check the head for flatness.

Place a straightedge across the gasket surface. Using feeler gauges, determine the clearance at the center of the straightedge. Measure across both diagonals, along the longitudinal centerline and across the cylinder head at several points. If the warpage exceeds 0.003 in. in a 6.0-in. span, or 0.006 in. over the total length of the head, the cylinder head must be resurfaced. If the warpage exceeds the manufacturer's maximum tolerance for material removal, the head must be replaced. After resurfacing the heads of a V-type engine, the intake manifold flange must be milled proportionately to allow for the change in its mounting position.

The cylinder head is machined if warpage exceeds specifications

VALVE GUIDES

Valve guides may be pressed, hammered, shrunk, or cast into the cylinder head. If a valve guide is worn beyond specifications, it will not guide the valve in a straight line, causing burnt valve faces or seats, loss of compression, and excessive oil consumption. If a worn guide is not repaired into true alignment, an accurate valve seat is impossible to grind or ream.

There are several methods of checking valve guide wear. The first and most simple is using a new valve.

Clean the valve guide thoroughly

One of the more important parts for correct valve operation is the valve guide. The guide should be checked for the proper inside diameter as well as bell-mouthing by using a split-ball gauge (Courtesy TRW, Inc.)

After the guide has been thoroughly cleaned, install the new valve into the valve guide so that the stem protrudes at the top and the valve face protrudes at the bottom. Apply sideway motion to the valve. If there is excessive wobble, chances are valve guide repair is necessary.

Another way of checking valve guide wear is with a split-ball gauge. The gauge is used to check the inside diameter of the guide as well as the top of the guide to see if a bell-mouth condition exists.

Excessive valve guide-to-stem clearance can also be checked with a dial indicator. Clean the valve stems with a solvent to remove all gum and varnish. Clean the valve guides using an expandable brush and solvent. Mount a dial indicator so that the stem is at a 90° angle to the valve stem, as close to the valve guide as possible. Move the valve off its seat, and measure the valve guide-to-stem clearance by rocking the stem back and forth to actuate the dial indicator. Measure the valve stems with a micrometer and compare the specifications to determine whether the stem of the valve or the guide is responsible for the excessive clearance.

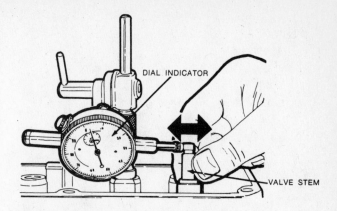

Checking the valve-stem-to-guide clearance

Replaceable Valve Guides

If the particular design of the cylinder head allows for replaceable valve guides and a guide repair is necessary, use a replacement guide instead of repairing the existing one.

On drive-in replaceable guides, carefully press or tap out the old valve guide using a stepped drift. Determine the height above the boss of the cylinder head that the guide must extend. Get a stack of flat washers that will fit over the outside diameter of the valve guide; place the washers over an installed guide until they reach the top. This will be the installed height necessary.

Insert the new valve guide into its bore. Place the stack of flat washers over the guide and press or tap the guide into position. The inside of the valve guide should be reamed to the size of the valve stem after installation.

Shrunk-fit valve guides (usually on aluminum heads) should be installed by a machine shop. The procedure requires heating the cylinder head and cooling the valve guide.

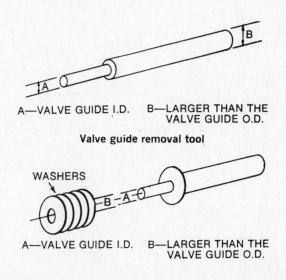

Valve guide removal tool. Use washers and a stepped drift for installing a valve guide

Pressing in replaceable valve guides

Knurling Valve Guides

In some cases, valve guides that are not excessively worn or distorted may be knurled. This applies to replaceable as well as cast guides. Knurling is a process in which metal is displaced and raised, thereby reducing clearance, giving a true center, and providing oil control. It is the least expensive way of repairing valve guides. However, the least expensive way is not necessarily the best, and in some cases, a knurled valve guide will not stand up for more than a short time. Following are better ways of repair.

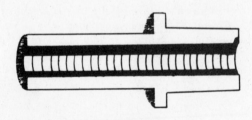

Cut-way view of a knurled valve guide

Reaming for Oversize Valves

To restore normal clearances and provide for a true valve seat, most cast guides can be reamed out to take a valve with an oversize stem. Standard oversize valves are generally 0.003 in., 0.005 in., 0.015 in., and 0.030 in.

Valve Guide Inserts

A coil insert can be installed in the valve guide. The guide is tapped and a bronze insert installed. The insert is then reamed to size.

A second type of guide insert, and probably the best way of repairing the cast valve guide is the thin-walled bronze insert. The guide is reamed slightly oversize and a split-sleeve thin-walled insert is installed. A special tool is run through the guide bore which expands the insert into the cast guide. The guide is reamed to standard size.

Replacement Guides

It is possible to have the old cast guide bored oversize and a replacement guide pressed into the enlarged hole. This is not a bad idea, but the thin-walled bronze insert is a better method.

VALVE SEAT INSERTS

Once the valve guides have been checked and repaired if necessary, the valve seats can be refinished. Many engines use a hardened valve seat insert pressed into the head. This is the standard practice with aluminum heads. Inserts must be replaced when they are cracked, loose, or badly worn. Inserts can be installed on heads (or blocks) with integrally cast valve seats. In the case of a loose or cast valve seat, the insert seat or casting is machined and an oversize or new insert installed.

REFACING VALVES

After the valve faces and stems are cleaned, the next step is to resurface the valve face. If the valve guides have been machined to accept an oversize valve stem, new valves will be used. If the valve guides are not worn much, or have been resized to standard, check the stems of the existing valves for wear.

Have the valve stem miked, or check them using a 0–1 in. micrometer. Check the unworn part of the stem (below or above the valve guide travel) against the worn part. A 0.001 in. wear is usually all right, but up to 0.002 in. is borderline. New "standard" valves should be used if the stem wear is greater than 0.002 in.

Next inspect the cleaned valve faces. Deeply grooved faces may not clean enough, or if they do, will not have

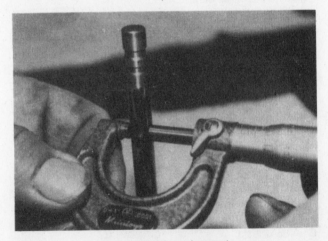

Measuring the valve stem with a micrometer

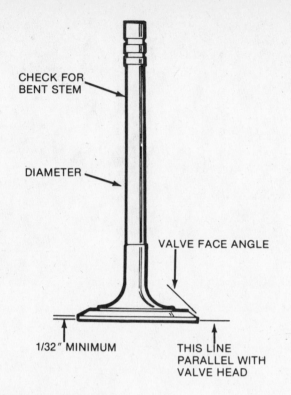

CHECK FOR
BENT STEM

DIAMETER

VALVE FACE ANGLE

1/32″ MINIMUM

THIS LINE
PARALLEL WITH
VALVE HEAD

Critical valve dimensions

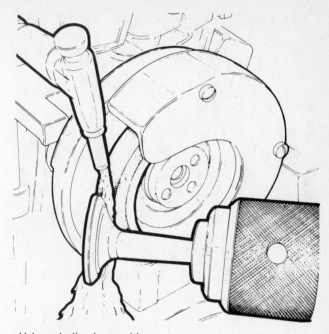

Valve grinding by machine

enough existing metal for good heat control. Burnt valves (usually exhaust) must be replaced. (Some light burning might be cleaned up by refacing.) Check the valve stem tips and keeper grooves. If the tip has been hammered by the rocker arm and worn to within $1/16$ in. of the keeper retainer, replace the valve.

The valves are refaced in a specialized piece of equipment called a valve grinder. It consists of a motor-driven chuck used to hold and rotate the valve face against a rotating grinding wheel. The chuck is adjustable to the correct angle required by the valve face. A cooling fluid is fed over the wheel and valve face while the valve is being ground. The wheel grinds the face of the valve, removing all burned spots and pits. Always

check the angle specifications before grinding the valves. The face angle is not always identical to the valve seat angle. A minimum margin of $1/32$ in. should remain at the edge of the valve after grinding. The valve stem top should always be dressed. This is done by placing the stem in the V-block of the grinder and rotating the valve stem while pressing lightly against the grinding wheel.

Sodium-filled exhaust valves must not be refaced on a machine. If the face is not too badly worn or burnt, the valve should be hand lapped. Valves that are in bad shape should be replaced.

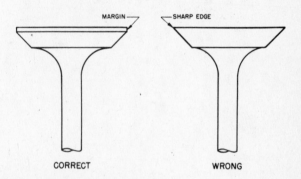

MARGIN

SHARP EDGE

CORRECT

WRONG

Proper edge thickness for a valve after refacing. Too thin an edge can lead to a melted valve

RECONDITIONING VALVE SEATS

Valve seats may be resurfaced either by reaming or by grinding. Valve seats in cast iron heads may be reamed, while hardened valve seat inserts must be ground. A reamed seat must be lapped with valve grinding com-

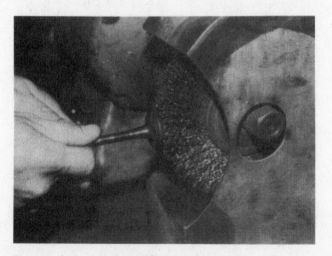

Clean the valve head and face on a wire wheel

The valve stem is refaced with the same machine

Turn the reamer clockwise while applying steady pressure

pound and the refaced or new valve that will be installed. It is not a bad idea to hand lap any valve when installing it in a newly machined seat.

Reaming the Valve Seat

Select a reamer of the correct seat angle, slightly larger than the diameter of the valve seat, and assemble it with the pilot of the correct size. Install the pilot in the valve guide and using steady pressure, turn the reamer clockwise (never turn the reamer counterclockwise, the cutters and the valve seat can be damaged). Remove only enough material to clean the seat. Check the concentricity (roundness) of the valve seat. (See the section on the use of a dial indicator.) This can be done by using

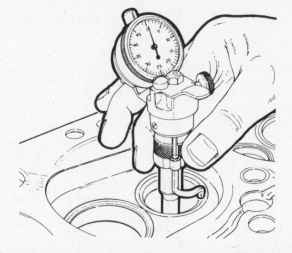

Checking the valve seat concentricity using a dial gauge

A set of valve seat reamers

Refacing Valve Seats with a Grinder

A high-speed grinder, driving a grinding stone mounted on a holder and riding on a valve-guide-mounted pilot probably is used more than any other method to reface valve seats.

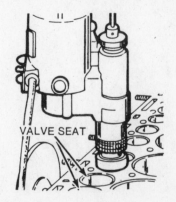

Grinding a valve seat

Prussian blue dye. Coat the face of the valve that is to be installed with the dye. Install and rotate the valve on the valve seat. Using the dye marked area as a centering guide, center and narrow the valve seat to specifications with correction cutters. If the specifications are not available, minimum seat width for exhaust valves should be $5/64$ in., intake valves $1/16$ in. After making any correction cuts, recheck with the seats and valves with the dye.

The finish on the valve seat depends on what grinding stone is used. By the correct use of various angle stones, the seat may be narrowed, stepped, or centered.

Checking Valve Seat Concentricity

Always check the concentricity of the valve seat after grinding either by the Prussian dye method (see Reaming the Valve Seat) or by using a dial indicator. Install the dial indicator pilot into the valve guide, rest the arm on the valve seat, and zero the gauge. Rotate the arm around the center of the seat. The run-out should not exceed. 0.002 in. Refinish the seat if the run-out is over 0.002. in.

Stepped Valve Seat Angles

Many miles on an automobile engine can cause "sunken" valve seats; that is, seats that are very wide after grinding. To prevent too large a diameter seat or one that is too deep in the head, the top and bottom of the seat are cut at different angles, and then the center. For example, a normal 45 percent seat would have the top portion at 30 percent, the center at 45 percent and the bottom at 60 percent. Not only does this method of grinding center the valve contact point, it also prevents the restriction of air flow.

If the stepped method of valve seat grinding is used, the width of the seat must be measured. If measurement is impossible, check the valve contact width by using the Prussian dye method. If the contact point is too wide or too narrow, a correction to the valve seat must be made or valve burning and face recession can occur.

Lapping Valves

To ensure tight sealing, the valves should be hand lapped to the valve seats. Even with the super fine finish provided by the new types of valve refacing equipment or the use of new valves, the small amount of time it takes to lap each valve is well worth the effort.

Lightly lubricate the valve stems and install the valves through their guides

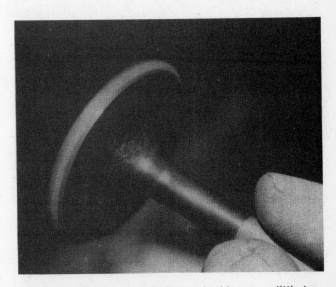

Rotate the lapping stick between the palms of your hands

Suction head of a valve-lapping stick

Circle indicating contact with seat, in this case a little too wide. Seat should be narrowed

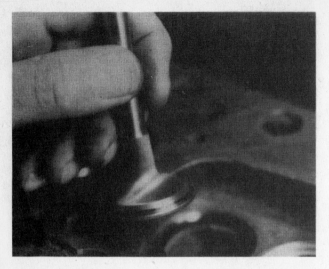

Correct seating valve

Invert the cylinder head. Lightly lubricate the valve stems. Install the valves into the head in their numbered order. Raise the valve from the seat and apply a small amount of fine lapping compound to the valve seat. Moisten the suction head of a hand-lapping tool and attach it to the head of the valve. Rotate the tool between the palms of both hands, changing the position of the valve on the valve seat and lifting the tool often to prevent grooving. Lap the valve until a smooth, polished circle is evident on the valve seat. Remove the tool and the valve. Wipe away all traces of the grinding compound and place the valve back into its proper numbered place in the valve stick. Do not get the valves out of numerical order after they have been lapped. They must be put back with the same valve seat they were lapped with.

Sodium-filled exhaust valves must be hand lapped; they must never be machine refaced.

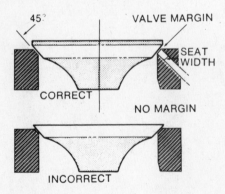

Valve seat width and centering

CAM BEARINGS—OVERHEAD CAM ENGINES

When reconditioning the cylinder head from an overhead cam engine, pay attention to the cam bearings. Some OHC engines use circular precision cam bearings that require a special tool to remove and install them. Other types of OHC engines have insert bearings mounted on caps that are very similar to connecting rod bearing caps. One-half of the cam bearing is mounted in the bearing cap, the other in a boss on the cylinder head. The cam is positioned on the head and retained by the caps. On another type of OHC engine the bearing surfaces are machined and finished as part of the head. If the bearing surfaces are badly worn, replacement of the cylinder head is required.

CHECKING THE CAMSHAFT—OHC ENGINES

The lobes (the parts of the camshaft that actuate the valves), the bearing journals (cam mounting points), and the trueness (straightness) of the camshaft can all be checked in the same way as an engine-block-mounted cam shaft (see Chapter Six).

OIL-BEARING CLEARANCE—OHC ENGINES

If the engine has circular precision bearings, the correct oil clearance is built-in, provided that the camshaft bearing journals are not too badly worn. If they are, a new camshaft or undersize bearings will be necessary.

The oil clearance on bearing-cap-mounted camshafts can be checked by using Plastigage (see Chapter Eight).

As mentioned before, cylinder heads that have the cam bearing surfaces machined into the head must be replaced if the surfaces are badly worn.

Oil pressure to the camshaft on OHC engines is of utmost importance. When the head is being cleaned, all oil passages should be checked with air pressure to make sure they are open. When circular cam bearings are installed, the oil holes in the bearings must be lined up with the cylinder head oil holes. If the camshaft uses an external oil feed tube, check that air will pass through with no restriction.

VALVE TRAIN COMPONENTS

All of the remaining valve train components should be cleaned and inspected.

VALVE SPRINGS, CAPS, RETAINERS, AND KEEPERS

The valve springs are a very important part of the valve train. It is their job to hold the valve tightly against the valve seat to seal in combustion chamber pressure and to return the valve to the closed position after feeding in the fuel air mixture or allowing the burned gases to exhaust from the combustion chamber.

Checking the valve spring pressure

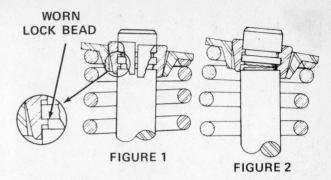

WORN
LOCK BEAD

FIGURE 1   FIGURE 2

Make a thorough inspection of the valve locks and beads. Always replace worn parts. However, as a precautionary measure, it is advisable to replace all locks. If an unworn lock is inadvertently mated with a worn lock (Figure 1), the retaining cap might shift, resulting in valve tip breakage (Figure 2)

ROCKER ARM MOUNTS

Rocker arms may be mounted on a stud, shaft, capscrew-mounted fulcrum seat, or a ball pivot and spring. A careful inspection of the mount is necessary, and worn parts should be replaced.

VALVE TRAIN FAILURE DIAGNOSIS

If the cylinder head is on an engine with high mileage, there is a very good chance that the valve springs have been weakened beyond specifications, and it would be best to install a complete set of new valve springs.

Valve spring pressure can be tested quickly with a special spring gauge. The spring is placed on the base of the tester and a hand-operated press assembly compresses the spring. Spring pressure is registered on the gauge. If the spring pressure is not at least 90 percent of the manufacturer's specification, the spring should be replaced.

Check the valve spring's height and squareness by placing the spring on a flat surface next to a carpenter's square. Measure the height of the spring and rotate it against the edge of the square to check for distortion. If the spring heights vary more than 1/16 in. or if the distortion exceeds 1/16 in., replace the spring.

Carefully inspect the spring coils. Valve spring breakage can be caused by surface imperfections, such as pitting or corrosion. If a valve spring breaks while the engine is running, major damage will occur. Replace any valve spring that shows suspicious markings.

Inspect the valve keepers, top retainers, top sleeves (if equipped), inner damper springs (if equipped), and lower spring seat (if equipped). Pay special attention to the keepers and retainer. If the edges of the keepers are rounded or the retainer grooved, replace them. Any out-of-round or grooved sleeve or bottom spring seat should be replaced.

Excessive valve train clearances allow the rocker arm to strike the valve tip with hammer-like blows, often producing a depression on the rocker arm pad. Improperly adjusted mechanical lifters, valve train wear, or a malfunctioning hydraulic lifter will cause this problem (Courtesy TRW, Inc.)

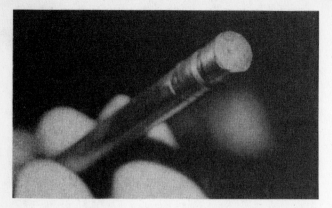

Excessive valve train clearance also hammers the valve tip

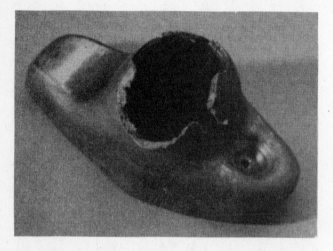

Broken rocker arms normally indicate interference in the valve train. This generally results from valve/piston collision due to excessive engine speed or insufficient piston-to-valve clearance. Lack of lubrication can also result in a similar condition (Courtesy TRW, Inc.)

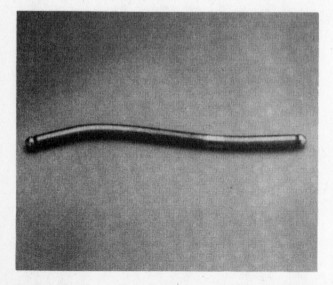

Bent or broken pushrods indicate interference in the valve train. Incorrect valve springs or an installed height less than specified can cause coil bind. Also insufficient valve-to-piston clearance can cause a collision between the valve and piston at high engine speeds (Courtesy TRW, Inc.)

VALVE SPRING FAILURE DIAGNOSIS

Valve springs that are out of square ($\frac{1}{32}$ in. or greater per inch of free height) can cause a side load on the valve. This can cause premature guide wear or even worse, valve breakage. Check spring squareness and replace the spring if the specification is exceeded (Courtesy TRW, Inc.)

Spring surge is the name given to the violent extending motion of the coils which results in abnormal oscillation. Spring surge results when the valve train does not follow the camshaft profile. This can be caused by weak valve springs, improper valve spring installed height, or excessive engine speeds. A good indication of surge is polished valve spring ends (as shown). Surge is a condition that can cause numerous valve train problems, such as seat recession, rocker arm failures, spring breakage, and even valve breakage (Courtesy TRW, Inc.)

Typical notched valve stem

The photograph compares the height of a new spring and a used spring. The used spring has collapsed slightly. The length reduction will lower open and closed pressures. Spring pressure should be at least 90 percent of the manufacturer's specification or valve spring surge may occur (Courtesy TRW, Inc.)

Valve spring breakage can be caused by surface imperfections, such as pitting or corrosion, as well as any of the previously mentioned conditions. When a valve spring breaks, disastrous engine failures can occur because the valve may contact the piston or cylinder wall. A careful visual inspection of the springs for surface imperfections is a must (Courtesy TRW, Inc.)

VALVE FAILURE DIAGNOSIS

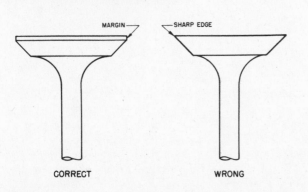

Proper edge thickness for a valve after refacing. Too thin an edge can lead to a melted valve

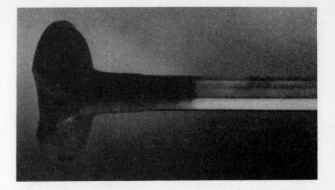

The picture illustrates the characteristic melting and blowing of material from the valve face from preignition. This condition develops when the fuel/air charge ignites prematurely. Potential causes of this failure include the glowing of sharp edges or deposits in the combusion chamber, improper spark plug heat range, knife thin valve head margins, and improper ignition timing (Courtesy TRW, Inc.)

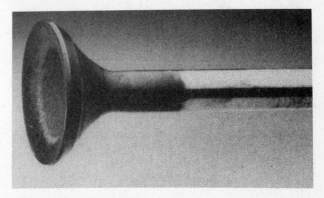

Valve cupping (tuliping) is descriptive of the valve appearance. This problem develops when abnormally high temperatures weaken the valve, allowing combustion pressures along with spring and inertial forces to deform the valve head. Commonly, elevated valve temperatures are caused by severe engine overloads, improper carburetion, and/or ignition settings and incorrect seat location or width (Courtesy TRW, Inc.)

Thermal shock occurs when a valve experiences extreme temperature variations. Extremely heavy engine loading, followed by abrupt unloading, or total engine shutdown creates excessively high internal stresses in the valve head. Consequently, radial cracks form through the valve margin. The cracks can interconnect, causing portions of the valve to break away as shown. Thermal shock can best be eliminated by avoiding severe fluctuations in engine load (Courtesy TRW, Inc.)

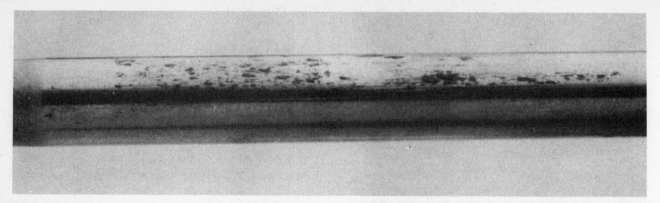

The picture shows what develops when lubrication film between the valve stem and guide breaks down. Although the damage itself does not appear to be severe, scuffing can cause the valve to stick in a partially open position. The valve can then burn from leakage or actually break, if struck by the piston. A careful review of both the stem-to-guide clearance and upper valve train oiling will usually prevent scuffing problems (Courtesy TRW, Inc.)

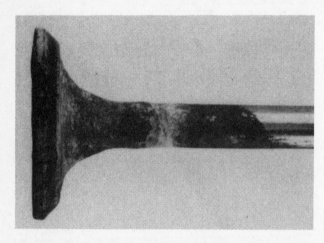

Valve burning is caused by high temperatures leaking past the valve face. The most common causes of leakage are seat distortion and deposit buildup. Seat distortion results from machining runout, thermal distortion (from overheating), and mechanical distortion (from warpage or improper torquing). The picture shows a valve that burned from deposits built up on the valve seat (Courtesy TRW, Inc.)

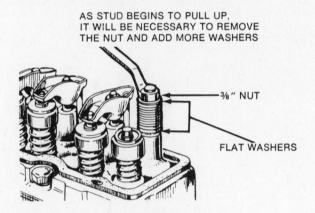

AS STUD BEGINS TO PULL UP, IT WILL BE NECESSARY TO REMOVE THE NUT AND ADD MORE WASHERS

⅜" NUT

FLAT WASHERS

Extracting a pressed in rocker stud

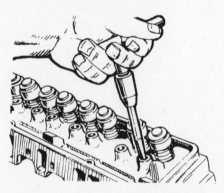

Reaming the stud bore for oversize rocker studs

Rocker Stud Replacement

If the rocker arm stud is cut (grooved) or pulling out of the head (measure height from head to the top of the stud), it will have to be replaced. A pressed-in stud is easy to replace. Put a number of flat washers over the stud until they cover the threads, leaving enough room to install the rocker arm adjusting nut. Put the nut on the stud and tighten with a socket and ratchet. Tightening the nut will pull the stud from its mounting hole.

Oversize base studs may be pressed into the head, but the best method of replacement is to use a screw-in stud. Depending on the brand of screw-in stud used, a special tapping tool or a regular tap is used to cut threads in the old stud mounting hole. The new rocker stud is then simply screwed into the threaded hole. Put some thread-locking compound on the threads before installing the stud.

Rocker Shafts

Rocker arm shafts are usually hollow and closed at each end by plugs. A bushing is usually installed in the rocker arm. This rides on a film of oil on the rocker shaft. If the engine has suffered from oil starvation, the rocker shaft will be scored. Replace the rocker shaft if scoring exists. When disassembling the rocker arm shaft for inspection or replacement, note if the rocker arms are designed for right- and left-hand operation or if the intake and exhaust rocker arms are different. The rocker arms must be installed in the same position from which they were removed.

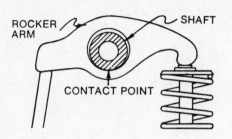

Wear points; rocker to rocker shaft

Rocker Arm Pivots

All rocker arms pivot on something. The rocker arm shaft has already been mentioned. Most common are ball seats or fulcrum mounts. The ball seat or the fulcrum fit inside the rocker arm and are mounted over a stud or have a cap screw passing through the center. Overhead camshaft engines sometimes have the rocker arms pivoting on a ball located underneath them. This is also the adjustment point for valve lash. If any of the pivot points are worn, replace them. If a worn pivot is not replaced, valve adjustment can be a problem and bad engine performance will occur.

ROCKER ARMS

Inspect all rocker arms for wear at the point where they contact the valve stem, push rod, cam lobe (OHC engines) and the pivot point. On rocker-shaft-mounted rocker arms, check the bushing insert (if equipped) for wear. Replace any rocker arm or pivot bushing that shows excessive wear.

The valve stem contact point may usually be refaced. This is done on a jig that fits onto the same machine that refaced the valves. If too much metal is removed to provide a smooth face, replace the rocker arm.

VALVE ROTATORS

Some engines use a valve rotating mechanism mounted on the top of the valve stem. Its purpose is to rotate the valve slowly, which helps prevent deposit buildup. If the engine is equipped with the rotators, be sure they are installed at the time of head assembly.

PUSHRODS

Although the pushrod is not part of the head reconditioning, it plays an important part in the valve train. Make sure that the pushrods are straight (roll them across a flat pane of glass) and not clogged (blow

through them). A bent pushrod is evidence of interference in the valve train. Check for incorrect pushrod length, incorrect valve springs, valve springs with less installed height than necessary, incorrect valve adjustment, and collision of the valve with the piston caused by incorrect clearance, or timing chain, belt, or gear problems.

VALVE LIFTERS

Like the pushrods, the lifter is usually not part of the cylinder head. Some OHC engines do have parts called cam followers that could be described as lifters.

The normal lifter has a convex radius at the bottom. If the bottom of the lifter is flat or concave, replace it. Lifters will be discussed further in Chapters Six and Eight.

RING   UMBRELLA   POSITIVE

Types of valve seals

POSITIVE VALVE STEM OIL SEALS

Due to the pressure differential that exists at the ends of the valve guides (atmospheric pressure above, manifold vacuum below), oil is drawn through the valve guides into the combustion chamber. While a certain amount of oil is needed for lubrication, an excess is not. An oil seal is mounted on the valve stem or over the tops of the valve guide to control the amount of oil that is sucked into the valve guides.

Positive oil seals are popular today. These seals fit over the top of the valve guide and contain a Teflon insert through which the valve stem rides. They are made for most engine applications and can be mounted, in most cases, without any machine work required. However, sometimes the top of the valve guide must be cut to accept the seal. The machine work can be done by renting or buying the cutter required from a parts store, or by having a machine shop do the work.

CYLINDER HEAD ASSEMBLY

After all the necessary machine work has been done, a final cleaning before assembly is required. Use solvent and thoroughly wash down the exterior of the head. Run solvent through all the ports and passages. Blow dry with air pressure or wipe with clean rags. Install any freeze plugs that were removed. For assembly procedures see Chapter Eight.

6

BLOCK INSPECTION AND RECONDITIONING

After the engine has been completely disassembled, inspect the block, crankshaft, connecting rods and pistons, the camshaft and timing components and so on. Pay attention to piston ring and bearing wear and try to diagnose any problems that may have existed.

Make a list, as you go along, of what parts are needed and what machine work needs to be done, whether the cylinders need boring, the crank turning, and so on. Complete the inspection before you order any parts or send any machine work out.

If the engine block was not leaking before it was removed from the car, an assumption can be made that there are no external cracks. If the oil drained from the crankcase did not contain coolant, an internal leak probably does not exist.

Some engines are susceptible to cracking at the bolt holes where the main bearing caps are mounted. If a crack is found and the engine is a common mode, scrap the block and get another. If the engine is not that common and a crack is suspected, refer to Chapter Five for various methods of crack detection. Most cracks in an engine block can be repaired. Consult your local automotive machine shop for their opinion. However, to repeat, if another good block can be found, scrap the cracked one.

An example of extreme cylinder wall wear

CYLINDER WALLS

Inspect and measure the cylinder walls. The bore should be checked for out-of-roundness, taper, and size. The results of this inspection will determine whether the cylinder can be used in its existing size or a rebore to the next oversize is required.

The amount of cylinder wall wear is greater at the top of the cylinder than at the bottom. This wear is known as taper. Any cylinder that has a taper of 0.012 in. or over should to rebored. However, if the engine will only be used in light service, or if obtaining oversize pistons would be a problem, the bottom of the cylinder can be honed to the same size as the top and specially fitted piston rings used.

Measuring cylinder wall taper with a dial indicator (Courtesy TRW, Inc.)

Two other factors contribute to the question of whether or not to rebore the block. First, are there any deep grooves caused by a broken piston ring or a sharp piece of carbon or dirt? Second, what is the condition of the pistons that were removed from the engine? Deep grooves in the cylinder walls cannot be honed out, so a bore job will be necessary. If the pistons are broken, cracked, or have broken ring grooves or excessive skirt-to-cylinder-wall clearance, and so on, the block should be rebored and new pistons fitted.

If just one cylinder wall is in need of repair and the other cylinders and pistons are in good shape, consider having a cylinder sleeve installed.

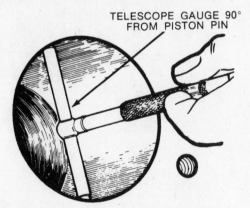

Measuring cylinder bore with a telescope gauge

MEASURING THE CYLINDER BORE

Make sure the cylinders are clean, especially at the top. Wire brush away any carbon deposits until bright metal shows.

Measurements can be made with a special dial indicator, telescope gauge and micrometer, or with an old compression ring taken from one of the pistons removed from the engine.

Measurements should be taken at a number of places in each cylinder: at the top, middle and bottom and at two points at each location; that is, at a point 90° from the crankshaft, as well as a point parallel to the crankshaft.

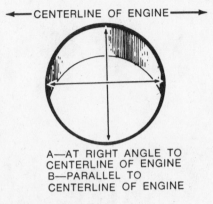

Cylinder bore measuring points

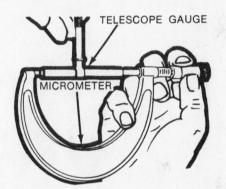

Determining cylinder bore by measuring telescope gauge with a micrometer

If the necessary precision tools to check the bore are not on hand, take the block to a machine shop and have them mike it. Also, if you do not have the mikes to check the cylinder bores, chances are you will not have the necessary devices to check the crankshaft. Take the crankshaft with you and save yourself an extra trip.

Another method of checking cylinder wear uses an old compression ring (taken from one of the pistons removed from the engine) and a set of feeler gauges. Place the piston ring in the bore just below the removed ridge. Make sure it is square in the bore (push it into place with a piston). Measure the end gap of the ring with the feeler gauge. Move the ring to the bottom of the bore and take another measurement. The taper of the cylinder is roughly 0.3 times the difference of the ring end gap readings. The amount of taper should not exceed 0.007 to 0.009 in. If it does, have the block rebored.

GLAZE BREAKING

If the cylinders are within specifications and no reboring is planned, the glazed finish caused by the old piston rings must be broken. The purpose of glaze breaking is not to remove a great deal of material from the cylinder wall, but just enough to leave a cross-hatch pattern to help the new piston rings seat.

Recheck the top of the cylinder to see if the ridge caused by the old top piston ring was completely

The upper ring shows where the ridge has been removed

Using a glaze breaker

removed. If not, use a ridge reamer and take off as much ridge as possible to match the bore. Take a glaze breaker or a spring-loaded, flexible shaft hone and run it up and down the cylinder wall. Remember, the object is to produce a cross-hatch pattern, not to remove a great deal of metal. There are several schools of thought as to the degree of cross-hatching. The current trend is to use a 22-to-32° pattern, as opposed to a 50-to-60° pattern. Check the instruction sheet that comes with the piston ring set (if on hand) or with the manufacturer of the rings for their recommendation.

Some newer engines using a thin block design require the use of a deck plate when honing the cylinders. The thin block has an inherent flexibility; the deck plate pre-stresses the block in the same manner the cylinder head would. Check with the machine shop to see if the use of the deck plate is necessary. If so, have them do the honing.

Using a flexible shaft cylinder hone

RESIZING THE CYLINDER BORE

If the cylinder taper is 0.012 in. or more, the block should be bored out to the next standard oversize and new pistons fitted. If the taper is less than 0.012 in. the bottom of the cylinder can be honed to match the top. The old pistons can be used, although they may need expanding.

When a block is rebored, the boring bar leaves a rough wall finish that requires honing to produce a wall that is acceptable to prevent excessive ring wear.

Honing with a deck plate (Courtesy TRW, Inc.)

Some boring equipment hones: the block is mounted in a fixture, and the cylinder walls are "bored" to size and finished with the same rigid hone. The hone is accurately controlled and leaves a highly desirable surface texture on the cylinder walls.

Sunnen CK 10 in action. An example of a rigid hone-boring a block

CYLINDER SLEEVES

If all but one or two cylinders can be reconditioned or if a cylinder wall is cracked and a replacement block cannot be found, a cylinder sleeve can be installed to repair the problem. The cylinder is bored to a size usually 0.001 in. less than the outside diameter of the sleeve. The boring bar is not allowed to run to the bottom of the bore but stopped so that a small step is left. The sleeve is chilled and then driven into the bored out cylinder until it bottoms on the step. The excess at the top of the sleeve is removed and the sleeve is bored and finished to match the other cylinders.

Example of the finish produced by a rigid hone

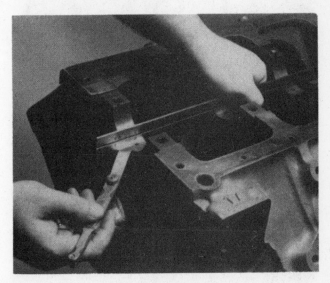

Checking block saddles for alignment (Courtesy TRW, Inc.)

Machines waiting to align bore an engine

CYLINDER BLOCK BEARING ALIGNMENT

Turn the engine block onto its top. Remove the main bearing caps and the main bearing inserts (if still installed) from the block-bearing saddles. Place a straight edge on the bearing saddles along the centerline of the crankshaft. If clearance exists between the straight edge and the center saddle, the block must be align-bored.

Align-boring consists of machining the main bearing block and cap saddles by means of a flycutter that runs through the bearing saddles.

Checking the deck for flatness

DECK FLATNESS

The top of the engine block where the cylinder head mounts is called the deck. Make sure the deck surface is clean of dirt, carbon deposits, and old gasket material by taking some sandpaper (fine grade for aluminum blocks) and sanding the deck surface until it is clean. Take a straight edge and place it across the deck surface. Using feeler gauges, check for clearance at the center of the deck. Measure across both diagonals and along the longitudinal centerline. If the warpage exceeds the manufacturer's specification, the deck will have to be resurfaced. The machine shop will do both decks on V-type engines even though one side is not warped. This ensures equal deck height (necessary for proper intake manifold seating).

CRANKSHAFT

Each crankshaft main journal and crank pin must be thoroughly inspected. They must be checked for surface condition and proper diameter. The journals must not be tapered or out-of-round. If any measurement is not within "specs", the shaft or pin should be ground and undersize bearings (or bearing) installed. Some engine manufacturers may install an undersize crankshaft or one with an undersize crankpin as stock; make sure this is not the case if an out of "spec" reading is taken. If the crankshaft checks out all right but the journals are a little rough, the crankshaft can be polished and standard or "one under" bearings used.

In order to save time and sometimes expense, crankshaft kits are available for most of the more popular engines. The kit consists of a reground crankshaft and the necessary undersize bearings.

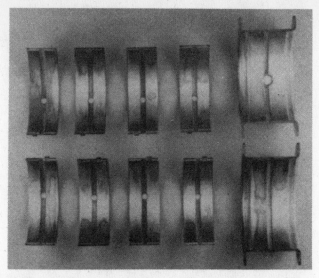

Main bearing misalignment is typified by irregular wear on the bearing overlay from uneven loading. To properly identify this condition, lay out the bearings in their respective position and examine the wear pattern. Misalignment causes an irregular pattern shown in the picture. Major cases include a warped crankcase, shifted main bearing caps, and/or a bowed crankshaft. Misaligned rod bearings display a similar abnormal pattern (Courtesy TRW, Inc.)

Crankshafts waiting to be machined

Checking the crankshaft journal with a micrometer

CAMSHAFT AND LIFTER FAILURE DIAGNOSIS

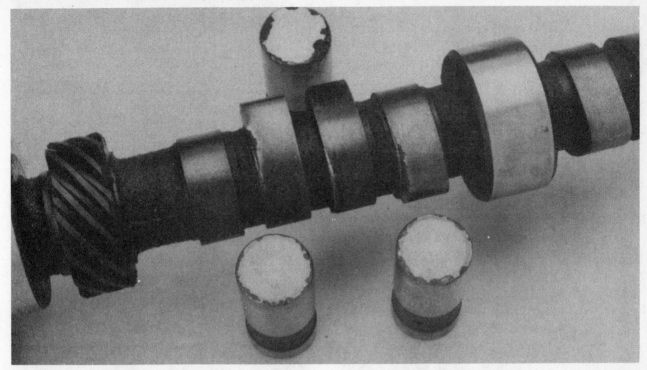

Lode and lifter interferene occurs primarily in engines originally equipped with a separate cam sprocket spacer (used to control end clearance). The problem develops when a replacement sprocket with a built-in spacer is installed without removing the original spacer. This forces the cam shaft rearward, allowing the lobes to strike adjacent lifters, chipping the edges of both. Interference will also develop if sprocket bolts are not tightened properly or if the cam sprocket/engine block thrust surfaces are worn excessively (Courtesy TRW, Inc.)

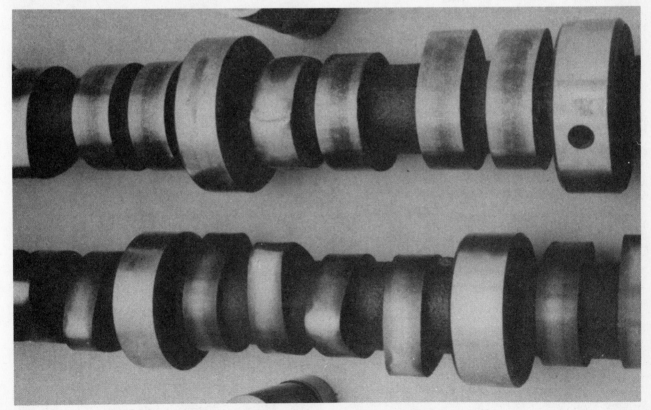

Edge wear on cam lobes occurs when used lifters are installed with a new camshaft. The bottoms of used lifters are often flat or slightly concave due to previous wear. Consequently, the lifters will contact the lobe along a narrow band at the lobe's edge. This tends to create high contact forces and rapid wear results. (Courtesy TRW, Inc.)

Do not despair if the crankshaft is damaged and a crank kit cannot be located. The crankshaft is very tough and can usually be repaired. If a journal or journals are worn or damaged beyond a normal oversize grind job, they can be welded and then reground. In fact, the whole crankshaft can be welded and ground to standard. High-performance engines have crankshafts welded, reground, chromed, and polished to standard size. This, however, is very expensive.

Another method used to gain greater engine performance is to have the entire lower end of the engine balanced; that is, the crankshaft, piston and rod assemblies, the flywheel, and so on. It is an expensive job. Ask the machine shop about this, but unless you are building a racing engine, it is not necessary.

Hand polishing a crankshaft journal

A damaged journal may require welding and grinding

Sometimes polishing is all that is necessary

CAMSHAFT AND LIFTERS

The camshaft should be cleaned using a solvent, and the lobes and bearing journals checked for wear. A visual inspection is done first; if a lobe or journal is damaged it usually is quite easy to see.

Check the camshaft with a micrometer. Measure the lobes from nose to heel and again at 90° from the origi-

nal measurement, record the reading, and go to the next lobe. The lift of the cam lobe is determined by subtracting the second measurement from the first. If all of the exhaust lobes and all of the intake lobes are not identical, the camshaft will have to be reground or replaced. Check the bearing journals with a micrometer. If they are within specifications, fine, if not the camshaft will have to be reground and undersize bearings installed.

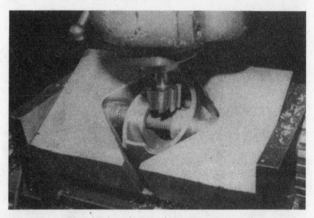

Pistons are checked and material removed in balancing

Connecting rods are weighted and matched

The crankshaft is balanced and polished

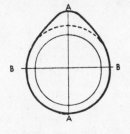

Camshaft lobe measurement

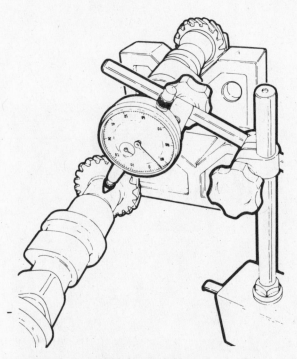

Checking the camshaft for straightness

If the lobes and journals check out, place the front and rear bearing journals in V-blocks and position a dial indicator on the center bearing journal. Slowly rotate the camshaft. If the dial indicator shows run-out (a 0.001 in. deviation) replace the camshaft because it is not straight.

Check the lifters. The bottom of the lifters, whether they are mechanical or hydraulic, should be convex. Rub the bottom of two of the lifters together. (Do not get the lifters out of order; if the old camshaft and lifters are to be reused, the lifters must go back in their original location.) If they rock back and forth, they are probably all right. If a visual inspection of the bottom of the lifter reveals flattening or concave wear, replace the lifter. If a lifter is worn badly, replace the camshaft as well, even if it did not show wear.

Hydraulic Lifters

Hydraulic lifters are designed to maintain zero-lash. That is, if any clearance exists in the valve train, the hydraulic lifter instantly takes out the lash. If the lifter is worn more than the clearance it can adjust, it will start to make noise.

If after inspecting the lifters the decision is made to reuse them, clean them. Clean the outside of the lifters by soaking them in a carburetor cleaner or strong solvent. After the outside is cleaned, take an oil squirt can filled with lacquer thinner and force some thinner through the oil hole in the top or side of the lifter. Force the lifter plunger up and down while continuing to squirt in the thinner. If the engine does not have high mileage, or has not suffered from the lack of oil changes, this method of cleaning should be enough.

Another way of cleaning is to disassemble the lifter. Should this be necessary, it is probably more practical to replace all the lifters.

Sludge, varnish, or metallic particles can cause the plunger to stick or hold the check valve open. A lifter with a stuck plunger can cause excessive valve lash. An open check valve will cause the lifter to collapse as the cam starts to raise it. Both problems will cause a noise and can lead to valve breakage (Courtesy TRW, Inc.)

Lifter Bores—Engine

Pay attention to the bores in the engine block where the lifters are mounted. Make sure they are clean and free of burrs. Check the oil feed holes to make sure they are not clogged.

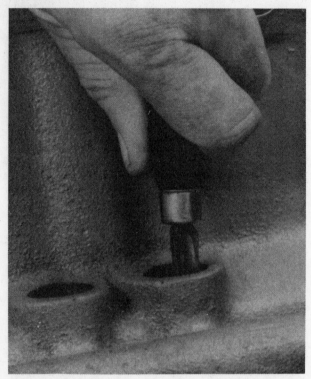

Clean the lifter bores in the block (Courtesy TRW, Inc.)

Piston skirt scuffing (the advanced state is scoring) on both thrust surfaces is an indication of insufficient piston-to-wall clearance. Scuffing of only one thrust surface (usually the major) points toward an inadequate supply of oil on the cylinder wall and/or high piston loading against the wall. Reasons for this could be use of the wrong viscosity oil for conditions, contaminated or fuel diluted oil, clogged oil squirt hole (if so equipped), or a deficiency somewhere in the lubrication system (Courtesy TRW, Inc.)

PISTON FAILURE DIAGNOSIS

(Figure 1) Preignition is an abnormal combustion condition occuring when the fuel/air mixture ignites prior to the regular spark. Often, localized hot spots in the combustion chamber, such as sharp edges on valves or gaskets, combustion deposits, or spark plugs of too high a heat range are the cause. The damaging effect of preignition is shown here. Note the melted, heat weakened appearance of the dome. (Figure 2) Detonation, (knock) also a form of abnormal combustion develops when a portion (yet unburned) of the fuel/air mixture suddenly explodes. Common causes are excessive ignition advance, too lean a fuel/air mixture, using a fuel of too low an octane rating, lugging or overheating. The picture shows detonation damage. Note the fractured head land and broken compression ring (Courtesy TRW, Inc.)

Piston skirt scuffing near the pin boss is due to abnormal thermal expansion. This results when a piston is exposed to excessively high operating temperatures. Common causes are abnormal combustion, low coolant level, contaminated coolant, scale or rust buildup in the water jacket (Courtesy TRW, Inc.)

Top land contact above the thrust surfaces develops when the piston rocks as it travels through the bore. Commonly, excessive skirt-to-wall clearance is the cause. Contact around all or most of the top land indicates excessive thermal expansion, due to prolonged high temperature exposure. If a contact pattern is found above the pin bore, a bent connecting rod is indicated. In any case, oil control and in some instances bearing wear problems are likely to occur (Courtesy TRW, Inc.)

PISTON RING FAILURE DIAGNOSIS

Abrasive wear is the major cause of premature ring failure. The grinding action of hard foreign particles will rapidly remove material from the rings and cylinder walls. Numerous fine vertical scratches which give the ring faces a dull gray appearance are characteristic of abrasive wear. The major cause of abrasive wear is the result of honing grit being left in the cylinder bores at the time of rebuild. Other sources of abrasives: infrequent air, oil, and breather filter maintenance; engine vacuum leaks and use of contaminated oil fill container (Courtesy TRW, Inc.)

Ring faces can scuff, or in extreme cases, score, due to metal-to-metal contact with the cylinder wall following breakdown of the oil film. Friction generated by the contact causes instantaneous welding, which is torn loose by the motion of the piston, leaving scratches and voids on the ring faces and cylinder wall. Causes include overheating, cylinder distortion, oil contaminated by coolant or fuel, improper bore finish, lack of lubrication, and insufficient piston to bore clearance (Courtesy TRW, Inc.)

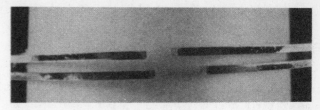

Worn grooves or a combination of worn grooves and worn rings increase the side clearance between the ring and groove, allowing abnormal shock loading during the power stroke. Broken rings have a characteristic area of carbon on both sides of the break (Courtesy TRW, Inc.)

Fuel wash causes light scuffing. The compression ring faces have a dull finish with occasional vertical scratches. An overly rich fuel mixture washes the oil film from the cylinder wall, causing metal-to-metal contact. Sources of trouble can be faulty carburetion or fuel injection, improper choke operation, and a clogged air filter (Courtesy TRW, Inc.)

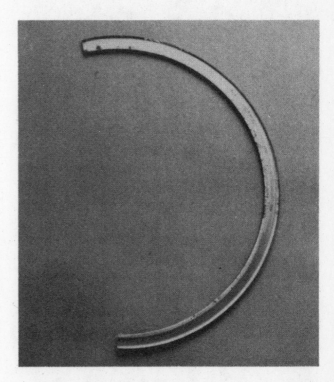

Tests with radioactive tracers have shown that top compression rings rotate slowly without ill effect on their service life. However, rapidly spinning rings create excessive side wear and polishing. This is caused by a bent or twisted connecting rod or a heavy one-directional honing pattern (Courtesy TRW, Inc.)

PISTONS AND CONNECTING RODS

The condition of the pistons relates to the question of boring the block to a standard oversize. In other words, if the pistons need replacing or have excessive piston-to-bore clearance, why not have the block bored to a larger oversize? The choice is up to you. If the condition of the cylinders is borderline and some of the pistons need to be replaced, why not?

Piston Inspection and Cylinder Wall Clearance

Take a piston and connecting rod assembly and clamp the rod in a vise just under the skirt of the piston. Use a ring expander to save wear and tear on the thumb tips and remove the rings from the piston. Clean the piston ring grooves using a special tool or a piece of broken piston ring. Break one of the rings you have just removed that is the same size as the groove you are about to clean. When cleaning the oil ring groove use the thickest compression ring (if they are of different thicknesses). Use a twist drill that will fit through the

Checking piston diameter

Insert piston into the bore

Clean the ring grooves with a special cleaning tool

small holes behind the oil ring to open up holes or slots that are clogged. Take care not to cut too deeply when cleaning the ring grooves. Scrape the carbon from the top of the piston. Never use a wire brush. After removing the rings and cleaning the ring grooves, put the pistons (head down) in a container of solvent and let them soak for a time. Take the pistons out of the solvent and blow or wipe them dry.

Inspect the pistons for skirt scuffing, scoring, cracks, broken ring lands, excessive ring groove wear, and pre-ignition or detonation damage (see Piston Failure Diagnosis illustrations).

Use a micrometer and measure the diameter of the piston perpendicular to the piston pin, on the skirt. Measure the cylinder the piston came from. Take the mea-

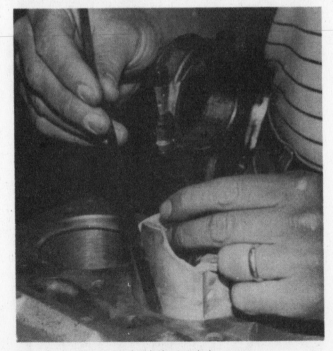
Use a feeler gauge to check the total clearance

surement about 2¼ in. (0.09 mm) below the top of the bore and perpendicular to the piston pin. The difference between the two measurements is the piston clearance. If the clearance is within specifications, the piston may be used as is. If the piston clearance is slightly below specifications, knurling the piston skirt may be considered. Knurling is really a stop-gap measure for patchwork. The best bet is to replace a piston that has too much side clearance.

If the necessary micrometer and telescope gauge for checking the clearance is not on hand, use the piston and rod assembly from the cylinder to be checked. The rings must be removed from the piston for this method.

Take the piston and place it in the cylinder bore. Take a feeler gauge and see how large a blade can be inserted between the cylinder wall and the piston. Check at a point 90° from the piston pin axis (the clearance between the piston skirt and cylinder wall). Slide the piston up and down in the cylinder and check the clearance at different points in the bore. Once again, if the clearance is greater than that in the specifications, replace the pistons or have the block rebored and new pistons fitted.

Piston Ring Groove Width

The top groove will show more wear than any of the others because it carries the heaviest loading. A badly worn ring groove will display a step on the lower part of the ring land. If you do not want to replace a piston that shows groove wear, the grooves can be machined wider and spacers provided to compensate for the additional clearance.

If the new set of piston rings is on hand, take the proper ring for the groove you are checking and roll the outside of the ring around the groove to check for burrs and deposits. If any are found, remove them with a fine file. Next take the ring and hold it in the ring groove.

Use a feeler gauge blade and check the clearance. If the clearance is too great, a new piston or the installation of a spacer is required. Most ring sets have a go/no-go depth gauge to check groove depth. Shallow piston ring grooves may be corrected by cutting them deeper. Deep grooves require some type of filler or expander behind the ring. Consult the machine shop or the manufacturer of the rings for the suggested method of repair.

Checking the Connecting Rod

If your engine does not require a rebore job and the existing pistons are all right, chances are that the piston-pin-to-piston clearance or the pin-to-rod bushing clearance is acceptable. A quick way of checking is to hold the head of the piston in one hand, take the rod in the other, and see if you can feel any wiggling while you twist the piston and rod in opposite directions. If no side motion is felt, there should be no problem.

If wiggling or side motion is felt, an oversize piston pin should be installed. This is usually a job for the machine shop. Of course, if new pistons are to be installed, they will come with piston pins and then the fit at the small end of the connecting rod needs attention.

If the piston shows diagonal wear on the skirt and the rod bearing insert shows wear on opposite sides of the upper and lower halves, the connecting rod is out of alignment with the piston. There are three main places for misalignment: the piston pin bore, the rod pin bore, and the crankshaft bearing bore. Many misalignment problems are caused by a bent or twisted connecting rod. Most of the time, the alignment problem can be corrected with an alignment fixture. The machine shop has one and usually can correct the situation by bending the rod.

"Identify and save the old bearings." Remember those words from Chapter Four? "Reading" the bearings can tell you a lot about the engine. If a rod bearing shows wear that cannot be blamed on dirt, lubrication

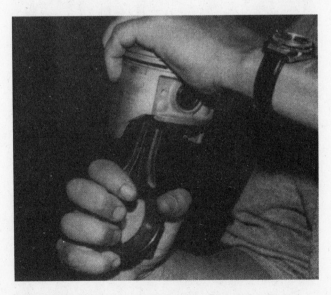

Twist the piston and rod assembly. There should be no motion

Diagonal skirt wear and pin end contact usually indicate a rod alignment problem (Courtesy TRW, Inc.)

BEARING FAILURE DIAGNOSIS

The primary cause of accelerated bearing wear is suspended dirt or other foreign particles in the lubricant. Debris commonly enters the engine through the air inlet or crankcase breathers. Metal chips from crank or block machining left behind at assembly will also cause problems. Careful attention to cleanliness of parts at assembly along with oil and filter changes at the proper intervals will prevent premature bearing wear (Courtesy TRW, Inc.)

Lack of oil is normally characterized by overall wiping marks on the bearing overlay and excessive heat discoloration (blueing) on the bearing backside. Some common causes incude plugged oil passages, internal oil leaks, a cracked or improperly installed pickup tube, low oil level, insufficient oil clearance, and/or oil pump relief stuck in the open position (Courtesy TRW, Inc.)

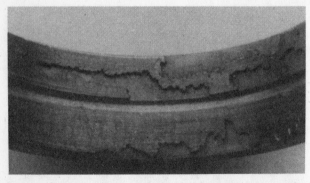

Bearing fatigue causes a separation of the bearing material from the steel backing at the bond line. This distress is normally confined to the more heavily loaded upper rod and/or the lower main bearing shells. The most common sources of fatigue are high loads from engine lugging, abnormal combustion (detonation or preignition), and/or a localized overloading from irregularities in the bearing bore (Courtesy TRW, Inc.)

Corrosion is indicated by pitting and discoloration of the bearing surface. Common causes are extreme blow-by, coolant leaks, incompatible oils, improper oil temperature (too low as well as too high), or clogged breathers, all of which either contaminate or chemically break down the lubricant (Courtesy TRW, Inc.)

failure, or fatigue, it could be that the connecting rod big end is out-of-round. If the backside of a bearing shows shiny spots or if a bearing has spun, the bearing bore of the rod is too big or there was insufficient bearing-to-crankshaft journal clearance. In any case, have the rods checked and reconditioned, or replaced if necessary.

A rod alignment fixture found in machine shops (Courtesy TRW, Inc.)

Piston and Rod Changing

The method by which the piston and connecting rod are attached determines whether you can slip them apart, or if a press and special fixtures are necessary. If the pin is retained in the piston by a spring clip (C-clip) at each end, simply remove the clips and push out the piston pin. Piston pins secured by a rod-mounted cap screw require the loosening of the screw and the use of a drift and hammer for removal.

The only mounting that requires special equipment is a pressed-in piston pin. This pin requires the use of a

Unless special care is taken, a piston can be easily damaged while the pin is being installed. This happens from the force needed to install the pin in the rod. It is advisable to apply moderate heat to the small end of the rod. Immersing it in hot oil is recommended to avoid concentrated overheating, as would be evidenced by a discoloring of the rod. This lets the bore expand and reduces the force needed to press the pin in (Courtesy TRW, Inc.)

press and special fixtures and sometimes the use of heat and cold for removal and installation. If you have a piston pin clearance problem, or are changing the rods or installing new pistons on press-in pin pistons, take the job to a machine shop. It's too easy to cause damage if the correct tools are not used.

When installing a piston that is retained by clips or attached by a cap screw, the connecting rod pin bushing should be checked. When installing new pistons on this type of rod, make sure there is not too much clearance in the bushing. If there is, a new bushing will have to be installed and reamed to take the new piston pin.

Whenever a connecting rod and piston are separated, it is imperative that they be put back together with proper orientation. Pistons and rods usually have a built-in offset. The notch in the head of the piston and the numbers on the connecting rod and cap must be in

the same relationship when assembled as they were before disassembly. All new pistons have a mark identifying the front.

One last thing before moving on to the next topic: the connecting rod bolts and nuts. If the engine has high mileage or if you suspect bolt fatigue, replace all the rod bolts and nuts.

Piston Rings

There are basically three different piston ring compositions: cast-iron, chromium, and molybdenum (moly). There are advantages and disadvantages for each type and the choice of one over the other depends on the job the engine must do and the conditions under which it must operate.

Cast-iron rings seat in the cylinder bore faster but wear out quickly and are less expensive than the other two types.

Chrome rings are very tough and last longer. This makes them an ideal choice if the engine is to operate in dusty or dirty conditions. They lend themselves well to heavy-duty service.

Moly rings are probably the best all around choice. They seat quickly and carry lubrication better than the other two types.

If you plan to use cast-iron or chrome rings and you are having the block bored and honed, tell the machine shop to give the bore a rough finish. This is required to help the rings seat faster. A set of moly rings requires a much smoother finish on the cylinder walls.

ENGINE BEARINGS

Bearing materials, design, and types were described in Chapter One. Before making a decision as to what type of bearing to install in the engine, review that information.

If a complete crankshaft kit is to be installed, you are pretty much at the mercy of the kit manufacturer as to what type of bearings are supplied, although heavy-duty bearings can be requested.

A good rule of the thumb is to stick with the type of bearings the engine manufacturer uses. The term *type* means material composition of the bearing. Installing heavy-duty bearings can never be a bad decision.

Cam bearings, with the exception of some OHC engines, require a special tool for removal and installation. Have the machine shop install them. Take the cam along or provide the new camshaft, if one is to be installed, so that it can be fitted with the new bearings. Remember, if the engine is hot tanked, the cam bearings will have to be replaced.

OIL PUMP

Depending on the design of the engine, the oil pump will be either rotary or gear. The oil pump is probably the most important part of the engine because it supplies

Most connecting rods and pistons have an offset. It is imperative that they be installed in the engine with the proper orientation. The F notch or arrow that appears on many pistons indicates which way the piston must be installed in the engine in order that the pin offset be utilized to reduce piston slap and noise (Courtesy TRW, Inc.)

OIL PUMP FAILURE DIAGNOSIS

Pump gears will jam if foreign particles are drawn into the pump. The photograph shows what happens when debris enters a pump through the bypass port in the pump screen. A lockup of the gears or rotors can result in a broken or twisted pump shaft or intermediate shaft (Courtesy TRW, Inc.)

Hard foreign particles (dirt, abrasive and metallic particles) that circulate through the lubrication system can lead to pitted or severely scratched rotors or gears in the oil pump. Cylindrical pressure relief valves may also be scratched. Particles hard enough to scratch pump components will also cause premature bearing and shaft wear. The increased clearance will cause a drop in oil pressure (Courtesy TRW, Inc.)

Oil aeration is caused by air being drawn through a leak on the suction side of the oil pump. A leak can result from a cracked seam in the screen housing or a loose connection to the oil pump. Aeration may also be caused by an over-filled crankcase. Such an error allows the crank counter-weights to churn the oil, forming air bubbles in the lubricant. Consequently, the oil pressure can fluctuate drastically (Courtesy TRW, Inc.)

Abnormal oil pressure can be caused by the oil pump relief valve being jammed by foreign particles. Low oil pressure will occur when the valve is stuck open. Excessively high pressure will occur when the relief valve is stuck in the closed position (Courtesy TRW, Inc.)

Pump casting breakage is caused by misalignment or failure to mount the pump squarely (Courtesy TRW, Inc.)

Prime the oil pump before installation (Courtesy TRW, Inc.)

Hammering gears into place can cause cracks through the keyway or possibly break off a tooth. Damage to chains can occur by rolling or prying them into position (Courtesy TRW, Inc.)

lubrication. Without proper lubrication, the most careful rebuild job will be in vain.

If you are sparing no expense, buy a new heavy-duty oil pump. If none is available, pay particular attention when checking or rebuilding the old pump.

Take apart the oil pump and check for scoring between the inner and outer gears or rotors. Get the specifications and check the clearances required. If they are too large, replace the necessary gear or rotor. Make sure no piece of scraped gasket material is in the oil feed passages. Replace or clean the pickup tube and screen. Check the pressure release valve to make sure it operates freely and is not full of gum. Prime the pump at installation or prior to starting the engine.

TIMING GEAR/CHAIN FAILURE DIAGNOSIS

Misalignment will cause heavy wear on the sides of the sprocket teeth. Commonly, alignment problems are the result of failing to tighten sprocket mounting bolts and/or excessive wear on the sprocket thrust surface (Courtesy TRW, Inc.)

A gear with cracks, spalling, or excessive wear on the tooth surface is an indication of improper backlash. With excessive backlash, operation will be noisy because the teeth will make violent impact contact. This overloading when coupled with the normal valve train loads causes accelerated tooth wear and often breakage. Insufficient backlash places a bind on the gears. High contact forces are generated which can rupture the lubrication film between the teeth, causing spalling and wear (Courtesy TRW, Inc.)

Under normal conditions, the load carried by the timing chain is far below its ultimate strength. However, foreign objects occasionally find their way into the timing case and lodge between the chain and gear. This causes an overload and a broken chain. The chain usually breaks straight across the links (Courtesy TRW, Inc.)

When the cam and crank gears are not properly aligned, the chain must twist in order to engage the teeth on the sprocket or gear. This puts an abnormally high stress on the teeth and chain. The chain will usually break diagonally across the links (Courtesy TRW, Inc.)

Timing Gears, Chains, and Belts

The camshaft is driven by gears, gears (sprockets) and chain(s), or gears (sprockets) and belt(s), depending entirely on the design of the engine.

Check all driving or driven parts. If a gear or sprocket shows worn or dull teeth, replace it. If a chain is suspected of stretch, replace it. If a belt has more than 25,000 miles on it, or if the teeth are not sharp or the fabric shows fatigue, replace the belt.

In all cases, if one gear or a chain needs replacement, replace both gears and the chain. It is always best to replace the parts in sets.

Some V–8 engines use a composition material on the cam drive gear that is subject to wear or breakage. Several aftermarket parts suppliers provide a metal tooth replacement gear, available by itself or in a timing set. Other types of gear and chain sets are available and should be considered if the engine you are rebuilding is to see heavy-duty service.

THE MACHINE SHOP

You have now completed the inspection of the engine block and internal parts and have a general idea of what parts and machine work is necessary. Take the block to the machine shop and let them start to work.

7

COMPONENT INSPECTION AND REPAIR

The same care and attention given to engine inspection and reconditioning should be given to the various "bolt on" components.

COOLING SYSTEM

RADIATOR

If the engine has been removed from the car for rebuilding, the radiator is already out of the car. Have it cleaned and pressure tested by a radiator repair shop.

WATER PUMP

Examine the water pump. Water pumps are generally serviced because they leak, but sometimes close examination will uncover potential problems before they happen. Pitted and eroded surfaces on the impeller and flow channels in the housing indicate contaminants or air entrapment in the cooling system. Contaminants attack the flow surfaces in the pump and, in some instances, damage the seal which may cause bearing or shaft damage. Replace a pump that is pitted or corroded.

Shaft failures (breakage) are the most destructive of all pump failures. Frequently, the cause for the failure is fatigue caused by a rotational imbalance. A shaft carrying an imbalanced load will flex as it rotates; consequently, small surface cracks develop that eventually progress into the shaft. A fatigue fracture is always flat and smooth. The depth of crack penetration is controlled by the severity of the imbalance and the load-carrying capacity of the remaining unbroken material. Once the critical depth is reached, the shaft will break. Check the shaft carefully and replace the pump if the shaft is suspect.

WATER PUMP FAILURE DIAGNOSIS

Check the water pump for pitted or eroded surfaces (Courtesy TRW, Inc.)

Left-hand picture shows fatigue crack and granular appearance of the inner region. Right side shows that with a light imbalance the crack travelled almost completely through the shaft (Courtesy TRW, Inc.)

Check for signs of leakage around the seal or at the casting hole under the shaft (Courtesy TRW, Inc.)

A water pump leak resulting from seal failure is generally the result of 1) excessive sealing surface erosion or wear caused by coolant contaminants; 2) cracking of the ceramic seat due to thermal shock (stress resulting from rapid temperature changes) produced by intermittent coolant flow, air entrapment, or a faulty thermostat; or 3) seal damage caused by vibrations created by rotational imbalance. Examine the seal and casting hole under the shaft in the casting. If any sign of leakage is present, replace the water pump.

THERMOSTAT

The most efficient operating temperature of an internal combustion engine is about 180 to 195°F (82 to 91°C). Below this temperature, the fuel will not fully vaporize, leading to crankcase dilution by raw gasoline. To warm the engine quickly and hold the coolant to the most efficient temperature, a thermostat is installed in the cooling system. The thermostat opens completely when the correct temperature is reached and reduces coolant flow until that time.

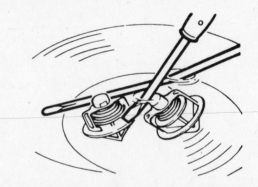

Check the operation of the thermostat

It is probably a good idea to replace the thermostat if a complete engine rebuild is in process. However, to check the operation of the existing (or new) thermostat, place the thermostat in a pan of water and heat on a stove. Use an over thermometer (stem and dial) to measure the temperature of the water. Observe the action of the thermostat. It should open as the water temperature increases and be fully opened when the rated temperature is reached. Turn off the stove. As the water temperature decreases, the thermostat should start to close. It is best to suspend the thermostat by a length of wire or string when performing this test; if the thermostat contacts the pan, its temperature will differ from that of the water, and the thermometer reading will be useless.

FAN CLUTCHES

Fan clutches are designed to engage at low engine speeds and in congested traffic conditions, but to shut off at high speeds, thus helping engine performance and reducing noise level.

The fan clutch mounts directly to the water pump flange, in front of the drive pulley. The clutch is composed of a body and clutch plate, each having grooves machined to mate with the other. The body is filled with a fluid. The fluid drive chamber operation is based on the shear resistance of the viscous fluid between the two members. Torque is transmitted from the shaft to the clutch plate through silicone fluid and into the body to which the fan is attached. The temperature adjustment is made by filling and evacuating the fluid chamber by means of a valve actuated by a bimetallic sensor. As the chamber fills, fan speed increases until the cut-off limit is reached.

A greasy dirt buildup or fluid around the outer seal on a fan clutch indicates seal and bearing wear. A worn-out fan clutch can produce a rotational imbalance that can damage the water pump. Replace the fan clutch if it is suspect.

FAN BLADES

Carefully inspect the fan blades. Replace any blade assembly that has a broken blade or loose rivets. Inspect fiberglass or plastic blades for cracks, and replace if necessary.

BATTERY

Every storage battery used in an outomobile has three key functions:

- To provide current for the starter and ignition system when cranking.
- To provide current (in addition to alternator current) to operate the radio, lights, and so on.
- To act as a voltage stabilizer or reservoir in the electrical system.

While the first two functions are obvious, the third may require some explanation. To understand it, first consider the battery and alternator (or generator) as opposing forces. Current will flow from the greater force to the lesser force. For example, after running the starter motor, the battery will be discharged because some of the acid has been absorbed into the plates. If the car is driven immediately (which is usually the case), current will flow back into the battery from the alternator. The voltage regulator will cut off the current when the battery is recharged.

The most important attribute of a lead-acid storage battery is its chemical reversibility. This means that unlike a dry cell battery, a storage battery is capable of being recharged by passing an electric current through it in the opposite direction of discharge. Through a chemical reaction, the battery's active chemicals will be restored to a state of charge.

To understand the charging process, you first have to understand how a battery is discharged.

The discharge process in a battery is begun as soon as an electrical circuit is completed, such as turning on the car lights. Current flows from the battery through the positive terminal. During the time that there is a drain on the battery (it is discharging), sulphuric acid in the battery works on both the positive and negative plates' active material, lead peroxide and sponge lead respectively. Hydrogen in the sulphuric acid combines with oxygen available at the positive plate to form water, which reduces the concentration of acid in the electrolyte. This is why the state of charge can be determined by measuring the strength (specific gravity) of the electrolyte.

The amount of acid consumed by the plates is in direct proportion to the amount of energy removed from the cell. When the acid is used up to the point where it can no longer deliver electricity at a useful voltage, the battery is effectively discharged.

To recharge the battery, it is only necessary to reverse the flow of current provided by the alternator through the positive terminal and out the negative battery terminal. The sulphate that formed on the plates during discharge is changed back to sponge lead and the sulphur returns to the electrolyte forming sulphuric acid again. At the positive plate, the lead sulphate changes to lead peroxide and returns even more sulphuric acid to the electrolyte.

When a car won't start, most people blame the battery, when in fact, it may be that the battery has run down in a futile attempt to start a car with other problems.

Battery output is affected by ambient temperatures; the battery becomes less efficient at low temperatures, while the power required to start the engine becomes greater. All this means that it pays to keep the battery in good shape so that power is there when it is needed.

A hydrometer is used to check the electrolyte specific gravity. The specific gravity is determined by the amount of sulfuric acid remaining in the electrolyte. The amount of sulfuric acid remaining in the electrolyte is directly proportional to the state of charge of the battery because the acid is absorbed by the plates during discharge, leaving only water behind. Test the battery specific gravity as follows.

- Remove the filler or vent caps from the battery top.
- Check the level of the electrolyte. It should be approximately 1/4 in. above the level of the plates. If it is not, add water.
- Insert the hydrometer into the battery cell and draw enough electrolyte into the tube to float the balls or the float. Ball hydrometers are probably easier to obtain than float hydrometers, but either one will work.
- Remove the hydrometer from the battery cell and hold it up to eye level in a vertical position. Read the float scale at the point where the surface of the liquid

meets it. Disregard any curvature of liquid against the float.

- Read and interpret the hydrometer results. A reading of 1,260 indicates a fully charged battery (reading corrected for temperature). Any reading below 1.220 is indicative of a poor charge condition. A reading of 1.150 or below indicates that the cell is dead. If any one cell is lower than the others by 0.50 or more, that cell is shorted and the battery must be replaced.

BATTERY CABLES

Inspect the cable terminals and the cable insulation. If the terminals are corroded but not worn, clean them. If excessive corrosion wear is present, replace the cables. Replace the cables if the insulation is cracked or the wires are bare.

CHARGING SYSTEM

When the ignition key is turned on, current movement is indicated by the glowing of the red charging indicator light or by the movement of the needle to the discharge side of the ammeter gauge.

Current passes through the ignition switch to the voltage regulator. The voltage regulator, through a series of resistors and transistors, sends a small amount of current to the alternator post which is connected to the brushes. The brushes contact slip-rings on the rotor, and pass the small amount of current into the windings of the rotor. This current passing through the rotor coils creates a magnetic field within the alternator.

As the engine is started and the rotor is rotated by the drive belt, the rotor induces a magnetic current in the stationary windings or stator located in the alternator housing and surrounding the rotor.

This induced current is alternating current (AC) and must be changed to direct current (DC); diodes are used for this purpose. The technical explanation of how a diode works is not important. Think of the diode as a form of an electrical check valve, allowing current to flow in one direction and blocking the current flow in the opposite direction. A negative diode will pass current traveling in a negative direction, while the positive diode will pass current traveling in a positive direction. The positive diodes make up the positive rectifier, while the negative diodes make up the negative rectifier.

The stationary windings or stator are wound into three sets of windings or phrases. Each phase winding is connected to a positive and a negative diode. When the phase winding is passing positive current, the current will flow through the positive diode and to the output terminal of the alternator.

When the phase winding is passing negative current, the negative diode allows the returning current from the ground circuit to pass into the windings to complete the circuit for another phase winding.

The direct current, flowing from the alternator output terminal to the battery, is used to provide the current to operate the electrical system and to recharge the battery. As electrical demand increases, the voltage regulator senses the low voltage condition and directs more current to pass through the rotor, thus increasing the magnetic field. This causes greater induction voltage to be produced, which increases the output of the alternator. As the voltage increases and the requirements of the electrical system decrease, the voltage regulator reduces the current flowing through the rotor, thereby lowering the magnetic field and decreasing the output of the alternator.

An alternator mounted on a test bench

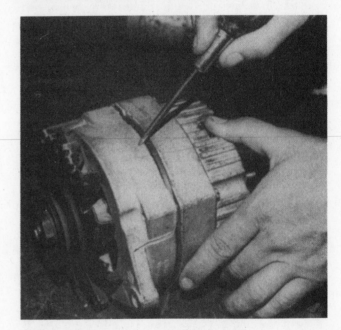

Scribe a reference mark across the alternator

ALTERNATOR

If you suspect less than normal output from the alternator, have it tested. The test will determine if the alternator needs to be rebuilt or replaced. Special tools and procedures are necessary for complete rebuilding; however, brush and bearing replacement can usually be handled without too much difficulty.

The general procedure for disassembling an alternator is as follows. Scribe a line across the end housing and stator frame for alignment reference when reassembling. Remove the housing through bolts. Separate the front housing and rotor assembly from the stator and rear housing assembly. It may be necessary to tap the front housing with a plastic-tipped hammer to loosen the front housing from the stator frame.

Remove the brush springs from the brush holder in the rear housing. Remove the nuts, washers, and insulators on the back of the rear housing. Note the location of the insulators for reassembly. Remove the stator and rectifer assembly from the rear housing. The rear bearing can be pressed out at this time.

Secure the front housing in a vise, using suitable protection so the housing will not be damaged. Remove the

pulley from the rotor shaft. Various alternators require different tools to remove the pulley. The front bearing may now be checked and serviced by removing the retaining cover. Install a new front and rear bearing.

Reassemble in the reverse order, replacing the brushes if they are worn shorter than 1/4 in. (0.01 mm). Some alternators use replacement brushes that come in a holder; others require a removable pin to hold them up until the alternator is fastened together. Check a manual for complete directions.

Parts of a typical alternator

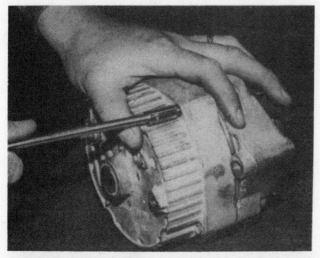

Remove the through bolts

STARTING SYSTEM

When the key is turned on, a small amount of current is sent to the starter solenoid, where it flows through a coil of wire wrapped around a metal core, encasing a metal plunger. As the current flows through the coil, a magnetic field is produced and the plunger is pulled into contact with the heavy wires of the battery-to-starter circuit. As contact is made, the current flows from the battery to the starter. The use of a starter switch or a relay controls the closing of the circuit between the battery and the starter only, and the drive gear is pushed into mesh with the flywheel by centrifugal force as the starter begins to rotate.

The solenoid is mounted on the starter and also used as an interrupter switch. Two functions must be performed: the closing of the circuit between the battery and the starter, and the starter drive gear moved to mesh with the engine flywheel gear teeth. The plunger is connected to the starter drive gear through mechanical linkage, and both the closing of the electrical circuit and the engagement of the starter drive gear occur at the same time.

Current to the starter is directed to the stationary coils around pole pieces or field coils and causes an

Remove the front pulley

increase in the magnetic field between them. A movable armature, made by looping heavy wire around a shaft is placed between the opposite field pieces. Part of the applied current is directed through brushes to a commutator, to which the ends of the wire loops on the armature are attached. As a result, a variable magnetic field is produced in both the armature and the field coils, which causes a repelling or kicking action between the two magnetic fields. The armature is the only part of the starter that is able to rotate and the mechanical force developed is transmitted to the engine by the starter drive unit.

The starting of the engine signals the driver to release the ignition key from the start position, stopping the flow of current to the solenoid or relay. The plunger is pulled out of contact with the battery-to-starter cables by a coil spring, and the flow of electricity to the starter is interrupted. This weakens the magnetic fields, and the starter ceases its rotation.

As the solenoid plunger is released, its movement also pulls the starter drive gear from its engagement with the engine flywheel.

STARTER MOTOR SERVICE

Diagnosis

STARTER WON'T CRANK THE ENGINE

1. Dead battery.
2. Open starter circuit, such as:
   a. Broken or loose battery cables.
   b. Inoperative starter motor solenoid.
   c. Broken or loose wire from the ignition switch to the solenoid.
   d. Poor solenoid or starter ground.
   e. Bad ignition switch.
   f. Defective seat belt interlock system—1974–75 cars only.
3. Defective starter internal circuit, such as:
   a. Dirty or burnt commutator.
   b. Stuck, worn, or broken brushes.
   c. Open or shorted armature.
   d. Open or grounded fields.
4. Starter motor mechanical faults, such as:
   a. Jammed armature end bearings.
   b. Bad bearing, allowing the armature to rub the fields.
   c. Bent shaft.
   d. Broken starter housing.
   e. Bad starter drive mechanism.
   f. Bad starter drive or flywheel-driven gear.
5. Engine is hard or impossible to crank, such as:
   a. Hydrostatic lock, water in the combustion chamber.
   b. Crankshaft seizing in bearings.
   c. Piston or ring seizing.
   d. Bent or broken connecting rod.
   e. Seizing of connecting rod bearing.
   f. Flywheel jammed or broken.

STARTER SPINS FREE, WON'T ENGAGE

Sticking or broken drive machanism.

SOLENOIDS WITHOUT RELAYS

This type of starter solenoid is always mounted on the starter. It makes electrical contact for the starter and pulls the starter and drive clutch into mesh with the flywheel. The Chrysler reduction gear starter has this solenoid embodied in the starter housing.

There is only one control terminal on the solenoid.

The ignition bypass terminal is usually marked R or IGN, if it is used.

SOLENOIDS WITH SEPARATE RELAYS

The solenoid itself is always mounted on the starter. In addition to making contact for the starter, it also pulls the starter drive clutch gear into mesh with the flywheel. A single control terminal is used on the solenoid itself. The relay is usually found mounted to the inner fender panel or on the firewall.

SOLENOIDS WITH BUILT-IN RELAYS

These units are always mounted on the starter and are connected, through linkage, to the starter drive clutch. The relay portion is built into and integral with the solenoid assembly.

NEUTRAL SAFETY SWITCHES

The neutral safety switch prevents the starter from cranking the engine except when the transmission is in Neutral or Park.

NOTE: *All Ford Motor Co. cars and Cadillacs starting 1974, and all 1977 and later full-size G.M. cars wth a column-mounted automatic transmission selector and steering column lock do not have a neutral safety switch; instead, the key can only be turned to the "START" position when the selector is in Park or Neutral.*

On some cars, the neutral safety switch is located on the transmission. It serves to ground the solenoid or magnetic switch, whichever is used.

On other cars, the neutral safety switch is located either at the bottom of the steering column, where it contacts the shift mechanism, on the steering column, underneath the dash, or on the shift linkage (console).

NOTE: *Recent cars with manual transmissions have a safety switch mounted on the clutch linkage to prevent starter operation unless the pedal is depressed.*

On most cars, the neutral safety switch and the backup light switch are combined into a single switch mechanism.

See the car sections for specific details.

Troubleshooting Neutral Safety Switches— Quick Test

If the starter fails to function and the neutral safety switch is to be checked, a jumper can be placed across its terminals. If the starter then functions, the safety switch is defective.

In the case of neutral safety switches with one wire, this wire must be grounded for testing purposes. If the starter works with the wire grounded, the switch is defective.

Neutral Safety Switch—Backup Light Switch

When the neutral safety switch is built in combination with the backup light switch, the easiest way to tell which terminals are for the backup lights is to take a jumper and cross every pair of wires. The pair of wires that light the backup lamps should be ignored when testing the neutral safety switch. Once the backup light wires have been located, jump the other pair of wires to test the neutral safety switch. If the starter functions only when the jumper is placed across these two wires, the neutral safety switch is defective or requires adjustment.

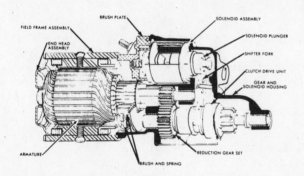

A reduction gear starter motor

REDUCTION-GEAR STARTER MOTOR

(Chrysler Corporation)

The housing is die-cast aluminum. A 3.5:1 reduction, combined with the starter-to-ring-gear ratio, results in a total gear reduction of about 45:1.

NOTE: *The high-pitched sound is caused by the higher starter speed.*

The positive shift solenoid is enclosed in the starter housing and is energized through the ignition switch. When the ignition switch is turned to start, the solenoid plunger engages the drive gear through a shifting fork. At the completion of travel, the plunger closes a switch to revolve the starter.

An overrunning clutch prevents motor damage if the key is held on after the engine starts.

No lubrication is required due to Oilite bearings.

1975 and later Chrysler Corporation cars with large V-8s (360 cu. in. and up) and some sixes use a larger reduction gear starter motor. It is similar to the previous models but is more powerful and has a 2:1 gear reduction rather than 3.5:1 The clutch drive unit in the new starter has been enlarged to handle the increased load as have the rest of the components. While the new starter is outwardly similar to the old one, parts are not interchangeable; however, removal, installation, disassembly, and assembly procedures are unchanged.

Disassembly

1. Support the assembly in a vise equipped with soft jaws. Do not clamp. Care must be used not to distort or damage the die-cast aluminum.
2. Remove the through bolts and the end housing.
3. Carefully pull the armature up and out of the gear housing, and the starter frame and field assembly.
4. Pull the field frame assembly out enough to get at the terminal screw. Remove the screw.
5. Remove the field frame assembly.
6. Remove the nuts holding the solenoid and brush holder plate to the gear housing. Remove the solenoid and brush plate.
7. Remove the nut, washer, and sealing washer from the solenoid brush terminal.
8. Unwind the solenoid lead wire from the brush terminal. Remove the screws and remove the solenoid from the brush plate. Remove the nut and battery terminal from the brush plate.
9. Remove the solenoid contact and plunger assembly, and the return spring.
10. Remove the gear housing dust cover. Remove the driven gear retainer clip.

NOTE: *The retainer is under tension; cover it with a cloth before removal to prevent loss.*

11. Remove the pinion shaft C-clip at the end of the housing. Push the pinion shaft in and remove the clutch assembly. Remove the driven gear and the washer.
12. Remove the retainer pin to remove the shifting fork.

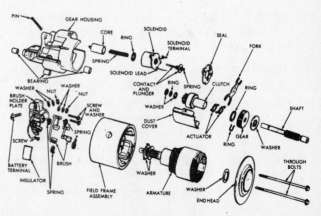

Exploded view of a reduction gear starter motor

Replacement of Brushes

1. Brushes that are worn more than one-half the length of new brushes, or are oil-soaked, should be replaced.
2. When resoldering the shunt field and solenoid lead, make a strong, low-resistance connection using a high-temperature solder and rosin flux. Do not use acid or acid-core solder. Do not break the shunt field wire units when removing and installing the brushes.
3. Brush spring tension should be 32 to 36 ounces.

Starter Clutch and Pinion Gear Inspection

1. Do not immerse the starter clutch unit in a cleaning solvent. The outside of the clutch and pinion must be cleaned with a cloth so as not to wash the lubricant from the inside of the clutch.
2. Rotate the pinion. The pinion gear should rotate smoothly (although it may require some force) and in one direction only. If the starter clutch unit does not function properly, or if the pinion is worn, chipped, or burred, replace the starter clutch unit.

Assembly

1. The shifter fork consists of two spring steel plates held together by two rivets. Before assembling the starter, check the plates for side movement. After the space between the plates has been lubricated with a small amount of SAE 10 engine oil, the plates should have about 1/16 in. side movement to ensure proper pinion-gear engagement.
2. Position the shift fork in the drive housing and install the shifting fork retainer pin. One tip of the pin should be straight and the other bent at a 15° angle away from the housing. The fork and retainer pin should operate freely after bending the tip of the pin.
3. Install the solenoid moving core and engage the shifting fork.
4. Place the pinion shaft into the drive housing and install the friction washer and drive gear.
5. Install the clutch and pinion assembly, thrust washer, and retaining washer.
6. Engage the shifting fork with the clutch actuators.

CAUTION: *The friction washer must be positioned on the shoulder of the splines of the pinion shaft before the driven gear is positioned.*

7. Install the driven gear snap ring.
8. Install the pinion shaft retaining ring.
9. The starter solenoid return spring can now be inserted in the movable core.
10. Check the condition of the starter solenoid switch washer; if burned, disassemble the plunger assembly and reverse the washer. Install the solenoid contact plunger assembly into the solenoid.
11. Assemble the battery terminal stud in the brush holder.
12. Position the seal on the brush holder plate.

13. Run the solenoid lead wire through the hole in the brush holder and attach the solenoid stud, insulating washer, flat washer, and nut.
14. Wrap the solenoid lead wire tightly around the brush terminal post and solder it (rosin core solder only).
15. Fix the brush holder to the solenoid attaching screws.
16. Gently lower the solenoid coil and brush plate into the gear housing.
17. Position the brush plate assembly into the starter gear housing, install the nuts, and tighten.
18. Position the brushes with the armature thrust washer.
19. Install the brush terminal screw.
20. Position the field frame on the gear housing and start the armature into the housing, carefully engaging the splines on the shaft with the reduction gear by rotating the armature.
21. Install the thrust washer on the armature shaft.
22. Replace the starter end housing and starter through bolts; tighten securely.

NIPPONDENSO OR BOSCH STARTER MOTOR

(Chrysler Corporation)

Either a Nippondenso or Bosch starter may be used in the Omni and Horizon. Service procedures are the same for both. The starter drive is an overrunning clutch with a solenoid on the motor.

Disassembly

1. Disconnect the field coil wire from the solenoid terminal.
2. Remove the solenoid mounting screws and work the solenoid off the shift fork.
3. On Nippondenso units, remove the bearing cover, armature shaft lock, washer, spring, and seal.

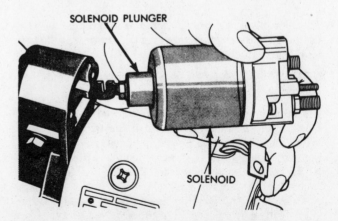

Nippondenso solenoid removal; Bosch similar

4. On Bosch units, remove the two screws holding down the end shield bearing cap, and remove the cap and washers.

5. Remove the two through bolts and the commutator end frame cover.

6. Remove the two brushes and the brush plate.

7. Slide the field frame off over the armature.

8. Take out the shift lever pivot bolt.

9. Take off the rubber gasket and metal plate.

10. Remove the armature assembly and shift lever from the drive end housing.

11. Press the stop collar off the snap ring. Remove the snap ring, stop collar, and clutch.

Inspection and Service

1. Brushes that are worn more than one-half the length of new brushes, or are oil-soaked, should be replaced. New brushes are $1\frac{1}{16}$ in. long.

2. Do not immerse the starter clutch unit in cleaning solvent. Solvent will wash the lubricant from the clutch.

3. Place the drive unit on the armature shaft and, while holding the armature, rotate the pinion. The drive pinion should rotate smoothly in one direction only. The pinion may not rotate easily, but as long as it rotates smoothly, it is in good condition. If the clutch unit does not function properly, or if the pinion is worn, chipped, or burred, replace the unit.

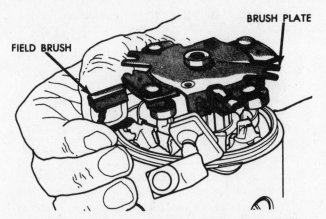

Field brush removal on Bosch starter; Nippondenso similar

Assembly

1. Lubricate the armature shaft and splines with SAE 10 or 30 W oil.

2. Install the clutch, stop collar, and lock ring on the armature.

3. Place the armature assembly and shift fork in the drive end housing. Install the shift lever pivot bolt.

4. Install the rubber gasket and metal plate.

5. Slide the field frame into position. Install the brush holder and brushes.

6. Position the commutator end frame cover and install the through bolts.

7. On Nippondenso units, install the seal, spring, washer, armature shaft lock, and bearing cover.

8. On Bosch units, install the shim and armature shaft lock. Check that end play is (0.05 to 0.3 mm). 0.002 to 0.012 in. Install the bearing cover.

9. Assemble the solenoid to the shift fork and install the mounting screws.

10. Connect the field coil wire to the solenoid.

AUTOLITE/MOTORCRAFT POSITIVE ENGAGEMENT STARTER MOTOR

(Ford Motor Co. and American Motors)

This starting motor is a series-parallel wound, four-pole, four-brush unit. It is equipped with an overrunning clutch drive pinion, which is engaged with the flywheel ring gear by an actuating lever, operated by a movable pole piece. This pole piece is hinged to the starter frame and can drop into position through an opening in the frame.

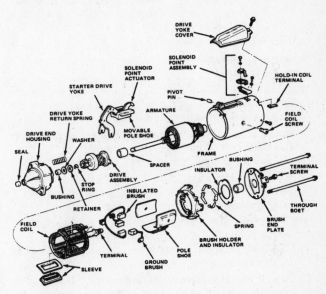

Exploded view of a Ford positive engagement starter motor

Three conventional field coils are located at three pole piece positions. The fourth field coil is designed to serve also as an engaging coil and a hold-in coil for the operation of the drive pinion.

When the ignition switch is turned to the start position, the starter relay is energized and current flows from the battery to the starter motor terminal. This prime surge of current first flows through the starter engaging coil, creating a very strong magnetic field. This magnetism draws the movable pole piece down toward the starter frame, which then causes the lever attached to it to move the starter pinion into engagement with the flywheel ring gear.

When the movable pole shoe is fully seated, it opens the field coil grounding contacts, and the starter is then in normal operation. A holding coil is used to hold the movable pole shoe in the fully seated position during the engine cranking operation.

Ford Motor Co. automatic transmission models with a floorshift lever have a neutral start switch; column shift models have a mechanical interlock.

This starter is used on both Ford and American Motors products. There are 4 and 4½ in. (0.16 and 18 mm) diameter versions.

Disassembly
Through 1977

1. Remove the brush cover band and starter drive gear actuating lever cover. Observe the brush lead locations for reassembly; then remove the brushes from their holders.
2. Remove the through bolts, starter drive gear housing, and the drive gear actuating lever return spring.
3. Remove the pivot pin retaining the starter gear actuating lever and remove the lever and the armature.
4. Remove the stop ring retainer. Remove and discard the stop ring holding the drive gear to the armature shaft; then remove the drive gear assembly.
5. Remove the brush end plate.
6. Remove the two screws holding the ground brushes to the frame.
7. On the field coil that operates the starter drive gear actuating lever, bend the tab up on the field retainer and remove the field coil retainer.
8. Remove the three-coil retaining screws. Unsolder the field coil leads from the terminal screw, then remove the pole shoes and coils from the frame (use a 300-watt iron).
9. Remove the starter terminal nut, washer, insulator, and terminal from the starter frame.
10. Check the commutator for runout. If the commutator is rough, has flat spots, or is more than 0.005 in. out-of-round, reface the commutator. Clean the grooves in the commutator face.
11. Inspect the armature shaft and the two bearings for scoring and excessive wear. Replace if necessary.
12. Inspect the starter drive. If the gear teeth are pitted, broken, or excessively worn, replace the starter drive.

NOTE: *Factory brush length is ½ in. (0.02 mm); wear limit is ¼ in. (0.01 mm).*

1978 and Later

1. Remove the cover screw, cover, through bolts, starter drive end housing, and the starter drive plunger lever return spring.
2. Remove the pivot pin that holds the starter gear plunger lever and remove the lever and the armature.
3. Remove the stop ring retainer and the stop ring from the armature shaft and discard the stop ring. Remove the starter drive gear assembly.

4. Remove the brush end plate and the insulator assembly.
5. Remove the brushes from the plastic holder and lift out the brush holder. For reassembly, note the position of the brush holder with respect to the end terminal.
6. Remove the two screws holding the ground brushes to the frame.
7. Bend up the edges of the sleeve that is inserted in the rectangular hole in the frame and remove the sleeve and the retainer. Detach the field coil ground wire from the copper tab.
8. Remove the three-coil retaining screws. Cut the field coil connection at the switch post lead and remove the pole shoes and the coils from the frame.
9. Cut the positive brush leads from the field coils as close to the field connection point as possible.
10. Check the armature and the armature windings for broken or burned insulation and open circuits and grounds.

Refer to Steps 10–12 of the 1974–77 disassembly procedure.

Assembly

1. Install the starter terminal, insulator, washers, and retaining nut in the frame. (Be sure to position the slot in the screw perpendicular to the frame end surface.)
2. Position coils and pole pieces, with the coil leads in the terminal screw slot; then install the retaining screws. As the pole screws are tightened, strike the frame several sharp hammer blows to align the pole shoes. Tighten, then stake the screws.
3. Install the solenoid coil and retainer and bend the tabs to hold the coils to the frame.
4. Solder the field coils and solenoid wire to the starter· terminal, using rosin core solder and a 300-watt iron.
5. Check for continuity and ground connections in the assembled coils.
6. Position the solenoid coil ground terminal over the nearest ground screw hole.
7. Position the ground brushes to the starter frame and install retaining screws.

NOTE: *For 1978–and later starters proceed to step 15.*

8. Position the brush end plate to the frame, with the end plate boss in the frame slot.
9. Lightly Lubriplate the armature shaft splines and install the starter drive gear assembly on the shaft. Install a new retaining stop ring and stop ring retainer.
10. Position the fiber thrust washer on the commutator end of the armature shaft; then position the armature in the starter frame.
11. Position the starter drive gear actuating lever to the frame and starter drive assembly, and install the pivot pin.

NOTE: *Fill drive gear housing bore one-quarter full of grease.*

12. Position the drive actuating lever return spring and the drive gear housing to the frame; then install and tighten the through bolts. Do not pinch brush leads between brush plate and frame. Be sure that the stop ring retainer is properly seated in the drive housing.

13. Install the brushes in the brush holders and center the brush springs on the brushes.

14. Position the drive gear actuating lever cover on the starter and install the brush cover band with a new gasket.

NOTE: *The following procedures are for 1978–and later starters.*

15. Apply a thin coating of Lubriplate on the armature shaft splines. Install the starter motor drive gear assembly to the armature shaft and install a new stop ring and stop ring retainer.

16. Install the armature in the starter frame.

17. Position the starter drive gear plunger lever to the frame and the starter drive assembly. Install the pivot pin. Place some grease into the end housing bore. Fill it about one-quarter full. Position the drive end housing to the frame.

18. Install the brush holder and install the brush springs. Positive brush leads should be positioned in their respective slots in the brush holder to prevent any grounding problems.

19. Install the brush end plate being certain that the end plate insulator is in the proper position on the end plate.

20. Install the two through bolts to the starter frame and torque them to 55–75 in. lbs.

21. Install the starter drive plunger lever cover and tighten the retaining screw.

AUTOLITE/MOTORCRAFT SOLENOID ACTUATED STARTER MOTOR

(Ford Motor Co.)

This starter motor, usually used with 429 and 460 engines through 1977, is a four-brush, four-field, four-pole wound unit. The frame encloses a wound armature, which is supported at the drive end by caged needle bearings and at the commutator end by a sintered copper bushing. The four-pole shoes are screwed to the frame by one pole screw apiece, and on each pole shoe is wound a ribbon-type field coil connected in series-parallel.

The solenoid is mounted to a flange on the starter drive housing, which encloses the entire shift mechanism and solenoid plunger. The solenoid, following standard industry practice, utilizes two windings—a pull-in winding and a hold-in winding.

Disassembly

1. Disconnect the copper strap from the solenoid starter terminal, remove the remaining screws, and remove the solenoid.

2. Loosen the retaining screw and slide the brush cover band back far enough to gain access to the brushes.

3. Remove the brushes from their holders; then remove the through bolts and separate the drive end housing from the frame and brush end plate.

NOTE: *Factory brush length is 1/2 in., wear limit is 1/4 in.*

4. Remove the solenoid plunger and shift fork. These two items can be separated from each other by removing the roll pin.

5. Remove the armature and drive assembly from the frame. Remove the drive stop ring and slide the drive off the armature shaft.

6. Remove the drive stop ring retainer from the drive housing.

7. Inspection of the commutator, armature and bearings, and pinion gear procedures is the same as the positive engagement starter procedures.

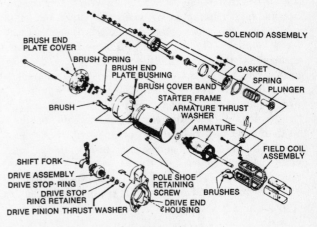

Ford solenoid actuated starter motor

Assembly

1. Lubricate the armature shaft splines with Lubriplate; then install the drive assembly and a new stop ring.

2. Lubricate the shift lever pivot pin with Lubriplate; then position the solenoid plunger and shift lever assembly in the drive housing.

3. Place a new retainer in the drive housing. Apply a small amount of Lubriplate to the drive end of the armature shaft; then place the armature and drive assembly into the drive housing, indexing the shift lever tangs with the drive assembly.

4. Apply a small amount of Lubriplate to the commutator end of the armature shaft; then position the frame and field assembly to the drive housing.

5. Position the brush plate assembly to the frame, making sure it properly indexes. Install through bolts and tighten to 45 to 85 in. lbs.

6. Install the brushes into their holders and make sure leads are not touching any interior starter components.

7. Place the rubber gasket between the solenoid mount and the frame surface.

8. Place the starter solenoid in position with the metal gasket and spring, install heat shield (if so equipped), and install solenoid screws.

9. Connect the copper strap and install the cover band.

DELCO-REMY STARTER MOTOR

(General Motors Corp. and American Motors)

There are many different vesions of the Delco-Remy starter, depending upon application. In general, six-cylinder engines use a unit having four field coils in series between the terminal and armature. Standard V-8 engines use, depending on displacement, one of three types: one has two field coils in series with the armature and parallel to each other; another has two field coils in parallel between the field terminal and ground; another has three field coils in series with the armature and one field connected between the motor terminal and ground. Heavy-duty starter motors have series compound windings. On the 1975 and later Delco starter, the terminal that connects the starter solenoid to the ignition coil has been removed because it is unnecessary with the High Energy Ignition System. Starting in 1978, a new starter design was used for some smaller engines. It is very similar to previous motors, but has the field coils and pole shoes integral with the motor frame. This motor is also used on 1980 and later four cylinder AMC engines.

Despite these differences, all Delco-Remy starters are disassembled and assembled in essentially the same manner.

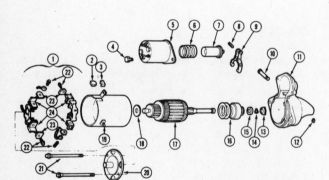

Exploded view of the Delco-Remy 5 MT starter, typical of all later models (© AMC)

1 Brush and holder set	13 Thrust collar
2 Grommet	14 Pinion stop retainer ring
3 Grommet	15 Pinion stop collar
4 Screw	16 Clutch and drive assembly
5 Solenoid	17 Armature
6 Plunger return spring	18 Washer
7 Plunger	19 Frame and field assembly
8 Plunger pin	20 Commutator end frame
9 Shift fork	21 Through bolts
10 Shift fork shaft	22 Screw
11 Drive end housing	23 Brush
12 Shift fork shaft retaining ring	24 Brush holder

Typical Delco starter motor

Disassembly

1. Detach the field coil connectors from the motor solenoid terminal.

NOTE: *On models so equipped, remove solenoid mounting screws.*

2. Remove the through bolts.

3. Remove commutator end frame, field frame and armature assembly from the drive housing. The diesel starter has an end frame insulator. The diesel armature will remain in the drive end frame. Remove the diesel shift lever pivot bolt and center bearing screws.

4. Remove the overrunning clutch from the armature shaft as follows:
   a. Slide the two-piece thrust collar off the end of the armature shaft.
   b. Slide a standard 1/2 in. pipe coupling or other spacer onto the shaft so that the end of the coupling butts against the edge of the retainer.
   c. Tap the end of the coupling with a hammer, driving the retainer toward the armature end of the snap-ring.
   d. Remove the snap-ring from its groove in the shaft using pliers. Slide the retainer and clutch from the armature shaft.

5. Disassemble the brush assembly from the field frame by releasing the V-spring and removing the support pin. The brush holders, brushes, and springs now can be pulled out as a unit and the leads disconnected. On integral frame units, remove the brush holder from the brush support and remove the brush screw.

6. On models so equipped, separate solenoid from the lever housing.

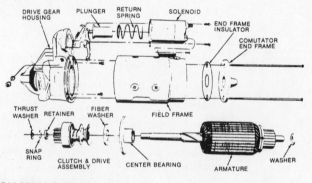

GM 350 V-8 diesel starter

Cleaning and Inspection

1. Clean the parts with a rag, but do not immerse the parts in a solvent. Immersion in a solvent will dissolve the grease that is packed in the clutch mechanism and damage the armature and field coil insulation.

2. Test overrunning clutch action. The pinion should turn freely in the overrunning direction and must not slip in the cranking direction. Check pinion teeth to see that they have not been chipped, cracked, or excessively worn. Replace the unit if necessary.

3. Inspect the armature commutator. If the commutator is rough or out-of-round, it should be turned down and undercut.

NOTE: *Undercut the insulation between the commutator bars by ¹/₃₂ in.*

This undercut must be the full width of the insulation and flat at the bottom; a triangular groove will not be satisfactory. Most later starter motor models use a molded armature commutator design and no attempt to undercut the insulation should be made or serious damage may result to the commutator.

Assembly

1. Install brushes into the holders. Install the solenoid, if so equipped.
2. Assemble the insulated and the grounded brush holder together using the V-spring and position the assembled unit on the support pin. Push the holders and spring to the bottom of the support pin and rotate the spring to engage the slot in the support. Attach the ground wire to the grounded brush and field lead wire to the insulated brush; repeat for other brush sets.
3. Assemble the overrunning clutch to armature shaft as follows:
   a. Lubricate the drive end of the shaft with silicone lubricant.
   b. Slide the clutch assembly onto the shaft with the pinion outward. On the diesel starter, install the center bearing and fiber washer first.
   c. Slide the retainer onto the shaft with the cupped surface facing away from the pinion.
   d. Stand the armature up on a wood surface, commutator side down. Position the snap-ring on the upper end of the shaft and drive it onto the shaft with a small block of wood and a hammer. Slide the snap-ring into the groove.
   e. Install the thrust collar onto the shaft with the shoulder next to the snap-ring.
   f. With the retainer on one side of the snap-ring and the thrust collar on the other side, squeeze together with two sets of pliers until the ring seats in the retainer. On models without a thrust collar, use a washer. Remember to remove the washer before continuing.
4. Lubricate the drive end bushing with silicone lubricant; then slide the armature and clutch assembly into place, at the same time engaging the shift lever with the clutch. On nonintegral starters, the shift lever may be installed in the drive gear housing first. Install the center bearing screws and shift lever pivot bolt on the diesel starter.
5. Position the field frame over the armature and apply sealer (silicone) between the frame and solenoid case. Position the frame against the drive housing, making sure the brushes are not damaged in the process.
6. Lubricate the commutator end bushing with silicone lubricant, place a washer on the armature shaft and slide the commutator end frame onto the shaft. Install the through bolts and tighten. On the diesel starter, install the insulator, then the end frame.
7. Reconnect the field coil connectors to the solenoid motor terminal. Install solenoid-mounting screws, if so equipped.
8. Check pinion clearance; it should be 0.010 to 0.140 in. (0.0004 to 0.0056 mm) with the pinion in cranking position on all models.

CARBURETOR

The carburetor mixes the liquid fuel with air in the correct proportions to provide the desired power output from the engine. The carburetor performs this function by metering, atomizing, and mixing the fuel with air drawn through the venturi and into the engine. The volume of the mixture is regulated by the throttle, which gives the operator control of engine speed.

FUNCTIONS

Metering

The automotive internal combustion engine operates efficiently within a relatively small range of fuel/air ratios. It is the function of the carburetor to meter the fuel in exact proportions to the air flowing into the engine, so that the optimum ratio of fuel/air is maintained under all operating conditions. Regulations governing exhaust gas emissions have made the proper metering of fuel by the carburetor an increasingly important factor. Too rich a mixture will result in poor economy and increased emissions, while too lean a mixture will result in loss of power and generally poor performance.

Carburetors are matched to engines so that metering can be accomplished by using carefully calibrated metering jets that allow fuel to enter the engine at a rate proportional to the engine's ability to draw air.

Atomization

The liquid fuel must be broken up into small particles so that it will more readily mix with air and vaporize. The more contact the fuel has with the air, the better the vaporization. Atomization can be accomplished in two ways: air may be drawn into a stream of fuel that will cause a turbulence and break the solid stream of fuel into smaller particles; or a nozzle can be positioned at the point of highest air velocity in the carburetor and the fuel will be torn into a fine spray as it enters the air stream.

Distribution

The carburetor is the primary device involved in the distribution of fuel to the engine. The more efficiently fuel and air are combined in the carburetor, the smoother the flow of vaporized mixture through the intake manifold to each combustion chamber; hence, the importance of the carburetor in fuel distribution.

PRINCIPLES

Vacuum

All carburetors operate on the basic principle of pressure difference. Any pressure less than atmospheric pressure is considered vacuum or a low pressure area. In the engine, as the piston moves down on the intake stroke with the intake valve open, a partial vacuum is created in the intake manifold. The farther the piston travels downward, the greater the vacuum created in the manifold. As vacuum increases in the manifold, a difference in pressure occurs between the carburetor and cylinder. The carburetor is positioned in such a way that the high pressure above it and the vacuum or low pressure beneath it cause air to be drawn through it. Fuel and air always move from high- to low-pressure areas.

Venturi Principle

To obtain greater pressure drop at the tip of the fuel nozzle so that fuel will flow, the principle of increasing the air velocity to create a low-pressure area is used. The device used to increase the velocity of the air flowing through the carburetor is called a venturi. A venturi is a specially designed restriction placed in the air flow. In order for the air to pass through the restriction, it must accelerate, causing a pressure drop or vacuum as it passes.

CARBURETOR CIRCUITS

Float Circuit

The float circuit includes the float, float bowl, and a needle valve and seat. This circuit controls the amount of gas allowed to flow into the carburetor.

As the fuel level rises, it causes the float to rise, which pushes the needle valve into its seat. As soon as the valve and seat make contact, the flow of gas is cut off from the fuel inlet. When the level of fuel drops, the float sinks and releases the needle valve from its seat, thus allowing the gas to flow in. In actual operation, the fuel is maintained at practically a constant level. The float tends to hold the needle valve partly closed so that the incoming fuel just balances the fuel being withdrawn.

Idle and Low-Speed Circuit

When the throttle is closed or only slightly opened, the air speed is low and practically no vacuum develops in the venturi. This means that the fuel nozzle will not feed. Thus, the carburetor must have another circuit to supply fuel during operation with a closed or slightly opened throttle.

This circuit is called the idle and low-speed circuit. It consists of passages in which air and gas can flow beneath the throttle plate. With the throttle plate closed, there is high vacuum from the intake manifold. Atmospheric pressure pushes the fuel/air mixture through the passages of the idle and low-speed circuit and past the tapered point of the idle adjustment screw, which regulates engine idle mixture volume.

High-Speed Partial-Load Circuit

When the throttle plate is opened sufficiently, there is little difference in vacuum between the upper and lower part of the air horn. Thus, little fuel/air mixture will discharge from the low speed and idle circuit. However, under this condition enough air is moving through the air horn to produce a vacuum in the venturi to cause the main, or high-speed, nozzle to discharge fuel. The circuit from the float bowl to the main nozzle is called the high-speed partial-load circuit. A nearly constant fuel/air ratio is maintained by this circuit from part to full-throttle.

High-Speed Full-Power Circuit

For high speed, full-power, wide open throttle operation, the fuel/air mixture must be enriched; this is done either mechanically or by intake manifold vacuum.

Full-Power Circuit (Mechanical)

This circuit includes a metering rod jet and a metering rod. The rod has two steps of different diameters and is attached to the throttle linkage.

When the throttle is wide open, the metering rod is lifted bringing the smaller diameter of the rod into the jet. When the throttle is partly closed, the larger diameter of the metering rod is in the jet. This restricts fuel flow to the main nozzle but adequate amounts of fuel do flow for part-throttle operation.

Full-Power Circuit (Vacuum)

This circuit is operated by intake manifold vacuum. It includes a vacuum diaphragm or piston linked to a valve.

When the throttle is opened so that intake manifold vacuum is reduced, the spring raises the diaphragm or piston. This allows more fuel to flow in, either by lifting a metering rod or by opening a power valve.

Accelerator Pump Circuit

For acceleration, the carburetor must deliver additional fuel. A sudden inrush of air is caused by rapid acceleration or applying full-throttle.

When the throttle is opened, the pump lever pushes the plunger down and this forces fuel to flow through

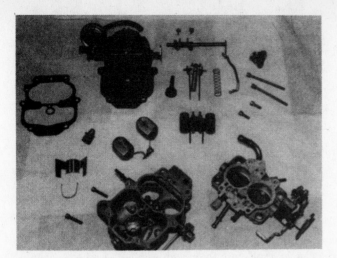

Parts of a typical two-barrel carburetor

the accelerator pump circuit and out the pump jet. This fuel enters the air passage through the carburetor to supply additional fuel demands.

Choke

When starting an engine, it is necessary to increase the amount of fuel delivered to the intake manifold. This increase is controlled by the choke.

The choke consists of a valve in the top of the air horn controlled mechanically by an automatic device. When the choke valve is closed, only a small amount of air can get past it. When the engine is cranked, a fairly high vacuum develops in the air horn. This vacuum causes the main nozzle to discharge a heavy stream of fuel. The quantity delivered is sufficient to produce the correct fuel/air mixture needed for starting the engine. The choke is released either manually or by heat from the engine.

REBUILDING

All kits should contain the necessary parts and some form of instructions for whatever phase of carburetor rebuilding is necessary. The instructions may vary between a simple exploded view and detailed step-by-step rebuilding instructions. Unless you are familiar with carburetor overhaul, the latter should be used.

There are some general overhaul procedures that should always be observed.

Efficient carburetion depends greatly on careful cleaning and inspection during overhaul because dirt, gum, water, or varnish in or on the carburetor parts are often responsible for poor performance.

Overhaul your carburetor in a clean, dustfree area. Carefully disassemble the carburetor, referring often to the exploded views. Keep all similar and lookalike parts segregated during disassembly and cleaning to avoid accidental interchange during assembly. Make a note of all jet sizes.

When the carburetor is disassembled, wash all parts (except diaphragms, electric choke units, pump plunger, and any other plastic, leather, fiber, or rubber parts) in clean carburetor solvent. Do not leave parts in the solvent any longer than is necessary to sufficiently loosen the deposits. Excessive cleaning may remove the special finish from the float bowl and choke valve bodies, leaving these parts unfit for service. Rinse all parts in clean solvent and blow them dry with compressed air or allow them to air dry. Wipe clean all cork, plastic, leather, and fiber parts with a clean, lint-free cloth.

Blow out all passages and jets with compressed air and be sure that there are no restrictions or blockages. Never use wire or similar tools to clean jets, fuel passages, or air bleeds. Clean all jets and valves separately to avoid accidental interchange.

Inspect all parts for wear or damage. If wear or damage is found, replace the defective parts. Especially check the following:

1. Check the float needle and seat for wear. If wear is found, replace the complete assembly.
2. Inspect the float hinge pin for wear and the float(s) for dents or distortion. Replace the float if fuel has leaked into it.
3. Check the throttle and choke shaft bores for wear or an out-of-round condition. Damage or wear to the throttle arm, shaft, or shaft bore will often require replacement of the throttle body. These parts require a close tolerance; wear may allow air leakage, which could affect starting and idling.

NOTE: *Throttle shafts and bushings are usually not included in overhaul kits. They can be purchased separately.*

4. Inspect the idle mixture adjusting needles for burrs or grooves. Any such condition requires replacement of the needle because you will not be able to obtain a satisfactory idle.
5. Test the accelerator pump check valves. They should pass air one way but not the other. Test for proper seating by blowing and sucking on the valve. Replace the valve if necessary. If the valve is satisfactory, wash the valve again to remove breath moisture.
6. Check the bowl cover for warped surfaces with a straightedge.
7. Closely inspect the valves and seats for wear and damage, replacing as necessary.
8. After the carburetor is assembled, check the choke valve for freedom of operation.

Carburetor overhaul kits are recommended for each overhaul. These kits contain all gaskets and new parts to replace those that deteriorate most rapidly. Failure to replace all parts supplied with the kit (especially gaskets) can result in poor performance later.

Some carburetor manufacturers supply overhaul kits: minor repair, major repair, and gasket kits. Basically, they contain the following:

Minor repair kits:
- All gaskets
- Float needle valve
- Volume control screw

- All diaphragms
- Spring for the pump diaphragm
  Major Repair Kits:
- All jets and gaskets
- All diaphragms
- Float needle valve
- Volume control screw
- Pump ball valve
- Main jet carrier
- Float
- Complete intermediate rod
- Intermediate pump lever
- Complete injector tube
- Some cover hold-down screws and washers
  Gasket Kits:
- All gaskets

After cleaning and checking all components, reassemble the carburetor, using new parts and referring to the exploded view. When reassembling, make sure that all screws and jets are tight in their seats, but do not overtighten, as the tips will be distorted. Tighten all screws gradually, in rotation. Do not tighten needle valves into their seats; uneven jetting will result. Always use new gaskets. Be sure to adjust the float level when reassembling.

DISTRIBUTOR

Like the alternator and starter, the distributor can be rebuilt or replaced with a new or remanufactured unit.

If the distributor was performing well, chances are that not much, if any, service will be necessary. Remove

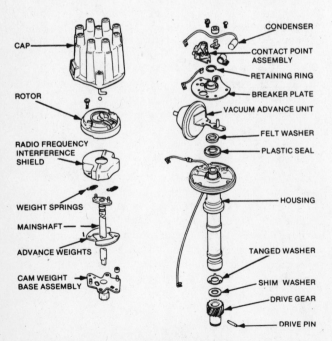

CAP

ROTOR

RADIO FREQUENCY
INTERFERENCE
SHIELD

WEIGHT SPRINGS

MAINSHAFT

ADVANCE WEIGHTS

CAM WEIGHT
BASE ASSEMBLY

CONDENSER

CONTACT POINT
ASSEMBLY

RETAINING RING

BREAKER PLATE

VACUUM ADVANCE UNIT

FELT WASHER

PLASTIC SEAL

HOUSING

TANGED WASHER

SHIM WASHER

DRIVE GEAR

DRIVE PIN

A typical non-Delco distributor, exploded view

the cap and rotor, if not already removed. Wiggle the cam and shaft where the rotor was mounted. If it moves excessively, the upper bushing, the inside of the cam, or the shaft may be worn. If you do not see excessive movement, take the distributor to a shop that has a distributor test stand. When the distributor is mounted on the stand, it can be checked for the proper centrifugal advance and vacuum advance or retard. Dwell can also be checked on point-type distributors. Various adjustments can be made to bring the distributor into specifications if no worn parts are detected.

If it is determined that excessive wear is present, the worn part or parts will have to be replaced or a new distributor installed. Before going through the trouble of tearing down the distributor, check to see if parts are available, or how long it will take to order them in. Concern yourself with the bushings, shaft, and cam. If they are on hand in the parts department or require a reasonable length of time to get, disassemble the distributor and determine what is needed. If not, replace the distributor with a rebuilt unit or a new one.

NON-DELCO-TYPE

Point-Equipped Distributors

Remove the points and condenser, vacuum advance/ retard unit, and breaker plate. Examine the breaker plate for wear or excessive movement. Remove the base plate screws and the base plate. Identify the weights and springs so they can be reinstalled in the same position. Remove the weights and springs. Remove the retainer clip from inside the cam, and remove the cam and thrust washer if equipped. Drive out the roll pins at the bottom of the shaft and gear. Support the gear and press it from the shaft. Do not allow the distributor body to fall on the floor when the shaft clears the gear. Support the housing and press the bushings out. Clean all parts in solvent and wipe or blow dry. Measure the worn and unworn parts of the distributor shaft, and check the cam points for wear and the cam for fit on the shaft. If the worn and unworn parts of the shaft show a great dimensional difference or if the cam is worn or does not fit, order the necessary parts and new bushings.

Electronic Distributors

Remove the armature with a small two-jawed puller. Do not lose the locator roll pin. Remove the vacuum advance/retard by unhooking it from the magnetic pickup and unbolting it from the housing. Remove the magnetic pickup assembly. Remove the base plate. The rest of the disassembly is the same as the point-type distributor.

Assembly

Assembly is in the reverse order. Lubricate the shaft

and make sure it rotates freely in the new bushings. Check the weights for free movement and the spring for proper tension. Have the distributor rechecked on the test bench.

DELCO-TYPE-DISTRIBUTORS

Point-Equipped Distributors

Remove the rotor, points, and condenser. Use a punch to remove the roll pin securing the gear to the distributor shaft. Remove the shaft from the distributor. Remove the C-clip holding the base plate to the distributor and remove the plate. Remove the vacuum advance unit. Clean all parts and check for wear. If the bearings in the housing are worn, check the shaft for wear first, then reinstall through the body and check for wobble. If

A distributor mounted on a tester

wear is excessive, obtain a new or good used body. Replace the shaft, gear, vacuum advance, or whatever is necessary, and reassemble in the reverse order of removal. Be sure to fill the grease well with new lubricant. Check the lead wire and replace if necessary.

HEI Ignition

The distributor comes apart in the same manner as the point-type. An HEI mechanical overhaul kit is available, which contains the shaft and centrifugal advance/ retard mechanism. Here again, be sure to fill the grease well with new lubricant.

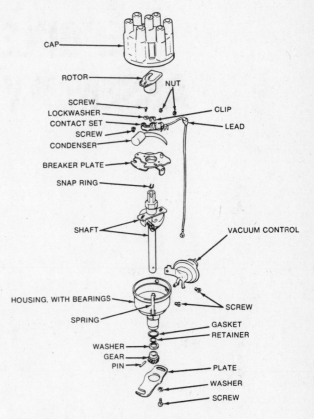

A typical Delco-type distributor, exploded view

8
ENGINE ASSEMBLY

Now that all of the cylinder head and engine parts have been inspected, the machine work completed, and all necessary replacement parts on hand, it is time to reassemble the engine. Once again a set series of steps is followed with slight variations, depending on the type of engine being rebuilt.

GASKET SETS

The amount of engine "tear down" determines what gasket set is necessary for reassembly. If just a valve job is required, a valve grind set should be ordered. Sometimes called a head set, it contains all of the gaskets and valve stem seals required for a valve job. There is, however, one exception. If the engine uses a large metal "cookie sheet" intake manifold gasket, this gasket will have to be purchased separately. If the engine is still mounted in the car and the head and oil pan have been removed, most of the time a head and pan set are all that are necessary. When just the front of the engine has been disassembled to replace a timing component or to replace the front seal, a timing cover gasket set is used. The set contains all necessary gaskets: water pump, case, cover, and oil seal. A complete engine rebuild is handled with a full set: every gasket and oil seal necessary is in the set. Once again, a "cookie sheet" intake gasket or, in the case of some imported cars, a conversion gasket set will have to be purchased separately.

GASKET SEALER

Various types of gasket sealers are available. The ones listed here work well in certain applications: silicone sealer for freeze plugs, intake manifold gaskets, and water or oil pressure points, yellow weatherstrip adhesive for oil pan, timing cover, and valve covers gaskets; brush on liquid sealer for use on some head gaskets or general sealing.

Make sure these sealers are on hand before starting the assembly.

FREEZE PLUG INSTALLATION

If the head and block have been hot tanked and the freeze plugs have been removed, new plugs will have to be installed. The old screw-in threaded oil galley plugs can be reused, but it is better to install new ones.

Take a piece of emery cloth or use a rotary wire brush and clean the core holes. Apply a small bead of silicone sealer around the outside edge of the core hole. Set the freeze plug squarely over the hole, cup side up if a cupped plug, curved side up if a dished plug. To prevent distortion, drive cup-shaped freeze plugs into the core hole with the largest size drift you have that is not bigger than the plug. Drive the plug in a little at a time making sure it is going in straight. Work the drift around the inside lip to keep the plug straight. When the outer edge of the cup is even with the outside of the core hole, the plug is installed deeply enough. Run an even bead of silicone around the outer edge of the freeze plug and the core hole. Dished freeze plugs are pushed into the core hole until they bottom on the flange. After they bottom, take a blunt drift and locate it in the center of the plug. Hit the drift sharply with a hammer to expand and lock the plug into position. Apply silicone sealer around the edge.

When installing threaded plugs, make sure the threads on both the plug and hole are clean. Apply a bead of sealer on the plug and screw into the hole.

CYLINDER HEAD ASSEMBLY

After all of the freeze and galley plugs have been installed and the sealer has been allowed to set, clean the head once more with solvent. Blow dry with air if it is available; if not, wipe dry with a lint-free clean rag. Pay attention to the valve seats. Make sure there is no trace of lapping compound left.

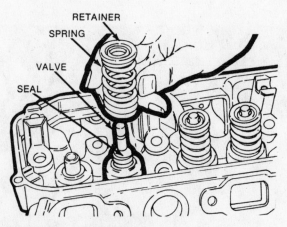

Umbrella oil seal installation

Place the head on the holding stands or support it with wooden blocks. Take the valves in numerical order, lubricate the stems with motor oil, and install them through the valve guides. If positive valve stem oil seals have been installed on the valve guides, be sure to place the plastic protector over the tip of the valve stem so the seal will not get cut. Remove the shield after the valve is in position. If an umbrella oil seal is used, install it at this time. The O-ring valve seals are installed after the top retainer and before the valve keys. Make sure that the seal is not twisted and is mounted firmly in its groove.

Assemble the valve lower spring seat, valve spring (if the spring has two close coils at one end, that end goes at the bottom), damper spring (if equipped), umbrella shield (if equipped), and keeper retainer on the valve

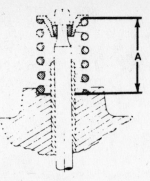

Measure the installed height from the seat to the keeper retainer

stem. Compress the spring with the C-clamp and install the keepers. Check the installed height of the valve spring.

VALVE SPRING INSTALLED HEIGHT

Measure the assembled height of each valve spring from the machined surface of the cylinder head spring pad to the underside of the spring retainer. Check the required specifications. If the height is not within "specs" shims will have to be installed under the valve spring. Special shims in different thicknesses are made for this purpose. The variation in installed height depends on the depth of the valve seat, so it is possible to need shims even if new springs have been installed. If the installed height is incorrect, the valve loading on the seat will not be right.

Measuring valve spring installed height

After the installed height has been corrected and the valve spring installed, take a plastic hammer and rap the tip of the valve stem sharply. This ensures proper keeper seating. Continue until all valves are installed.

ASSEMBLING THE ENGINE

Clean the block, oil holes and especially the cylinder bores with solvent and blow dry or wipe dry with a lean lint free rag. Next take soap and water and a clean lint

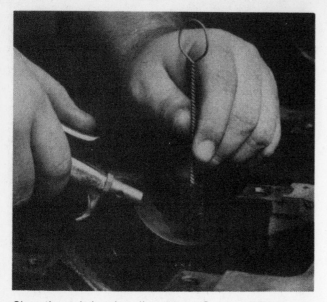

Clean the main bearing oil passages (Courtesy TRW, Inc.)

free rag and scrub the cylinder walls. Change rags frequently until they stay clean while scrubbing. The importance of a clean block and cylinders cannot be overemphasized. The whole engine rebuild job depends on it.

CAMSHAFT INSTALLATION

The cam bearings require a special tool for installation, except in the case of some Overhead Cam engines that use insert type bearings. New cam bearings must be installed if the block was hot tanked. Since some experience and the cam bearing driver are necessary have the machine shop install the bearings. After they are installed, check the oil feed holes for alignment. Be sure a new rear core plug is installed at the rear of the block.

Wipe the cam bearings gently with a clean lint-free rag and some lacquer thinner; then lubricate them with some oil or molybdenum disulfide (moly) grease. Install the long bolt into the camshaft gear mounting bolt hole or temporarily install the cam gear to use as a handle to install the camshaft. Use moly grease and evenly apply it to the cam lobes. Lubricate the bearing journals with oil or moly grease. If the engine is on the floor, stand it up on the flywheel/flexplate end.

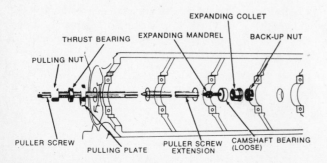

Camshaft bearing removal and installation tool (typical)

If the engine is mounted on a stand, use extreme care during the next step. Install the camshaft into the engine block. Support it with the long bolt or gear and carefully feed it through the cam bearings. Take care to keep it straight, to prevent it from cutting or grooving the bearings. When it is in place, remove the gear or bolt. Install the thrust retainer (if equipped) using the special mounting bolts. The thrust plate should have the oil groove installed toward the block.

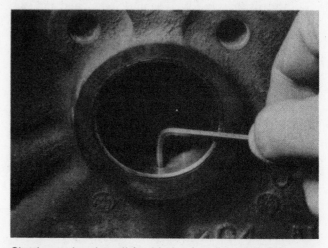

Check cam bearing oil feed holes for alignment (Courtesy TRW, Inc.)

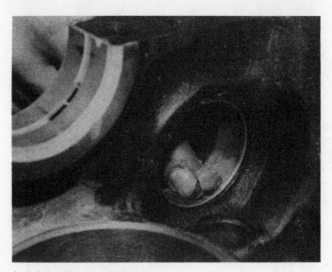

Lubricate the cam bearings

CAMSHAFT END PLAY INSPECTION

Using a feeler gauge, determine whether the clearance between the camshaft boss (or gear) and backing plate is within specifications. Install shims behind the thrust plate, or reposition the camshaft gear and retest end play. In some cases, adjustment is made by replacing the thrust plate.

To check end play using a dial indicator, mount the dial indicator stand so that the stem of the dial indicator rests on the nose of the camshaft, parallel to the cam-

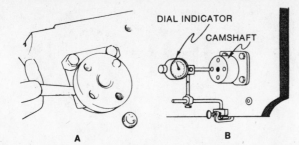

Check camshaft end play (A) with feeler gauge (B) with dial indicator

shaft axis. Push the camshaft in as far as possible and zero the gauge. Move the camshaft outward as far as possible to determine the amount of camshaft end play.

Turn the engine on to its top. The crankshaft will be installed next, but first the block half of the rear main oil seal has to be installed. Two types of seals are generally used: "rope" or a split neoprene. If a choice is offered, pick neoprene. If you are going to check oil clearances with Plastigage, the neoprene seal may be installed at this time. However, if a rope is used, it must be installed after the oil clearance check because of its thickness interference when initially installed.

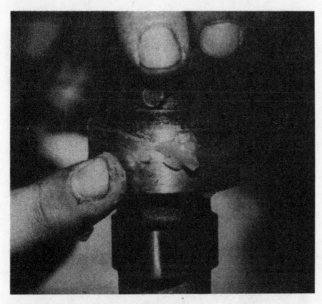

Lubricate the cam bearing journals

Installing the camshaft

Lay a piece of Plastigage on the crank journal or bearing insert

OIL CLEARANCE INSPECTION WITH PLASTIGAGE

Install the main bearings or rod bearings as described in the following paragraphs. Install the crankshaft. Lay a piece of Plastigage cut to the width of the bearing insert to be checked, on top of the bearing journal or in the middle of the bearing. Install the main bearing or rod cap and torque the bolts or nuts to specification. Do not rotate the shaft or it will be necessary to use a new piece of Plastigage. Remove the bearing cap and measure the squeezed width of the material with the gauge of the Plastigage package. If the clearance is within specification proceed to the next step.

Plastigage and container envelope

REAR MAIN SEAL, MAIN BEARING AND CRANKSHAFT INSTALLATION

As mentioned before there are two type rear main oil seals, refer to the appropriate paragraph for installation instructions.

Rope Type Oil Seal

Lay one piece of the seal across the seal groove in the rear of the block. Install it into the groove edgeways by

Measure crush of the Plastigage

Install rope seal in groove edgeways

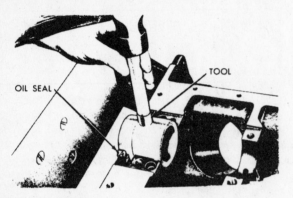

OIL SEAL

TOOL

Rope seal installing tool

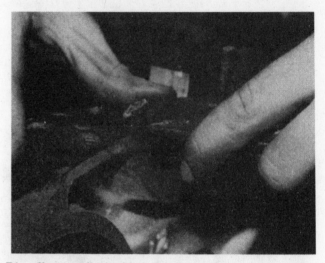

Trim off excess flush with the block

pushing it down with your thumbs. Allow both ends to extend out of the block. Take a large socket and a hammer and tap on the socket while rolling it along the seal. When the seal is fully seated in the groove, trim off the excess flush with the block. Install the other half of the oil seal into the rear main bearing cap groove using the same method. When it is fully seated trim off the excess material flush with the cap flanges.

Neoprene Seal

If a rope seal is being replaced with a neoprene seal, check the main bearing cap and block groove for a locating pin. This pin must be removed before installing a neoprene seal. Fill the pin hole with silicone sealer after removal. Lubricate the seal halfs with oil. Install the seals into the mounting grooves of the block and cap. Install the seal with the lip pointed toward the front of the engine. Do not install the seal flush with the flange surface of the block or cap; allow a little overhang so that the seal ends mate inside the groove instead of where the cap and block mate.

CRANKSHAFT INSTALLATION

Wipe the block bearing saddles and the main bearing caps clean and free from oil with a paper towel. Inspect

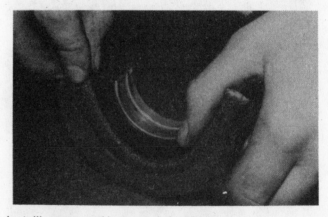

Installing rope seal in rear main bearing cap

the oil feed holes in the block to be sure they are not clogged or full of dirt. Install the main bearing inserts into the block and bearing caps. Clean the crankshaft with solvent and paper towels. Check the oil holes for dirt or clogging, inspect the edges of the oil holes for burrs. Lightly coat the rear main seal and the block-mounted bearing inserts with oil. Gently lower the crankshaft into position, and when it is in place, turn it one revolution. Check the mounting flanges of the bearing caps for a pieces of dirt, oil the inserts and place the caps over the crankshaft and into position. Apply a small amount of silicone sealer to the edges of the rear main cap and seal ends. Place a drop or two of oil on the cap mounting bolts and screw them in place. Make sure they are in the right position and pointed in the right direction. Do not tighten the bolts completely at this time. Make sure the caps are seated properly by locating one edge against the block cut out and gently tapping the cap with a plastic hamamer. The cap should slip into the correct position. Tighten the rear main bearing cap first. Alternate bolts and tighten in stages. Torque to specifications. Install the crankshaft pulley bolt and turn the crankshaft. If a rope seal was installed, turning the crank will indicate the resistance that will be encountered from the seal. With the exception of a center mounted thrust bearing, tighten the rest of the main bearing caps in the same manner as the rear cap. Turn the crank each time to check for excessive drag. On the thrust bearing cap, run the bolts in finger tight, take two flat pry bars insert them between a tighten cap and crank counter weight and move the crank back and forth a few times. This will seat the thrust surfaces of the bearing. Pry the crank forward,

hold in this position and torque the thrust bearing cap bolts. Turn the crankshaft, more resistance should now be encountered.

Check the crankshaft end play by mounting a dial indicator stand on the front of the block, with the dial indicator stem resting on the noise of the crankshaft, parallel to the crankshaft axis. Pry the crankshaft the extent of its travel rearwards and zero the indicator. Pry the crankshaft forward to measure the end play. It is possible to measure the end play with a feeler gauge by pry the crankshaft rearwards and measuring the clearance between a cap the counterweight with a

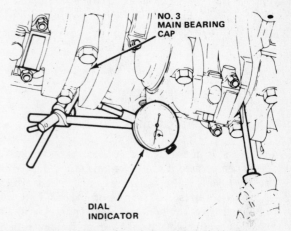
Checking the crankshaft end play with a dial indicator

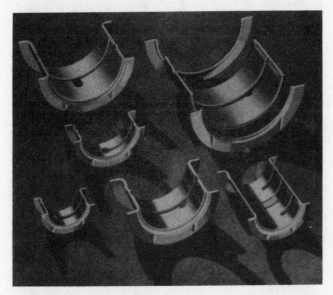
Different type of thrust main bearings

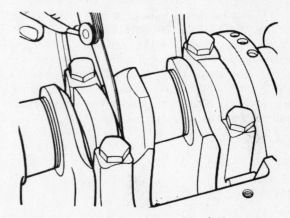
Checking the crankshaft end play with a feeler gauge

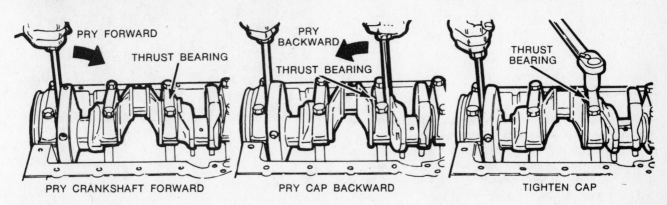
Aligning the thrust bearing

blade. If the end play is less than specs the thrust bearing surfaces will have to be sanded down. If the end play is too great a new crankshaft must be installed or the old one built up. In either case the crankshaft will have to be removed.

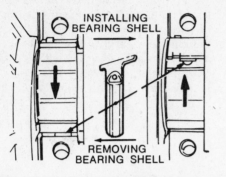

Removal and installation of upper main bearing shell using a roll-out pin

Measure the piston ring end gap (Courtesy TRW, Inc.)

Main Bearing Installation—Engine in Car

In most cases, if necessary, main bearing replacement may be accomplished with the engine still mounted in the car. Remove a main bearing cap and locate which side the locking tap is on. Turn the crankshaft until the journal oil hole is at the bottom. Insert a special roll pin into the oil hole or make one as shown in the illustration. Turn the shaft in the opposite direction of the locking tap and slowly "roll" the upper insert from the saddle. Install the new insert by rolling the shaft in the opposite direction from removal. Stop turning the shaft when the lock tab is in position. Turn the crankshaft back slightly and remove the roll pin. Install a new insert in the lower bearing cap and install on engine. Torque to specifications. Proceed to the next bearing. In most cases, rear main seals may be installed with a special tool. Follow the directions that come with the tool.

Use a ring expander to install the piston rings

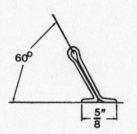

A homemade roll-out pin

Installing Piston Rings

Before installing the piston rings on the pistons measure the end gap in a cylinder. If the machine shop has already installed the rings, carefully remove the top compression ring from one of the pistons. Compress the ring into a cylinder and locate it squarely about an inch below the top of the cylinder. Use a feeler gauge and measure the gap between the ends of the piston ring. If

After installing the rings on pistons, use a feeler gauge to check the ring side clearance. This is the clearance between the side of the ring and the groove. Side clearance should not exceed 0.005 in. for automobile engines and 0.006 in. for truck engines. Pistons with worn or damaged grooves should be replaced (Courtesy TRW, Inc.)

the gap is within specifications, the rest of the rings are probably all right. If the gap is too close, the ends of the ring must be filed. In that case, all the rings should be checked and adjusted.

If the rings are not installed on the pistons, install them now. Start with the lowest ring first (oil ring) and work toward the top. Use a ring expanding tool for installation. Refer to the ring manufacturer's instruction sheet for the proper oil ring installation.

Always check the backlash between the mating gear teeth with a feeler gauge. The backlash should not be too loose (over 0.008 in.) or too tight (less than 0.003 in.) on the gears pitch line. Clearance should always be checked on the same side of the tooth. For best accuracy, check the gear at four different meshings approximately 90° apart (Courtesy TRW, Inc.)

Timing Gear Installation

On OHV engines, install the key into the camshaft and slide the timing gear onto the camshaft. Locate the correct timing mark alignment in a shop manual and set the cam gear mark in the required position. Slide the crank gear over the key on the crankshaft and turn the crank until the gear mark is in its proper position. Remove the two gears, taking care not to rotate either the cam or crank. Install the timing chain on the gears. Carefully remount and secure the two gears on their respective shafts. Turn the engine two complete revolutions and check for the required alignment of the gear marks. If

Camshaft thrust plate retainer in position

Crank and cam gear marks aligned (check engine manual for proper alignment)

Chain in position between the gears

the marks do not line up, remove the gears, realign, and install the gears and chain. Recheck the alignment. The same method is used if two gears are meshed and no chain is used. Install the fuel pump eccentric on the cam in front of the gear and tighten the bolt to specifications.

For overhead cam engines refer to the car shop manual or a Chilton repair manual or repair and tune up guide for the correct timing gear, chain or belt alignment, and installation.

Piston and Rod Assembly Installation

The following procedure can be used for installing the pistons and rods in an engine still mounted in the car or one that is out. Remove the connecting rod bearing cap, wipe the rod and cap clean, and install the bearing inserts. Turn the crank so the journal that the connecting rod is to be attached is at the bottom of its travel. Place the plastic protectors or the pieces of hose over the rod bolts. Lubricate the piston and rings with oil and clamp the ring compressor around the top of the piston. Put some oil on the upper bearing insert and install the piston and rod into the correctly numbered cylinder. Be sure the notch identifying the front of the piston is fac-

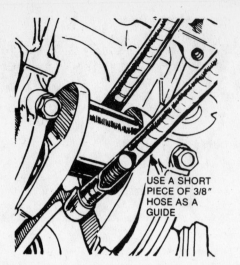

USE A SHORT
PIECE OF 3/8"
HOSE AS A
GUIDE

Tubing used to protect crankshaft journals and cylinder walls during piston installation

Push or gently tap the piston into the cylinder

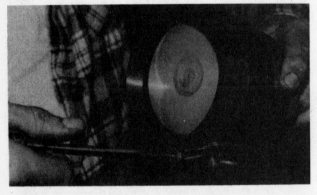

Tighten the ring compressor over the piston

ing forward. Push the piston down into the cylinder with a wooden hammer handle (some slight tapping with the base of the handle may be necessary), but do not hammer. If you encounter resistance, check the ring compressor for straightness and tightness. Reinstall the compressor if necessary. Do not push the piston down into the cylinder until you are sure the connecting rod is lined up over the crank journal. Pull or push the rod over the crank, oil the bottom insert, and install the rod cap, making sure the numbers correspond to ensure correct installation. Install the rod nuts and torque to correct specifications. Install the remaining pistons in a like manner.

Timing Case and Timing Case Cover Installation

Install the crankshaft oil slinger (if equipped). Use weatherstrip adhesive or brush-on sealer and mount a new gasket on the timing case cover (if equipped). Install the cover on the front of the engine and tighten the bolts to the required torque. Install a new oil seal in the timing case cover. Apply sealer and install a new gasket on the cover. Install the cover to the timing case or the front of the engine. Examine the front balancer

(pulley). If the rubber insert looks worn, replace the pulley. Install the front pulley on the engine. If the retaining bolt was installed while setting the crank, it must be removed before the pulley can be installed. Torque the bolt as required.

Oil Pump and Oil Pan Installation

Always install a new oil pump drive shaft if one is used in the engine. Prime the oil pump by immersing it in oil and turning the driveshaft or by filling the pump with petroleum jelly. Use new pump-to-block gaskets (do not use sealer on these gaskets). Install the oil pump, oil pump pickup tube, and screen. Apply sealer to the oil pan and position new gaskets on the pan if the engine is still mounted in the car. Apply the sealer and mount the gaskets to the block if the engine is out of the car. Attach the pan with the mounting bolts. The size of the front and rear oil pan mounting bolts is usually different from that of the side bolts, so do not get them mixed up. Tighten the pan bolts in two or three passes. Pay attention when installing the end seals to the oil pan. Make sure they do not slip out of place.

Water Pump Installation

Install the water pump at this time. Depending on the engine, one or two gaskets are used. Apply sealer to the block and mount the pump.

Cylinder Head Installation—OHV Engines

Turn the engine onto the oil pan and support it in a stable position. Check the block and head surfaces for dirt and remove any gasket material that might still be stuck on the surfaces. On some engines, the valve lifters must be installed at this time. Apply sealer to the block surface, position the gasket on the block, and apply sealer to the gasket. On some engines, the head gaskets are marked Top or Front. If the gaskets are not installed in the correct position, some water passages could be blocked and an overheating problem might arise. Position the cylinder head(s) on the engine. Dowel pins are usually installed in the block to locate the head(s). Install the cylinder head mounting bolts. If different length bolts are used, make sure they end up in the right locations. Run the bolts in until they are snug. Tighten them to the proper torque in stages. Start from the center of the head and alternate from right to left, working your way to the ends of the head. Install the valve lifters and the pushrods. Install the rocker arms or the rocker arm shafts and arms. Lubricate all of the parts generously with oil. Coat the bottom and sides of the lifters with moly grease.

Cylinder Head Installation—OHC Engines

The basic procedures for installing the head on an OHC engine are the same as those for an OHV engine. If the engine is still in the car and the camshaft is retained and rides on circle bearings, the cam must be installed on the cylinder head before the head is mounted on the engine.

Intake Manifold Installation

Certain engines use two side gaskets and two end seals to mount the intake manifold. In this case, to prevent leaks it is critical to interlock the end seals and gaskets, to apply a bead of silicone sealer, and to prevent the intake manifold and gaskets from shifting when they are positioned and mounted on the heads. Always tighten the mounting bolts from the middle to the ends, alternating sides and tightening in stages until the correct torque is reached.

Flywheel or Flexplate Installation

Align the location mark on the crankshaft and flywheel or flexplate (the mark made when it was removed). Install with the new special bolts and torque to specifications.

Miscellaneous Parts

Install a new thermostat and bypass hose (if equipped). Make sure the thermostat is installed according to the arrow or position indicated on its top. Mount any driven equipment that was removed with the engine. Mount the fuel pump.

Distributor Installation

Mark the crankshaft pulley notch or TDC (top dead center) mark and the timing cover pointer on TDC mark with a daub of white paint. Turn the crankshaft until No. 1 piston, coming up on the compression stroke, aligns the TDC mark with the pulley or pointer. Watch the rocker arms on No. 1 cylinder just after the intake arm closes and before the exhaust arm opens. The exhaust valve is TDC when the marks are aligned. Install the distributor with the rotor pointing to the mark on the body that indicates No. 1 position. It may be necessary to turn the rotor about 15° away from the mark and wiggle the rotor slightly to engage the intermediate driveshaft or oil pump drive. Once the distributor base slides into solid contact with the block or manifold mounting, align the reference marks and tighten the mounting bolt slightly. You will have to check the ignition timing later, so do not tighten completely at this time.

Initial Valve Adjustment

On valve trains with adjustment provisions, adjust the lifters according to the manufacturer's specifications. Never use power tools to tighten the rocker arms on an engine with hydraulic lifters because this might bend the pushrods.

Clutch and Pressure Plate Installation

Install the clutch and pressure plate to the flywheel using a special pilot tool or dummy shaft to ensure proper clutch disc alignment. Torque the mounting bolts to specifications.

9

ENGINE INSTALLATION AND TUNE-UP

ENGINE INSTALLATION

Installation of the engine is the reverse of removal. Clean the engine compartment, if not already done, and make sure all necessary tools are available.

Install a new throwout bearing, or the old one (if removed) on the manual transmission clutch fork. Connect the transmission, or converter and transmission to the engine if it was removed as a unit. Reconnect the engine sling to the engine mounting points and connect it to the hoist or portable crane.

Raise the engine, or engine and transmission assembly and position the car underneath the assembly. If the engine has been removed with the transmission still in the car, place a jack under it and loosen the temporary supports. Lower the engine into the engine compartment. If the transmission is still attached lower and slide the end of the transmission under the transmission tunnel. Move the portable crane or the car as necessary. If the transmission is still in the car, jack up to match the angle of the rear of the engine. Lower the engine.

If the engine is to be attached to the transmission mounted in the car: if an automatic, lower the engine and raise the transmission until the converter mounting bolts and flexplate bolts align. Most engines will have alignment dowels to engage the transmission bell housing. Check the alignment, lower the engine and engage the dowels and converter mounting bolts. Install the lower bell housing bolts. If installing the engine to a manual transmission: lower the engine and raise the transmission until the transmission spline and clutch disc hub line up. Push rearward on the engine and engage the splines. Sometimes it may be necessary to turn the crankshaft with a wrench while working the engine into alignment. Once the spline engages, lower the engine until it is even with the transmission and slide it into position. Make sure the engine block dowel pins are engaged. Install the transmission-to-engine mounting bolts.

If the engine and transmission are installed as a unit, support the transmission tail on a jack as it slides under the transmission tunnel. Move the car while lowering the engine or move the jack until the assembly is in position. Raise the transmission and install the crossmember.

Install all engine-to-bell housing or transmission-to-engine mounting bolts and tighten. Lower the engine and install the front motor mounts. Install the rear mount and crossmember. Remove the jack and engine sling.

Raise the car and support it on jack stands. Install the starter motor, driveshaft and all items disconnected from under the car. Make sure that the converter-to-flexplate mounting bolts are secure after the wire that kept it in position was removed. Install the exhaust manifolds with new gaskets. Install all other accessories in the order of removal, including a new oil filter. Adjust the clutch after installing any removed linkage. Fill the manual transmission (if necessary).

Install all driven items including the power steering

pump and air conditioner compressor. Install the fan clutch (if equipped) shroud and fan blades. Install the radiator, connect the shroud, radiator hoses and transmission cooler lines. Connect all linkage, wire harnesses and fuel lines. Make sure the oil pan drain plug is installed and fill the engine with the correct amount and type of oil. Fill the radiator with a 50/50 mixture of coolant and water, or enough coolant for cold weather protection to at least −20°F. Install and connect the battery. Make sure all drive belts are installed and correctly adjusted. Crank the engine until oil pressure is observed. The light will go out on the dash or the gauge will read pressure. Check that oil is present at the rocker arms. Install the valve covers, without gaskets or use old gaskets (if they must be removed after the engine is warm) for valve adjustment. Install new spark plugs and connect the plug wires. Cranking the engine to get oil pressure should have pumped gas to the carburetor. Make sure the choke is working and crank the engine. It should start quickly. Run the engine at 1000–2000 rpm for 20–30 minutes until it is thoroughly warm. If the engine is equipped with hydraulic lifters it will be noisy for a few minutes. Readjust the rocker arms if necessary according to the manufacturer's recommendations. After the engine has warmed up completely, shut it off. Check for oil and water leaks. Check the fluid levels. Add transmission fluid if necessary. Retorque the head bolts.

NOTE: *Engines with aluminum heads or blocks must cool to room temperature before retorquing the heads.*

Install new gaskets (if necessary) and tighten the valve covers. Lower the car from the jackstands and install the hood. Make sure all emission equipment (except the air cleaner) is connected or installed. Be sure to install a new PCU valve and that the EGR valve is working.

Once again start the engine and allow it to reach normal operating temperature. Check the ignition timing, idle speed and mixture. Install the air cleaner.

(Refer to the next section on tune up). After the engine has a few miles on it, have it checked and set up on an electronic engine analyzer. The few dollars it will cost are worth the performance and reduced emissions.

TUNE-UP

The procedures below are used to indicate where adjustments, parts service or replacement are necessary within the realm of a normal tune-up.

- Remove the distributor cap, and inspect it inside and out for cracks and/or carbon tracks, and inside for excessive wear or burning of the rotor contacts. If any of these faults are evident, the cap must be replaced.
- If the distributor cap is to be reused, clean the inside with a dry rag, and remove corrosion from the rotor contact points with fine emery cloth. Remove the spark plug wires one by one, and clean the wire ends and the inside of the towers. If the boots are loose, they should be replaced.

If the cap is to be replaced, transfer the wires one by one, cleaning the wire ends and replacing the boots if necessary.

- Check the breaker points (if equipped) for burning, pitting or wear, and the contact heel resting on the distributor cam for excessive wear. If defects are noted, replace the entire breaker point set.
- If the original points are to remain in service, clean them lightly with emery cloth, lubricate the contact heel with grease specifically designed for this purpose. Rotate the crankshaft until the heel rests on a high point of the distributor cam, and adjust the point gap to specifications.

When replacing the points, remove the original points and condenser, and wipe out the inside of the distributor housing with a clean, dry rag. Lightly lubricate the contact heel and pivot point, and install the points and condenser. Rotate the crankshaft until the heel rests on a high point of the distributor cam, and adjust the point gap to specifications.

NOTE: *Always replace the condenser when changing the points.*

- Remove and inspect the rotor. If the contacts are burned or worn, or if the rotor is excessively loose on the distributor shaft (where applicable), the rotor must be replaced.
- If the rotor is to be reused, clean the contacts with solvent. Do not alter the spring tension of the rotor center contact. Install the rotor and the distributor cap.
- Inspect the spark plug leads and the coil high tension lead for cracks or brittleness. If any of the wires appear defective, the entire set should be replaced.
- Check the air filter to ensure that it is functioning properly.
- Install a new fuel filter.
- Test the PCV valve (if so equipped), and clean or replace as indicated. Clean all crankcase ventilation hoses, or replace if cracked or hardened.

IGNITION TIMING

Ignition timing is the measurement in degrees of crankshaft rotation of the instant the spark plugs in the cylinders fire, in relation to the location of the piston, while the piston is on its compression stroke.

Ignition timing is adjusted by loosening the distributor locking device and turning the distributor in the engine.

NOTE: *To advance timing, rotate distributor opposite normal direction of rotor rotation, and vice-versa.*

Timing the Engine with a Timing Light

1. If the timing light operates from the battery, connect the red lead to the battery positive terminal, and the black lead to a ground. With all lights, connect the trigger lead in series with No. 1 spark plug wire.

2. Disconnect and plug the required vacuum hoses, as in the manufacturer's specifications. Connect the red lead of a tachometer to the distributor side of the coil and the black lead to ground. Start the engine, put the (automatic) transmission in gear (if required), and read the tachometer. Adjust the carburetor idle screw to the proper speed for setting the timing. Aim the timing light at the crankshaft pulley to determine where the timing point is. If the point is hard to see, it may help to stop the engine and mark it with chalk or day-glow, luminescent paint.

3. Loosen the distributor holding clamp and rotate the distributor slowly in either direction until the timing is correct. Tighten the clamp and observe the timing mark again to determine that the timing is still correct. Readjust the position of the distributor, if necessary.

4. Accelerate the engine in Neutral, while watching the timing point. If the distributor advance mechanisms are working, the timing point should advance as the engine is accelerated. If the engine's vacuum advance is engaged with the transmission in Neutral, check the vacuum advance operation by running the engine at about 1,500 rpm and connecting and disconnecting the vacuum advance hose.

Static Timing

1. Make sure the engine is at the correct temperature for timing adjustment (either fully warmed or cold, as specified in the factory manual or a Chilton repair manual).

2. Locate No. 1 cylinder and trace its wire back to the distributor cap. Then, remove the cap.

3. Rotate the engine until the proper timing mark on the crankshaft pulley is lined up with the timing mark on the block. Observe the direction of distributor shaft rotation when the engine is turned in its normal direction of rotation.

4. Connect a test lamp from the coil terminal (the distributor side) to ground. Make sure the tip of the rotor lines up with No. 1 cylinder. If it does not, turn the engine one full revolution and line up the timing marks again.

5. Loosen the clamp that holds the distributor in position and turn the distributor body in the direction of normal shaft rotation until the points close and the test lamp goes out. Now turn the distributor in the opposite direction very slowly, just until the test lamp comes on. Tighten the distributor clamp.

6. To test the adjustment, turn the engine backward until the light again goes out, and then forward just until the light comes back on.

NOTE: *Engines with a belt-driven camshaft must not be rotated backward.*

If the timing marks are lined up, the engine is accurately timed. If the timing is too far advanced, loosen the distributor and turn it just slightly in the direction of shaft rotation, and retighten the clamp. If the timing is retarded, turn the distributor in the opposite direction and then repeat the test. Repeat this procedure until the light comes on just as the two timing marks are aligned.

CARBURETOR ADJUSTMENTS

The curb idle speed adjusting screw contacts a lever (the throttle lever) on the outside of the carburetor. When the screw is turned in, it opens the throttle plate on the carburetor, raising the idle speed of the engine.

Since the early seventies, most engines have been equipped with throttle solenoids. Due to the power-robbing effects of emission control systems, car manufacturers have found it necessary to raise the idle speed on almost all engines in order to obtain a smooth idle. Ordinarily, when the key is turned to "off," the current to the spark plugs is cut off, and the engine normally stops running. However, if an engine has a high operating temperature and a high idle speed (conditions common to emission-controlled engines), it is possible for the temperature of the cylinder instead of the spark plug to ignite the fuel/air mixture. When this happens, the engine continues to run after the key is turned off. To solve this problem, a throttle solenoid was added to the carburetor. The solenoid is a cylinder with an adjustable plunger and an electrical lead. When the ignition key is turned to "on," the solenoid plunger extends to contact the carburetor throttle lever and raise the idle speed of the engine. When the ignition key is turned to "off," the solenoid is de-energized and the solenoid plunger falls back from the throttle lever. This allows the throttle lever to fall back and rest on the curb idle adjusting screw. This drops the engine idle speed back far enough so that the engine will not "run-on."

Since it is difficult for the engine to draw the fuel/air mixture from the carburetor with the small amount of throttle plate opening that is present when the engine is idling, an idle mixture passage is provided in the carburetor. This passage delivers fuel/air mixture to the engine from a hole which is located in the bottom of the carburetor below the throttle plates. This idle mixture passage contains an adjusting screw which restricts the amount of fuel/air mixture that enters the engine at idle. The idle mixture screws are capped on late-model cars due to emission-control regulations.

Idle Speed Adjustment

Generally, the idle speed is adjusted before the idle mixture is adjusted. You will need a tachometer to adjust the carburetor to the specified rpm. Connect the tachometer red lead to the negative terminal of the coil and connect the black lead to ground. This procedure is for conventional ignition systems only. Electronic ignition systems generally have specific tach hook-up procedures, and in addition, will not necessarily work with all tachometers. Locate the idle speed screw or the idle solenoid. With the engine at operating temperature, adjust the screw or the solenoid until the correct idle speed is reached. Ordinarily, on cars equipped with idle solenoids, there are two idle speeds listed. The higher of the two speeds is with the solenoid connected, while the lower is obviously with the solenoid disconnected. Set both speeds and then go on to the mixture adjustment.

Idle Mixture Adjustment

Locate the idle mixture screw or screws. All vehicles manufactured after 1972 have their idle mixture screws capped in accordance with Federal emission control regulations. As a result of this, there is only a very limited range of adjustment possible on these carburetors. To comply with emission regulations, the caps should not be removed or the mixture adjusted without them. After you have found the mixture screws, adjust them according to the manufacturer's instructions. In general, the procedure is:

1. On early vehicles without capped mixture screws, adjust the mixture screw or screws for the highest idle speed you can obtain on the tachometer. An alternative method is to use a vacuum gauge and adjust the screws until the highest possible vacuum reading is obtained.

2. On vehicles with capped mixture screws, adjust the mixture screws (within the limits imposed by the caps) until the highest possible idle is obtained. Then adjust the screws inward from highest idle until the specified rpm drop is obtained.

After the mixture has been adjusted, it is quite often necessary to reset the idle speed with the idle speed screw or solenoid. As a general rule, idle mixture adjustments will raise the idle above that which is called for, necessitating a readjustment with the idle speed screw or solenoid.

VALVE ADJUSTMENT

Periodic valve adjustments are not required on most engines with hydraulic valve lifters. In fact, many engines no longer have any provision whatsoever for valve adjustment, hydraulic valve lifter technology being what it is. Most import car engines, however, have adjustable valves, since a tightly controlled valve lash is the key to wringing horsepower out of these smaller motors. Exact valve adjustment procedures for all engines cannot be given here, but here are some general guidelines:

1. Bring the engine to the condition specified for valve adjustment (cold, hot, running, etc). Some manufacturers give procedures for both hot and cold adjustment. A note of caution about hot valve adjustment: oil temperature is far more critical to valve adjustment than water temperature; if the adjustment procedure calls for the engine to be at operating temperature, make sure the engine runs for at least fifteen

minutes to allow the oil temperature to stabilize and parts to reach their full expansion.

2. Remove the valve or cam cover. If the valves are to be adjusted while the engine is running, oil deflector clips are available which install on the rocker arms and prevent oil spray.

3. If the valves must be adjusted with the engine stopped, follow the manufacturer's instructions for positioning the engine properly. For example, on Volkswagens, number one cylinder is adjusted while it is on the compression stroke at TDC, number two with the crankshaft turned 180 backward, etc.

4. Generally on overhead camshaft engines, valve adjustment is fairly simple. Turn the engine over (either manually or with a remote starter switch) until the highest part of the cam lobe is pointing directly away from the rocker arm or lifter. In the event you are unsure of how to do it, consult a Chilton manual.

5. Adjust solid lifters by pushing a leaf type feeler gauge of the specified thickness (consult the manual) between the valve stem and rocker arm. Loosen the locking nut and tighten the screw until a light resistance to the movement of the feeler blade is encountered. Hold the adjusting screw while tightening the locking nut. Some adjusting screws are fitted snugly into the rocker arm so no locknut is required. If the feeler is too snug, the adjustment should be loosened to permit the passage of the blade. Remember that a slightly loose adjustment is easier on the valves than an overly tight one, so adjust the valves accordingly. Always recheck the adjustment after the locknut has been tightened.

Refer to a Chilton manual for details on hydraulic valve lifter adjustment.

6. Replace the valve cover, cleaning all traces of old gasket material from both surfaces and installing a new gasket. Tighten valve cover nuts alternately, in several stages, to ensure proper seating.

BREAK-IN

Make the first miles on the new engine, easy ones. Vary the speed but do not accelerate hard. Most importantly, do not lug the engine, and avoid sustained high speeds for at least 100 miles. Check the engine oil and radiator coolant levels frequently. Expect the engine to use a little oil until the rings seat. Change the engine oil and the filter after the first five hundred miles. After that, drive normally.

10

REBUILDING VOLKSWAGEN AND PORSCHE ENGINES

This section describes, in detail, the procedures involved in rebuilding a horizontally opposed, air-cooled Volkswagen/Porsche four cylinder engine. It is divided into two sections. The first section, Cylinder Head Reconditioning, assumes that the cylinder head is removed from the engine, all manifolds and sheet metal shrouding is removed, and the cylinder head is on a workbench. The second section, Crankcase Reconditioning, covers the crankcase halves, the connecting rods, crankshaft, camshaft and lifters. It is assumed that the engine is mounted on a work stand (which can be rented), with the cylinder heads, cylinders, pistons, and all accessories removed.

In some cases, a choice of methods is provided. The choice of a method for a procedure is at the discretion of the user. It may be limited by the tools available to a user, or the proximity of a local engine rebuilding or machine shop.

Aluminum is used liberally in VW and Porsche engines due to its low weight and excellent heat transfer characteristics. Both the cylinder heads and the crankcase are aluminum alloy castings. However, a few precautions must be observed when handling aluminum alloy castings. However, a few precautions must be observed when handling aluminum engine parts:— Never hot-tank aluminum parts, unless the hot-tanking solution is specified for aluminum application (i.e. Oakite ® Aluminum Cleaner 164, or ZEP® Hot Vat Aluminum Cleaner). Most hot-tanking solutions are used for ferrous metals only, and "cook" at much higher temperatures than the 175°F used for aluminum cleaners. The result would be a dissolved head or crankcase.

—Always coat threads lightly with engine oil or anti-seize compound before installation, to prevent seizure.

—Never overtorque bolts or spark plugs in aluminum threads. Should stripping occur, threads can be restored using inserts such as the Heli-Coil®, K-D® Insert for Keenserts® kits.

Any parts that will be in frictional contact must be pre-lubricated before assembly to provide protection on initial start-up. Many different pre-lubes are available and each mechanic has his own favorite. However, any product specifically formulated for this purpose or even a good grade of white grease may be used. Do not use engine oil for pre-lube.

CYLINDER HEAD

Identify the Valves

Keep the valves in order, so that you know which valve (intake and exhaust) goes in which combustion chamber. If the valve faces are not full of carbon, number them, front to rear, with a permanent felt tip marker.

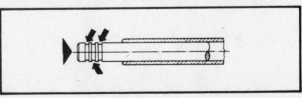

Valve keeper seating surfaces

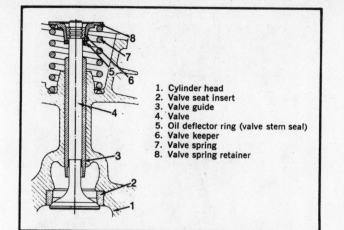

1. Cylinder head
2. Valve seat insert
3. Valve guide
4. Valve
5. Oil deflector ring (valve stem seal)
6. Valve keeper
7. Valve spring
8. Valve spring retainer

Cross section of valve and related parts

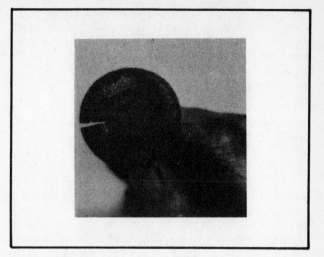

Burnt exhaust valve

Lever type valve spring compressor

Removing carbon from combustion chamber

REMOVE THE VALVES AND SPRINGS

Using a valve spring compressor, compress the valve springs and lift out the keepers with needlenosed pliers. Slowly release the compressor, and remove the valve, spring and spring retainer. Check the keeper seating surfaces on the valve stem for burrs which may scratch the valve guide during installation of the valve. Remove any burrs with a fine file.

This section assumes that the cylinder head is removed for this operation. However, if it is desired to remove the valve springs with the head installed, it will be necessary to screw a compressed air adaptor into the subject spark plug hole and maintain a pressure of 85 psi to keep the valve from dropping down.

Inspect the exhaust valves closely. More often than not, the cause of low compression is a burned exhaust valve. The classic burned valve is cracked on the valve face from the edge of the seat to the stem the way you could cut a pie. Remove all carbon, gum and varnish from the valve stem with a hardwood chisel, or with a wire brush and solvent (i.e. carburetor cleaner, lacquer thinner).

Hot-Tank the Cylinder Head

Hot-tank the cylinder head to remove grease, corrosion, carbon deposits and scale.

NOTE: *Make sure that the hot-tanking solution is designed to clean aluminum, not to dissolve it.*

After hot-tanking, inspect the combustion chambers (around the spark plug hole) and the exhaust ports for cracks. Also, check the plug threads, manifold studs, and rocker arm studs for damage and looseness.

De-grease the Remaining Cylinder Head Parts

Using solvent (i.e. Gunk® or Zep® carburetor cleaner), clean the rockers, rocker shafts, valve springs, spring retainers, keepers and the pushrods. You may also use solvent to clean the cylinder head although it will not clean as well as hot-tanking. Also clean the sheet metal shrouding at this time. Do not clean the pushrod tubes in solvent.

Decarbon the Cylinder Head

Chip carbon away from the combustion chambers and exhaust ports using a hardwood chisel. Remove the remaining deposits with a stiff wire brush. You may also use a power drill with wire attachment if you use a very light touch. Remember that you are working with a relatively soft metal (aluminum), and you do not want to grind into the metal. You can also have the cylinder head glass-beaded.

Check the Valve Stem-To-Guide Clearance (Valve Rock)

Clean the valve stem with lacquer thinner or carburetor cleaner to remove all gum and varnish. Clean the valve guides using solvent and an expanding wire-type valve guide cleaner or brass bristle brush. Mount a dial indicator to the head so that the gauge pin is at a 90° angle to the valve stem, up against the edge of the valve head. Insert the valve by hand so that the stem end is flush with the end of the guide. Move the valve off its seat, and measure the clearance by rocking the stem back and forth. Maximum rock should not exceed the wear limit.

Check whether excessive rock is due to worn valve stems or guides (or both). If a new valve is available, recheck the valve rock. If rock is still excessive the guide is at fault. Or, you may measure the old valve stem with a micrometer, and determine if it has passed its wear limit.

Knurling the Valve Guides

Although this operation can be performed on VW and Porsche engines, it is not recommended. Replacement of the worn guides should be done when excessive wear is noted.

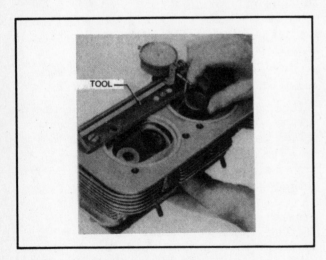

Checking valve stem-to-guide clearance

Replace the Valve Guides

The valve guides are a press fit into the head.

NOTE: *If the replacement valve guides do not have a collar at the top, measure the distance the old guides protrude above the head.*

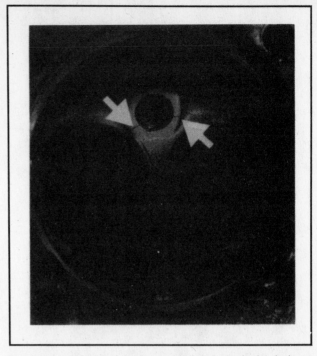

Cracks in combustion chamber adjoining spark plug hole

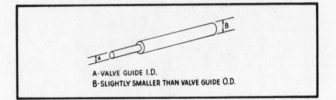

A-VALVE GUIDE I.D.
B-SLIGHTLY SMALLER THAN VALVE GUIDE O.D.

Valve guide removal tool

Several different methods may be used to remove worn valve guides. One method is to press or tap the guides out of the head using a stepped drift. The problem with this method is the risk of cracking the head. Another method, which reduces this risk, is to first drill out the guide about ⅔ of the length of the guide so that the walls of the guide at the top are paper thin (1/32 in. or so). This relieves most of the tension from the cylinder head guide bore, but still provides a solid base at the bottom of the guide to drift out the guide from the top. A third method of removing guides is to tap threads into the guide and pull it out from the top. After tapping the guide, place an old wrist pin (or some other type of sleeve) over the guide, so that the wrist pin rests squarely on the boss on the cylinder head around the guide. Then, take a long bolt (about 4 or 5 inches long with threads running all the way up to the bolt head) and thread a nut about half way up the bolt. Place a washer on top of the wrist pin and thread the bolt into the valve guide until the nut contacts the washer and wrist pin. Finally, screw the nut down against the washer and wrist pin to pull out the guide.

If you are installing the guides without the aid of a press, using only hand tools, it will help to place the new valve guides in the freezer for an hour or so, and the

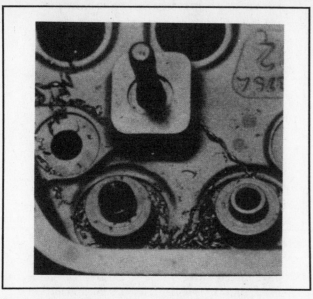

Valve guide drilled to relieve tension for removal

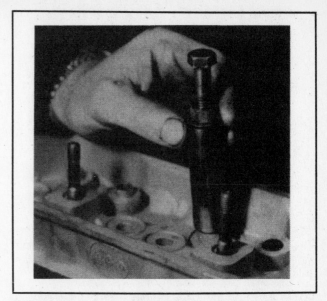

Valve guide removal using long bolt, washer, nut and wrist pin

clean, bare cylinder head in the oven at 350–400°F for ½ hour to 45 minutes. Controlling the temperature of the metals in this manner will slightly shrink the valve guides and slightly expand the guide bore in the cylinder head, allowing easier installation and lessening the risk of cracking the head in the process.

Most replacement valve guides, other than those manufactured by VW, have a collar at the top which provides a positive stop to seat the guides in the head. However, VW guides have no such collar. Therefore, on these guides, you will have to determine the height above the cylinder head boss that the guide must extend (about ¼ in.). Then obtain a stack of washers, their inner diameter slightly larger than the outer diameter of the guide at the top of the guide. If the guide should extend ¼ in. in., use a ¼ in. thick stack of washers around the guide.

To install the valve guides in the head, use a collared drift, or a special valve guide installation tool of the proper outside diameter. If the replacement guide is collared, drive in the guide until it seats against the boss on the cylinder head. If the guide is not collared, drive in the guide until the installation tool butts against the stack of washers (approx. ¼ in. thick) on the head.

NOTE: *If you do not heat the head to aid installation, use penetrating lubricant in the guide bore instead.*

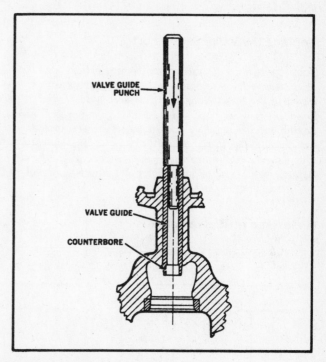

Cross section of valve guide and punch

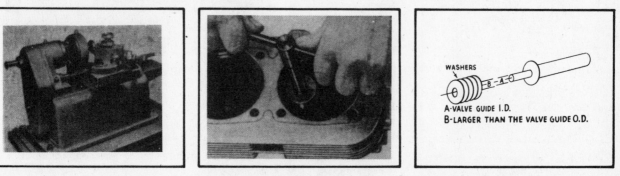

Grinding a valve

Installing a pilot in the valve guide

Valve guide removal tool

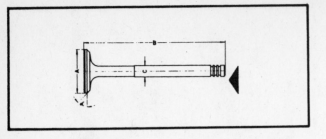

Critical valve dimensions

Resurfacing (Grinding) the Valve Face

Resurface the valves according to specifications.

The valve stem tip should also be squared and resurfaced, by placing the stem in the V-block of the grinder, and turning it while pressing lightly against the grinding wheel.

NOTE: *After grinding, the minimum valve head margin must be 0.50mm (.020 in.). The valve head margin is the straight surface on the edge of the valve head, parallel with the valve stem.*

Replace the Valve Seat Inserts

This operation is not normally performed on VW engines due to its expense and special shrink fit of the insert in the head. Usually, if the seat is destroyed, the head is also in bad shape. Some high-performance engine builders will replace the inserts to accommodate larger diameter valve heads. Otherwise, the operation will usually cost more than replacement of the head. Also, a replacement insert, if not installed correctly, could come out of the head.

Resurface the Valve Seats

Most valve seats can be reconditioned by resurfacing. This is done with a reamer or grinder. First, a pilot is

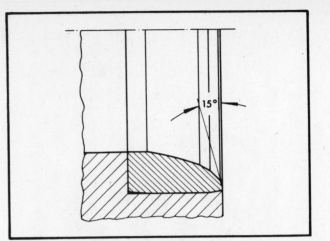

15° finish cut on upper (outer) edge of seat

installed in the valve guide (a worn valve guide will allow the pilot to wobble, causing an inaccurate seat cut). When using a reamer, apply steady pressure while rotating clockwise. The seat should be clean up in about four complete turns, taking care to remove only as much metal as necessary. Never rotate a reamer counterclockwise. When using a grinder, lift the cutting stone on and off the seat at approximately two cycles per second, until all flaws are removed.

It takes three separate cuts to recondition a VW valve seat. After each cut, check the position of the valve seat using Prussian blue dye. First cut the center of the seat using a 45° cutter (30° cutter on 1700, 1800 and 2000 cc intake valve seat). Then, you cut the bottom of the seat with a 75° cutter and narrow the top of the seat with a 15° stone. The center of the seat must be maintained as per the following chart:

Equally as important as the width of the seat is its location in relation to the valve. Using a caliper, measure the distance between the center of the valve face on both sides of a valve. Then, place the caliper on the valve seat, and check that the pointers of the caliper locate in the center of the seat.

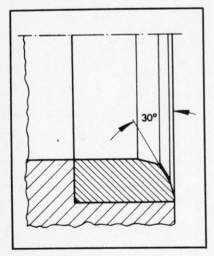

30° contact facing on seat of 1700, 1800 and 2000 exhaust valves

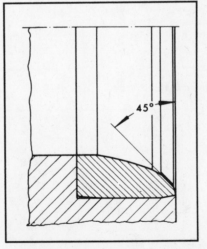

45° contact facing on seat of all 1600 valves and on 1700, 1800 and 2000 exhaust valves

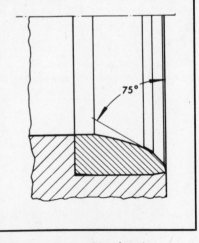

75° cut on lower edge of seat

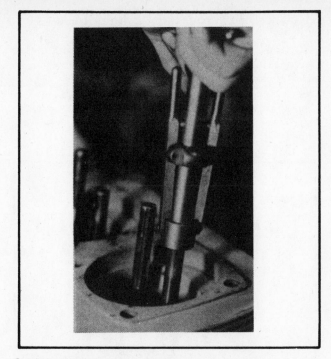

Cutting valve seat using a reamer

Check the Valve Seat Concentricity

The valve seat must be concentric with the valve guide. To check concentricity, coat the valve face with Prussian blue dye and install the valve in its guide. Applying light pressure, rotate the valve 1/4 turn in its valve seat. If the entire valve seat face becomes coated, and the valve is known to be concentric, the seat is concentric.

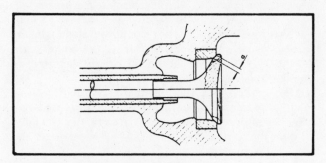

Seat contact width (dimension "a")

Lap the Valves

With accurately refaced valve seat inserts and new valves, it is not usually necessary to lap the valves. Valve lapping alone is not recommended for use as a resurfacing procedure.

Prior to lapping, invert the cylinder head, lightly lubricate the valve stem and install the valves in their respective guides. Coat the valve seats with fine carborundum grinding compound, and attach the lapping tool suction cup to the valve head. Then, rotate the tool between your palms, changing direction and lifting the

Hand lapping the valves

tool often to prevent grooving. Lap the valve until a smooth, polished seat is evident. Finally, remove the tool and thoroughly wash away all traces of grinding compound. Make sure that no compound accumulates in the guides as rapid wear would result.

Check the Valve Springs

Measure the height of the spring and compare that valve to that of the other springs. All springs should be the same height. Rotate the spring against the edge of the square to measure distortion. Replace any spring that varies (in both height and distortion) more than 1/16 in.

Use the following specifications to check the springs under a load.

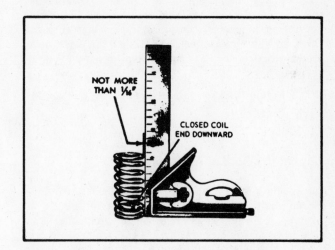

Checking valve spring free length and squareness

Install the Valves

Lubricate the valve stems with white grease (molybdenum disulphide), and install the valves in their respective guides. Lubricate and install the valve stem seals.

Checking valve spring loaded length and tension

NOTE: *VW does not install stem seals on new engines. The reason is, control, the guides tend to run "dry" which only hastens their demise. This is especially true for exhaust valves which run at much greater temperatures.*

Position the valve springs on the head. The spring is positioned with the closely coiled end facing the head.

Check the valve stem keys (keepers) for burrs or scoring. The keys should be machined so that the valve may still rotate with the keys held together. Finally, install the spring retainers, compress the springs (using a valve spring compressor), and insert the keys using needle-nosed pliers or a special tool designed for this purpose.

NOTE: *Retain the keys with wheel bearing grease during installation.*

Inspect the Rocker Arms and Shafts

Remove the rocker arms, springs and washers from the rocker shaft. Inspect the rocker arms for pitting or wear on the valve stem contact point, and check for excessive rocker arm bushing wear where the arm rides on the shaft. If the shaft is grooved noticeably, replace it.

Minor scoring may be removed with an emery cloth. If the valve stem contact point of the rocker arm is worn, grind it smooth, removing as little as necessary. If it is noticed at this point that the valve stem is worn concave where it contacts the rocker arm, and it is not desired to disassemble the valve from the head, a cap may be installed over the stem prior to installing the rocker shaft assembly.

Inspect the Pushrods and Pushrod Tubes

After soaking the pushrods in solvent, clean out the oil passages using fine wire, then blow through them to make sure there are no obstructions. Roll each pushrod over a piece of clean, flat glass. Check for run-out. If a distinct, clicking sound is heard as the pushrod rolls, the rod is bent, necessitating replacement. All pushrods must be of equal length.

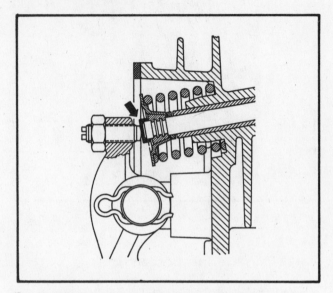

Cap installed over a valve stem tip worn concave

Inspect the pushrod tubes for cracks or other damage to the tube that would let oil out and dirt into the engine. The tubes on the 1600 engine are particularly susceptible to damage at the stretchable bellows. Also, on the 1600 engine, the tubes may be maintained at length "a" (see illustration) which is 190–191 mm or 7.4–7.52 in. If a tube is too short, it may be carefully stretched, taking care to avoid cracking. However, if the bellows are damaged or if a gritty, rusty sound occurs when stretching the tube, replace it. Always use new seals. When installing tubes in a 1600 engine, rotate the tubes so that the seams face upwards. When installing tubes in a 1700, 1800 or 2000 engine, make sure the retaining wire for the tubes engages the slots in the supports and rests on the lower edges of the tubes.

If, on an assembled, installed 1600 engine, it is desired to replace a damaged or leaky pushrod tube without pulling the engine, it can be done using a "quick-change" pushrod tube available from several different specialty manufacturers. The special two-piece aluminum replacement tube is installed after

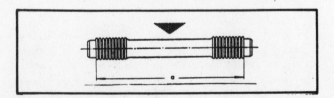

Pushrod tube required length

num or magnesium alloy, clean the crankcase to remove all sludge, scale, or foreign particles. You can also cold-tank the case, using a strong degreasing solvent, but you will have to use a brush and a lot of elbow grease to get the same results.

After cleaning, blow out all oil passages with compressed air. Remove all old gasket sealing compound from the mating surfaces.

Inspect the Crankcase

Check the case for cracks using the methods described earlier in this section.

Inspect all sealing or mating surfaces, especially along the crankcase seam, as the crankcase halves are machined in pairs and use no gasket.

Check the tightness of the oil suction pipe. The pipe must be centered over the strainer opening. On 1600 engines, peen over the crankcase where the suction pipe enters the camshaft bearing web.

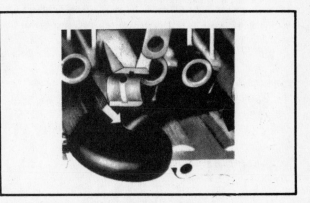

Checking tightness of the oil suction tube

Check all studs for tightness. Replace any defective studs as mentioned earlier in this section. Check all bearing bores for nicks and scratches. Remove light marks with a file. Deeper scratches and scoring must be removed by align boring the crankshaft bearing bores.

Align Bore the Crankcase

There are two surfaces on a VW crankcase that take quite a hammering in normal service. One is the main bearing saddles and the other the thrust flange of #1 bearing (at the flywheel end). Because the case is constructed of softer metal than the bearings, it is more malleable. The main bearing saddles are slowly hammered in by the rotation of the heavy crankshaft working against the bearings. This is especially true for an out-of-round crankshaft. The thrust flange of #1 main bearing receives its beating trying to control the end-play of the crankshaft. This beating is more severe in cases of a driver with a heavy clutch foot. Popping the clutch bangs the pressure plate against the clutch disc, against the flywheel, against the crankcase flange, and finally against the thrust flange. All of this hammering leaves its mark on the case, but can be cleaned up by align boring.

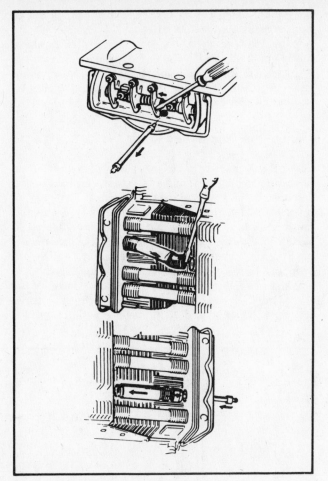

Quick change tube installation

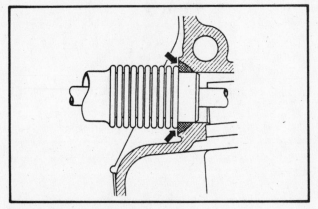

Silicone seat at pushrod tube ends

removing the valve cover, rocker arm assembly and pushrod of the subject cylinder. The old tube has to be pried loose. Using new seals, the replacement tube is positioned between the head and crankshaft, and expanded into place, with a pair of threaded, locking nuts.

ENGINE BLOCK AND CRANKCASE

Disassemble and Hot-tank the Crankcase

Using only a hot-tanking solution formulated for alumi-

Most VW engine rebuilders who want their engines to stay together will align bore the case. This assures proper bearing bore alignment. Then, main bearings with the correct oversize outer diameter (and oversize thrust shoulder on #1) are installed.

Also, as the split crankcase is constructed of light aluminum and magnesium alloy, it is particularly susceptible to warpage due to overheating. Align boring the case will clean up any bearing saddle misalignment due to warpage.

Check Connecting Rod Side Clearance and Connecting Rods for Straightness

Before removing the connecting rods from the crankshaft, check the clearance between the rod and the crank throw using a feeler gauge. Replace any rod exceeding the wear limit. Proper side clearance is given in the specifications.

Also, prior to removing the rods from the crankshaft, check them for straightness. This is accomplished easily using an old wrist pin, and sliding the wrist pin through each connecting rod (small end) in succession. Position each rod, in turn, so that as the pin begins to leave one rod, it is entering the next rod. Any binding indicates a scored wrist pin bushing or misaligned (bent) connecting rod. If the wrist pin absolutely will not slide from one adjacent rod to another, then you've got a severely bent rod.

Disassemble the Crankshaft

Number the connecting rods (1 through 4 from the flywheel side) and matchmark their bearing halves. Remove the connecting rod retaining nuts (do not remove the bolts) from the big end and remove the rods. Slide off the oil thrower (1600 only) and #4 main bearing. Slide off #1 main bearing from the flywheel end. Remove the snap-ring. #2 main bearing is the split-type, each half of which should remain in its respective crankcase half. Using a large gear puller, or an arbor or hydraulic press, remove the distributor drive gear and crankshaft timing gear and spacer. Don't lose the Woodruff key(s).

NOTE: *The 1600 engine has two Woodruff keys. The 1700, 1800 and 2000 engines have only one.*

Finally, slide off #3 main bearing.

Inspect the Crankshaft

Clean the crankshaft with solvent. Run all oil holes through with a brass bristle brush. Blow them through with compressed air. Lightly oil the crankshaft to prevent rusting.

Measure the crankshaft journals for wear. The maximum wear limit for all journals is .0012 in. (0.03 mm).

Check the crankshaft run-out. With main bearing journals #1 and #3 supported on V-blocks and a dial gauge set up perpendicular to the crankshaft, measure the run-out at #2 and #4 main bearing journals. Maximum permissible run-out of .0008 in. (0.02 mm).

Inspect the crankshaft journals for scratches, ridges, scoring and nicks. All small nicks and scratches necessitate regrinding of the crankshaft. Journals worn to a taper or slightly out-of-round must also be reground. Standard undersizes are .010, .020, .030 in.

Inspect the Connecting Rods

Check the connecting rods for cracks, bends and burns. Check the rod bolts for damage, replace any rod with a damaged bolt. Check the rods for twists and Magnaflux them for hidden cracks. Also, the rods must be checked for straightness, using the wrist pin method described earlier. If you did not perform this check before removing the rods from the crankshaft, definitely do so before dropping the assembled crankshaft into the case.

Weigh the rods on a gram scale. On 1600 engines, the rods should all weigh within 10 grams (lightest to heaviest); on 1700, 1800 and 2000 engines, within 6 grams.

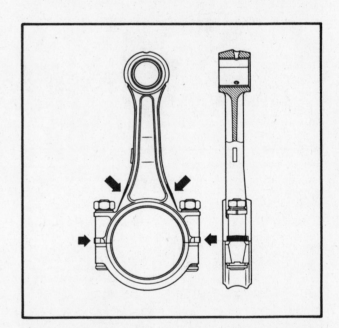

Metal can be removed from locations indicated to lighten connecting rods

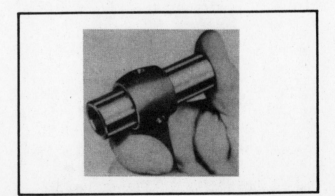

Checking wrist pin fit

All rods should ideally weigh the same. If not, find the lightest rod and lighten the others to match. Up to 8 grams of metal can be removed from a rod by filing or grinding at the low stress points shown in the illustration.

Check the fit of the wrist pin bushing. The pin should slide through the bushing with only light thumb pressure.

Check Connecting Rod Bearing Clearance

It is always good practice to replace the connecting rod bearings at every teardown. The bearing size is stamped on the back of the inserts. However, if it is desired to reuse the bearings, two methods may be used to determine bearing clearance.

Use Plastigage® to check bearing clearance. This method can only be used on the split-type bearings and not on the ring-type bearings used to support the crankshaft. First, clean all oil from the bearing surface and crankshaft journal being checked. Pllastigage® is soluble in oil. Cut a piece of Plastigage® the width of the rod bearing and insert it between the journal and bearing insert.

NOTE: *Do not rotate the rod on the crankshaft.*

Tighten the rod cap nuts to specifications. Remove the bearing insert and check the thickness of the flattened Plastigage® using the Plastigage® scale. Journal taper is determined by comparing the width of the Plastigage® strip near its ends. To check for journal eccentricity, rotate the crankshat 90° and retest. After checking all four connecting rod bearings in this manner, remove all traces of Plastigage® from the journal and bearing. Oil the crankshaft to prevent rusting.

If the oil clearance is .0006 in. (0.15 mm) or greater, it will be necessary to have the crankshaft ground to the nearest undersize (.010 in.) and use oversize connecting rod bearings.

Check Main Bearing Oil Clearance

It is also good practice to replace the main bearings at every engine teardown as their replacement cost is minimal compared to the replacement cost of a crankshaft or short block. However, if it becomes necessary to reuse the bearings, you may do so after checking the bearing clearance.

Main bearings #1, 3 and 4 are ring-type bearings that slip over the crankshaft. These bearings cannot be checked using the Plastigage® method. Only the split-type #2 main bearing can be checked using Plastigage®. However, since this involves bolting together and unbolting the crankcase halves several times, it is not recommended. Therefore, the main bearings are checked using a micrometer. Use the following chart to determine if the bearing (oil) clearance exceeds its wear limit.

Never reuse a bearing that shows signs of wear, scoring or blueing. If the bearing clearance exceeds its wear limit, it will be necessary to regrind the crankshaft to the nearest undersize and use oversize main bearings.

Clean and Inspect the Camshaft

Degrease the camshaft using solvent. Clean out all oil holes and blow through with compressed air. Visually inspect the cam lobes and bearing journals for excessive wear. The edges of the camshaft lobes should be square. Slight damage can be removed with silicone carbide oilstone. To check for lobe wear not visible to the eye, mike the camshaft diameter from the tip of the

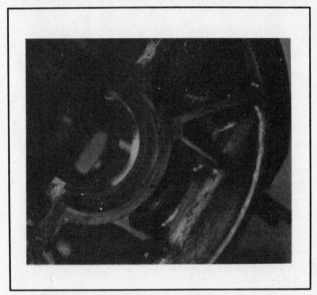

No. 1 main thrust bearing flange

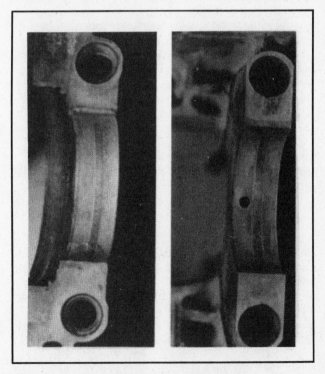

Ridged main bearing bores prior to align boring

lobe to base (distance A) and then mike the diameter of the camshaft at a 90° angle to the previous measurement (distance B). This will give you camshaft lift. Measure lift for each lobe. If any lobe differs more than .025 in., replace the camshaft.

Check the camshaft for run-out. Place the #1 and #3 journals in V-blocks and rest a dial indicator on #2 journal. Rotate the camshaft and check the reading. Run-out must not exceed 0.0015 in. (0.04 mm). Repair is by replacement.

Check the camshaft timing gear rivets for tightness. If any of the gear rivets are loose, or if the gear teeth show a poor contact pattern, replace the camshaft and timing gear assembly. Check the axial (end) play of the timing gear. Place the camshaft in the left crankcase half. The wear limit is .0063 in. (0.16 mm). If the end-play is excessive, the thrust shoulder of #3 camshaft bearing is probably worn, necessitating replacement of the cam bearings.

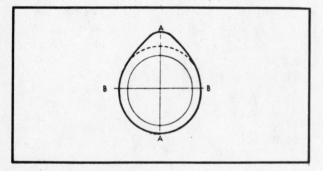

Camshaft lobe measurement

Check the Camshaft Bearings

The camshaft bearings are the split-type, #3 camshaft bearing has shoulders on it to control axial play. Since there is no load on the camshaft, the bearings are not normally replaced. However, if the bearings are scored or imbedded with dirt, if the camshaft itself is being replaced, or if the thrust shoulders of #3 bearing are worn (permitting excessive axial play), the bearings should be replaced.

In all cases, clean the bearing saddles and check the oil feed holes for cleanliness. Make sure that the oil holes for the bearing inserts align with those in the crankcase. Coat the bearing surfaces with prelube.

Check the Lifters

Remove all gum and varnish from the lifters using a tooth brush and carburetor cleaner. The cam following surface of the lifter is slightly convex when new. In service, this surface will wear flat which is OK to reinstall. However, if the cam following surface of the lifter is worn concave, the lifter should be replaced. To check this, place the cam following surface of one lifter against the side of another, using the one lifter as a straightedge. After checking, coat the lifters with oil to prevent rusting.

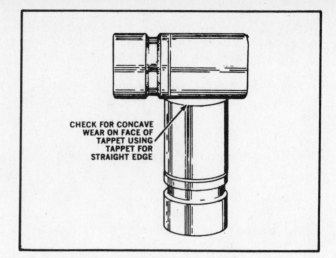

CHECK FOR CONCAVE WEAR ON FACE OF TAPPET USING TAPPET FOR STRAIGHT EDGE

Checking lifter face for wear

Assemble the Crankshaft

NOTE: *All dowel pin holes in the main bearings must locate to the flywheel end of the bearing saddles.*

Coat #3 main bearing journal with assembly lubricant. Slide the #3 bearing onto the pulley side of the crankshaft and install the large Woodruff key in its recess (the hole in the bearing should be nearest to the flywheel end of the crankshaft). In the meantime, heat both the crankshaft timing gear and distributor drive gears to 176°F in an oil bath. Press on the timing gear, taking care to keep the slot for the Woodruff key aligned, the timing marks facing away from the flywheel, and the chamber in the gear bore facing #3 main bearing journal. The Woodruff key must lie flat in its recess. Then, slide on the spacer ring and align it with the Woodruff key. On 1600 engines install the smaller Woodruff key. Now, press or drive on the distributor drive gear in the same manner as the crankshaft timing gear. Make sure it seats against the spacer ring. Install the snap-ring (circlip) using snap-ring pliers. Take care not to scratch #4 main bearing journal. Prelube main bearings #1 and #4 and slide them on the crankshaft. On 1600 engines, install the oil slinger, concave side out.

NOTE: *Make sure crankshaft timing gear and distributor drive gear fit snugly on the crankshaft once they return to room temperature.*

Install the bearing inserts for the connecting rods and rod caps by pressing in on bearing ends with both thumbs. Make sure the tangs fit in the notches. Don't press in the middle as the inserts may soil or crack. Prelube the connecting rod bearings and journals. Then, install the connecting rods on the crankshaft, making sure the forge marks are up (as they would be installed in the crankcase [3, 1, 4, 2 from flywheel end]), and the rod and bearing cap matchmarks align. Use new connecting rod nuts. After tightening the nuts, make sure that each rod swings freely 180° on the crankshaft by its own weight.

Checking camshaft run-out

Checking camshaft and timing gear axial play

Camshaft bearing inserts

NOTE: *A slight pretension (binding) of the rod on the crankshaft may be relieved by lightly rapping on the flat side of the big end of the rod with a hammer.*

If the connecting rod nuts are not of the self-locking type (very rare), peen the nuts into the slot on the rods to lock them in place and prevent the possibility of throwing a rod.

Install the Crankshaft and Camshaft

Pencil mark a line on the edge of each ring-type main bearing to indicate the location of the dowel pin hole. Install the lower half of #2 main bearing in the left side of the crankcase so that the shell fits securely over its dowel pin. Prelube the bearing surface.

Lift the crankshaft by two of the connecting rods and lower the assembly into the left crankcase half. Make sure the other connecting rods protrude through their corresponding cylinder openings. Then rotate each ring-type main bearing (#1, then #3, then #4) until the pencil marks made previously align with the center of the bearing bore. As each bearing is aligned with its dowel pin, a distinctive click should be heard and the crankshaft should be felt dropping into position. After each bearing is seated, you should not be able to rock any of the main bearing or the crankshaft in the case. Just to be sure, check the bearing installation by placing the other half of #2 main bearing over the top of its

crankshaft journal. If the upper half rocks, the bearing or bearings are not seated properly on their dowels. Then, install the other half of #2 main bearing in the right crankcase half. Prelube the bearing surface.

Rotate the crankshaft until the timing marks (twin punch marks on two adjacent teeth) on the timing gear point towards the camshaft side of the case. Lubricate and install the lifters. Coat the lifters for the right half of the case with grease to keep them from falling out during assembly. Coat the camshaft journals and bearing surfaces with assembly lubricant. Install the camshaft so that the single timing mark (0) on the camshaft timing gear aligns (lies between) with the two on the crankshaft timing gear. This is critical as it establishes valve timing.

Install the camshaft end plug using oil-resistant sealer. On cars with manual transmission, the hollow end of the plug faces in toward the engine. On cars equipped with automatic or automatic stick shift transmission, the hollow end faces out towards the front of the car to provide clearance for the torque converter drive plate retaining bolts.

The timing gear mesh is correct if the camshaft does not lift from its bearings when the crankshaft is rotated backwards (opposite normal direction of rotation).

Check Timing Gear Backlash

Mount a dial indicator to the crankcase with its stem

Aligning timing marks (arrow)

Camshaft and plug installation

Checking timing gear backlash

resting on a tooth of the camshaft gear. Rotate the gear until all slack is removed, and zero the indicator. Then, rotate the gear in the opposite direction until all slack is removed and record gear backlash. The reading should be between .000 and .002 in.

Assemble the Crankcase

1. Make sure all bearing surfaces are prelubed.
2. Always install new crankcase stud seals.
3. Apply only non-hardening oil resistant sealer to all crankcase mating surfaces.
4. Always use new case nuts. Self-sealing nuts must be installed with the red coated side down.
5. All small crankcase retaining nuts are first torqued to 10 ft-lbs, then 14 ft-lbs. All large crankcase retaining nuts are torqued to 20 ft-lbs, then 25 ft-lbs (except self-sealing large nuts red plastic insert, which are torqued to a single figure of 18 ft-lbs). Use a criss-cross torque sequence. On 1700, 1800 and 2000 engines, you will have to keep the long case bolt heads from turning.
6. While assembling the crankcase halves, always rotate the crankshaft periodically to check for binding. If any binding occurs, immediately disassemble and investigate the case. Usually, a main bearing has come off its dowel pin, or maybe a warped crankcase wasn't aligned bored.

Check Crankshaft End-play

After assembling the case, crankshaft end-play can be checked. End-play is controlled by the thickness of 3 shims located between the flywheel and #1 main bearing flange. End-play is checked with the flywheel installed as follows. Attach a dial indicator to the crankcase with the stem positioned on the face of the flywheel. Move the flywheel in and out and check the reading. End-play should be between .003–.005 in. The wear limit is .006 in.

To adjust end-play, remove the flywheel and reinstall, this time using only two shims. Remeasure the end-play. The difference between the second reading and the .003–.005 in. figure is the required thickness of the third shim. Shims come in the following sizes:

0.24 mm—.0095 in.
0.30 mm—.0118 in.
0.32 mm—.0126 in.
0.34 mm—.0134 in.
0.36 mm—.0142 in.
0.38 mm—.0150 in. (1700, 1800 and 2000 only.)

Checking crankshaft end-play

11

REBUILDING DIESEL ENGINES

DIESEL ENGINES—GENERAL INFORMATION

The diesel engines have basically the same internal components as do the gasoline powered engines. The major differences are the type of fuel used and the manner in which the fuel is directed to the combustion chamber. The diesel engine also lacks the conventional spark type ignition, but depends upon the increase of temperature of the air in the cylinder as it is compressed by the upward piston movement within the cylinder. As the piston nears its top dead center (TDC) position, the fuel is injected into the cylinder in a spray or atomized state and, due to the high temperature of the compressed air, the mixture of fuel and air ignites, forcing the piston downward in a power developing stroke due to the expanding gases.

The diesel is normally a four cycle engine, with 4, 5, 6 or 8 cylinders used to develop the necessary power. Two cycle diesel engines are manufactured, but have a different application in the transportation field.

It is easier to understand the function of the diesel engine parts when a general understanding of what happens in the combustion chamber during each of the four piston strokes, comprising the four cycles, is explained.

In order for the diesel engine to function properly, valves and injectors must act in direct relation to each other and to the four strokes of the engine. The intake and exhaust valves are camshaft operated, linked by tappets or cam followers, pushrods and rocker arms. The injectors are operated by a pump, timed to the crankshaft and/or camshaft rotation to provide a spray of fuel into the combustion chamber at the precise moment for efficient combustion.

STROKES OF THE FOUR CYCLE DIESEL ENGINE

Intake Stroke

During the intake stroke, the piston travels downward with the intake valve open and the exhaust valve closed. The downward travel of the piston allows and draws atmospheric air into the cylinder from the induction system. On turbocharged engines, the induction system is pressurized as the turbocharger forces more air into the cylinder. The intake charge consists of air only and contains no fuel mixture.

FUEL FEED OPERATING PRINCIPLE COMPARISON CHART

Stroke	Diesel	Fuel Injection	Carburetor
INDUCTION OR INTAKE	Intake of air only	Intake of air only. Injection of fuel during induction	Intake of an air-fuel mixture, measured by the carburetor
COMPRESSION	High compression of the air: Example—Ratio of 22.2/1. Temperature 600°C.	Compression of the mixture Example—Ratio of 8.8/1. Temperature 380°C.	
End of stroke	Injection of fuel which ignites spontaneously	Ignition of the mixture by the spark plug.	
IGNITION OR POWER	Combustion and expansion	Combustion and expansion	
EXHAUST	Discharge of the burnt gasses		

Compression Stroke

At the end of the intake stroke with the piston at bottom dead center (BDC), the intake valve closes and the piston starts upward on its compression stroke. The exhaust valve remains closed. At the end of the compression stroke, air in the combustion chamber has been forced by the piston to occupy a smaller space than it occupied at the beginning of the stroke. Thus, compression ratio is the direct proportion of the amount of space the air occupied in the combustion chamber before and after being compressed. Diesel engine compression ratios range from approximately 14:1 to 22:1 in comparison to the gasoline engine compression of from 7.5:1 to 9.5:1. Compressing the air into a small space causes the temperature of the air to rise to a point high enough to ignite the fuel, which has a flash point under the temperature level. During the last part of the compression stroke and the early part of the power stroke, a small metered charge of fuel is injected into the combustion chamber and ignited by the existing hot compressed air.

Power Stroke

During the beginning of the power stroke, the piston is pushed downward by the burning and expanding gases. Both the intake and exhaust valves remain closed. As more fuel is added to the cylinder and burns, the gases become hotter and expand more to force the piston downward and thus add driving force to the crankshaft rotation.

Exhaust Stroke

As the piston reaches its bottom dead center (BDC), the exhaust valve opens and the piston moves upward. The intake valve remains closed. The upward travel of the piston forces the burned gases from the combustion

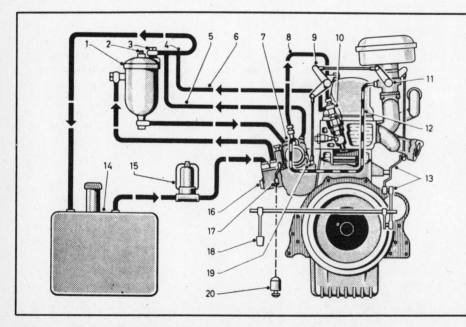

1. Main fuel filter
2. Vent screw
3. Hollow screw with throttle screw
4. Fuel return line
5. Overflow line
6. Injection nozzle leakage line
7. Injection pump
8. Pressure line from injection pump to injection nozzle
9. Angular lever for auxiliary mechanical control
10. Injection nozzle
11. Venturi control unit
12. Vacuum line with throttle screw
13. Linkage and lever for accelerator pedal control
14. Fuel tank
15. Fuel prefilter
16. Fuel feed pump with hand pump
17. Adjusting lever
18. Accelerator pedal
19. Lever for auxiliary mechanical control
20. Heater plug starting switch with starting and stopping cable

Diesel engine fuel supply system—typical

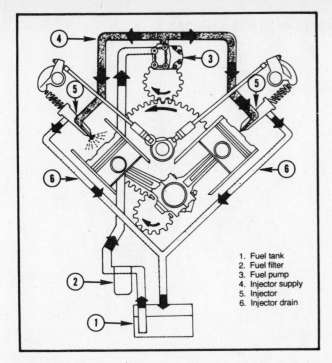

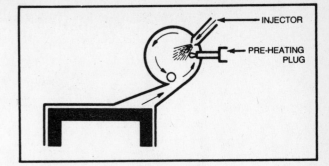

Direction of air flow in the swirl chamber

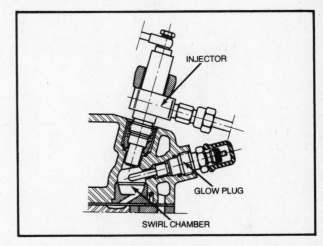

Location of injector and glow plug in the swirl chamber

Cross section of a cam operated injection nozzle and fuel supply

1. Fuel tank
2. Fuel filter
3. Fuel pump
4. Injector supply
5. Injector
6. Injector drain

chamber through the open exhaust valve port and into the exhaust manifold. As the piston reaches the top dead center (TDC) and starts its downward movement, the intake stroke is repeated and the cycling strokes continue.

It must be remembered that proper engine operation depends on two things. There must be compression for ignition and fuel must be metered and injected at the proper time.

SWIRL CHAMBER

Many diesel engines are equipped with a removable swirl chamber, located in the cylinder head. The fuel injector and the glow plug assemblies are normally installed so that their operating ends are exposed in the chamber. The chamber capacity is normally equal to ¾

of the total volume of the air at the end of the compression stroke.

The purpose of the swirl chamber is to produce a strong turbulence of air, which progressively increases as the piston approaches top dead center (TDC) on the compression stroke. The fuel is injected and swirled by the air and, as soon as ignition begins, the pressure in the chamber increases, forcing the air, the burned gases and the unburned fuel towards the cylinder. This causes the piston to descend and reverse the direction of the swirl, causing a more intense turbulence and a better combustion of the fuel. This aids in obtaining a low fuel consumption rate.

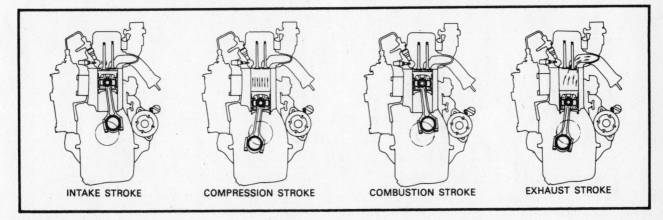

| INTAKE STROKE | COMPRESSION STROKE | COMBUSTION STROKE | EXHAUST STROKE |

Diesel engine stroke cycles

DIESEL ENGINE TROUBLESHOOTING CHART

Engine Won't Start

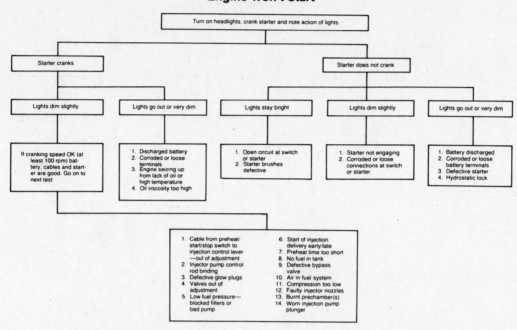

Turn on headlights: crank starter and note action of lights

Starter cranks | **Starter does not crank**

Lights dim slightly
If cranking speed OK (at least 100 rpm) battery, cables and starter are good. Go on to next test

Lights go out or very dim
1. Discharged battery
2. Corroded or loose terminals
3. Engine seizing up from lack of oil or high temperature
4. Oil viscosity too high

Lights stay bright
1. Open circuit at switch or starter
2. Starter brushes defective

Lights dim slightly
1. Starter not engaging
2. Corroded or loose connections at switch or starter

Lights go out or very dim
1. Battery discharged
2. Corroded or loose battery terminals
3. Defective starter
4. Hydrostatic lock

1. Cable from preheat/start/stop switch to injection control lever—out of adjustment
2. Injector pump control rod binding
3. Defective glow plugs
4. Valves out of adjustment
5. Low fuel pressure—blocked filters or bad pump
6. Start of injection delivery early/late
7. Preheat time too short
8. No fuel in tank
9. Defective bypass valve
10. Air in fuel system
11. Compression too low
12. Faulty injector nozzles
13. Burnt prechamber(s)
14. Worn injection pump plunger

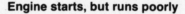

Engine starts, but runs poorly

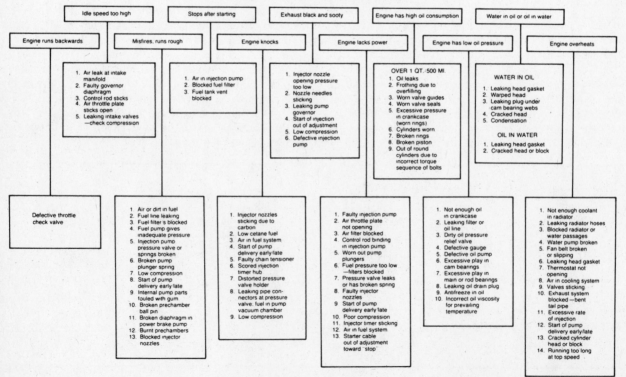

Idle speed too high | **Stops after starting** | **Exhaust black and sooty** | **Engine has high oil consumption** | **Water in oil or oil in water**

Engine runs backwards | **Misfires, runs rough** | **Engine knocks** | **Engine lacks power** | **Engine has low oil pressure** | **Engine overheats**

Misfires, runs rough
1. Air leak at intake manifold
2. Faulty governor diaphragm
3. Control rod sticks
4. Air throttle plate sticks open
5. Leaking intake valves—check compression

Stops after starting
1. Air in injection pump
2. Blocked fuel filter
3. Fuel tank vent blocked

Engine knocks
1. Injector nozzle opening pressure too low
2. Nozzle needles sticking
3. Leaking pump governor
4. Start of injection out of adjustment
5. Low compression
6. Defective injection pump

OVER 1 QT./500 MI.
1. Oil leaks
2. Frothing due to overfilling
3. Worn valve guides
4. Worn valve seals
5. Excessive pressure in crankcase (worn rings)
6. Cylinders worn
7. Broken rings
8. Broken piston
9. Out of round cylinders due to incorrect torque sequence of bolts

WATER IN OIL
1. Leaking head gasket
2. Warped head
3. Leaking plug under cam bearing webs
4. Cracked head
5. Condensation

OIL IN WATER
1. Leaking head gasket
2. Cracked head or block

Defective throttle check valve

1. Air or dirt in fuel
2. Fuel line leaking
3. Fuel filter's blocked
4. Fuel pump gives inadequate pressure
5. Injection pump pressure valve or springs broken
6. Broken pump plunger spring
7. Low compression
8. Start of pump delivery early/late
9. Internal pump parts fouled with gum
10. Broken prechamber ball pin
11. Broken diaphragm in power brake pump
12. Burnt prechambers
13. Blocked injector nozzles

1. Injector nozzles sticking due to carbon
2. Low cetane fuel
3. Air in fuel system
4. Start of pump delivery early/late
5. Faulty chain tensioner
6. Scored injection timer hub
7. Distorted pressure valve holder
8. Leaking pipe connectors at pressure valve; fuel in pump vacuum chamber
9. Low compression

1. Faulty injection pump
2. Air throttle plate not opening
3. Air filter blocked
4. Control rod binding in injection pump
5. Worn out pump plungers
6. Fuel pressure too low—filters blocked
7. Pressure valve leaks or has broken spring
8. Faulty injector nozzles
9. Start of pump delivery early/late
10. Poor compression
11. Injector timer sticking
12. Air in fuel system
13. Starter cable out of adjustment toward "stop"

1. Not enough oil in crankcase
2. Leaking filter or oil line
3. Dirty oil pressure relief valve
4. Defective gauge
5. Defective oil pump
6. Excessive play in cam bearings
7. Excessive play in main or rod bearings
8. Leaking oil drain plug
9. Antifreeze in oil
10. Incorrect oil viscosity for prevailing temperature

1. Not enough coolant in radiator
2. Leaking radiator hoses
3. Blocked radiator or water passages
4. Water pump broken
5. Fan belt broken or slipping
6. Leaking head gasket
7. Thermostat not opening
8. Air in cooling system
9. Valves sticking
10. Exhaust system blocked—bent tail pipe
11. Excessive rate of injection
12. Start of pump delivery early/late
13. Cracked cylinder head or block
14. Running too long at top speed

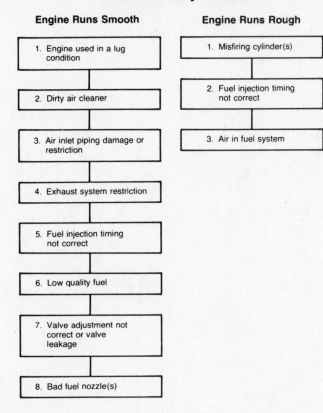

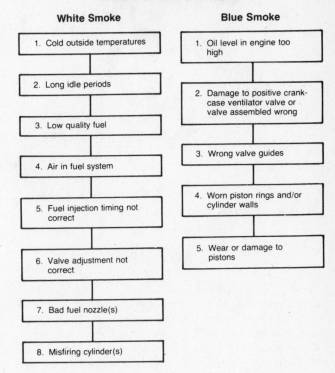

GLOW PLUGS

Electrically operated glow plugs are used to heat the combustion chambers prior to cold weather and initial engine starts. The glow plugs resemble the spark plugs of the conventional gasoline powered engine. A relay controls the length of time the glow plugs are in use. During cold weather, the relay may have to be reactivated through a second glow plug cycle in order to start the engine.

TURBOCHARGER—GENERAL INFORMATION

In a normal breathing or naturally aspirated engine, the air enters the induction system at atmospheric pressure, mixes with a predetermined amount of fuel and is burned in the combustion chamber, producing a certain amount of power. By testing, a determination was made that if more air were forced through the induction system and into the combustion chambers, more fuel could be burned and greater power could be developed from the same sized engine.

The development of the turbocharger system is the direct result of the tests. Therefore, the purpose of the turbocharger on an engine is to increase engine power by supplying compressed air into the combustion chamber, permitting greater fuel addition to increase the engine power at an efficient air/fuel ratio.

DESCRIPTION

The turbocharger is basically an exhaust driven blower. The assembly consists of the turbine wheel and shaft assembly, turbine wheel housing, compressor wheel and housing, and the center housing. The turbine wheel housing, bolted to the center housing, receives the exhaust gases from the engine. The exhaust gases can spin the turbine wheel and shaft in excess of 75,000 r.p.m. This speed is transferred to the compressor wheel, secured to the other end of the shaft. The outside air is piped to the compressor housing where it is compressed by the rotating compressor impeller and directed to the induction system (intake manifold).

The center housing supports the shaft on two bearings which float on a film of oil and touch neither the housing or shaft. The oil to lubricate and cool the bearings is supplied under pressure from the engine. A sealing ring or carbon face seal is used at each end of the shaft, preventing oil from leaking into the turbine or compressor wheel housings and exhaust gases and compressed air from leaking into the center housing. Thrust collars or thrust washers control axial shaft movement.

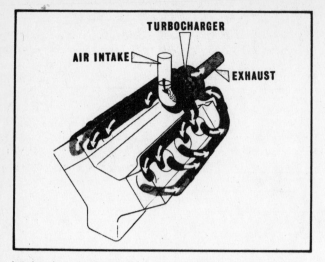

Intake air and exhaust flow through a typical turbocharger

OPERATION OF THE TURBOCHARGER

The engine exhaust is directed into the turbine housing of the turbocharger. As the exhaust gases pass through the nozzle ring vanes, it gains velocity and strikes the turbine wheel vanes. This in turn causes the compressor wheel to turn, which is attached to a common shaft. As the compressor wheel turns, it draws air from the air cleaner into the compressor housing, compresses it and forces it into the combustion chamber. Because a greater volume of air is forced into the combustion chamber, a greater amount of fuel is needed to obtain a correct air/fuel mixture. This increase of air and fuel results in the increased power output.

Since the turbine speed is governed by the exhaust energy of the engine at any speed, the turbocharger delivers the correct volume of air at any throttle position. In addition to the exhaust volume and velocity, the turbocharger depends upon exhaust heat to be efficient and supply the increased air volume needed to support proper combustion.

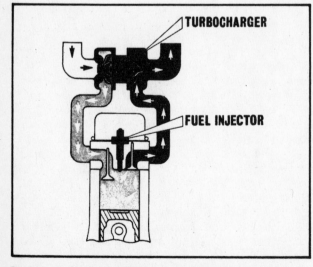

Basic operation of a typical turbocharger

It should be noted that the increased fuel usage requires greater air intake and that the exhaust temperatures increase with greater fuel usage. This increased exhaust temperature results in greater expansion of the exhaust gases within the turbine housing. This causes the compressor wheel to increase in speed, therefore having what is known as a turbocharger operating cycle.

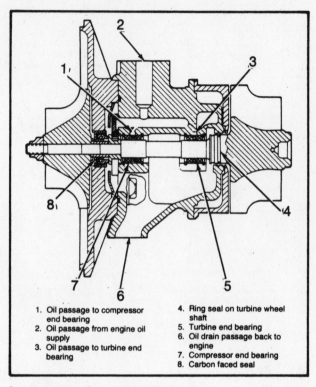

1. Oil passage to compressor end bearing
2. Oil passage from engine oil supply
3. Oil passage to turbine end bearing
4. Ring seal on turbine wheel shaft
5. Turbine end bearing
6. Oil drain passage back to engine
7. Compressor end bearing
8. Carbon faced seal

Cross section of a typical turbocharger

SERVICE PRECAUTIONS

The internal parts of a turbocharger must be handled with extreme care. The turbine wheel, compressor wheel (impeller), shaft and related parts form a balanced assembly which rotates at an extremely high r.p.m. Care must be exercised to prevent damage to the components which could result in a serious out-of-balance condition which could quickly destroy the turbocharger. Because of the close tolerances, the internal parts are very sensitive to the accumulation of dirt which can cause nicks and scratches on the operating surfaces. Because of this, the air intake system must be kept clean by replacement of the air filter at recommended or regular intervals.

TURBOCHARGER INSTALLATIONS

Turbocharging an engine is more than merely bolting a turbocharger to the induction system, connecting the exhaust to it and driving away. The installation of the turbocharger must be carefully engineered to provide the best performance and to avoid overcharging of the engine which could be destructive. In addition, the engine must be designed to handle the increase in air and fuel, higher pressures and temperatures, and the increase in the torque and power output.

The Audi diesel engine is a 5 cylinder, overhead cam, in-line engine. It has a displacement of 1986 cc and is capable of developing 67 horsepower at 4800 r.p.m. The engine is water-cooled and is equipped with a thermo-statically controlled electric fan. The engine is equipped with a gear-type oil pump and a full flow oil filter system. The crankshaft is supported by six main bearings. No. 2 diesel fuel is supplied to the injectors from an injection pump, belt driven from the engine camshaft.

The ignition switch has three positions, an off and lock position, a pre-glow position and the start position. When starting the engine, the key switch must be turned to the pre-glow position until the indicator light on the dash goes out, indicating the glow plugs have warmed the combustion area sufficiently. The key is then turned to the start position and the engine started.

TURBOCHARGER TROUBLESHOOTING CHART

Condition	Possible Cause	Correction
Shaft And Turbine Wheel		
a) Bearing surfaces scratched and worn	a) Dirty or insufficient oil Wheel overspeeding	a) Replace
b) Discoloration	b) Overheating or insufficient oil	b) Reuse if slightly discolored and not deeply scratched
c) Worn on one side only	c) Operating with unbalanced wheel	c) Replace
d) Cracked, bent or damaged blades	d) Foreign objects, heat or fatigue	d) Replace
Bearings		
a) Both ID and OD scratched and worn	a) Dirty or insufficient oil Wheel overspeeding	a) Replace
b) Seized on shaft or excessive OD wear	b) Overheating or lubrication failure	b) Replace
c) Worn on one side only	c) Operating with unbalanced wheel	c) Replace
Bearing Housing		
a) Bore scratched or worn	a) Dirty or insufficient oil	a) Replace
b) Carbon deposits	b) Oil leaking. Overfueling	b) Clean housing. Remove any restriction from air intake system or oil drain
Compressor End Dirty	a) Excessive intake restriction or a restricted oil drain line	a) Check for clogged air cleaner element, collapsed hose or leaks in air inlet pipe. Clean compressor end and oil drain line
	b) Insufficient air filtration	b) Secure the connections between the air cleaner and turbocharger
	c) Long period of operation without cleaning	c) Disassemble and clean the unit
Compressor Wheel		
a) Rubbing on OD of blades	a) Worn bearing or unbalanced turbine wheel	a) Replace parts as necessary
b) Rubbing on cover or back face	b) Insufficient clearance, cover damaged or thrust washer worn	b) Improper end-play. Replace damaged or worn parts
c) Inlet leading edge of blades either worn or pieces broken off	c) Loose pieces in air intake system	c) Check air intake system for loose nuts, bolts or other foreign material. Replace wheel assembly

TURBOCHARGER TROUBLESHOOTING CHART

Condition	Possible Cause	Correction
Shaft Rotation Wheel drags	a) Carbon buildup behind turbine wheel or dirt accumulation behind compressor wheel b) Bearing worn excessively or seized to shaft due to dirty oil or low oil pressure	a) Disassemble and clean the unit b) Replace bearing and change oil
Shaft End-Play a) End-play exceeds specifications b) End-play less than specifications	a) Thrust bearing or thrust rings worn or distorted b) Carbon buildup behind turbine wheel or dirt buildup behind compressor wheel	a) Replace parts as necessary b) Disassemble and clean the unit
Turbine Wheel Radial Movement a) Radial movement exceeds specifications	a) Worn bearings or shaft, or bore in bearing housing worn	a) Replace worn parts

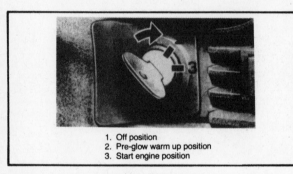

1. Off position
2. Pre-glow warm up position
3. Start engine position

Ignition switch positions

AUDI 4000/5000 DIESEL ENGINE

ENGINE TUNE-UP

The Audi diesel engine tune-up should include the following inspections and/or repairs.

1. Compression test
2. Valve adjustment
3. Injector pressure test and inspection
4. Injector timing
5. Valve timing
6. Idle speed adjustment
7. Glow plug operation

Compression Test

1. Start the engine and bring it to normal operating temperature.
2. Stop the engine and remove the fuel line from the injectors. Allow the fuel to drain into a clean container.

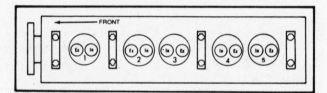

Valve arrangement—Audi 5000 diesel engine

3. Remove the injectors from the cylinder head.
4. Remove the fuel cut-off valve fuse from the fuse holder to prevent the pumping of fuel.
5. Install the compression gauge into the injector port and crank the engine over approximately 5–6 times. Record the pressure indicated on the gauge.
6. Continue the compression test on the remaining cylinders and record the results. Compare the results with the specifications of 398 to 483 psi. A maximum pressure variation of 71 psi between cylinder compression is allowable.

Valve Adjustment

The valve clearances should be adjusted in firing order with the cylinder head moderately warm (coolant temperature about 95°F.). Firing order is 1–2–4–5–3. Clearance adjustment is made by replacing shims in the tappets. Special tools are available to make this job easier. Replacement shims must be purchased in groups of varying sizes, since the size and number of shims needed won't be known until the clearance is checked and the size of the existing shims is determined. The thickness of the shim is etched on its underside.

TO CHECK THE CLEARANCES
1. Remove the camshaft cover.
2. Using a wrench on the crankshaft pulley, turn the

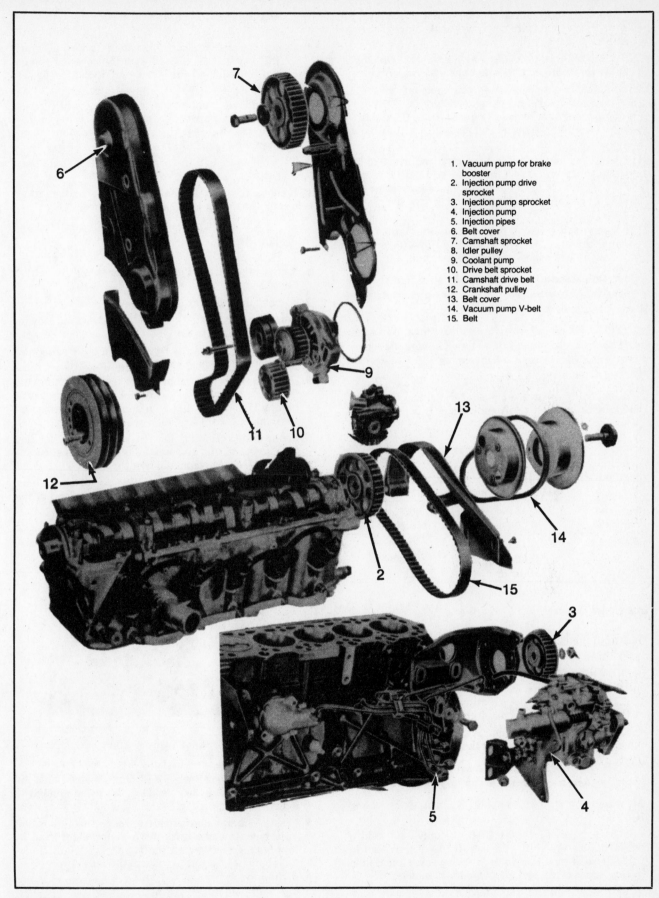

1. Vacuum pump for brake booster
2. Injection pump drive sprocket
3. Injection pump sprocket
4. Injection pump
5. Injection pipes
6. Belt cover
7. Camshaft sprocket
8. Idler pulley
9. Coolant pump
10. Drive belt sprocket
11. Camshaft drive belt
12. Crankshaft pulley
13. Belt cover
14. Vacuum pump V-belt
15. Belt

Injection pump and components

engine in the normal rotation direction until the camshaft lobes of the cylinder to be checked are pointing upward.

CAUTION: *Do not turn the engine by the camshaft sprocket retaining bolt. Belt damage may result.*

3. Slip a feeler gauge between the camshaft lobe and the tappet. Intake clearance should be .008–.012 inch; exhaust clearance should be .016–.020 inch. A slight drag should be felt when inserting the feeler gauge.

4. If the clearance is larger than required, remove the existing shim and insert the required thicker shim. If the clearance is less than required, remove the existing shim and insert a thinner shim to give the proper clearance.

5. To replace the shim, press down the tappet and remove the shim. Audi tools 2078 and 10–208, or their equivalent, are necessary for this procedure.

NOTE: *When installing a shim make sure that the size etching faces downward. Shims can be reused if not damaged or excessively worn.*

CAUTION: *When adjusting the valves, turn the crankshaft about ¼ turn past TDC to avoid having the valves contact the piston tops when the cam followers are pressed down.*

6. The following is an example for the use of the selective shims during the valve adjustment operation.

	Intake	Exhaust
Specified clearance	0.20–0.30 mm (0.008–0.012 in.)	0.40–0.50 mm (0.016–0.020 in.)
Measured clearance	0.15 mm (0.006 in.)	0.55 mm (0.022 in.)
Insert disc	0.10 mm (0.004 in.) thicker	0.10 mm (0.004 in.) thinner

Injection Timing

1. Rotate the crankshaft to TDC with the Number one cylinder at its firing stroke.

2. Align the mark on the flywheel with the mark on the clutch housing.

3. Align the mark on the injection pump sprocket with the mark on the pump mounting bracket.

4. Loosen the cold start control cable by loosening the screw on the clamp nearest the rubber cable boot.

CAUTION: *Do not loosen the screw on the cable clamp that is furthest away from the rubber boot.*

5. Loosen the cold start cable by turning the clamp 90°.

6. Install the tool adapter 2066 or equivalent, and a dial indicator with a 2.5 mm (0.100 in.) preload in the bore of the timing plug, after removal, located in the center of the fuel injection line cluster.

7. Turn the crankshaft counterclockwise, slowly, until the indicator needle stops moving.

8. Adjust the dial indicator to a 1 mm (0.040 in.) preload.

9. Rotate the crankcase clockwise until the TDC mark on the flywheel is aligned with the reference mark on the clutch housing. The dial indicator should show a lift of 0.85 mm (0.034 in.).

10. If the indicator shows more or less of a lift, loosen the injector pump bolts and adjust the lift to 0.85 mm (0.034 in.) by turning the injection pump. Tighten the pump bolts.

11. Turn the clamp on the cold start control cable back 90° and tighten the locking screw.

12. Remove the dial indicator assembly and adaptor. Install the timing plug back into its bore.

Valve Timing

1. Remove the covers for both the front and rear drive belts.

2. Remove the cylinder head top cover.

3. Rotate the crankshaft to TDC with Number 1 cylinder on its firing stroke.

4. Align the marks on the flywheel/clutch housing and the injection pump sprocket/mounting plate.

5. Lock the injection pump sprocket with a pin tool 2064 or its equivalent, and lock the vacuum pump belt pulley and the injection pump drive sprocket on the camshaft with tool 3063 or its equivalent.

6. Remove the retaining bolt from the camshaft pulley and sprocket, and remove the pulley, drive sprocket and belt from the camshaft end.

7. Install a special tool 2065 setting bar or equivalent, in the camshaft slot on the injector pump end of the camshaft.

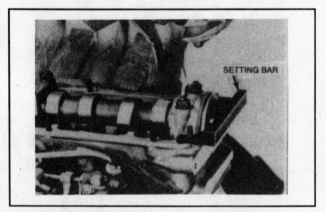

Installation of setting bar tool in camshaft slot

8. If the setting bar does not fit into the slots, turn the crankshaft until the camshaft is turned enough to accept the setting bar.

9. Loosen the camshaft drive sprocket retaining bolt approximately one turn and loosen the sprocket by tapping it from the camshaft taper with a drift and light hammer, through a hole in the rear cover.

10. Realign the TDC mark on the flywheel/clutch housing and retighten the camshaft drive sprocket retaining bolt to 45 Nm (33 ft-lbs).

11. Remove the setting bar tool and install the injection pump drive sprocket with the drive belt. Install and tighten the drive sprocket retaining bolt until it is just possible to turn the sprocket by hand.

12. Check the drive belt tension with special tool VW 210 or equivalent to a scale of 12 to 13, as marked on the tool. If no tool is available, adjust the drive belt tension by loosening the injection pump mounting bolts and moving the assembly to provide a slight deflection in the belt surface between the drive pulley and the injector pulley.

13. Recheck the crankshaft timing marks and correct if necessary. Hold the injector pump drive pulley stationary and tighten the retaining bolt to 100 Nm (72 ft-lbs).

14. Remove the setting pin tool from the injection pump pulley.

15. Check the injection pump timing and adjust as required, as previously outlined.

16. Install the belt covers and cylinder head top cover.

Checking the Injector Opening Pressure

1. Remove the injector from the engine and install in the injector test stand.

2. Pump the tester pump several times to remove any air from the injector and line.

3. Press the tester pump lever down slowly and note the injector opening spray pressure.

4. The opening pressure should be 120 to 130 BAR (1706 to 1849 psi).

5. If the opening pressure is not to specifications, the injector can be adjusted by the changing of selective shims, located within the injector. Refer to the Fuel Injector Diagnosis chapter for procedures.

6. Install either a repaired or new injector into the engine. Connect the fuel line.

Idle Speed Adjustment

The idle speed of the engine can be adjusted by turning a control knob, located on the dash, either right or left. Turning the knob to the right increases the engine speed, while turning the knob to the left, decreases the engine speed.

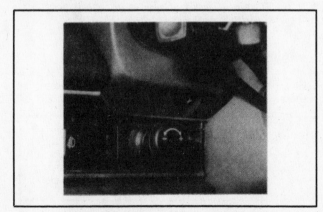

Idle control knob on dash

INITIAL IDLE AND NO-LOAD SPEED ADJUSTMENT

1. Install a meter on the engine to register the r.p.m.

2. Start the engine and bring to normal operating temperature. Turn the control knob to the left until it touches the stop.

3. Using the adjuster screw on the injector pump, adjust the idle speed to 720 to 880 r.p.m. Use a locking substance or a dab of paint to lock the idle adjuster screw into place on the pump.

CAUTION: *Use extreme care when adjusting the maximum/no-load engine speed. Over-revving the engine could result in engine damage and personal injury.*

4. Increase the engine speed to 5350 to 5450 r.p.m. and set with the maximum speed adjuster screw, located on the injector pump. Lock the screw with a locking substance or a dab of paint.

5. By using the control knob, the engine idle can be controlled by the operator.

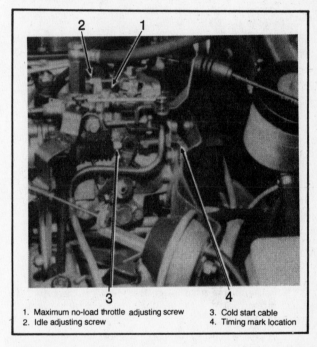

| 1. Maximum no-load throttle adjusting screw | 3. Cold start cable |
| 2. Idle adjusting screw | 4. Timing mark location |

Injection pump adjustment points and timing mark location

Glow Plug System

When the diesel engine starts hard, the problem may be in the glow plug system. Before the diesel engine can be started, the glow plug preheat period and delay glow period are necessary. A warning light on the dash goes out when the preheat period is ended. At the end of the preheat period, the glow plug continues to receive voltage (delay glow period) for 10 to 25 seconds. Test for this voltage without engaging the starter. If no voltage is present for this 10 to 25 seconds, then replace the glow plug relay.

When the starter is engaged, there should be current at the glow plugs. If there is no current during starter engagement, repair the connection from terminal 50 of the relay to the relay board. If the connection is okay at terminal 50, replace the relay.

NOTE: *The test lamp procedures are done with the ignition key on to the glow plug position.*

1. Check for current at all 5 glow plugs.
   a. Test lamp on at all 5 glow plugs.
   b. Connect test lamp between each glow plug and the positive battery terminal.
   c. Test lamp on—glow plugs are OK.
   d. Test lamp off—replace glow plug.
   e. Test lamp off at all glow plugs.
   f. Check 80 amp fuse located in the instrument panel to the left of the steering column.
   g. Fuse okay—go to next test.
   h. Fuse not okay—replace.
2. Check for current at terminal 30 of relay.
   a. Test lamp lights at terminal 30.
   b. Check terminal 86 of relay.
   c. Test lamplights at terminal 86.
   d. Repair terminal from 85 on the relay to ground—if connector okay, replace relay.
   e. Test lamp off at terminal 86.
   f. Repair the connection from terminal 86 on the relay to the relay board—if connection okay, replace the relay board.
   g. Test lamp off at terminal 30.
   h. Check connection between relay board, terminal 30 and relay terminal 30—if connection is okay, replace the relay board.

DIESEL INJECTOR PUMP

Removal and Installation

1. Remove the vacuum pump V-belt and pulley.
2. Take off the injection pump drive belt cover.
3. Set the crankshaft to TDC on the number 1 cylinder and align the marks on the flywheel with the clutch housing mark. Also, align the mark on the injection pump sprocket with the mark on the sprocket mounting plate.
4. Secure the injection pump sprocket with special pin tool 2064 or equivalent.
5. Secure the vacuum pump belt pulley and the injection pump drive sprocket with tool 3036 or equivalent.
6. Loosen and remove retaining bolt and detach drive sprocket together with drive belt.
7. Loosen the injection pump sprocket retaining nut about one turn and remove setting pin.
8. Tighten injection pump sprocket with puller.
9. Loosen injection pump sprocket by tapping lightly on the puller spindle.
10. Remove retaining nut and detach injection pump sprocket.
11. Disconnect the injector pipes, fuel supply and return pipes, wire for shutoff solenoid on injector pump and detach accelerator cable.
12. Remove bolts from injection pump mounting plate and support and remove pump.

13. Install the injection pump in reverse order of removal. Torque pump retaining nut to 45 Nm (33 ft-lbs).
14. Set drive belt tension with special tool VW210 or equivalent, to a scale value of 12–13.
15. Torque drive sprocket retaining bolt to 100 Nm (72 ft-lbs).
16. Check and set the injection timing.

Overhaul

The injector pump should be replaced with either a new or factory rebuilt unit. The average repair shops do not have the required rebuilding and testing equipment needed to properly service the injector pump.

DIESEL FUEL INJECTORS

Diagnosis

The first sign of an injector problem may appear as any one of the following.

1. Knocking in one or more cylinders
2. Engine overheating
3. Loss of power
4. Smoky black exhaust
5. Increased fuel consumption

A faulty injector may be located by loosening the pipe union at each injector in turn, with the engine at fast idle. If the engine speed does not drop when the pipe union is loosened, then the injector at that union is faulty.

CAUTION: *Always keep injection parts clean when working on them.*

Removal

1. Clean all pipe fittings and remove the injector pipes.
2. Disconnect the fuel return hoses.
3. Remove the injectors using Audi tool US 2775 or equivalent.
4. Take off the old heat shields and install new heat shields before installation.

Cleaning

1. Clamp upper part of the injector in vise and loosen the lower part.

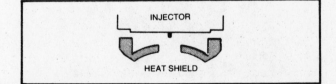

Injector heat shield

2. Turn the injector over and clamp it lightly in a vise for disassembly.

3. Clean the parts of the injector in diesel fuel. If carbon deposits won't clean, gasoline may be used, but all parts must immediately be rinsed in diesel fuel.

4. Check all injector parts for wear or damage.

5. Reassemble the injector and tighten halves to 70 Nm (51 ft-lbs).

Testing

SPRAY TEST

1. Using Audi test stand US 1111 or equivalent, fill the container with clean fuel and attach the injector to the tester.

2. Pump the tester with rapid short strokes, 4 to 6 times per second.

3. The spray should be even, well atomized and stop cleanly. The injector must not drip after it stops spraying.

OPENING PRESSURE TEST

1. Turn the valve on the tester so the pressure gauge is on.

2. Press the pump lever down slowly and note the opening spray pressure. The opening pressure should be 120–130 bar (1706–1849 psi).

3. If the opening pressure is not within specifications, remove the injector and disassemble it.

4. Remove and measure the injector shim.

5. Select a shim of the proper thickness to correct the pressure.

6. A thicker shim will increase the pressure.

7. A change of 0.05 mm (0.0019 in.) will change the pressure approximately 5 bar (71 psi).

8. Shims are available from 1 to 1.95 mm (0.039–0.076 in.) in steps of 0.05 mm (0.0019 in.).

9. Reassemble the injector and retest until the proper pressure is reached.

LEAKAGE TEST

1. Leave the pressure gauge on and press the pump lever down slowly.

2. Hold the pressure at approximately 110 bar (1564 psi) for 10 seconds.

3. The fuel should not drip from the injector. If needed replace the injector.

Installation

1. Make sure the injectors have new heat shields.

2. Install the injectors in the head and torque them to 70 Nm (51 ft-lbs).

3. Install and torque the injector pipes to 25 Nm (18 ft-lbs).

4. Reconnect the fuel return hoses.

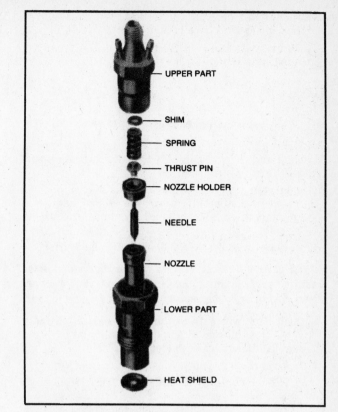

Exploded view of injector components

5. Start the engine and accelerate a few times to clear the air bubbles.

6. Check for fuel leaks.

CYLINDER HEAD

Removal

CAUTION: *No dirt must be allowed to contaminate the injectors or lines.*

1. Disconnect the battery ground strap.

2. Remove the coolant hoses and drain the coolant.

3. Disconnect the glow plug wires, injector lines and all sensor or sending unit wires.

4. Remove the vacuum pump pulley and belt at the rear of the engine.

5. Remove the injection pump drive belt cover.

6. Secure the vacuum pump belt pulley and the injection pump drive sprocket with tool 3036 or equivalent.

7. Loosen and remove the retaining bolt and detach the injection pump drive sprocket together with the drive belt.

8. Disconnect the injector fuel supply and return pipes.

9. Take off two intake to exhaust manifold supports.

10. Remove the exhaust and intake manifolds.

11. Take off the camshaft drive belt cover and remove the camshaft drive belt (timing belt).

12. Loosen and remove the head bolts in reverse order of the installation sequence.

Overhaul

NOTE: *Diesel cylinder heads should not be machined.*

1. Remove the marked camshaft bearing caps from the head and lift the camshaft from the bearing seats. Mark each bearing cap.

2. Remove the cam followers. Mark each cam follower for identification, if to be reused, so each can be placed in their original location, during the assembly.

3. Remove the valve stem keepers and valve springs.

NOTE: *It may be necessary to tap on the valve spring remover tool spindle to loosen the valve stem keepers from the upper spring seats.*

4. Push each valve from the head and discard the valve stem oil seal. Mark the valves to match their seat locations in the cylinder head.

5. Remove the valve spring lower seats from the valve spring bores in the cylinder head with the use of an expanding tool.

6. Remove the glow plugs from the cylinder head. Place a drift through the glow plug hole and tap the combustion chamber inserts from the combustion chamber.

7. Examine the cylinder head for damage or cracks.

8. If the cylinder head is usable, clean the carbon deposits from the valve guides and insert a new intake or exhaust valve into the respective guide until the end of the valve stem is flush with the end of the guide.

9. Install a dial indicator and measure the side movement of the valve stem in the guide.

10. The maximum side clearance is 1.3 mm (0.051 in.)

11. If the valve guides are worn beyond the specifications, new guides can be replaced.

12. Using a special guide remover tool or its equivalent, press the valve guide from the head by exerting pressure from the combustion chamber side.

13. Remove all valve guides and again inspect the cylinder head for cracks or for valve seats that cannot be refaced. Replace the cylinder head if required.

14. Considering the cylinder head to be usable, coat the new valve guides with oil and press into the cylinder head while cold, from the camshaft side.

CAUTION: *Once the guide shoulder is seated, do not use more than one ton of pressure or the guide shoulder may be broken.*

15. Ream the valve guides using proper cutting lubricant. Do not ream the valve guides oversize. Mate each valve stem to the proper sized guide. Mark the valves as required.

16. Reface the valve seats to obtain a seat surface of 2.0 mm (0.078 in.) for the intake valves and a seat surface of 2.4 mm (0.096 in.) for the exhaust valves. The seat angle for both the intake and exhaust valves is 45° with a correction angle of 15. The top of the valve head should not be lower than 1.5 mm (0.059 in.) from the combustion chamber surface.

NOTE: *Valve seats that are worn or burned can be refaced providing the correction angle and seat width are maintained. Otherwise, the cylinder head must be replaced.*

17. Reface the intake valve on a machine. Hand grind the exhaust valve only. A valve margin of no less than 0.5 mm (0.019 in.) should remain on both the intake and exhaust valve heads.

18. Coat the seats with a fine grinding compound and lap the valves to the seats, to insure correct valve to seat contact. When finished, remove all traces of the grinding compound from the valves and seats.

19. Install the valves into their respective guides and install the lower spring seats.

20. Install the valve guide seals using the plastic sleeve over the valve stem before installing the seal to avoid seal damage.

21. Install the valve springs, upper spring seats and with the use of the spring compressor tools, install the valve stem keepers.

22. Place the camshaft into the bearing seats, install the top bearing caps and tighten. Check the end-play of the shaft which should not exceed a maximum of 0.15 mm (0.006 in.).

NOTE: *Do not install the cam followers. This will insure freedom of movement when checking the end-play.*

23. Remove the bearing caps and the camshaft. Install the cam followers in their respective bores. Reinstall the camshaft and the bearing caps in the following order.
   a. Lubricate the bearing seats, journals and the contact areas of the caps.

Installation of valve guide seals

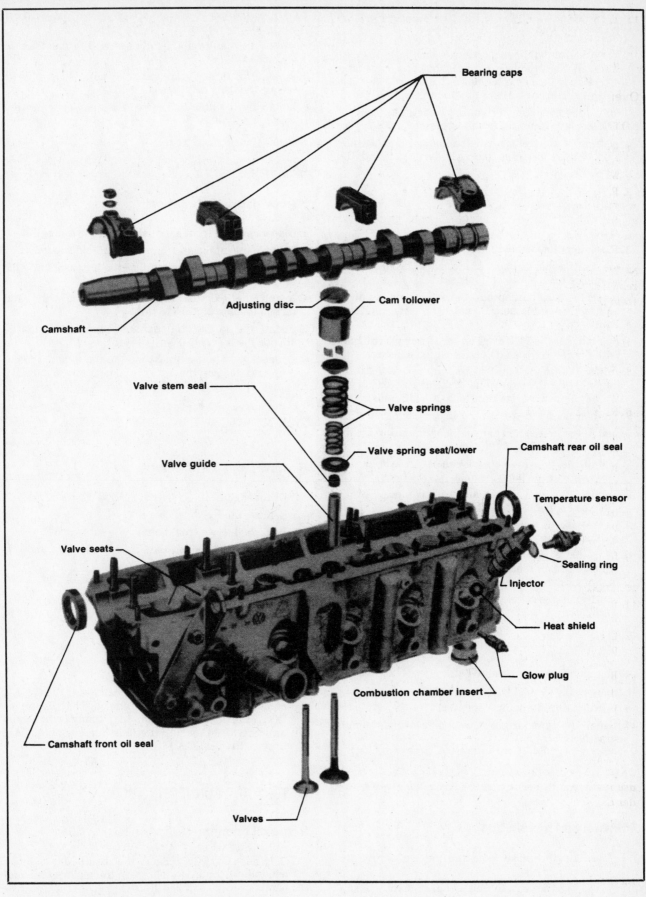

Bearing caps

Adjusting disc — Cam follower

Camshaft —

Valve stem seal —

Valve springs

Camshaft rear oil seal

Temperature sensor

Valve spring seat/lower

Valve guide —

Valve seats —

Sealing ring

Injector

Heat shield

Glow plug

Combustion chamber insert —

Camshaft front oil seal —

Valves —

Exploded view of cylinder head components

b. The cam lobes for the Number One cylinder must face upward.

c. Bearing caps Number 2 and 3 must be installed offset and tightened alternately and diagonally.

d. Install the Number 1 and 4 bearing caps and tighten in the same manner as Numbers 2 and 3.

e. Torque all bearing caps to 20 Nm (14 ft-lbs).

24. Install the combustion chamber insert. The insert is held in place by a groove and a retainer.

25. Install the glow plugs and the injectors, using new heat shields between the cylinder head and the injectors.

Installation

1. Install the head guide pins in sequence holes 9 and 10 to align the head with the block.

2. Install the head bolts and torque in numerical sequence to 90 Nm (65 ft-lbs) cold.

3. Insert the camshaft sprocket together with the drive belt and retaining bolt. Do not tighten the retaining bolt.

4. Be sure that the TDC mark on the flywheel is aligned with the reference mark on the clutch housing.

5. Adjust the timing belt tension with tool VW 210 or equivalent to a scale value of 12 to 13. Torque the water pump mounting bolts to 20 Nm (18 ft-lbs).

6. Tighten camshaft sprocket to 45 Nm (33 ft-lbs).

7. Install the intake and exhaust manifolds and torque the bolts to 25 Nm (18 ft-lbs).

8. Install the two intake and exhaust manifold supports and torque the bolts to 20 Nm (14 ft-lbs).

9. Connect the fuel supply and return pipes. Torque the pipe connectors to 25 Nm (18–ft lbs).

10. Install the injection pump drive belt and drive sprocket. Tighten the drive sprocket until it can just be turned by hand.

11. Adjust the belt tension with tool VW 210 or equivalent to a scale value of 12 to 13.

12. Make sure the crankshaft is still at TDC on Number 1 cylinder.

13. Secure the injection pump drive sprocket with tool 3036 or equivalent and tighten the retaining bolt to 100 Nm (72 ft-lbs).

14. Install the vacuum pump V-belt.

15. Remove the special tools.

16. Install the front timing belt cover.

17. Install the cylinder head cover and torque the nuts to 10 Nm (7 ft-lbs).

INTAKE MANIFOLD

Removal and Installation

1. Remove flexible hose from the air cleaner to the intake manifold.

2. Remove the two intake and exhaust manifold supports.

3. Remove the intake manifold to head bolts and lift off the intake manifold.

4. Install the manifold to head bolts and torque them to 25 Nm (18 ft-lbs).

5. Install the intake and exhaust manifold supports, torque the bolts to 20 Nm (14 ft-lbs).

6. Install the flexible hose from the air cleaner to the intake manifold.

EXHAUST MANIFOLD

Removal and Installation

1. Disconnect the front exhaust pipe at the flange.

2. Remove the intake and exhaust manifold supports.

3. Remove the exhaust manifold attaching bolts and lift off the exhaust manifold.

4. Install the exhaust manifold attaching bolts and torque them to 25 Nm (18 ft-lbs).

5. Install the intake and exhaust manifold supports. Torque the bolts to 20 Nm (14 ft-lbs).

6. Connect the front exhaust pipe to the exhaust manifold and torque the attaching nuts to 30 Nm (22 ft-lbs).

OIL PAN

Removal and Installation

1. Drain engine oil.

2. Remove the flywheel cover.

3. Remove the two front bolts in the subframe.

4. Turn the flywheel so that the recesses are lined up vertically on flywheel.

5. Remove the pan bolts and take out the oil pan.

6. Clean all gasket surfaces and install a new gasket.

7. Install the pan bolts and torque them to 20 Nm (14 ft-lbs).

8. Install the subframe bolts.

9. Install the flywheel cover and torque the bolts to 25 Nm (18 ft-lbs).

10. Install 4.8 qts. of engine oil or 5.3 qts. if the filter is changed. Use only API/CC grade oil. That means the CC will appear on the container singly or in combination with other designations (for example: "API Service SE, SD/CC, CD").

PISTONS AND CONNECTING RODS

Removal and Installation

1. It is necessary to remove the manifolds, cylinder head and the oil pan to expose the pistons and connecting rod assemblies. Refer to the appropriate disassembly section.

Marking the piston tops before removal

Marking the connecting rod and cap before removal

2. Note the direction of the arrows on the piston tops. Each arrow should point towards the crankshaft pulley.

3. Mark the cylinder number on the top of the piston before removal.

4. Mark the cylinder number on the connecting rod and cap before removal.

5. Note the direction of the connecting rod casting nipples before removal. The nipples should face the oil filter side.

6. Remove the bearing cap and push the piston and rod assembly from the block from the bottom to the top.

NOTE: *Should there be a ridge on the top of the cylinders from ring wear, this ridge would have to be removed before the piston assembly is pushed out of the block to avoid piston and ring breakage.*

7. Remove the rings from the piston and clean the ring grooves of carbon buildup.

8. If the pistons are reusable after inspection and cleaning, install new rings in the ring grooves and measure the side clearance between the ring and the piston ring groove.

9. If the piston pins are to be removed, evenly heat the piston with heated water or heated wet towels, to a temperature of 140° F (60° C). Drive the pins from the pistons, using a pin removal tool. Install the new pins in the same manner as the pin removal.

10. Check the piston diameter by measuring the piston skirt approximately $9/16$ inch from the bottom and 180° from the wrist pin bore.

11. Measure the cylinder bore walls at three points, starting from the top under ridge mark, followed by a measurement one-half way down the bore, and again approximately $9/16$ inch from the bottom. Record the measurements. Remeasure the bore in the same areas but 180° from the original measuring locations. Record the measurements from the second reading. By subtracting the lesser amount from the higher reading, the amount of cylinder taper and out-of-round is determined.

12. The maximum bore out-of-round is 0.04 mm (0.0016 inch). The clearance relationship between the cylinder bore and the piston is shown in the following chart, listing standard sizes and three oversizes. The piston to cylinder clearance for a new part

should be 0.03 mm (0.011 in.) and a wear limit of 0.07 mm (0.027 in.) for service parts.

13. To check the piston ring gap, push the ring down into the bore until it is approximately 15 mm (0.591 inch) from the top and measure the width of the gap with a feeler gauge. Repeat the measuring operation with the ring approximately $9/16$ inch from the bottom. The ring gap should be 0.3 to 0.5 mm (0.012 to 0.020 inch) for the two compression rings and a gap of 0.25 to 0.40 mm (0.010 to 0.016 inch) for the oil control ring. A wear limit of 1.0 mm (0.040 inch) is allowed for all ring gaps.

14. Install the piston rings with the "TOP" marking towards the crown of the pistons.

15. Using a piston/ring installer, insert the piston and rod assembly into the top of the cyinder bore and force it into the cylinder, being careful not to break rings during the piston movement from the installer tool to the cylinder bore.

16. Install the connecting rod to the crankshaft with either new or the old bearing inserts and torque the caps to the rods. The torque should be 33 ft-lbs (45 Nm).

17. Turn each piston and connecting rod assembly to TDC and measure the piston height above the engine block to determine the thickness of the head gasket to be used during the cylinder head assembly. A dial indicator is used for this measurement operation.

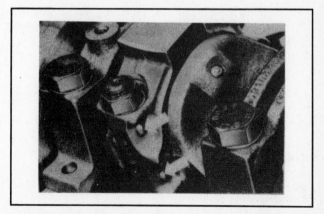

Location of the casting nipples on the connecting rods and caps

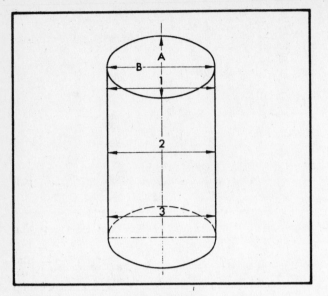

Measuring points of the cylinder bore

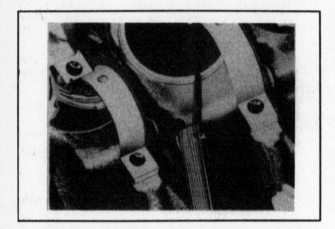

Measuring the ring gap

18. The head gaskets are selective and come in three different sizes and are identified by notches in the side of the gasket, along with part numbers.

19. Complete the assembly by installing the oil pan, cylinder head and manifolds by referring to the appropriate sections.

CYLINDER HEAD GASKET, IDENTIFICATION CHART

Piston Height mm (In.)	Identification (notches in gasket)	Part No.
0.67-0.80 (0.026-0.031)	1	069 103 383
0.81-0.90 (0.032-0.035)	2	069 103 383A
0.91-1.02 (0.036-0.040)	3	069 103 383B

CRANKSHAFT

Removal

1. Using tool 10-201 or equivalent to hold the flywheel from rotating, unscrew the flywheel bolts.
2. Remove the pistons.
3. Check the main bearing end clearance at bearing Number 4. The clearance should be 0.07–0.18 mm (0.003–0.007 in.) for a new part. The clearance should be 0.25 mm (0.010 in.) maximum for service parts.
4. Crankshaft main bearing clearances can be checked with the engine installed.
   a. Remove the bearing caps.
   b. Clean the shells and journals.
   c. Insert Plastigage® across the journal surface.
   d. Install the bearing caps and tighten to 65 Nm (47 ft-lbs).
   e. Remove the bearing caps.
   f. Compare the width of the Plastigage® for new bearings at 0.016–0.075 mm (0.0006 to 0.003 in.), and to a wear limit of 0.16 mm (0.006).
5. Replace the pilot bearing by removing it with tool 10-202 or equivalent and installing the new bearing, letter side visible, with tool 2026 or equivalent. The bearing should be seated 5.5 mm (0.216 in.) past the edge of the surrounding steel lip.
6. Remove the rear crankshaft oil seal by prying it out with tool 2086 or equivalent.
7. Install a new rear crankshaft oil seal using tool 2003/1 or equivalent. Coat the lip of the seal lightly with oil before installing.
8. Install the bearings and caps; Number 1 on the drive belt end of the engine and Number 6 of the flywheel end. Torque the bearing cap bolts to 65 Nm (47 ft-lbs).
9. Install the pistons.
10. Install the flywheel, using thread locking compound on the bolts. Torque the bolts to 75 Nm (54 ft-lbs).

CAMSHAFT

Removal

1. Remove the cylinder head cover and gasket.
2. Remove the alternator V-belt.
3. Remove the outboard half of the vacuum pump V-belt pulley and the belt.
4. Remove the covers on the timing (camshaft drive belt) and the injection pump drive belt.
5. Set the crankshaft to TDC on No. 1 cylinder and align the marks on the flywheel to clutch housing and injection pump sprocket to mounting plate.
6. Lock the injection pump sprocket with tool 2064 or equivalent.
7. Hold inboard half of the vacuum pump pulley and injection pump drive sprocket with tool 3036 or equivalent.

8. Remove the injection pump drive sprocket retaining bolt.

9. Take off the pump drive sprocket and the injection pump drive belt.

10. Using tools 2084 and 2079 or equivalents, loosen the crankshaft pulley center bolt.

11. Fix the camshaft in position with setting tool 2065A or its equivalent.

12. Loosen the water pump in order to remove the camshaft drive belt (timing belt).

13. Remove the crankshaft pulley, drive belt sprocket and drive belt.

14. Remove camshaft bearing caps 1 and 4.

15. Loosen the nuts of bearing caps 2 and 3 diagonally.

16. Remove bearing caps 2 and 3 and lift out the camshaft.

Installation

1. Lubricate the bearing shells, journals and contact faces of caps.

2. Set in the camshaft with cylinder Number 1 lobes facing upward.

3. Install bearing caps 2 and 3, and tighten alternately and diagonally.

CAUTION: *Check for direction of offset when installing caps 2 and 3.*

4. Install bearinga caps 1 and 4. Torque camshaft caps to 20 Nm (14 ft-lbs).

5. Install the crankshaft pulley, drive belt sprocket and drive belt. Torque the crankshaft pulley bolt to 350 Nm (250 ft-lbs) or to 35 Nm (25 ft-lbs) when using extension tool 2079 and a torque wrench.

6. Using tool VW210 or equivalent, position the water pump to tension the timing belt (scale 12 to 13 on tool VW210).

7. Torque the water pump bolts to 20 Nm (14 ft-lbs).

8. Check the position of the camshaft with setting bar tool 2065A. If the bar does not fit, rotate the crankshaft until the tool enters the camshaft notch. Loosen the camshaft sprocket retaining bolt and loosen the camshaft sprocket by tapping it with a brass drift. Turn the crankshaft until the TDC mark on the flywheel and the boss on the clutch housing are aligned. Torque the camshaft sprocket bolt to 45 Nm (33 ft-lbs) and remove the setting bar tool.

9. Install the injection pump drive sprocket with the drive belt. Tighten the bolt hand tight.

10. Check the drive belt tension to a scale of 12 to 13 on tool VW210. Adjust the drive belt tension by moving the pump mounting plate.

11. Align the TDC mark on the flywheel to clutch housing, if not aligned.

12. Secure the injection pump drive sprocket with tool 3036 and torque the retaining bolt to 100 Nm (72 ft-lbs).

13. Remove setting pin tool 2064 from the injection pump.

14. Set the injection timing, as previously outlined.

15. Install the injection and timing belt covers.

16. Install a new gasket and the cylinder head cover.

OIL PUMP

Removal and Installation

1. Remove alternator V-belt.

2. Remove the outboard half of the vacuum pump pulley and V-belt.

3. Remove the cylinder head cover and gasket.

4. Remove the injection pump drive belt cover and the camshaft (timing) belt cover.

5. Set the crankshaft to TDC on Number 1 cylinder and align the marks on the flywheel to the clutch housing. Also, align the marks on the injection pump mounting plate.

6. Lock the injection pump sprocket with tool 2064, or equivalent.

7. Hold the inboard half of the vacuum pump pulley and the injection pump drive sprocket with tool 3036 or equivalent.

8. Remove the center retaining bolt and take off the half pulley and pump drive sprocket along with the injection drive belt.

9. Using special tools 2084 and 2079 or equivalents, loosen the crankshaft pulley center bolt.

10. Position the camshaft with tool 2065A or equivalent.

11. Remove the crankshaft pulley, drive belt sprocket and drive belt.

12. Remove the camshaft drive belt idler pulley bolt.

13. Using tool 3034 or equivalent, remove the camshaft drive belt idler pulley.

14. Remove the oil dipstick and drain the engine oil.

15. Remove the front bolts on the subframe and remove the oil pan and gasket.

16. Remove the oil pump suction pipe from the base of the oil pump and the 2 bolts holding the suction pipe braces to the engine block.

17. Using tool 2086 or equivalent, remove the front crankshaft oil seal.

18. Remove the oil pump bolts and remove the oil pump from the front of the engine.

19. Replace the entire oil pump as an assembly.

20. When installing oil pump onto the crankshaft align the driving dog on the crankshaft with the pump.

21. Install the pump and gasket. Torque the 8 mm bolts to 25 Nm (18 ft-lbs) and the 6 mm bolts to 10 Nm (7 ft-lbs).

22. Using tool 2080 or equivalent and the crankshaft pulley retaining bolt, install a new crankshaft oil seal. Coat outer lip of seal with oil before installing.

23. Install the oil suction pipe. Always use a new lock plate when installing the pipe on the oil pump. Torque 10 Nm (7 ft-lbs).

24. Install a new gasket and the oil pan. Install the 2 subframe bolts.

25. Torque the oil drain plug to 50 Nm (36 ft-lbs).
26. Install the camshaft drive belt idler pulley and torque the bolt to 10 Nm (7 ft-lbs).
27. Install the crankshaft pulley, drive belt sprocket and drive belt. Use a locking compound on the crankshaft pulley bolt and torque it to 350 Nm (250 ft-lbs).
28. Install the 2 drive belt sprocket bolts and torque them to 20 Nm (14 ft-lbs).
29. Use tool VW210 or equivalent to adjust the drive belt to 12–13 on the scale.
30. Loosen coolant pump bolts and turn the pump to adjust drive belt tension. Retorque coolant pump bolts to 20 Nm (14 ft-lbs).
31. Check for crankshaft TDC position and torque the camshaft sprocket to 45 Nm (33 ft-lbs).
32. Remove the tool 2065A from the rear of the camshaft.
33. Install the alternator V-belt.
34. Adjust the injection drive belt tension with tool VW210 or equivalent, to a scale reading of 12 to 13.
35. Check the TDC mark on the flywheel for alignment.

36. Hold the injection pump drive sprocket and vacuum pump half pulley with tool 3036 or equivalent and torque the retaining bolt to 10 Nm (7 ft-lbs).
37. Attach the vacuum pump V-belt and pulley half.
38. Remove tool 2064 from the injection pump sprocket.
39. Install the belt covers and cylinder head cover.

WATER PUMP

The diesel engine is water cooled by a belt driven water pump. The system uses a main radiator plus an auxiliary radiator to cool the engine. The cooling fan is run by a thermostatically controlled electric motor.

Removal

1. Drain the coolant.
2. Remove the power steering belt.
3. Remove the power steering pump with the hoses connected and lay the pump aside.

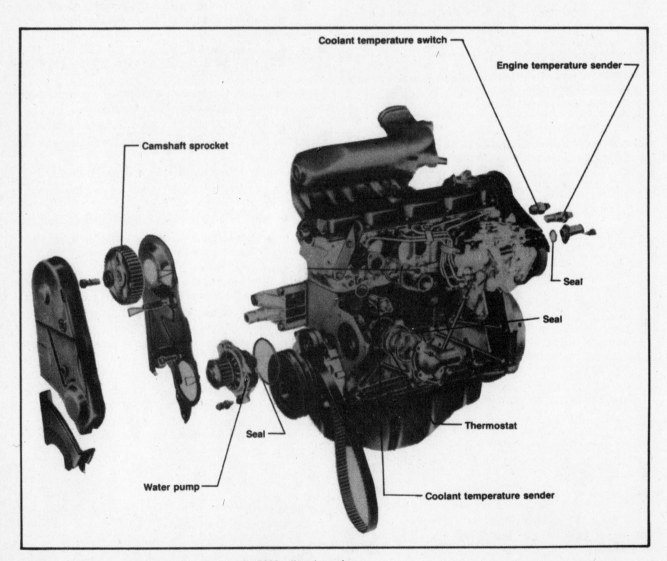

Cooling system components for the Audi 5000 diesel engine

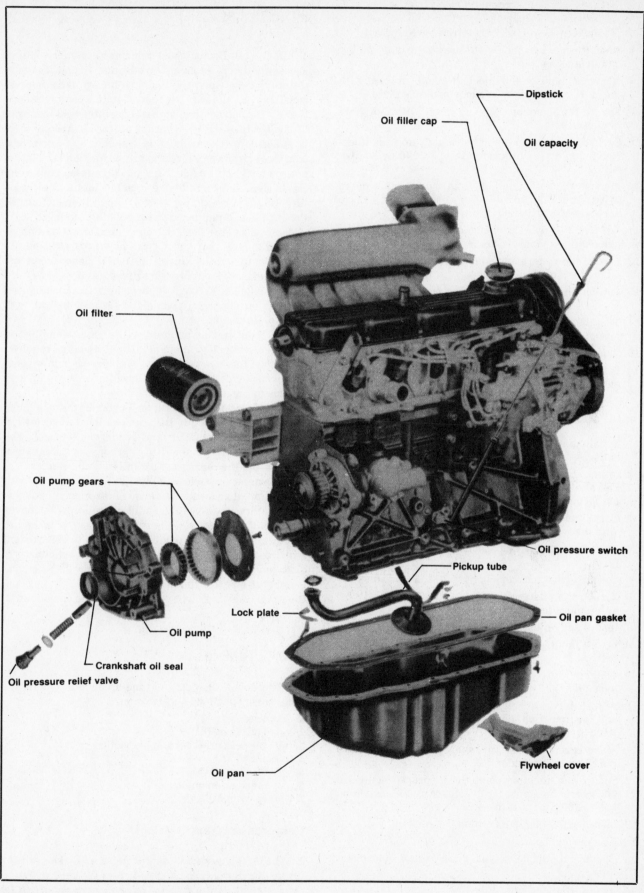

Exploded view of the lubricating system components

4. Remove both drive belt covers.

5. Set the crankshaft to TDC on cylinder Number 1.

6. Align the mark on the flywheel with the mark on the clutch housing.

7. Align the mark on the injection pump sprocket with the mark on the injection pump mounting plate.

8. Secure the injection pump sprocket with tool 2064 or equivalent.

9. Secure the vacuum pump belt pulley and the injection pump drive sprocket with tool 3036 or equivalent.

10. Remove the retaining bolt from the injection pump drive sprocket. Take off the injection pump drive sprocket and drive belt.

11. Remove the cylinder head cover and secure the camshaft with tool 2065A or equivalent.

12. Loosen the water pump and turn it to relieve tension on the timing belt.

13. Loosen the camshaft sprocket retaining bolt one turn.

14. Tap the camshaft sprocket with a brass drift to loosen it and remove the sprocket.

15. Remove the water pump.

16. If the water pump is defective, always replace the entire assembly.

Installation

1. Install the water pump loosely. Do not tighten the bolts.

2. Insert the camshaft sprocket together with drive belt and screw in the camshaft sprocket bolt, but do not torque the sprocket bolt.

3. Check the TDC mark on the flywheel for alignment with the reference mark and adjust if necessary.

4. Adjust the timing belt tension by turning the water pump.

5. Torque the water pump bolts to 20 Nm (14 ft-lbs).

6. Torque the camshaft sprocket to 45 Nm (33 ft-lbs) and remove tool 2065A.

7. Install and adjust the alternator belt.

8. Install the injection pump drive sprocket and drive belt.

9. Tighten the drive sprocket until it can just be turned by hand.

10. Adjust the drive belt tension by loosening and moving the injection pump. Adjust to 12–13 on the VW210 tool scale.

11. Make sure that the crankshaft remains at TDC on the Number 1 cylinder.

12. Secure the injection pump drive sprocket with tool 2064 or equivalent. Tighten the sprocket retaining bolt to 100 Nm (72 ft-lbs).

13. Install and adjust the vacuum pump V-belt.

14. Remove tool 2064.

15. Check and adjust injection timing as previously outlined.

16. Install front and rear drive belt covers.

17. Install the cylinder head cover and a new gasket.

MERCEDES-BENZ

The Mercedes-Benz diesel engine used in their vehicles is essentially the same as the gasoline engine. The only differences between the two engines are the compression ratio and the way the fuel is ignited. Both types are four cycle engines; that is, their operating cycles consist of (1) an intake stroke, whereby air (or air-fuel mixture) is pulled into the combustion chamber, (2) a compression stroke, during which the air (or air-fuel mixture) is compressed and heated, (3) a power stroke, caused by the burning (ignition) of the injected fuel and air mixture, and (4) an exhaust stroke, which literally pushes the burned and unburned gases out of the engine.

A diesel engine does not have an ignition system as such, although there are glow plugs for starting. To ignite its fuel-air mixture, the diesel depends on the heating effect of compression pressure. If the pressure is high enough, through high compression ratios and combustion chamber design, the fuel-air mixture will ignite of its own accord.

The diesel, having no ignition system, is simplified to an extent, although the timed fuel injection required may offset this to a degree. Advantages lie in increased fuel economy using lower grades of fuel, along with long life due to rugged construction.

The 300 series uses a unique 5-cylinder diesel engine. This engine is basically the same as the 240 series but with an added cylinder and a larger flywheel. The rocker arms are mounted in 2 groups as on previous engines, but the rear group extends over 3 cylinders.

This engine also uses a 5 plunger injection pump with a mechanical governor. Because of the mechanical governor, a throttle valve in the intake manifold is no longer used. With the key start ignition, the key is turned to position 2 and left there until the light in the instrument panel goes out, indicating that this is the optimum preglow time at a given engine temperature. If the engine is not started after the preglow indicator light goes on, the preglow system will remain energized for about 10 seconds.

ENGINE TUNE-UP

The Mercedes-Benz engine tune-up should include the following inspections and/or repairs.

1. Compression test
2. Valve adjustment
3. Injector pressure test and inspection
4. Injector timing
5. Valve timing
6. Idle speed adjustment
7. Glow plug operation

Compression Test

NOTE: *Valve clearances set too close will result in poor compression readings. Some engines have a valve rotator installed. If the rotator fails, compression will be low.*

Compression on a diesel engine can be checked just like a gasoline engine. The only difference in testing is that the glow plugs instead of the spark plugs are removed for the test and a screw-in compression gauge with a capacity of at least 500 psi. Individual cylinder pressures should not vary more than 10%.

Valve Adjustment

1. Remove the valve cover and note the position of the intake and exhaust valves.
2. Turn the engine with a socket and breaker bar on the crankshaft pulley or by using a remote starter. Due to extremely high compression pressures in the diesel engine, it will be considerably easier to use a remote starter. If a starter is not available, the engine can be bumped into position with the normal starter.

NOTE: *Do not turn the engine backwards or use the camshaft sprocket bolt to rotate the engine.*

3. Measure the valve clearance when the heel of the camshaft lobe is directly over the sliding surface of the rocker arm. The lobe of the camshaft should be vertical to the surface of the rocker arm. The clearance is correct when the specified feeler gauge can be pulled out with a very slight drag.
4. To adjust the clearance, loosen the cap nut while holding the hex nut. Adjust the valve clearance by turning the hex nut.
5. After adjustment hold the cap nut and lock it in place with the hex nut. Recheck the clearance.
6. Check the gasket and install the rocker arm cover.

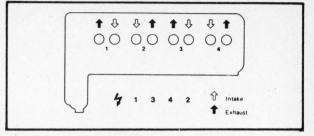

Valve arrangement—4 cylinder

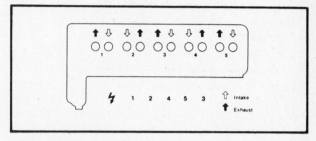

Valve arrangement—5 cylinder

Injection Timing

As the piston comes up on the compression stroke, there is a delay caused by the fuel having to come from the pump to the injector nozzle. For example, if injection takes place too early, temperatures may not yet be high enough for ignition (piston has not come up far enough

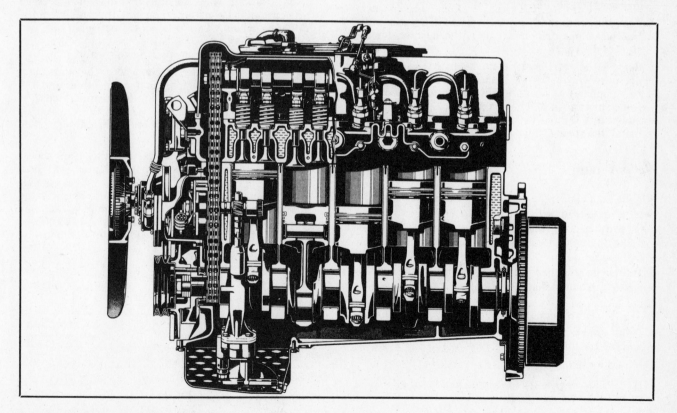

Diesel engine cross section—typical

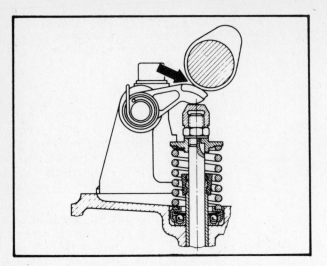

Measure valve clearance at the arrow

to compress the air). To compensate for this lag, the injection pump begins to deliver fuel to the nozzle before the piston reaches TDC. You will also need an overflow pipe to check the start of delivery.

1. On the 1976 and earlier 240D, set the preheat starter switch to the driving position. On all other models, remove the vacuum hose from the vacuum box.

2. Unscrew the connection from the first injection pump valve (No. 1 cylinder) and remove the spring and pressure valve.

3. Replace these with an overflow pipe.

4. While making the measurement, set the regulating lever on the injection pump at the Full Load stop.

5. Turn the crankshaft in the direction of rotation until fuel just stops dripping. This is the position for the start of delivery.

6. Remove the overflow pipe and replace the spring and pressure valve. On 1976 and earlier 240D's, use a new copper washer and tighten the connection to 22 ft-lbs, loosen and tighten again to 22 ft-lbs, loosen again, and tighten to 26 ft-lbs. On all others, simply install the spring, valve and pipe connection.

Valve Timing

Ideally, this operation should be performed by a dealer who is equipped with the necessary tools and knowledge to do the job properly.

Checking valve timing is too inaccurate at the standard tappet clearance, therefore timing values are given for an assumed tappet clearance of 0.4 mm. The engines are not measured at 0.4 mm, but rather at 2 mm.

1. To check the timing, remove the rocker arm cover and spark plugs. Remove the tensioning springs. Eliminate all valve clearance.

2. Install a degree wheel.

NOTE: *If the degree wheel is attached to the camshaft, values read from it must be doubled.*

3. A pointer must be made out of a bent section of ³/₁₆

in. brazing rod or coathanger wire, and attached to the engine.

4. With a 22 mm wrench on the crankshaft pulley, turn the engine, in the direction of rotation, until the TDC mark on the vibration damper registers with the pointer and the distributor rotor points to the No. 1 cylinder mark on the housing.

5. Turn the loosened degree wheel until the pointer lines up with the 0° (OT) mark, then tighten it in this position.

6. Continue turning the crankshaft in the direction of rotation until the camshaft lobe of the associated valve is vertical (e.g., points away from the rocker arm surface). To take up tappet clearance, insert a feeler gauge (thick enough to raise the valve slightly from its seat) between the rocker arm cone and the pressure piece.

7. Attach the indicator to the cylinder head so that the feeler rests against the valve spring retainer of No. 1 cylinder intake valve. Preload the indicator at least 0.008 in. then set to zero, making sure the feeler is exactly perpendicular on the valve spring retainer. It may be necessary to bleed down the chain tensioner at this time to facilitate readings.

8. Turn the crankshaft in the normal direction of rotation, again using a wrench on the crankshaft pulley, until the indicator reads 0.016 in. less than zero reading.

9. Note the reading of the degree wheel at this time, remembering to double the reading if the wheel is mounted to the camshaft sprocket.

10. Again turn the crankshaft until the valve is closing and the indicator again reads 0.016 in. less than zero reading. Make sure, at this time, that preload has remained constant, then note the reading of the degree wheel. The difference between the two degree wheel readings is the timing angle (number of degrees the valve is open) for that valve.

11. The other valves may be checked in the same manner, comparing them against each other and the opening values given in "Tune-up Specifications." It must be remembered that turning the crankshaft contrary to the normal direction of rotation results in inaccurate readings.

12. If valve timing is not to specification, the easiest way of bringing it in line is to install an offset Woodruff key in the camshaft sprocket. This is far simpler than replacing the entire timing chain and it is the factory-recommended way of changing valve timing provided the timing chain is not stretched too far or worn out. Offset keys are available in the following sizes.

VALVE TIMING OFFSET KEYS

Offset	Part No.	For a Correction at Crankshaft of
2° (0.7)	621 991 04 67	4°
3°20' (0.9)	621 991 02 67	6½°
4° (1.1)	621 991 01 67	8°
5° (1.3)	621 991 00 67	10°

13. The Woodruff key must be installed with the offset toward the "right", in the normal direction of rotation, to effect advanced valve opening; toward the "left" to retard.

14. Advancing the intake valve opening too much can result in piston and/or valve damage (the valve will hit the piston). To check the clearance between the valve head and the piston, the crankshaft must be positioned at 5° ATDC (on intake stroke). The procedure is essentially the same as for measuring valve timing.

15. As before, the dial indicator is set to zero after being preloaded, then the valve is depressed until it touches the top of the piston. As the normal valve head-to-piston clearance is approximately 0.035 in., you can see that the dial indicator must be preloaded at least 0.042 in. so there will be enough movement for the feeler.

   If the clearance is much less than 0.035 in., the cylinder head must be removed and checked for carbon deposits. If none exist, the valve seat must be cut deeper into the head. Always set the injection timing after installing an offset key.

Injector Pressure

NOTE: *Never remove the injector to check fuel pressure. The working pressure of the nozzle is over 1400 PSI and fuel under that pressure can penetrate the skin.*

The fuel pump is mounted on the side of the fuel injection pump and can be easily identified by the hand priming pump. With the diesel engine it is extremely important that the fuel is airfree, without bubbles. A fuel bypass valve is located in the injection pump to maintain constant fuel pressure for the engine load. This valve opens at a pressure of 14.7–22 psi, sending excess fuel back into the supply system.

   A general check of fuel pressure can be made if it is assumed that the bypass valve is functioning properly.

1. Disconnect the return line and hold the line over a container.

2. Start the engine and watch the line. If fuel comes out, it can be assumed that the fuel pressure is sufficient, as a pressure of at least 14.7 psi is required to open a good bypass valve.

3. Check the discharge line from the fuel filter.

4. Check the tank before assuming the worst about a fuel pump. Disconnect the input line from the fuel tank and blow back through it with low-pressure compressed air. A line free of debris will allow the air to bubble in the tank.

CAUTION: *High pressure air will blow out the fuel tank filter.*

5. Unscrew the hand pump and remove the suction valve. Unscrew the plug which covers the pressure valve and remove the valve. Worn valve seats can be reground sometimes, but it is better to replace them.

6. To check the plunger, remove the plug and pull the plunger and spring. If it is badly scored or worn, the pump must be replaced. If the pump is only clogged

with gum, it is possible to clean it with lacquer thinner or carbon tetrachloride but a new rubber O-ring should be used on the hand pump during reassembly.

Glow Plug System

The glow plugs provide a means for ignition during starting and perform the same function as normal spark plugs, although they do so in a different manner.

   The light on the dashboard which indicates when the glow plugs are hot enough to fire can also serve as a troubleshooting aid. If the light does not glow, it usually indicates a faulty plug.

1. Test the plugs by having an assistant hold the starting knob or key (1975, and later 5-cylinder) in the preheat position while shorting the plugs to ground, in turn, with a suitable tool. Each plug should produce a spark if working properly. While bridging the connections, the light on the dashboard should light.

2. If, after disconnecting the ground lead of the preheating system, the light still stays lit, a short circuit in the system is indicated. This is usually caused by a carbon-fouled plug electrode or by a lead touching the cylinder head. Check the leads first.

3. If they seem satisfactory pull the knob or turn the key to the preheat position and disconnect one plug power lead at a time, starting from the ground end, until the light goes out, indicating the faulty plug.

4. Glow plugs can be cleaned, but it is better to replace them if they are badly fouled.

5. To remove the plugs, loosen the cable, if this has not been done already, by removing the knurled nut.

6. Unscrew the other nuts and remove the insulators and the bus bars.

7. Remove the glow plugs.

8. Before installing new plugs, clean the ducts and prechamber bores with a stiff bristle brush or a small scraper. The ball pin in the prechamber is easy to

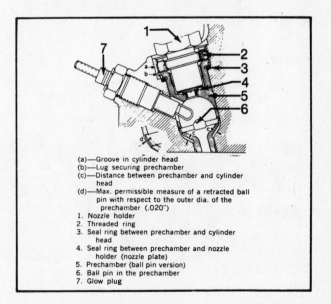

(a)—Groove in cylinder head
(b)—Lug securing prechamber
(c)—Distance between prechamber and cylinder head
(d)—Max. permissible measure of a retracted ball pin with respect to the outer dia. of the prechamber (.020")
1. Nozzle holder
2. Threaded ring
3. Seal ring between prechamber and cylinder head
4. Seal ring between prechamber and nozzle holder (nozzle plate)
5. Prechamber (ball pin version)
6. Ball pin in the prechamber
7. Glow plug

Position of glow plug and injection nozzle in the prechamber

break, so don't go much deeper than 2 in. into the plug hole.

9. Crank the engine a few times to blow out any carbon particles loosened by the scraping, then insert the plugs. Do not exceed 35 ft-lbs torque.

Idle Speed Adjustment

Since the diesel engine has no ignition distributor or ignition coil there is no way to connect an external tachometer to measure idle speed. While using the built-in tachometer on the dash is not the most accurate way, the only other possibility is to set the idle speed by ear.

1. On models before 1977, turn the knob on the instrument completely clockwise. Turn it again counterclockwise. The travel before the idle speed is raised should not exceed about 1/2 turn. If required, adjust the travel with the nut.

2. On 1977 and later models, turn the knob on the instrument panel completely clockwise and check the distance between the adjusting ring and the specially shaped spring. It should be approximately .04 in.

3. With the engine stopped, depress the accelerator pedal while turning the idle knob counterclockwise.

4. Start the engine. The idle should be 1000–1100 r.p.m. Adjust this with the adjusting screw, but do not exceed 1100 r.p.m.

5. On 1977 and later models, be sure the special spring is installed correctly.

6. Run the engine to operating temperature.

7. Turn the idle adjusting knob on the dash fully to the right.

8. Disconnect the regulating rod and adjust the idle speed with the idle speed adjusting screw. 1977 and later models have a locknut on the idle speed adjusting screw.

9. Reconnect the regulating rod.

DIESEL INJECTOR PUMP

Removal and Installation

In many cases of poor running, the injection pump itself is at fault. Fuel that is extremely gritty will cause wear of the pump plungers and plunger springs can break in service. Accurate testing of the pump must be carried out on a test stand. Aside from testing the governor vacuum and control rod, little else other than visual inspection for broken or worn parts can be accomplished.

1. To remove the pump for service, unscrew all the injection lines, the vacuum line and fuel lines.

2. Plug the lines, then detach the connecting rod for the auxiliary mechanical control and the starting cable at the adjusting lever.

3. Turn the crankshaft, in the normal direction of rotation, to align the 45° BTDC mark with the pointer (No. 1 piston on compression stroke).

4. Matchmark the pump and flange.

5. Unscrew the nut at the bell-shaped support, then the front flange hold-down nuts. Pull the pump from the crankcase, then remove the coupling sleeve from the pump drive collar or driveshaft. New pumps do not come with the splined drive collar, therefore the old one must be removed if the pump is to be exchanged.

6. Using a puller, carefully remove the collar and Woodruff key.

7. To install the pump, be sure that the crankshaft has not moved from the 45° BTDC position, then insert the Woodruff key into its groove in the driveshaft, making sure the shaft is dirt free.

8. Install the drive collar and hex nut, using a pair of pliers wrapped in tape to hold the collar while tightening the nut. It is extremely important that the splines are not damaged in any way during this operation.

9. Try sliding the coupling sleeve onto the drive collar. If it slides on easily, it can be pressed onto the driveshaft. Remove the oil overflow pipe plug at the rear of the injection pump and adjust start of delivery position by aligning the marks. Apply light finger pressure to the follower in a direction opposite normal direction of rotation (left). This pressure should cause the drive collar to jump two teeth.

10. Grease the paper gaskets with petroleum jelly and install them to side of crankcase, then install pump, finger-tightening the bolts in the slotted holes.

11. Turn the crankshaft in the direction of rotation to 24° BTDC and check the start of delivery.

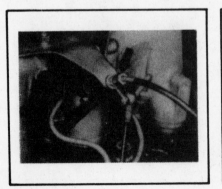

Adjusting nut for dashboard idle speed knob

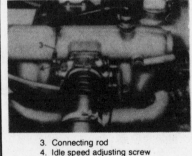

3. Connecting rod
4. Idle speed adjusting screw

Diesel engine idle speed adjustment—4 cylinder

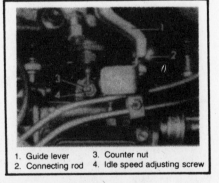

1. Guide lever   3. Counter nut
2. Connecting rod   4. Idle speed adjusting screw

Diesel engine idle speed adjustment—300D, 300CD

Overhaul

The injector pump should be replaced with either a new or factory rebuilt unit. The average repair shops do not have the required rebuilding and testing equipment needed to properly service the injector pump.

DIESEL FUEL INJECTORS

Diagnosis

The first sign of an injector problem may appear as one of the following.

1. Knocking in one or more cylinders
2. Engine overheating
3. Loss of power
4. Black exhaust smoke
5. Increased fuel consumption

To determine which injector may be malfunctioning, allow the engine to idle. Loosen the cap nuts of each injector tube, one at a time, about ½ turn then retighten. If there is no change in the rough idle, it indicates a faulty injector. A good injector will be indicated by a further roughening of the idle when the cap nut is unscrewed.

NOTE: *Always keep injector parts clean when you are working with them.*

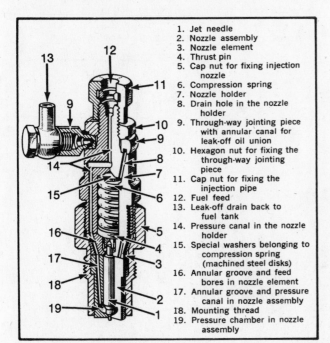

1. Jet needle
2. Nozzle assembly
3. Nozzle element
4. Thrust pin
5. Cap nut for fixing injection nozzle
6. Compression spring
7. Nozzle holder
8. Drain hole in the nozzle holder
9. Through-way jointing piece with annular canal for leak-off oil union
10. Hexagon nut for fixing the through-way jointing piece
11. Cap nut for fixing the injection pipe
12. Fuel feed
13. Leak-off drain back to fuel tank
14. Pressure canal in the nozzle holder
15. Special washers belonging to compression spring (machined steel disks)
16. Annular groove and feed bores in nozzle element
17. Annular groove and pressure canal in nozzle assembly
18. Mounting thread
19. Pressure chamber in nozzle assembly

Cross section of fuel injector

Removal and Installation

1. Remove the cap nut and unscrew the nut that holds the banjo fitting.

2. Remove the bolt and the overflow line. Unscrew the nozzle assembly and the seal.

3. To disassemble the nozzle holder, remove the cap nut with a 27 mm box wrench, then pull out the nozzle assembly and jet needle.

4. Remove the nozzle element, thrust pin, and spring from the nozzle holder. It is very easy to crush or distort the nozzle holder. Individual nozzle components are run-in together and never should be interchanged.

5. Nozzle testing requires special equipment. Since this equipment is not readily available, it is recommended that a dealer do any nozzle testing.

6. Malfunctioning nozzles are usually only fouled and, if care is exercised, can be hand-cleaned.

7. Brush any carbon away using a brass-bristle brush or a piece of kerosene-soaked wood.

8. Examine for burrs or scratches and out-of-round injection holes, then make sure that the jet needle moves freely in the nozzle.

9. Immerse the assembly in diesel fuel and pull the jet needle about one-third out of the nozzle, then release it. The jet should fall of its own weight.

10. In emergency situations only, burrs keeping the jet from sliding may be removed by lapping with fine valve grinding compound. Damaged seating surfaces, however, usually will not be restored by lapping. It is best to replace such damaged units.

11. Assemble the unit carefully, as any dirt or foreign matter will prevent free operation of the jet.

12. When tightening the cap nut, do not exceed 50 ft-lbs. Excessive torque may distort the nozzle and cause the jet needle to bind.

NOTE: *Always use new seals when reassembling and installing the injectors. Never try to stop leaks by overtightening connections.*

GOVERNOR

Mercedes-Benz vehicles are equipped with two different types of governors. The governor is attached to the injection pump. Should this unit require service, it should be replaced with either a new or factory rebuilt part.

CYLINDER HEAD

Removal

In order to perform a valve job or to inspect cylinder bores for wear, the head must be removed. While this may seem fairly straightforward, some caution must be observed to ensure that valve timing is not disturbed.

1. Drain the radiator and remove all hoses and wires.

2. Remove the camshaft cover and associated throttle linkage, then press out the spring clamp from the notch in the rocker arm.

3. Push the clamp outward over the ball cap of the

rocker, then depress the valve with a suitable tool and lift the rocker arm out of the ball pin head.

4. Remove the rocker arm supports and the camshaft sprocket nut.

NOTE: *The rockers and their supports must be removed together.*

5. Using a suitable puller, remove the camshaft sprocket, after having first marked the chain, sprocket and cam for ease in assembly.

6. Remove the sprocket and chain and wire it out of the way.

CAUTION: *Make sure the chain is securely wired so that it will not slide down into the engine.*

7. Unbolt the manifolds and exhaust header pipe and push them out of the way.

8. Then loosen the cylinder head hold-down bolts in the reverse order of that shown in torque diagrams for each model. It is good practice to loosen each bolt a little at a time, working round the head, until all are free. This prevents unequal stresses in the metal.

9. Reach into the engine compartment and gradually work the head loose from each end by rocking it. Never, under any circumstances, use a screwdriver between the head and block to pry, as the head will be scarred badly and may be ruined.

Overhaul

NOTE: *Diesel cylinder heads should not be machined.*

1. Remove the marked camshaft bearing caps from the head and lift the camshaft from the bearing seats. Mark each bearing cap.

2. Remove the cam followers. Mark each cam follower for identification, if to be reused, so each can be placed in their original location, during the assembly.

3. Remove the valve stem keepers and valve springs.

NOTE: *It may be necessary to tap on the valve spring remover tool spindle to loosen the valve stem keepers from the upper spring seats.*

4. Push each valve from the head and discard the valve stem oil seal. Mark the valves to match their seat locations in the cylinder head.

5. Remove the valve spring lower seats from the valve spring bores in the cylinder head with the use of an expanding tool.

6. Remove the glow plugs from the cylinder head. Place a drift through the glow plug hole and tap the combustion chamber inserts out from the combustion chamber.

7. Examine the cylinder head for damage or cracks.

8. If the cylinder head is usable, clean the carbon deposits from the valve guides and insert a new intake or exhaust valve into the respective guide until the end of the valve stem is flush with the end of the guide.

9. Install a dial indicator and measure the side movement of the valve stem in the guide.

10. The generally accepted maximum side clearance is 1.3 mm (0.051 in.)

11. If the valve guides are worn beyond the specifications, new guides can be replaced.

12. Using a special guide remover tool or its equivalent, press the valve guide from the head by exerting pressure from the combustion chamber side.

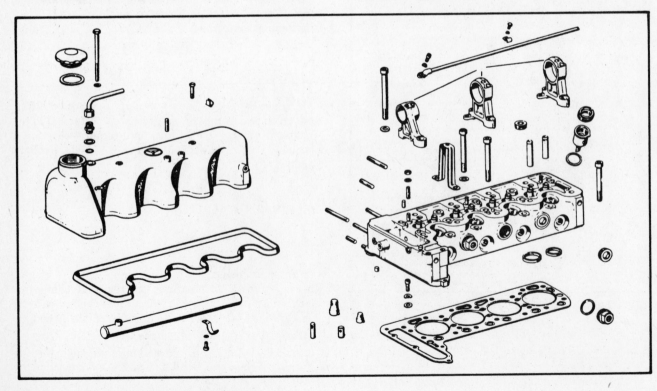

4-cylinder diesel head assembly—exploded view

13. Remove all valve guides and again inspect the cylinder head for cracks or for valve seats that cannot be refaced. Replace the cylinder head if required.

14. Considering the cylinder head to be usable, coat the new valve guides with oil and press into the cylinder head while cold, from the camshaft side.

CAUTION: *Once the guide shoulder is seated, do not use more than one ton of pressure or the guide shoulder may be broken.*

15. Ream the valve guides using proper cutting lubricant. Do not ream the valve guides oversize. Mate each valve stem to the proper sized guide. Mark the valves as required.

16. Reface the valve seats to obtain the proper seat surface for both the intake and exhaust valves.

NOTE: *Valve seats that are worn or burned can be refaced providing the correction angle and seat width are maintained. Otherwise, the cylinder head must be replaced.*

17. Reface the intake valve on a machine. Hand grind the exhaust valve only. A valve margin of no less than 0.5 mm (0.019 in.) should remain on both the intake and exhaust valve heads.

18. Coat the seats with a fine grinding compound and lap the valves to the seats, to insure correct valve to seat contact. When finished, remove all traces of the grinding compound from the valves and seats.

19. Install the valves into their respective guides and install the lower spring seats.

20. Install the valve guide seals, using the plastic sleeve over the valve stem before installing the seal to avoid seal damage.

21. Install the valve springs, upper spring seats and with the use of the spring compressor tools, install the valve stem keepers.

22. Place the camshaft into the bearing seats, install the top bearing caps and tighten. Check the end-play of the shaft which should not exceed the generally acceptable maximum of 0.15 mm (0.006 in.).

NOTE: *Do not install the cam followers. This will insure freedom of movement when checking the end play.*

23. Remove the bearing caps and the camshaft. Install the cam followers in their respective bores. Reinstall the camshaft and the bearing caps in the following order.
    a. Lubricate the bearing seats, journals and the contact areas of the caps.
    b. The cam lobes for the Number One cylinder must face upward.
    c. Bearing caps Numbers 2 and 3 must be installed offset and tightened alternately and diagonally.
    d. Install the Number 1 and 4 bearing caps and tighten in the same manner as Numbers 2 and 3.
    e. Torque all bearing caps to 20 Nm (14 ft-lbs).

24. Install the combustion chamber insert. The insert is held in place by a groove and a retainer.

25. Install the glow plugs and the injectors. Install new heat shields between the cylinder head and the injectors.

Installation

1. Using cylinder head guide pins, install the head on the engine block. Install the head bolts and torque them to the proper specification and sequence.

2. Continue the installation in the reverse order of the removal procedure.

3. Fill the radiator with the proper grade and type solution. Start the engine and check for leaks.

ROCKER ARM

Removal and Installation

Rocker arms on diesel engines can only be removed as a unit with the respective rocker arm blocks.

1. Detach the connecting rod for the venturi control unit from the bearing bracket lever and remove the bearing bracket from the rocker arm cover.

2. Remove the air vent line from the rocker arm cover and remove the rocker arm cover.

3. Remove the stretchbolts from the rocker arm blocks and remove the blocks with the rocker arms. Turn the crankshaft in each case so that the camshaft does not put any load on the rocker arms.

NOTE: *Turn the crankshaft with a socket wrench on the crankshaft pulley bolt. Do not rotate the engine by turning the camshaft sprocket.*

4. Before installing the rocker arms, check the sliding surfaces of the ball cup and rocker arms. Replace any defective parts.

5. To install, assemble the rocker arm blocks and insert new stretchbolts.

6. Tighten the stretchbolts. In each case, position the camshaft so that there is no load on the rocker arms. See the previous NOTE.

7. Check to be sure that the tension clamps have engaged with the notches of the rocker arm blocks.

8. Adjust the valve clearance.

9. Reinstall the rocker arm cover, air vent line, and bearing bracket for the reverse lever. Attach the connecting rod for the venturi control unit to the reversing lever.

10. Make sure that during acceleration, the control cable can move freely without binding.

11. Start the engine and check the rocker arm cover for leaks.

INTAKE MANIFOLD

Removal and Installation

1. Remove the air cleaner assembly.

2. Remove all hoses and supports from the intake manifold.

3. Remove the intake manifold retaining bolts. Remove the unit from the vehicle.

4. Installation is the reverse of removal. Torque the retaining bolts to 25 Nm (18 ft-lbs).

EXHAUST MANIFOLD

Removal and Installation

1. Disconnect the front exhaust pipe at the flange.
2. Remove all hoses and supports where necessary to gain access to the exhaust manifold.
3. Remove the exhaust manifold retaining bolts. Remove the assembly from the vehicle.
4. Installation is the reverse of removal. Torque the attaching bolts to 25 Nm (18 ft-lbs).

OIL PAN

Removal and Installation

1. Raise the vehicle on the hoist and support it safely.
2. Drain the engine oil.
3. Suspend the engine using Mercedes-Benz engine carrier #107589026100.
4. Remove the front axle.
5. Remove the power steering pump and carrier from the vehicle.
6. Remove the oil pan retaining bolts. Remove the pan from the vehicle.
7. Installation is the reverse of removal. Fill the vehicle with the proper grade and type engine oil. Lower the vehicle from the hoist, start the engine and check for leaks.

CAMSHAFT

Removal and Installation

When the camshaft is replaced, be sure the rocker arms are also replaced.

1. Remove the valve cover.
2. Remove the chain tensioner.
3. Remove the rocker arms.
4. Set the crankshaft at TDC for No. 1 cylinder and be sure that the camshaft timing marks are aligned.
5. Hold the camshaft and loosen the cam gear bolt. Remove the cam gear and wire it securely so that the chain does not lose tension nor slip down into the chain case.
6. Remove the camshaft.
7. Installation is the reverse of removal. Be sure to check that the valve timing marks align when No. 1 cylinder is at TDC. Check the valve clearance.

OIL PUMP

Removal and Installation

1. Raise the vehicle on a hoist and support it safely.
2. Remove the engine oil pan.
3. Remove the oil pump retaining bolts and remove the oil pump assembly from the vehicle.
4. Installation is the reverse of removal.

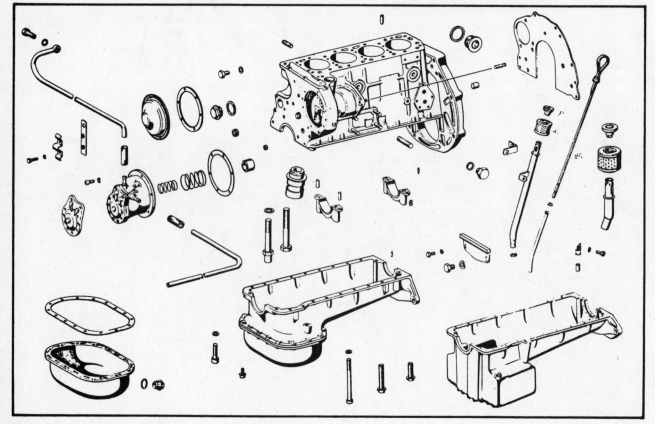

Cylinder block and related parts

WATER PUMP

Mercedes-Benz passenger car engines are all equipped with closed, pressurized, water cooling systems. Care should be exercised when dealing with the cooling system. Always turn the radiator cap to the first notch and allow the pressure to decrease before completely removing the cap.

Removal and Installation

1. Drain the water from the radiator.
2. Loosen the radiator shell and remove the radiator.
3. Remove the fan with the coupling and set it aside in an upright position.
4. Loosen the belt around the water pump pulley and remove the belt.
5. Remove the bolts from the harmonic balancer and remove the balancer and pulley.
6. Unbolt and remove the water pump.
7. Installation is the reverse of removal. Tighten the belt and fill the cooling system.

PEUGEOT DIESEL ENGINE

The Peugeot diesel engine is a four cylinder, in-line engine of the camshaft-in-block design. The crankshaft is supported by five main bearings. The engine is lubricated by a gear-type oil pump and a full-flow oiling system. The cooling system incorporates a belt driven water pump and a thermostatically controlled electric fan. The Peugeot diesel engine is designed to operate on No. 2 diesel fuel and uses Bosch fuel injection components. A pre-glow position is provided in the starting system to preheat the glow plugs for easier cold starting.

Peugeot diesels (of the same basic design) have been available in three versions: 1948cc/50 hp, 2112 cc/60 hp, and 2304 cc/70 hp for the XD88, XD90, and the XD2, respectively.

ENGINE TUNE-UP

Compression Test

1. The engine must be at normal operating temperature. Remove all of the fuel injectors.
2. Move the injection pump stop control to the "cut-off" position.
3. Connect a compression gauge to the first cylinder. Crank the engine for approximately four seconds (cranking speed must be at least 300 r.p.m.).
4. Repeat Step 3 for all cylinders. Compression pressure for all cylinders should be 362 psi. Cylinder compressions should not vary over 10% between cylinders. Remove the compression gauge and reinstall the fuel injectors.

Valve Adjustment

1. Remove the rocker cover. The valves must be adjusted in the sequence shown in the accompanying valve adjustment diagram.
2. To attain the necessary valve clearance (as listed in the valve specifications chart at the beginning of this section), loosen the rocker arm adjusting screw locknut and turn the adjusting screw the required amount.

Injection Timing
Engine Preparation (W/Pump Removed)

1. Bring the #1 cylinder to the top dead center (TDC) position.
2. Compress the #4 exhaust valve spring using Peugeot tool #8.0105 or its equivalent. Slide the #4 exhaust valve rocker arm towards the rear of the engine with the valve side of the rocker arm facing upwards.

NOTE: *Do not change the position of the adjusting screw or the locknut.*

3. Remove the #4 exhaust valve spring. Make sure that the valve moves freely then allow the valve to rest on the piston.

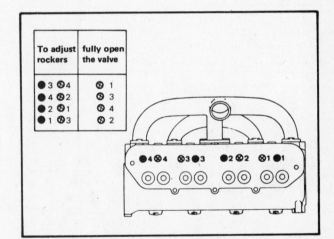

Rocker arm (valve clearance) adjusting sequence

Removing the exhaust valve spring

4. Remove the plug connector bar and the No. 2 and 4 cylinder plugs. Install a dial indicator above the #4 exhaust valve and set the indicator stem directly on the top of the valve stem (the indicator stem should be in line with the centerline of the valve stem to attain correct indicator readings). The indicator will read piston movement; actually using the exhaust valve as an extension. After finding an appropriate position for the indicator, lock the indicator attaching apparatus and "zero" the indicator dial.

5. Rotate the crankshaft counterclockwise 4 dial indicator revolutions.

6. Very slowly rotate the crankshaft clockwise until a reading of 1.40 mm (for the AR5, 7 or 8 injection pump) or 1.46 mm (for the AR10 or 12 injection pump) is obtained.

NOTE: *Leave the dial indicator in place on the engine; it will be utilized in a later procedure. Do not change the position or the reading of the indicator.*

Injection Pump Preparation for Timing with the Engine (Bosch EP/VM Injection Pump)

1. Obtain a Peugeot injection timing tool #6.0168 or its equivalent. Insert the feeler probe of the special tool into the pump body and attach the tool securely to the pump.

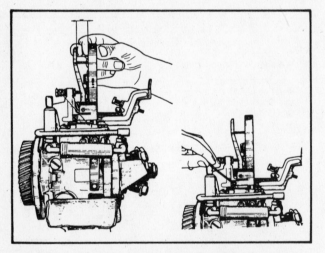

Installing the injection pump timing tool (EP/VM pump)

2. The distance between the feeler arm and the dial indicator mounting arm should be 20 mm. Mount a dial indicator (designed to be used with the timing tool) onto the indicator mounting arm of the timing tool. Check that the pump, feeler arm and the indicator move freely.

3. If the engine uses a chain driven injection pump, align the double width tooth of the pump gear along the axis of the #4 cylinder outlet coupling. If the engine uses a gear driven injection pump, align the timing mark of the pump gear with the axis of the outlet coupling marked with a "D".

4. Set the dial indicator to zero in the bottom dead center (BDC) range. Rotate the pump drive gear a very slight amount in each direction. The indicator reading should remain at zero.

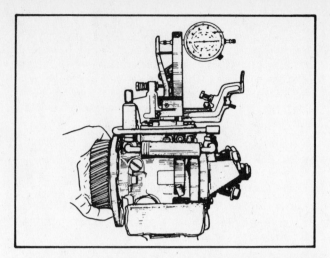

Mounting the dial indicator on the timing tool (EP/VM pump)

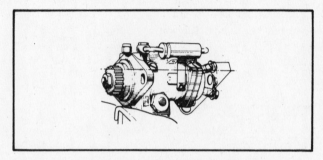

Aligning the pump gear with the outlet coupling (chain driven EP/VM pump)

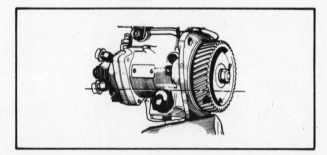

Aligning the pump gear with the outlet coupling (gear driven EP/VM pump)

5. Rotate the pump gear slowly in the direction of normal rotation. Stop as soon as the needle of the indicator begins to register the start of the upstroke (approx. 0.02 mm). The injection pump is now prepared for installation.

Bosch EP/VA and EP/VE Injection Pumps

1. On the EP/VA injection pump, remove the deferred injection accumulator.

2. Look through the hole located in the center of the outlet coupling cluster and identify the timing groove. Rotate the driveshaft of the pump to align the timing groove with the outlet coupling marked with a "B".

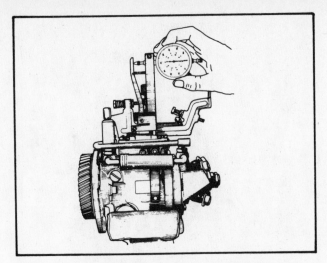

Setting the dial indicator in the BDC range (EP/VM pump)

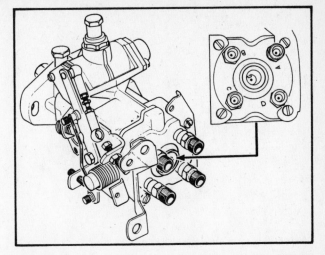

Removing the deferred injection accumulator (EP/VM pump)

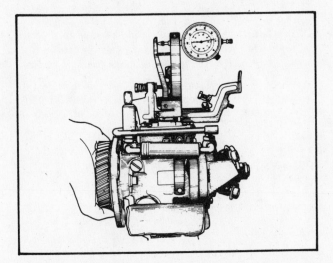

Registering the upstroke of the pump (EP/VM pump)

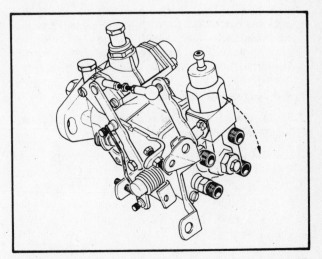

Aligning the timing groove with the outlet coupling (exc. EP/VM pump)

3. Install the dial indicator support (Peugeot tool #8.0117F or its equivalent). Attach the proper feeler extension to a dial indicator and fit the indicator to the injection pump. The injection pump is now prepared for installation.

Installing and Timing the Pump on the Engine

1. Using Peugeot tool #6.0168 or its equivalent, position the pump onto the engine as follows:
   a. For a chain driven injection pump, align the double width tooth of the pump drive gear with the hub.
   b. For a gear driven injection pump, rotate the pump drive gear slightly outward and engage with the mating gear.

2. When the injector pump is engaged with the drive mechanism (chain or gear), install the pump mounting bolts loosely and turn the injection pump as necessary (by means of the slotted bolt holes) to obtain the following pump lift reading on the pump mounted indicator.

Bosch Pump Model	Pump Lift
EP/VM AR5 and AR 7	0.38 mm
EP/VM AR8, AR10, AR12	0.55 mm
EP/VA	0.65 mm
EP/VE	0.50 mm

3. Tighten the pump mounting screws.

NOTE: *For models equipped with a gear driven injection pump, if there is not enough spacing in the pump mounting bolt hole slots to attain the proper pump lift reading, the injection pump drive gear teeth are incorrectly meshed by at least one tooth. If this situation occurs, the pump must be removed, retimed and reinstalled, in that order.*

4. The setting should be rechecked at this point, Make sure that the engine mounted indicator indicates that the piston is still at TDC.

5. Rotate the crankshaft counterclockwise 7 dial indicator revolutions.

6. As the indicator needle nears the end of the 7th revolution, check that the pump mounted indicator has

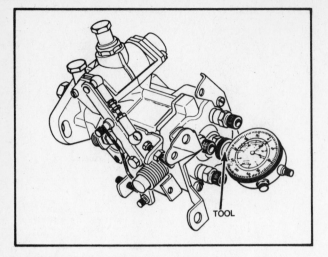

Installing the dial indicator (exc. EP/VM pump)

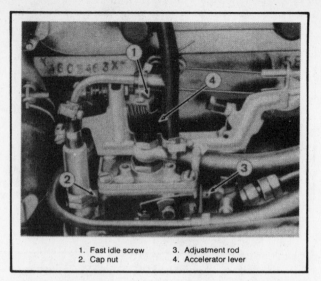

| 1. Fast idle screw | 3. Adjustment rod |
| 2. Cap nut | 4. Accelerator lever |

Idle adjustment

stabilized in the BDC range. Check the pump mounted indicator reading. Slowly rotate the crankshaft clockwise and check that the piston position and the pump lift correspond to the setting for the particular model of pump being used. Settings are listed in Step 2.

7. Remove the dial indicators.

NOTE: *On models equipped with the EP/VA type pump, install the deferred injection accumulator.*

8. Install the exhaust valve spring, retainer, split locks and the rocker arm.

9. Install the rear injection pump mounting bracket.

10. Check the valve clearances and adjust as necessary.

11. Reconnect any cables or wiring that had been previously disconnected.

Injector Pressure

Injector pressure is determined by the thickness of the washer(s) between the injector cap nut and the pressure setting spring. Adjustments and specifications associated with injector pressure are covered in the Injection Nozzle section.

Idle Speed Adjustment

1. Bring the engine to normal operating temperature and disconnect the accelerator cable.

2. Loosen the locknut and turn the fast idle screw in approximately 3 turns. Do not use the fast idle screw to adjust the low idle.

3. Hold the adjustment rod and loosen the cap nut.

4. Turn the adjustment rod to adjust the idle speed. Hold the adjustment rod and tighten the cap nut after the adjustment is complete.

5. Recheck the idling r.p.m.

6. Turn the fast idle screw out until the engine speed increases.

7. Turn the fast idle screw in exactly one full turn and tighten the locknut.

NOTE: *About 1 mm free-play should exist so that when the engine is throttled from the fast idle position, the engine speed will not actually increase for a moment.*

8. Connect the accelerator cable and check that full movement of the accelerator pedal results in complete depression of the accelerator lever at the injection pump.

FUEL SYSTEM

Injection Pump Removal

1. Disconnect the negative battery cable at the battery.

2. Turn the ignition switch to the "on" position.

3. Disconnect the stop, fast idle, and accelerator controls.

4. Disconnect the fuel return hose and the fuel inlet line at the injection pump.

5. Disconnect the injection lines at the injection pump and the injectors. Remove the injection line cluster.

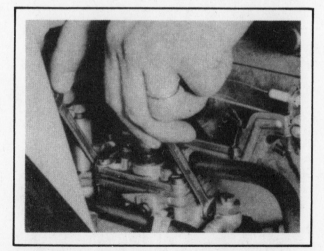

Holding the adjustment rod and loosening the cap nut

6. Remove the rear injection pump support from the engine.

7. For engines with a chain driven injection pump, remove the two pump-to-bearing support retaining screws. For engines with a gear driven injection pump, remove the two pump intermediate flange-to-timing gear housing retaining screws.

8. Move the injection pump backwards, pivot it towards the engine, and remove.

The injection pump and the engine must both be re-timed to accurately reinstall the injection pump. Refer to the Injection Timing section for the proper procedure.

Overhaul

Should an injection pump malfunction occur, the injection pump assembly should be replaced with either a new unit from the manufacturer or a rebuilt unit from a Bosch distributor.

INJECTION NOZZLE REMOVAL

1. Disconnect the negative battery cable at the battery.

2. Clean the portion of the cylinder head surrounding each injector.

3. Remove the injection and return lines.

4. Remove the injector.

Installation

1. Replace the wave washer and the copper seal if required.

2. Position the injector but do not tighten.

3. Carefully position the injection lines so as to prevent abrasion with any engine compartment component.

4. Lightly tighten the injection line couplings, first at the injection pump, then at the injector(s).

5. Tighten the injection line couplings to 11 ft-lbs (14.9 Nm) and reconnect the return line(s).

CAUTION: *Should fuel leakage occur at a coupling, loosen the coupling and retighten to specifications. Do not tighten the coupling further.*

Overhaul

Overhaul of this type of injector requires only a careful disassembly, inspection and a thorough cleaning.

Disassembly

Disassemble the injector by removing the parts in the following order:

1. Cap nut

2. Adjusting shims

3. Spring

4. Pushrod

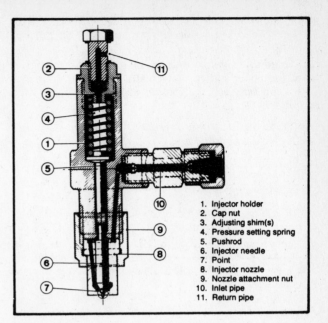

1. Injector holder
2. Cap nut
3. Adjusting shim(s)
4. Pressure setting spring
5. Pushrod
6. Injector needle
7. Point
8. Injector nozzle
9. Nozzle attachment nut
10. Inlet pipe
11. Return pipe

Fuel injector

5. Nozzle attachment nut

6. Nozzle

7. Needle

CAUTION: *Be especially careful when handling the needle. If the needle is dropped, it is no longer fit for service and must be replaced.*

When clamping the injector in a vise, be sure to use soft-faced jaws to prevent damage to the injector. Each injector should be cleaned separately to avoid mixing parts. Use only diesel fuel to clean the injectors and always keep a thin film of diesel fuel on each part to avoid corrosion. Do not use any type of abrasive compound or an injector part. No attempt should be made to lap any surface of this type of injector. Do not use metal instruments of any kind to clean carbon from any injector part. Use wood only.

Assembly

1. Insert the needle into the nozzle and make sure that the needle moves freely.

2. Assemble the injector nozzle onto the injector with the nozzle attachment nut. Tighten the nozzle attachment nut to 43–58 ft-lbs (58.3–78.6 Nm).

3. Install the plunger, the spring, and the adjustment washer(s).

4. Install the cap nut with a new copper seal. Tighten the cap nut to 22 ft-lbs (29.8 Nm).

Checks and Adjustments

OPENING PRESSURE

1. Attach the injector securely to an injector tester. A gauge reading is necessary for this test.

2. Depress the tester lever and gradually raise the pressure. Note the pressure gauge reading at the point of injector opening.

3. Should the opening pressure be too low (as compared to the specification chart listings), install a thicker washer between the pressure setting spring and the cap nut.

NOTE: *Every 0.10 mm increase in washer thickness will raise the opening pressure approximately 70 psi.*

4. Assemble the injector and retest.

SPRAY PATTERN

1. Attach the injector securely to an injector tester. A gauge reading is not required for this test.

2. Pump the tester lever quickly (approximately 4–6 strokes per second). The spray pattern should be sharply defined, evenly atomized, and have a narrow cone-type shape.

NOISE

1. Attach the injector securely to an injector tester. A gauge reading is not required for this test.

2. Pump the tester lever at a rate of about 1–2 strokes per second. This type of injector should produce a distinct "humming" noise. If a "hum" is not noticed, another problem most likely exists with the injector (such as incorrect opening pressure, pattern, etc.).

LEAKAGE

1. Attach the injector securely to an injector tester. A gauge reading is necessary for this test.

2. Depress the tester lever and gradually raise the pressure to approximately 285 psi below the injector opening pressure, and hold this pressure for 10 seconds. Any dripping of fuel from the injector is to be considered unsatisfactory, although a very slight amount of seepage (wetness around the nozzle) is considered normal.

CYLINDER HEAD

Removal

1. It is not necessary to remove the engine to take off the cylinder head. However, the engine must be cold, to lessen the chance of head warpage. Drain the cooling system using the radiator petcock as well as the block drain located between the oil filter and the dipstick.

2. Remove the air filter assembly, the water hoses and the vacuum pump inlet pipe, where so equipped.

3. On models so equipped, remove the vacuum pump and belt. Remove the water pump belt and the idler pulley.

4. If equipped with air conditioning, disconnect the bracket at the firewall. Do not disconnect the air conditioning pipe itself. Disconnect the small tube on the side of the cylinder head. This carries oil to the rocker shaft. Disconnect the exhaust at the flange.

Removing the cylinder head—do not pry between the mating surfaces

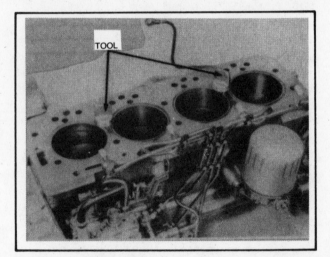

Retaining the cylinder liners

5. Disconnect the fuel injection pipes from the top of the injectors and remove the fuel return pipes from their unions on the side of the injectors. Disconnect any wires that will interfere with removing the head.

6. Remove the rocker cover. Remove the rocker shaft assembly. Take note that there is an oil seal at the base of the oil inlet pipe. Remove the pushrods carefully with a twisting motion so that the tappets will not be stuck to the ends of the pushrods and pulled from their bores.

7. Remove the injector holders and loosen the head bolts. Lift off the cylinder head. Peugeot has a special tool (#0.0149) that acts as a long handle that rocks the head to one side to break the seal since the head may be difficult to lift. However, do not insert a prying tool between the head and block or the gasket surfaces will be damaged.

8. If the engine is mounted in a stand or remains in the vehicle so that the crankshaft can be rotated, it is possible for the cylinder liners to become loosened. To

prevent this, Peugeot has special tools (#8.0110F) that screw into two head bolt holes to hold the liners in place. A substitute might be made using metric bolts, spacers and large washers.

Overhaul

1. With the cylinder head secure in a holding fixture, remove the intake and exhaust manifolds, the preheater plugs, the water pump, the valve springs and related parts. The valves and springs must be marked or otherwise kept separate so that they can be replaced in the proper places.

2. Inspect the head before any further work is done. Look for obvious cracks, stripped bolt holes or broken studs. If satisfied that the head is in reusable condition, clean thoroughly in solvent.

CAUTION: *The valve springs are protected against rust and corrosion by a special synthetic varnish finish. DO NOT clean them in solvent. Rinse clean with diesel fuel only.*

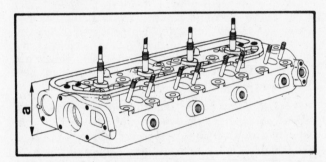

Measure the cylinder head thickness illustrated as dimensions "a"

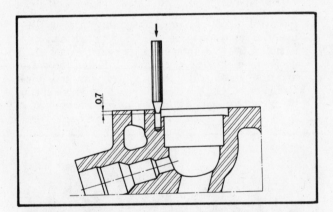

Driving the swirl chamber wedge pins into the head (no more than 0.7mm)

3. A wire brush and a power drill can be used to decarbonize the combustion chambers, valve heads and guides. Check and clean the exhaust ports. Be careful not to damage the cylinder head with any sharp tool or scrapers. Clean all parts well and dry with compressed air.

4. The cylinder head should be checked for warpage. This operation requires some care. With the cylinder head secured, lay a straightedge along the face of the head. Measure with a feeler gauge for distortion. The head should be measured along its length, width and diagonally. Be careful that the straightedge does not touch the swirl chambers. The swirl chambers normally protrude from 0.000 to 0.0012 inch (0.0–0.03 mm). The maximum out of true, or distortion allowed is 0.006 inch (0.15 mm).

5. The valves may be reground or lapped with a power driven grinder to save time and to produce a more uniform finish. However, be sure to use only fine grinding compound. An oil base paste is recommended. After lapping, remove all traces of the compound, cleaning the valve guides carefully with a small brush. Check the valve seats for an even color. The seating of the valves can be checked with blueing. Proper valve seating is absolutely important for the proper operation of this or any other engine.

6. If the cylinder head needs to be cut, or surfaced, the following points should be followed. Surface the head only if distortion exceeds 0.006 inch (0.15 mm). Before machining, check the overall thickness of the head. A large micrometer will be required. Measure

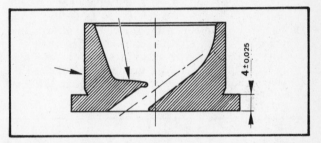

Check the condition of the swirl chambers at the points illustrated (arrows)

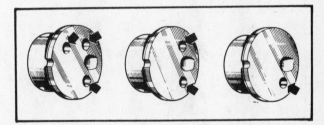

Identification of the various swirl chambers (see text)

from the rocker cover gasket surface to the head gasket surface. The normal head thickness should be 3.600 ± 0.006 inches (90 ± 0.15 mm). The maximum amount that can be cut is 0.020 inch (0.5 mm). Under no circumstances must the overall thickness of the head be less than 3.574 inches (89.35 mm), or the engine operation will be seriously affected. If the head must be cut, the swirl chambers must be removed, as well as the injector hold-down studs and the rocker shaft studs.

7. To remove the swirl chambers for either head surfacing or chamber replacement, first locate the wedge pins that lock the swirl chambers to the head. With a punch or tapered drift pin, drive the wedge pins carefully into the head. The hole in the head is a blind one, so only tap the pin in just enough to unlock the swirl chamber, which would be about 0.028 inch (0.7 mm).

8. Mark the swirl chambers 1 to 4 so that they will be returned to their original locations. With a brass drift, drive the chambers out. Tap lightly so that the chambers will not be damaged.

CAUTION: *Due to the design of the chambers, the drift bears on the chamber in an offset manner. Therefore, often the chamber may stick or twist, jamming it in the head. Do not force it. Turn the head over and straighten the chamber by tapping it back in place with a soft-face mallet. Use care in this operation to avoid damage to the swirl chamber, the head or both. Remove the wedge pins from the head.*

9. The swirl chambers should be checked carefully. The inner lip or gas outlet, must not be cracked or damaged, as might happen during the removal process. Check the outer portion of the chamber for cracks. Measure the flange. The minimum thickness is 0.160 ± 0.008 inch (4 ± 0.025 mm). If doubtful about the condition of the swirl chamber, replace it. Note, however, that the swirl chamber may be cracked slightly around the fuel outlet. These cracks will not affect the operation of the engine, and therefore the chambers can be reused.

10. The swirl chambers can be reinstalled after following these precautions. Remove any dirt, carbon or burrs from the swirl chambers and the chamber bores in the head. Make sure that the flange on the swirl chamber and its mating surface in the head are both clean.

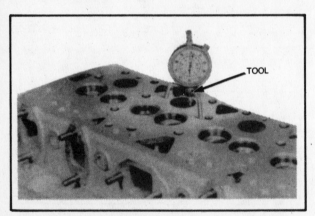

Checking the swirl chamber installation

11. Insert the chambers in the head in their original locations. Do not use a hammer to force them to fit. Tap in with a soft face mallet. The swirl chambers must be a tight fit. If not, rebore the recesses and fit oversize chambers. Note that the swirl chambers for the XD-XDP 88/90 engines and those uses in the XD-XD2P engines are NOT interchangeable, due to their difference in volume. To identify swirl chambers, the 88 engine used chambers with 1 recess, the 90 engine uses 2 recesses, while the XD2 engine uses 3 recesses or cavities in the face of the chamber. Also, 1st and 2nd oversize repair chambers are identified by the Number 1 or 2 stamped in the center. To fit oversize chambers, the recesses for the chamber flange is machined out from its original size of 1.4036 inch (35.09 mm) to 1.4200 inch (35.50 mm).

12. Once the swirl chamber is installed, it should be checked for flatness. A dial indicator can be used. The Peugeot factory tool (#0.0141) allows the indicator to sit above the chamber. After zeroing the indicator, take a reading at a number of points around the chamber. The maximum difference between the highest and lowest points must not be more than 0.0012 inch (0.03 mm), nor may it protrude from the head more than this amount. If it does protrude more than this figure, the chamber must be removed and the back side of the chamber machined on a lathe to correct it. Note that there should be a clearance between the back side of the chamber and the bottom of the chamber bore in the head. This clearance should be held to between 0.004 inch (0.1 mm) and 0.020 inch (0.5 mm). From the reading obtained with the dial indicator, subtract 0.0012 inch (0.03 mm). This difference is the amount to be removed from the two faces of the chamber. By machining both surfaces of the chamber, the clearance of 0.004–0.020 inch (0.1–0.5 mm) can be retained.

13. If the head has been cut or surfaced, or the valves ground, the depth of the valves should be checked. With a dial indicator or depth micrometer, check that the depth of the valves is from 0.030–0.046 inch (0.75–1.15 mm). If the depth is insufficient, the valve seats must be recut. If the depth is too much, new valves must be installed. If, after new valves are installed, there is still too much clearance, new valve seats will have to be installed.

NOTE: *All of the above checking and machine work, where required, is a time-consuming operation, requiring skill and precision on the part of the technician. Nevertheless, it is important and should not be sidestepped or short-cut. This is required to hold the high compression pressures required by a diesel engine to operate properly.*

14. After all the above work has been performed, the cylinder head should again be cleaned, then reassembled. Begin by lubricating the valve stems with a good assembly lube or engine oil. Install the valves and the valve train parts. Start with the lower spring cup first, the oil seal next, the valve spring, the upper spring cup and new valve keys, or locks.

Rocker shaft oil feed pipe seal

Installation

1. Make certain that the head and block gasket surfaces are clean. Obtain new washers for use under the cylinder head bolts.

2. Run an 11 × 150 metric tap through the cylinder head bolt holes. This cleans the corrosion and rust and any other obstruction so that the bolts will seat properly and also give a true torque reading. The holes must be free from oil and water. Clean the bolt threads with a wire brush and lightly lubricate with clean engine oil.

3. Note that on the XD2/XD2P engines, there are several head gaskets that can be used, depending on the amount that the piston protrudes above the top of the block, or deck surface. If the piston protrudes 0.0336 inch (0.84 mm) or less, use the 0.0632 inch (1.58 mm) head gasket which will compress to 0.0592 inch (1.48 mm). There is an identification tab on the gasket that has two notches. If the piston protrudes more than 0.0336 inch (0.84 mm) use the 0.068 inch (1.70 mm) head gasket which will compress to 0.064 inch (1.60 mm). There should be three notches on the gasket identification tab.

4. The head gasket is installed dry, with the larger crimped area toward the engine block. If necessary, guide pins can be made from metric bolts of the proper size and appropriate length.

5. Install the manifolds and preheater plugs into the heat. Install the water pump using new gaskets.

6. Note that there are three different length head bolts. Measure and mark them and separate them into three groups. The six bolts that are 4.720 inch (118 mm) long can be called group "1". The seven bolts that are 4.340 inch (108.5 mm) long can be called group "2". The eight bolts that are 3.660 inch (91.5 mm) long can be called group "3".

7. Carefully lower the cylinder head into place. Check that the gasket has not shifted out of place. Install the head bolts. Group "1", the longest, go in the row in the middle. Group "2" bolts, the middle size, go in the rows closest to the intake manifold. Group "3" bolts, the shortest, go in the row on the injector side of the head.

8. The bolts should be torqued in the following manner. On the XD/XDP 88/90 engines, tighten the bolts in sequence, first to 29 ft-lbs (39 Nm) then, in the same sequence, loosen each bolt a quarter turn, then tighten to a torque of 51 ft-lbs (69 Nm). On the XD2/XD2P engines, tighten the bolts in sequence, first to 33 ft-lbs (45 Nm), then in the same sequence, loosen each bolt a quarter turn, then tighten to a torque of 47 ft-lbs (64 Nm).

9. Install the injector holders using new seals. Install the pushrods, with a light coat of engine oil. Fit a new oil seal on the feed pipe to the rocker shafts, and install the rocker shaft assembly.

10. Torque the rocker shaft nuts to 36 ft-lbs (49 Nm). Insert a feeler gauge on the outside of the intake rockers on No. 1 and No. 4 cylinders. The amount of side-play should be between 0.014–0.022 inch (0.35–0.55 mm). If the side-play is out of specification, thrust washers are available to adjust the side-play.

11. Adjust the valves carefully to the clearances listed in the valve specification chart.

12. Install all hoses, belts and wires. Connect the oil feed line to the side of the head.

13. After the cylinder head has been installed, the following factory recommendations should be followed.

    a. After driving the vehicle between 30 and 60 miles (50–100 km) allow the engine to cool down completely, at least six hours minimum. Then retighten the cylinder head bolts to the specified torque.

    b. Do this by loosening each bolt in the same sequence that they were tightened, backing off one quarter turn, then tightening to the specified torque. Repeat this operation a second time.

    c. After 600 miles (1000 km) of operation, repeat the tightening operation, this time adjusting the valves to 0.008 inch (0.20 mm) on the intake side, and 0.012 inch (0.30 mm) on the exhaust side.

    d. It is advisable to instruct the vehicle operator not to fully load the engine prior to the retightening operation, to be done at 600 miles (1000 km).

ROCKER ARM

Removal

1. Remove the rocker arm cover.

2. Remove the four nuts that hold the rocker assembly to the head. Take note that there is an oil seal at the base of the oil inlet pipe.

Overhaul

1. Clean the rocker arm assembly in solvent.

2. Hold the rocker arm assembly in a vise with soft jaws by clamping lightly on the center fitting from the sides.

3. Remove the end bearings, the rockers, the shaft supports, springs and washers. Take note of the order in which the parts are removed.

4. Remove the locating screw on the center fitting, then remove the shaft. Do not lose the copper washer that should be on the screw.

5. Carefully inspect all parts for wear. Check the adjusting screws for wear or damage. Replace any rockers if they show signs of galling or binding. An oil stone can be used to smooth any rocker tips if the faces are not marked excessively. However, *do not grind rocker faces.*

6. Assemble the rocker parts by sliding the shaft into the center fitting. Use care since this is a lubrication fitting, that is, the lubrication holes should be on the same side as the attachment hole in the fitting. Make sure that the threaded hole in the fitting is perfectly lined up with its attachment hole in the shaft (with the chamfered side facing the shaft locating screw).

7. Install and tighten the shaft locating screw. Be sure to install the copper washer under the screw head.

8. Hold the center fitting and shaft in a vise with soft jaws, clamping lightly on the center fitting from the sides.

9. Coat the shaft lightly with clean engine oil and install the rocker shaft parts.

10. Work from the center out, in both directions.
    a. First install the backing washers on either side of the center fitting.
    b. Install the weak springs on both sides, two rockers, two inner shaft supports and two more rocker arms, again, one to each side of the center fitting.
    c. Install the heavier springs on each side, and two more rockers.
    d. Install the end supports and the outer rockers.

11. Install a new oil seal on the feed pipe to the rocker shaft, and install the rocker shaft assembly.

12. Torque the rocker shaft nuts to 36 ft-lbs (49 Nm). Insert a feeler gauge on the outside of the intake rockers on No. 1 and No. 4 cylinders. The amount of side play should be between 0.014–0.022 inch (0.35–0.55 mm). If the side play is out of specification, thrust washers are available to adjust the side play.

13. Adjust the valves carefully to the clearances listed in the valve specification chart.

14. Install the rocker cover.

INTAKE MANIFOLD

Removal and Installation

1. Removal of the manifolds follows conventional procedure. It is recommended that the engine be cold to avoid warpage. Remove the air filter, vacuum hoses and heater hoses as equipped, depending on year and model.

2. Remove attaching parts and remove the manifold from the engine.

3. Clean all surfaces well and inspect for cracks.

4. Reverse the procedure to install. Check all hoses and fittings for leaks.

EXHAUST MANIFOLD

Removal and Installation

1. Remove the nuts and clamps retaining the exhaust pipe to the manifold. A generous application of solvent is recommended.

2. Remove the nuts holding the manifold to the head and remove the manifold from the engine.

3. Clean all surfaces well and inspect for cracks.

4. Reverse the procedure to install, using new gaskets as required. Lubricate the stud threads to allow the nuts to be drawn down evenly and to prevent breakage.

OIL PAN

Removal and Installation

The engine need not be raised to remove the oil pan. The oil pan is fastened to the engine block in a conventional manner. Removal and installation is a basic procedure that is nearly identical to any gasoline engine.

PISTONS AND CONNECTING RODS

The engine must be removed from the vehicle and the cylinder head removed from the engine. Immediately after removing the cylinder head, install two Peugeot tool #8.0110 thumb screws or their equivalents between the Numbers 1 and 2 and 3 and 4 cylinders at the top of the block to retain the cylinder liners.

CAUTION: *The cylinder liners must be securely retained.*

Remove the oil pan and the oil pump, then remove the piston and connecting rod assemblies. Carefully inspect the connecting rods, pistons and the cylinder liners for damage and replace parts as needed.

CRANKSHAFT

Removal and Installation

1. The engine must be removed from the vehicle and the cylinder head removed from the engine. Immediately after removing the cylinder head, install two Peugeot tool #8.0110 thumb screws or their equivalents between the Numbers 1 and 2 and 3 and 4 cylinders at the top of the block to retain the cylinder liners.

CAUTION: *The cylinder liners must be securely retained.*

2. Remove the oil pan and the oil pump, then mark the connecting rod caps and the connecting rods so that the caps and rods may be reassembled in their proper relationship.

3. Remove the timing cover.

4. If the engine uses a chain driven camshaft, release the chain tensioner by turning the set screw using a 3 mm Allen wrench. Loosen the eccentric rod gear fastening nut and move the pinion to its slackest position. This should allow enough slack in the timing chain to slip the chain from around the crankshaft gear during crankshaft removal.

   If the engine uses a gear drive camshaft, locate the timing marks on each of the gears. Turn the crankshaft to align the timing marks as follows: crankshaft to idler, idler to camshaft, and idler to injection pump gear. Note that these timing marks will line up correctly only once in every 22 revolutions of the crankshaft. Aligning the marks at this time (before disassembly) will save time later in the procedure.

5. Mark and remove the main bearing caps and note the markings on the thrust bearings indicating the side of

the thrust bearing which faces the crankshaft. Inspect the crankshaft, the main bearings, connecting rod bearings and the thrust bearings; replace parts as needed.

6. Installation of the crankshaft is the reverse of the removal procedure.

CAMSHAFT

Removal and Installation

CHAIN DRIVEN VERSION

1. The engine should be removed to allow easier access to various components.
2. Remove the engine cooling fan, belts, pulleys and related components necessary to gain access to both the timing and the valve lifter access covers.
3. Remove the rocker cover and the rocker shaft assembly.
4. Remove the pushrods and the valve lifter access covers. Remove the valve lifters.

CAUTION: *Keep the pushrods and lifters in order so that they may be reinstalled in their original locations.*

5. Remove the oil pan and the timing cover.
6. Release the timing chain tensioner, loosen the eccentric rod gear fastening nut and move the pinion gear to slacken the timing chain.
7. Remove the rod gear along with the rod gear eccentric and the timing chain tensioner.
8. Remove the timing chain and carefully withdraw the camshaft from the engine.

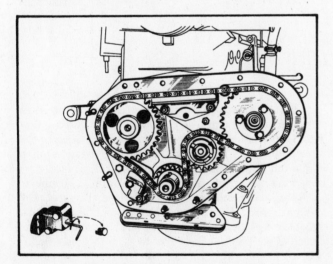

Moving the pinion gear to slacken the timing chain

Installation

1. Reinstall the camshaft and the camshaft gear.
2. Point the timing gears in approximately the following directions as viewed from the front of the engine.

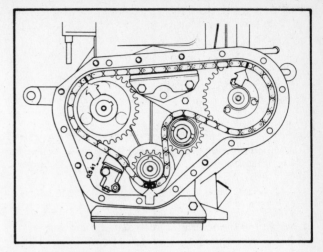

Timing mark alignment

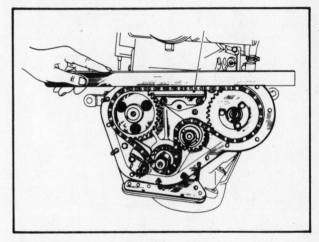

Adjusting the chain guide pad

    a. Camshaft gear timing mark is at 11:00 o'clock.
    b. Injection timing gear timing mark is at 1:00 o'clock.
    c. Crankshaft gear timing mark is at 6:00 o'clock.

3. Locate the following markings on the timing chain: two links marked with lines and one copper colored link.
4. Align the dot on the crankshaft gear with the center of the copper link. Align each line of the camshaft and injection timing gears with the respective reference lines on the timing chain as shown.
5. Rotate the idler pinion eccentric counterclockwise until the clearance between the tensioner pad and its support is from .020–.040 inches (.5–1.0 mm).
6. Tighten the eccentric fastening nut to 36 ft-lbs (48.8 Nm).
7. Turn the hex head key to the right until the tensioner pad contacts the timing chain. Screw in and lock the tensioner.
8. To adjust the chain guide pad on models so equipped, place a straightedge on the length of chain between the cam and the injection timing gears. Loosen the guide pad nuts, position the guide pad evenly against the chain and tighten the guide pad nuts.

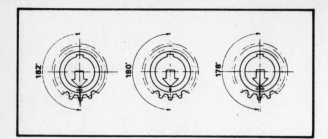

Valve timing adjustment using one of the three available crankshaft sprockets

9. Install the cylinder head and related components.

10. The valve timing must be checked any time a timing component is replaced. Check the valve timing as follows. Install the valve lifters, pushrods and the rocker shaft assembly. Remove either a glow plug or an injector from each cylinder to create a compression release. Adjust the valve clearances to the values listed in the valve specification chart. After all of the valves have been adjusted, insert a .016″ (.40 mm) feeler gauge between the intake valve stem and the rocker arm face. Slowly turn the engine by hand (with the feeler gauge installed) to determine if any interference exists between the valve and the piston. If valve to piston contact is noted, replace the crankshaft sprocket marked with three dots, with a sprocket marked with one dot (available from parts suppliers).

11. Assemble the engine in the reverse of the removal procedure, Steps One through Eight. Install the engine into the vehicle.

CYLINDER LINERS

Removal and Installation

1. The engine must be removed from the vehicle and the cylinder head removed from the engine. Remove the oil pan and the oil pump.

2. Mark the proper relationship of the connecting rods and the caps.

3. Remove the piston and connecting rod assemblies.

4. Remove the cylinder liner(s) to be replaced with Peugeot tool #0.0101 or its equivalent.

NOTE: *The cylinder liners are available only with new pistons matched to each cylinder liner. Do not interchange pistons or liners between unmatched sets.*

5. Install the new liner without the lower gaskets.

6. Retain the cylinder liners with two Peugeot tool #8.0110 thumb screws or their equivalents.

7. Check the amount of cylinder liner protrusion from the deck surface to the highest point of the cylinder liner protruding above the deck surface. Protrusion should be .012–.028 inches (.03–.07 mm).

8. Remove the thumb screws and the cylinder liners.

9. Fit a new lower gasket to each of the cylinder liners.

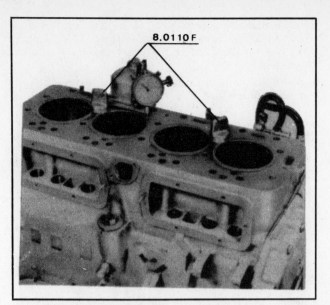

Checking cylinder liner protrusion

10. Install the cylinders and again retain them with the thumb screws.

11. Thoroughly clean and inspect the pistons and the connecting rods. Stagger the piston ring end gaps 120° apart.

12. Install the piston and connecting rod assemblies; torque the rod caps to 43 ft-lbs (58.3 Nm).

13. Install the oil pump and the oil pan.

14. Remove the liner retaining thumb screws, install the cylinder head and related components.

15. Install the engine into the vehicle.

VOLVO

The Volvo diesel is a six cylinder in-line engine which develops 82 hp at 4800 r.p.m. and 102 ft-lbs of torque at 3000 r.p.m. The piston displacement is 145 cubic inches (2383 cc). The lubrication system uses API Service SE/CC quality oil, a crankshaft-driven gear type oil pump and a full flow oil filter. The crankshaft is supported by seven main bearings, and the reciprocating assembly is both internally and externally balanced. The fuel tank capacity is 15.8 US gallons of No. 2 diesel fuel, having a minimum cetane rating of 45. Fuel is supplied to the Bosch DNO SD 193 injectors by a belt-driven Bosch VE6/10 F2400 L32 (VE6/10 F2400 L32–1 for automatic transmission models) injection pump. The cooling system uses a conventional radiator, V-belt driven cooling fan, Thermostat and a water pump driven off of the toothed camshaft drive (timing) belt. Valve actuation is performed by a belt-driven overhead camshaft which rotates on insert-type bearing halves (similar to conventional rod or main bearings). The camshaft is attached to the cylinder head with bearing caps similar in design to a conventional main bearing cap.

ENGINE TUNE-UP

Compression Test

1. Disconnect the wire at the stop valve to prevent injection during fuel system disassembly.
2. Remove the vacuum pump and the vacuum pump plunger.

NOTE: *Clean all injection line connections with compressed air.*

3. Remove the injection lines, but leave the arrangement looms intact if possible.
4. Remove the injectors using a $^{11}/_{16}$" socket. Make sure that the injector heat shields are left in place. Install a compression test adaptor (Volvo #5191 or its equivalent) and seal, and connect a high-pressure compression gauge.
5. Crank the engine and record the compression reading. Compression pressure should be 400–485 psi. Repeat Steps 4 and 5 for all cylinders. Maximum pressure variation between cylinders is 70 psi.
6. Using new heat shields, reinstall the injectors. Torque the injectors to 50 ft-lbs (70 Nm).
7. Reinstall the injection lines and torque the connections to 18 ft-lbs (25 Nm).
8. Replace the vacuum pump O-ring if necessary. Then reinstall the vacuum pump plunger and the vacuum pump.

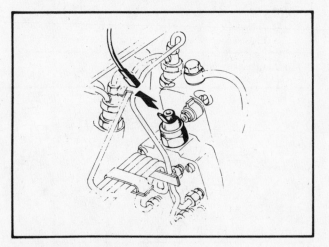

Disconnecting the stop valve

Valve Adjustment

1. Remove the valve cover. Using a $1^1/_{16}$" socket on the vibration damper bolt, turn the engine to the #1 firing position. The base circle should be contacting the valve depressor/disc assemblies. Both cam lobes should be pointed upward in equal amounts.
2. Check the valve clearance for the #1 cylinder. For a cold engine (room temperature), intake valve clearance should be .006"–.010", exhaust valve clearance should be .014"–.018". For a warm engine (approx. normal operating temperature), intake valve clearance should be .008"–.012", exhaust

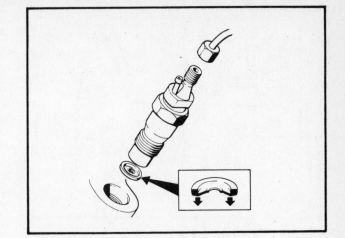

Positioning of the injector heat shields

valve clearance should be .016"–.020". No adjustment is necessary if the clearances are within these specifications.

3. When adjustment is necessary, turn the engine approx. $^1/_4$ turn after top dead center. At TDC, not enough clearance exists to sufficiently depress the valves for shim removal. Line up both the intake and exhaust valve depressors so that both notches are pointed slightly inward.
4. Depress the valve depressors with Volvo special tool #5196 or its equivalent.
5. Remove the valve depressor disc (wafer that actually contacts the cam lobe) with Volvo special tool #5195 or its equivalent.
6. Measure the thickness of the existing valve depressor disc with a micrometer, and calculate the dimension of the new disc needed to obtain the following valve clearances: cold engine—.008" intake/.016" exhaust, warm engine—.010" intake/.018" exhaust. Discs are available in thicknesses ranging from .1299" to .1673" in .002" increments. Use only new discs.
7. Coat the new disc with engine oil and install the disc with the marking side down.
8. Check the valve clearances of the remaining cylinders and adjust as necessary using Steps 2 through 7.

NOTE: *Each piston must be situated at TDC as the respective valve clearances are being checked. When setting valve clearances, always turn the engine $^1/_4$ turn after TDC.*

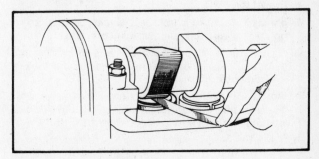

Checking the valve clearance

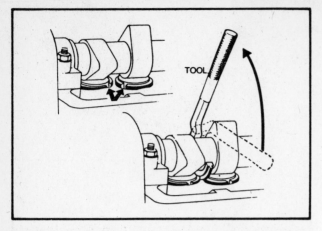

Aligning the depressor notches/depressing the depressors

9. After all the valve clearances have been checked and/or adjusted, rotate the engine several complete revolutions and recheck all the valve clearances.

10. Using a new valve cover gasket if necessary, install the valve cover and check engine operation.

Injection Timing

1. Rotate the crankshaft until the #1 cylinder is at the TDC firing position. Make sure that the flywheel and the clutch housing reference marks are aligned.

2. Loosen the cold start control cable screw (#1) which is closest to the rubber cable boot and push the lever forward.

CAUTION: *Do not loosen the control cable screw (#2) which is farthest away from the rubber cable boot.*

Turn the control cable clamp 90° and push the lever back against its stop to loosen the control cable.

3. Align the reference markings of the injection pump and the pump bracket by loosening the pump retaining screws. Tighten the screws after the alignment is completed.

4. Once again, make sure that the #1 cylinder is at TDC/firing position and that the flywheel and the clutch housing marks are aligned. Remove the timing plug which is located in the center of the injection line cluster at the injection pump.

5. Install Volvo adaptor #5194 (or its equivalent) in place of the plug. Attach a dial indicator (range of 0–3 mm/0–.160″) to the adaptor.

6. Preset the dial indicator to 2 mm (.085″).

7. Slowly rotate the crankshaft clockwise to align the pump gear and the pump bracket markings.

8. Slowly rotate the crankshaft counterclockwise until the dial indicator reaches its lowest reading. Set the dial indicator to zero.

9. Slowly rotate the crankshaft clockwise to align the flywheel and the clutch housing marks. The indicator gauge should now read .70 mm (.028″).

10. If the indicator needle reading is incorrect, loosen the injection pump retaining bolts and rotate the injection pump to obtain the correct dial indicator

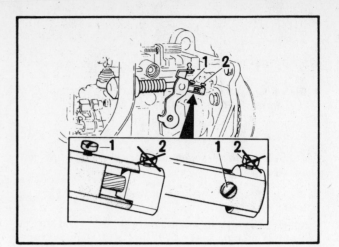

Aligning the injection pump marks

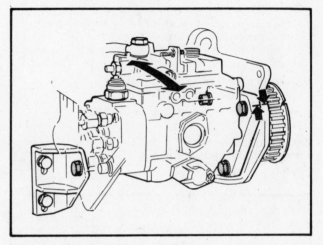

Disconnecting the cold start device

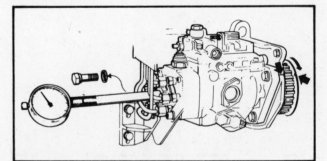

Installing the dial indicator

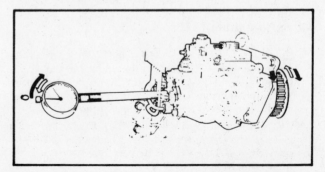

Set the dial indicator at zero after the minimum reading has been obtained

reading. After the adjustment is completed, tighten the pump bolts, remove the dial indicator and the adaptor, reinstall the timing plug (torque to 9 Nm/6.5 ft-lbs) and tighten the control cable clamp screw.

INJECTION NOZZLE

Removal and Installation

1. Disconnect the wire at the stop valve to prevent injection pump operation during fuel system disassembly.
2. Remove the vacuum pump and the vacuum pump plunger.

NOTE: *Clean all injection line connections with compressed air.*

3. Remove the injection lines, but leave the arrangement looms intact.
4. Remove the injectors using a 1¹/₁₆″ socket. Reverse the removal procedure to install. Torque the injector to 50 ft-lbs (70 Nm), and the injection line connections to 18 ft-lbs (25 Nm).

Testing

When testing the fuel injectors, pay special attention to both the opening pressure and the injector tightness. Evaluating the condition of an injector *strictly* by sound or spray pattern should be considered inaccurate. Incorrect sound or spray pattern will usually accompany another defect. In the engine, injection takes place in an environment much different than that of a workshop area. Many injectors will function properly in the engine although the sound or spray pattern may have been questionable on the bench tester.

NOTE: *Perform the testing or repair of diesel fuel system components in a well ventilated, meticulously clean area. Even the most minute particle of dirt will cause a fuel system malfunction, sometimes resulting in very costly damage. Use only diesel fuel in the injectors during testing.*

CAUTION: *Do not use gasoline in the injectors during testing. Fuel under injection pressure must not be allowed to come in contact with the skin; pressure will cause the diesel fuel to actually puncture the skin, and blood poisoning could result. Do not inhale fumes from unburned diesel fuel.*

1. Connect the injector to an injector tester. Make sure that all connections are absolutely leak-proof.
2. Check the spray pattern. Pump the injector tester lever with fast, short strokes (about 4–6 strokes per second). The spray pattern should be fairly compact and stop abruptly with no dripping.
3. Check the injection sound. Slowly depress the injector tester lever; usually a good injector will create a "whirring" or "buzzing" sound.
4. Check the injector opening pressure. Slowly depress the injector tester lever; opening pressure should be

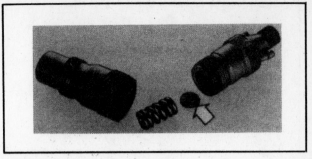

Opening pressure adjustment washer

1700–1850 psi. Perform the next test before any adjustment is made.
5. Check injector leakage. Carefully clean the injection nozzle before proceeding. Pump the injector tester to 1560 psi and hold this pressure for approx. 10 seconds. Any dripping of the injector is unacceptable, although a very slight amount of moisture can be considered normal.

Disassembly

Make sure that the outside of the injector is clean before proceeding. Carefully disassemble the injector. Do not drop the nozzle needle; if it is dropped, replacement of the needle and sleeve unit is necessary. Immerse the injector components in clean diesel fuel immediately following disassembly. Do not mix parts between the injectors. Replace any damaged injector components.

Adjustment

The washer between the spring and the upper nozzle controls the opening pressure. Washers in thicknesses ranging from .040″–.0768″ in increments of .002″ are available. Each additional .002″ increase in washer thickness will increase the opening pressure by approx. 72 psi. Adjust the pressure accordingly.

Assembly

Any new parts that are used must be thoroughly washed in clean gasoline and immersed in diesel fuel before injector assembly. Assemble the injector, torque to 50 ft-lbs (70 Nm) and retest.

Injector Pressure

Injector pressure is determined by the thickness of the washer between the spring and the upper nozzle retainer. Each 0.05 mm increase in washer thickness will increase the injector opening pressure approximately seven (7) psi. Procedures pertaining to injector service can be found in the injector nozzle section.

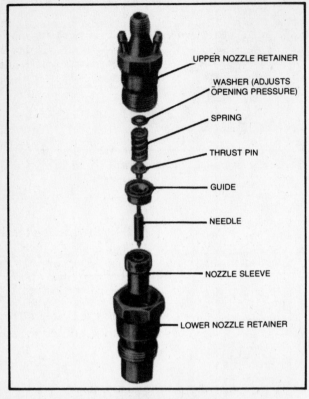

UPPER NOZZLE RETAINER

WASHER (ADJUSTS OPENING PRESSURE)

SPRING

THRUST PIN

GUIDE

NEEDLE

NOZZLE SLEEVE

LOWER NOZZLE RETAINER

Exploded view of the injector assembly

High idle adjustment screw (arrow)

Low idle adjustment screw (arrow)

IDLE SPEED ADJUSTMENT

1. Bring the engine to normal operating temperature and connect a tachometer to the engine.
2. Check the low idle speed which should be 800 ± 80 r.p.m. Adjust the low idle as necessary by turning the adjustment nut closest to the injectors.
3. The maximum r.p.m. adjustment nut is located opposite the low idle adjustment nut, farthest away from the injectors. Open the throttle completely and set the maximum engine r.p.m. which should be 5200 ± 100 r.p.m.

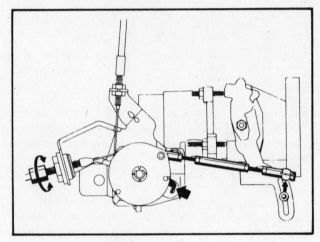

Adjusting the accelerator cable

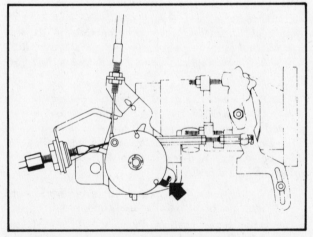

Adjusting the maximum accelerator position

CAUTION: *Do not hold the engine at maximum r.p.m. any longer than is absolutely necessary—personal injury could result.*

4. Remove the tachometer.

NOTE: *Any time the idle speed is adjusted, the cold start device, accelerator cable, and the maximum accelerator position should also be adjusted.*

5. Adjusting the cold start device (engine off):
   a. The engine temperature should be cold. Disconnect the cold start device.
   b. Loosen the screw (1) which is closest to the rubber boot. Do not loosen the screw (2) which is furthest away from the rubber boot.
   c. Push the accelerator lever forward and turn the cable sleeve 90°. Tighten the screw (1), and reconnect the cold start device.
6. Adjusting the accelerator cable (engine off):
   a. Disconnect the link rod at the lever on the injection pump.
   b. Turn the accelerator cable sheath until the cable is stretched but so that it does not alter the pulley position. The pulley should touch the idle stop.
   c. Reconnect the link rod at the lever on the injection pump.
7. Check the maximum accelerator position (engine off):
   a. Fully depress the accelerator pedal.
   b. The pulley should touch the full speed stop.

FUEL SYSTEM

Injection Pump Removal and Installation

NOTE: *Rotate the crankshaft by using a socket on the vibration damper bolt. Do not rotate the crankshaft while the drive belts are disconnected.*

1. Remove the vacuum pump and the vacuum pump plunger.
2. Remove the injection pump drive belt cover.
3. Rotate the crankshaft to set the number one (1) cylinder at TDC. Be sure that the "O" mark on the flywheel and the reference point on the clutch housing are aligned and that the mark on the injection pump and the mark on the sprocket mounting plate are also aligned.
4. Brace the rear camshaft sprocket and remove the rear camshaft sprocket retaining bolt.

CAUTION: *The rear camshaft sprocket must not be rotated.*

5. Remove the rear camshaft sprocket along with the injection pump drive belt.
6. Disconnect the following items from the injection pump:
   a. Injection lines
   b. Fuel supply and return pipes
   c. Shutoff solenoid
   d. Accelerator cable
7. Remove the injection pump mounting bolts and remove the injection pump.
8. Install the injection pump in the reverse order of the removal procedure. Torque the pump retaining screws to approximately 35 ft-lbs (45 Nm).
9. Check and adjust the injection timing.

Overhaul

Should any injection pump malfunction occur, the injection pump assembly should be replaced with either a new unit from the manufacturer or a rebuilt unit from a Bosch distributor.

CYLINDER HEAD

Removal

NOTE: *Do not rotate the crankshaft while the drive belts are disconnected.*

1. Rotate the crankshaft to set the Number one(1) cylinder at TDC. Be sure that the "O" mark on the flywheel and the reference point on the clutch housing are aligned, and that the mark on the injection pump and the mark on the sprocket mounting plate are also aligned.
2. Disconnect the negative battery cable at the battery.
3. Drain the engine coolant and remove the coolant hoses at the cylinder head.
4. Disconnect the following items:
   a. Glow plug wires

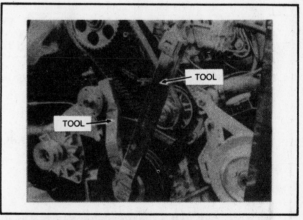

Removing the vibration damper center bolt

To slacken the timing belt, loosen the water pump bolts

b. Injection lines

c. Wiring related to the cylinder head the the manifolds

5. Brace the vibration damper and remove the center damper bolt.

6. Remove the vibration damper and check that the Number One (1) cylinder has remained at TDC. If necessary, rotate the flywheel with a flywheel turning wrench to adjust.

NOTE: *If the vibration damper and the crankshaft gear are stuck together, gently tap them apart.*

7. Remove the accessory drive V-belts, the cooling fan, and the camshaft timing belt cover.

8. Loosen the water pump retaining bolts and pivot the pump on the bolts in order to loosen the timing belt.

9. Remove the camshaft timing belt.

NOTE: *If the camshaft timing belt is to be replaced, the idler pulley must also be replaced. If necessary, remove the idler pulley with the appropriate puller and tap the new idler pulley into place.*

10. Remove the injection pump drive belt cover.

11. Remove the valve cover and the gasket.

12. Brace the rear camshaft sprocket and remove the rear camshaft sprocket retaining bolt.

13. Remove the rear camshaft sprocket along with the injection pump drive belt.

14. Install a camshaft locking tool (Volvo #5190 or its equivalent) onto the camshaft at the rear of the cylinder head with an .008″ (0.2 mm) feeler gauge on the left side of the tool, between the tool and the cylinder head.

15. Brace the front camshaft sprocket and remove the front camshaft retaining bolt.

16. Remove the front camshaft sprocket.

17. Remove the intake and the exhaust manifolds.

18. Remove the cylinder head bolts in the reverse order of the cylinder head bolt tightening sequence.

Overhaul

NOTE: *Machining the cylinder head is not recommended.*

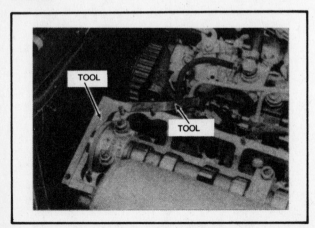

Installation of the camshaft locking tool

1. Mark and remove the camshaft bearing caps. Lift the camshaft from the bearing seats.

2. Mark and remove the cam followers. The followers should be replaced in their original locations.

3. Remove the valve stem locks, retainers, and the valve springs.

NOTE: *It may be necessary to tap on the valve spring remover tool spindle to loosen the valve locks from the retainers.*

4. Mark and remove the valves. The valves should be replaced in their original locations during reassembly. Discard the valve stem oil seals.

5. Using an appropriate (expanding) tool, remove the lower valve spring seats.

6. Remove the glow plugs from the cylinder head.

7. Using an appropriate (drift) tool positioned through the glow plug holes, tap the combustion chamber inserts out of the cylinder head. Examine the cylinder head for damage and/or cracks. Then thoroughly clean the cylinder head.

NOTE: *It is recommended that a Magnaflux (or similar) inspection be performed to locate cracks. Some hairline cracks could escape detection during a visual inspection.*

8. Install the valves in their respective positions without the valve springs, retainers, etc.

9. Install a dial indicator and measure the stem to guide clearance, which should not exceed 0.051″ (1.3 mm). If the clearance is greater than the specification, first check the stem diameters of the valves in question with a micrometer. The stem diameters should be 0.314″ (7.97 mm) intake, and 0.313″ (7.95 mm) exhaust. Replace any valve which has worn past the specification limit and recheck the stem to guide clearance. If the clearance is still too large, the valve guides must be replaced.

10. Should the valve guides need replacement, press the guides out of the head from the combustion chamber side. Once again, inspect the cylinder head for cracks.

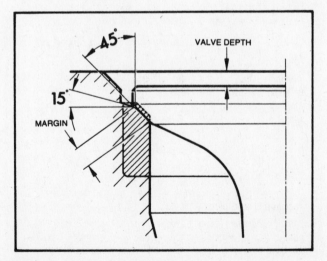

Valve and seat grinding dimensions

11. If the cylinder head is reuseable, obtain new valve guides and coat them liberally with oil. Press the guides into the cylinder head from the camshaft side of the head.

CAUTION: *The cylinder head must be cold. Once the shoulder of the guide has seated, do not exceed one ton pressure. The shoulder could break.*

12. Ream the valve guides to standard size using a hand reamer and a good quality cutting lubricant. Match each valve to a properly sized guide and mark the valve locations accordingly.

13. Reface the valve seats to obtain seat surfaces of 0.078″ (2.0 mm) for the intake seat and 0.096″ (2.4 mm) for the exhaust seat. The seat angles should be 45° for both the intake and exhaust. If adjustment of the seat width is needed, use a 15° correction angle. Valve depth (measured from the combustion chamber surface to the valve head) should not exceed 0.059″ (1.5 mm).

NOTE: *Valve seats that are worn or burned can be refaced, providing the correction angle and seat width dimensions are maintained; otherwise, the cylinder head must be replaced.*

14. Reface the intake valves on a machine. Hand grind the exhaust valves only. A valve margin of no less than 0.019″ (0.5 mm) should remain on the valve heads.

15. Lightly coat the seats with a fine grinding compound and lap the valves to the seats, which insures correct valve to seat contact. Thoroughly clean the valves and the seats when finished.

16. Install the valves into their respective guides and install the lower spring seats.

17. Position a seal protector sleeve over the valve stem lock grooves and install the valve seals.

18. Install the valve springs, retainers and locks.

19. Carefully place the camshaft into the bearing seats and install the bearing caps. Tighten the bearing caps to 14 ft-lbs (20 Nm) and check the camshaft end-play with a dial indicator. The end-play should not exceed 0.006″ (0.15 mm).

NOTE: *The cam followers must not be installed prior to checking the camshaft end-play. The cam must be free to move when checking the end-play.*

20. After the end-play has been determined, remove the bearing caps and the camshaft and install the cam followers. Reinstall the camshaft and the bearing caps as follows.
    a. Lubricate the bearings and the cam journals.
    b. Rotate the camshaft so that the cam lobes of the Number One cylinder face upward at equally large angles. Install the numbers 2 and 3 bearing caps and tighten the retaining bolts to 14 ft-lbs (20 Nm) in an alternate and diagonal manner.
    c. Install the remaining bearing caps and tighten the bolts in the same manner as numbers 2 and 3.

21. Install the following items:
    a. Combustion chamber inserts
    b. Glow plugs
    c. Fuel injectors (w/new heat shields)

Installation

1. Position a new cylinder head gasket on the block and place the cylinder head carefully on the block using guide pins.
2. Remove the guide pins and install the cylinder head bolts. Use the head bolt tightening sequence diagram and torque the head bolts to 65 ft-lbs (90 Nm) in increments of approximately 20 ft-lbs (27.1 Nm).
3. Install the front camshaft sprocket together with the camshaft drive belt and the retaining bolt. Do not tighten the retaining bolt.
4. Align the TDC mark on the flywheel with the reference mark on the clutch housing.
5. Using the appropriate special tool, adjust the camshaft drive belt tension to a scale value of 12 to 13. Torque the water pump mounting bolts to 14 ft-lbs (20 Nm).
6. Torque the front camshaft sprocket retaining bolt to 33 ft-lbs (45 Nm).
7. Install the intake and exhaust manifolds and torque the bolts to 18 ft-lbs (25 Nm).
8. Install the two intake and exhaust manifold supports and torque the bolts to 14 ft-lbs (20 Nm).
9. Connect the fuel supply and return pipes and torque the connectors to 18 ft-lbs (25 Nm).
10. Install the rear camshaft sprocket together with the injection pump drive belt and the sprocket retaining bolt.
11. Be sure the flywheel and clutch housing TDC marks are still aligned.
12. Using the appropriate special tool, adjust the injection pump drive belt tension to a value of 12 to 13. Tighten the rear camshaft sprocket retaining bolt.
13. Install the following items:
    a. Vacuum pump V-belt
    b. Accessory drive V-belts
    c. Front timing belt cover
    d. Related hoses and wiring
    e. Valve cover (torque the fasteners to 7 ft-lbs [9.5 Nm])
14. Check the injection pump timing and adjust as necessary.
15. Install the injection pump drive belt cover.

INTAKE MANIFOLD

Removal and Installation

1. Remove the flexible air intake hose from the air cleaner and the intake manifold.
2. Remove the two intake and exhaust manifold supports.
3. Remove the intake manifold fasteners and lift off the intake manifold.
4. Installation is the reverse of the removal procedure. Torque the manifold support fasteners to 14 ft-lbs (20 Nm), and the intake manifold-to-head fasteners to 18 ft-lbs (25 Nm).

EXHAUST MANIFOLD

Removal and Installation

1. Disconnect the front exhaust pipe at the flange.
2. Remove the intake and exhaust manifold supports.
3. Remove the exhaust manifold fasteners and lift off the exhaust manifold.
4. Installation is the reverse of the removal procedure. Torque the exhaust manifold fasteners to 18 ft-lbs (25 Nm), the manifold support fasteners to 14 ft-lbs (20 Nm), and the exhaust pipe flange fasteners to 22 ft-lbs (30 Nm).

OIL PAN

Removal and Installation

The oil pan is fastened to the block in a conventional manner. Removal and installation is a basic procedure which is nearly identical to that of a common gasoline engine.

PISTONS AND CONNECTING RODS

Removal, Overhaul, Installation

1. It is necessary to remove the manifolds, cylinder head and the oil pan to gain access to the pistons and the connecting rods. Refer to the appropriate disassembly section.
2. Mark the pistons and the connecting rods so that they may be reinstalled in their original locations and directions.
3. Where necessary, remove the ridge at the top of the cylinder(s).
4. Remove each connecting rod bearing cap and push each piston and connecting rod assembly out through the top of the block.
5. Remove the piston rings and thoroughly clean the pistons. Inspect the pistons for excessive wear, cracks, distortion, etc., and replace if necessary.
6. Check the piston diameter by measuring the piston skirt approximately 9/16″ from the bottom and 180° from the wrist pin bore.
7. If the piston must be removed or replaced, evenly heat the piston with hot water or heated wet towels (140° F. – 60° C.). Drive the pins from the pistons using a wrist pin removing tool. Install the pistons and pins in the same manner.
8. Measure the cylinder bore diameter at three points, starting from the top under the ridge mark, followed by a measurement one-half way down the bore, and another at approximately 9/16″ from the bottom. Record the measurements. Remeasure the bore in the same vertical areas, but rotate the measuring device 180° from the original points. Record the measurement from the second set of readings. To

determine the amount of cylinder taper and out-of-round, subtract the lesser reading from the higher reading. Maximum out-of-round is .0016″ (0.04 mm).

9. Measure the piston ring end gaps by placing the rings (one at a time) squarely in the cylinder, first, at approximately 1/2″ from the top of the cylinder, then at approximately 9/16″ from the bottom. End gap measurement should be .012″–.020″ (0.3–0.5 mm) for the compression rings, and .010″–.016″ for the oil control rings. A wear limit of .040″ (1.0 mm) is allowed for all ring end gaps.
10. Install the rings on the pistons (noting the "top" markings) and measure the side clearance between the ring and the piston ring groove. Refer to the accompanying chart.
11. Install the connecting rod halves of the rod bearings and lubricate the contact surface.
12. Using a suitable piston ring compressor, install the piston and connecting rod assemblies into the appropriate cylinders.

PISTON RING SIDE CLEARANCE SPECIFICATIONS

	Clearance (mm)	Wear Limit (mm)
Upper ring	0.06-0.09 mm (0.002-0.0035 in.)	0.2 mm (0.008 in.)
Lower ring	0.05-0.08 mm (0.002-0.003 in.)	0.2 mm (0.008 in.)
Oil scraper ring	0.03-0.06 mm (0.001-0.002 in.)	0.15 mm (0.006 in.)

NOTE: *Use some type of rod bolt protectors to prevent damage to the crankshaft as the rod bolts pass over the crank journals.*

13. Install the connecting rod cap bearing halves (lubricate the contact surfaces) and the rod cap. Torque the rod nuts to 33 ft-lbs (45 Nm).
14. Once all of the piston and connecting rod assemblies have been installed, slowly rotate the crankshaft to bring the Number One cylinder to TDC. Measure the piston height above the engine block using a dial indicator. Repeat this step for the remaining cylinders.
15. Install the oil pan, cylinder head, and the manifolds. Refer to the appropriate sections.

CRANKSHAFT

Removal and Installation

1. Remove the engine from the vehicle.
2. Refer to the appropriate sections and remove the following items from the engine:
   a. Intake and exhaust manifolds.
   b. Cylinder head.
   c. Oil pan.
   d. Piston and connecting rod assemblies.

3. Brace the flywheel against rotation and remove the flywheel.

4. Using a feeler gauge between the thrust bearing and the crankshaft thrust surface, measure the amount of crankshaft end play by rocking the crankshaft back and forth. End play should not exceed 0.010″ (.25 mm). Should the end play be excessive, record the amount of total end play and replace the thrust bearing during Step 8.

5. Remove the crankshaft and carefully lift the crankshaft out of the block.

6. Thoroughly clean and inspect the crankshaft. Make sure that the journal passages are clear.

7. Check the main bearing clearances as follows:
   a. Install the block halves of the main bearings into the bearing saddles. The bearings should be clean and dry.
   b. Carefully lower the crankshaft into the block.
   c. Install the cap halves of the main bearings into the main caps. The bearings should be clean and dry.
   d. Lay a small strip of Plastigage® across each of the main journals.
   e. Install the bearing caps and tighten the bolts to 47 ft-lbs (65 Nm).

NOTE: *Do not turn the crankshaft.*

   f. Remove the bearing caps.
   g. Gauge the width of the Plastigage® against the scale which is printed on the Plastigage® package to determine the amount of bearing clearance. Clearance should be .0006″–.003″. Size the replacement bearings accordingly.

8. Lubricate the main bearings, reinstall the crankshaft, and torque the cap bolts to 47 ft-lbs (65 Nm).

9. Replace the pilot bearing if necessary, using the appropriate puller and driving tools to remove and reinstall.

10. Install the rear seal flange and if necessary, replace the rear seal as follows:
    a. Pry the seal out of the flange with the appropriate tool.
    b. Lightly coat the outer lip of the new seal with oil.
    c. Install the seal with the appropriate tool which draws the seal into the flange. The tool is made from a metal disc approximately ¼″ thick with the same diameter as the seal. The disc is drilled with two holes which align with two opposite flywheel mounting holes in the crankshaft. Tightening the bolts draws the seal towards the crankshaft.

11. Refer to the appropriate sections and reinstall the following items:
    a. Piston and connecting rod assemblies
    b. Oil pan
    c. Cylinder head
    d. Intake and exhaust manifolds

CAMSHAFT

Removal

1. Remove the splash guard from under the engine.

2. Disconnect the radiator hoses.

3. Remove the following items:
   a. Radiator
   b. Cooling fan, spacer, and pulley
   c. Power steering and alternator V-belts
   d. Camshaft drive (timing) belt cover

4. Set the Number one cylinder at TDC. Align the flywheel mark with the clutch housing reference mark and the injection pump sprocket mark with the injection pump mounting plate reference mark.

5. Brace the vibration damper against rotation and remove the center vibration damper bolt.

6. Check that the Number one cylinder is still at TDC. Remove the vibration damper.

NOTE: *If the vibration damper and the crankshaft gear are stuck together, gently tap them apart.*

7. Remove the lower camshaft drive (timing) belt shield.

8. Loosen the coolant pump retaining bolts, move the pump and remove the camshaft drive (timing) belt.

9. Brace the rear camshaft gear against rotation. Remove the center bolt of the rear camshaft gear, and remove the gear along with the injection pump drive belt.

10. Lock the camshaft in position by installing Volvo tool #5190 (or its equivalent) in place of the rear camshaft gear.

11. Using a special spanner wrench (Volvo tool #5199 or its equivalent), hold the front camshaft gear in position and remove the center bolt of the front camshaft gear.

12. Gently tap the front camshaft gear off the camshaft.

13. Mark the position of the camshaft in relation to the cylinder head and remove the camshaft locking tool.

14. Mark and remove the Numbers 1 and 4 cam bearing caps and diagonally loosen the nuts of the Numbers 2 and 3 caps.

15. Mark and remove the Numbers 2 and 3 caps and carefully lift the camshaft out of the cylinder head.

Installation

1. Lubricate the contact surfaces of the bearings.

2. Carefully place the camshaft into the cylinder head. The cam lobes of the Number one cylinder should face upward at equally large amounts.

3. Install the Numbers 2 and 3 bearing caps; tighten the nuts alternately and diagonally to 14 ft-lbs (20 Nm).

4. Install the Numbers 1 and 4 bearing caps and tighten in the same manner as in Step three.

5. Install the camshaft locking tool (Volvo #5190 or its equivalent) onto the rear of the camshaft, thereby preventing camshaft rotation.

6. Install the front camshaft gear together with the camshaft drive (timing) belt. Install the center bolt but do not tighten.

NOTE: *The gear should be allowed to rotate, not the camshaft.*

7. Install the lower camshaft drive (timing) belt shield and the vibration damper. Torque the Allen screws to 15 ft-lbs (20 Nm).

NOTE: *The vibration damper must align with the pin on the crankshaft gear.*

8. Apply Loctite® to the threads of the center vibration damper bolt and install the bolt.

9. While holding the vibration damper with Volvo tool #5187 (or its exact equivalent), torque the center vibration damper bolt to 255 ft-lbs (350 Nm) using only Volvo tool #5188 (or its exact equivalent).

NOTE: *This torque reading applies only when using the Volvo special tools or their equivalents.*

10. Check that the Number One cylinder is still at TDC.

11. Using a Volvo belt tension gauge (tool #5197 or its equivalent), adjust the tension of the camshaft drive (timing) belt to a scale value of 12.5 and tighten the cooling pump mounting bolts.

12. Install the front camshaft gear and tighten the center bolt to 33 ft-lbs (45 Nm).

13. Remove the camshaft locking tool and install the rear camshaft gear together with the injection pump drive belt.

14. Check and adjust the injection timing; refer to the appropriate section.

OIL PUMP

Removal and Installation

1. Remove the splash guard from under the engine.

2. Disconnect the radiator hoses.

3. Remove the following items:
   a. Radiator
   b. Cooling fan, spacer, and pulley
   c. Power steering and alternator V-belts
   d. Camshaft drive (timing) belt cover

4. Set the Number One cylinder at TDC. Align the flywheel mark with the clutch housing reference mark, and the pump sprocket mark with the injection pump mounting plate reference mark.

5. Brace the vibration damper against rotation and remove the center vibration damper bolt.

6. Check that the Number One cylinder is still at TDC and remove the vibration damper.

NOTE: *If the vibration damper and the crankshaft gear are stuck together, gently tap them apart.*

7. Remove the lower camshaft drive (timing) belt shield.

8. Loosen the coolant pump retaining bolts, turn the pump and remove the camshaft drive (timing) belt.

9. Drain the engine oil and remove the oil pan.

10. Remove the oil pump suction pipe from the oil pump.

11. Remove the oil pump bolts and remove the oil pump from the engine.

12. Should the oil pump be defective, the oil pump assembly must be replaced.

13. When installing the oil pump onto the crankshaft, align the driving key on the crankshaft with the corresponding slot in the pump gear.

14. Torque the 8 mm pump bolts to 18 ft-lbs (25 Nm), and the 6 mm pump bolts to 7 ft-lbs (10 Nm).

15. Using the appropriate special tool, install a new crankshaft oil seal.

16. Install the oil suction pipe and torque the fasteners to 7 ft-lbs (10 Nm).

17. Install the oil pan with a new gasket and torque the bolts to 14 ft-lbs (20 Nm).

18. Install the oil drain plug and torque to 36 ft-lbs (50 Nm).

19. Install the camshaft drive (timing) belt, adjust the belt to the proper tension and torque the coolant pump mounting bolts to 14 ft-lbs (20 Nm).

20. Install the following items:
   a. Vibration damper
   b. Belt cover
   c. V-belts
   d. Cooling fan, spacer and pulley
   e. Radiator and hoses

WATER PUMP

The Volvo diesel engine is water cooled in a conventional manner, using a radiator, expansion tank, pressure cap, and a belt-driven fan and water pump.

The pressure setting of the expansion tank is 9–12 psi. The thermostat is designed to begin opening at 186° F (87° C), and fully open at 236° F (102° C).

Removal and Installation

1. Drain the engine coolant.

2. Remove the alternator belt and the power steering belt.

3. Remove the camshaft drive (timing) belt cover.

4. Set the Number One cylinder to TDC. The flywheel mark and the clutch housing reference mark should be aligned, also, the injection pump sprocket mark and the injection pump mounting plate mark should be aligned.

5. Loosen the water pump mounting bolts, turn the water pump to loosen the camshaft drive (timing) belt and remove the belt.

CAUTION: *Do not under any circumstance rotate the engine while the timing belt is removed.*

6. Remove the water pump and clean the gasket surfaces. Installation is the reverse of the removal procedure.

NOTE: *Do not tighten the water pump mounting bolts until after the camshaft drive (timing) belt has been properly tensioned.*

VOLKSWAGEN

The VW Diesel engine is an inline four cylinder engine with a single overhead camshaft. The crankshaft runs in five main bearings, with the thrust taken on the center bearing. The cylinder block is cast iron. A reinforced rubber belt drives the intermediate shaft and the camshaft.

The cylinder head is lightweight aluminum alloy. The valves are opened and closed by the camshaft lobes operating on cupped cam followers (tappets) which fit over the valves and the springs.

This engine should only be run on #2 diesel fuel. In addition, use only motor oil graded as API/CC or better.

ENGINE TUNE-UP

The Volkswagen diesel engine tune-up should include the following inspections and/or repairs.

1. Compression test
2. Valve adjustment
3. Injector pressure test and inspection
4. Injector timing
5. Valve timing
6. Idle speed adjustment
7. Glow plug operation

Compression Test

NOTE: *The injectors are easily damaged and great care must be used to keep them clean.*

1. Disconnect the wire from the fuel shutoff solenoid on the injection pump. Insulate this connection.
2. Clean all the injector fittings, then remove the injection pipes.
3. Disconnect the fuel return hoses.
4. Remove the injectors from the cylinder head. Use VW tool US 2775 or equivalent.
5. Remove the heat shields from the injector bores.
6. Place an old heat shield in the cylinder to be checked and screw in adapter #1323/2 and attach the compression gauge to it.
7. Set the parking brake and place the transmission in Neutral.
8. Crank the starter and record the pressures.

Compression on the diesel engine should be between 398 and 483. The maximum pressure differential between the highest and lowest cylinder is 71 psi.

1. After checking and recording the cylinder pressures, install new heat shields and reinstall the injectors.
2. Reconnect the fuel return lines.
3. Install the injector pipes and torque the nuts to 18 ft-lbs.
4. Reconnect the wire to the fuel shutoff solenoid on the injection pump.
5. Start the engine and accelerate a few times to clear the air bubbles.

Valve Adjustment

1. The engine should be warm, with the coolant temperature about 95° F.

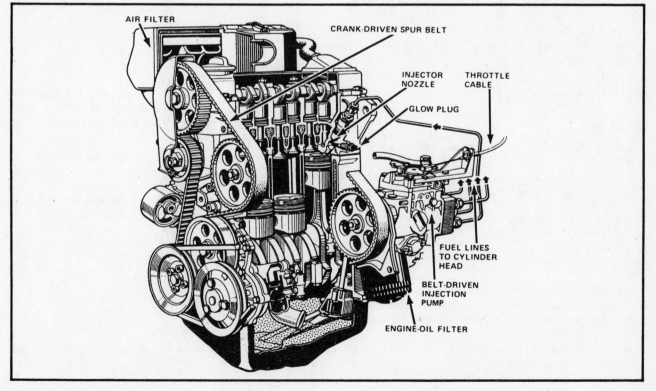

Diesel engine—exploded view

2. On vehicles with automatic transmission, remove the accelerator cable. Use care since it is easy to kink the cable. Remember to check for smooth operation at reassembly.

3. Remove the cylinder head cover.

4. Place the vehicle in 4th gear if equipped with manual transmission, and turn the camshaft by rocking and pushing the vehicle.

CAUTION: *Do not turn the camshaft mounting bolt. This will stretch the drive belt.*

5. The cam lobes should be pointing upward on the cylinder to be checked or adjusted. Clearances should be 0.008 to 0.012 inch on the intake valve and 0.016 to 0.020 inch on the exhaust side of a warm engine.

6. Measure the clearance with a feeler gauge. If the measured clearance is larger than the specification, remove the existing adjusting disc, or shim, and insert a thicker disc to close the gap to the proper specification. If the measured valve clearance is smaller than the specification, remove the existing disc and insert a thinner disc to open the gap to the proper specification.

7. VW has special tools (VW 546 and US4476) to depress the cam followers and remove the discs. If substitutions are used be very careful not to damage the camshaft, followers or the head. The thickness of each adjusting disc is etched on one side. Install the disc with these markings downward (toward the cam follower). If the discs are not damaged or worn, they can be reused.

CAUTION: *When adjusting the valves, the pistons MUST NOT be at TDC. Turn the crankshaft about ¼ turn past TDC so that the valves do not contact the pistons as the followers are depressed. This is most important. In addition, before depressing the followers, turn them so that the openings are at right angles to the camshaft. This will help with removing the adjusting disc.*

Injection Pump Timing

CHECKING

1. Remove the cylinder head cover as well as the timing belt cover.

2. If the engine is in the car, set the engine to TDC of No. 1 cylinder by turning the engine until the TDC mark on the flywheel is in line with the boss on the bellhousing. If the engine is out of the car, VW tool 2068 or 2068A is used to gauge the setting.

3. A setting bar is required and it is installed on the cylinder head. Turn the camshaft until one end of the setting bar touches the cylinder head. Measure the gap at the other end with a feeler gauge.

4. Divide this measurement in half and select a feeler gauge of this thickness between the setting bar and the cylinder head.

5. Turn the camshaft so that the bar rests on the feeler gauge of this thickness between the other end of the bar and the cylinder head. All of this is to set up the valve timing in the proper relationship with the injector.

6. VW tool 2064 is a special pin-like tool that fits into the holes in the pump sprocket and into the pump mounting plate. If it fits, the timing is correct. If not, the pump and valve timing will need to be adjusted.

ADJUSTING

1. With the cylinder head cover and the drive belt cover removed, set the engine to TDC on No. 1 cylinder.

2. Set the camshaft in postion with the setting bar as described previously.

3. Loosen the camshaft sprocket bolt one turn.

4. Tap the back of the camshaft sprocket with a rubber hammer until loose. Hand tighten the sprocket bolt until the end play is eliminated but the sprocket turns on the camshaft. The setting bar will keep the camshaft locked in the proper location while the sprocket can be turned as needed to mesh properly with the teeth on the belt.

5. Loosen the belt tension and remove the belt from the injection pump sprocket. Turn the pump sprocket until the marks on the sprocket and the mounting plate line up. Use VW tool 2064 to lock the pump sprocket.

6. Reinstall the drive belt.

7. Tighten the camshaft bolt to 33 ft-lbs and remove the setting tool. Remove the pin (VW tool 2064) from the pump sprocket by turning the tensioner counterclockwise slightly.

8. Rotate the crankshaft 2 complete turns and check the belt tension. Eliminate the play in the drive belt by striking it once, midway between the camshaft and pump sprocket with a rubber hammer.

9. At this point, the injection pump and valve timing have been checked and verified to be correct, or adjusted as necessary. The injection timing should be checked next.

Injection Timing

CAUTION: *Before checking or adjusting the injection timing, always push in the Cold Start Device completely. The knob to control the Cold Start Device is on the instrument panel.*

1. Locate the plug in the center of the injection pump cover. Remove this plug. Note that the seal must always be replaced whenever the plug is removed.

2. VW has an adapter (VW tool 2066) that fits the plug opening to which a dial indicator is attached. If this tool is not available, a dial indicator that is substituted must have a range of at least 0–0.120 inch (0–3 mm). Place the gauge so that the plunger will be in the hole from which the plug was removed. Preload the gauge approximately 0.095 inch.

3. Turn the engine slowly counterclockwise, which is opposite the normal rotation, until the needle on the dial indicator stops moving. Zero the gauge.

CAUTION: *Do not try to rotate the engine by turning the camshaft drive nut. This will only damage the drive belt.*

4. With the dial indicator zeroed, turn the engine clock-

wise, which is the normal rotation, until the TDC mark on the flywheel is aligned with the boss on the bell housing. The gauge should read 0.032 inch.

5. If this reading cannot be obtained, loosen the bolts on the mounting plate and injector support. Set the lift of the pump to 0.032 inch by turning the pump. Tighten the mounting bolts and recheck the injection timing.

6. Replace the seal on the center plug and install the plug.

Idle Speed Adjustment

CHECKING LOW IDLE

Since the diesel engine has no electrical ignition system to which a conventional Dwell-Tach can be attached, an engine r.p.m. sensor will be required. VW tool US 1324 or an equivalent will be required. The positive lead of a Dwell-Tach that is compatible with the r.p.m. sensor is attached to the sensor and the negative to ground.

1. Once the test equipment is hooked up, start the engine and allow to warm up.
2. Check the idle speed. It should be 770–870 r.p.m. with the oil temperature warm (140° F.).

ADJUSTING LOW IDLE

1. If the engine idle speed is not to this specification, loosen the locknut on the idle speed screw. There are two screws on the injector pump flange bearing against the control lever. The low speed or idle speed screw is the one closest to the engine.
2. Adjust the screw to obtain the correct idle speed. Note that turning the screw clockwise increases the r.p.m.
3. Tighten the locknut after adjusting.

CHECKING HIGH IDLE

1. For this check, the engine should be thoroughly warmed, with the oil temperature around 175° F.
2. With the test equipment hooked up as before, check that the maximum speed is 5500 to 5600 r.p.m.

ADJUSTING HIGH IDLE

1. If the engine speed is not to this specification, loosen the locknut on the high speed or maximum speed screw. Of the two adjustment screws on the injector pump, the high speed screw is the one toward the front of the vehicle, towards the radiator.
2. Adjust the screw to obtain the correct maximum engine speed. Note that turning the screw clockwise decreases the r.p.m.
3. Tighten the locknut after adjusting.

Cold Start Cable Adjustment

1. Locate the cold start cable connection on the back, or engine side of the injection pump.
2. Loosen the clamping screw. Move the cold starting cable to the zero position, which would be toward the right or passenger side of the vehicle.

3. Pull the cable tight and secure with the clamping screw.

Accelerator Cable Adjustment

CAUTION: *Before attempting to make any adjustments to the accelerator cable, check and adjust both the idle speed and maximum speed (no load) as outlined previously.*

1. Note that the accelerator cable attaches to a ball stud on the pump lever. The ball stud must be in the center of the slot, or elongated hole in the pump lever.
2. The accelerator pedal must be in the full throttle position. Note the two nuts on the cable at the attaching bracket. Adjust these two nuts so that the pump lever contacts the stop (high speed screw) without strain on the cable.

Glow Plug System

When the diesel engine starts hard the problem may be in the glow plug system. Before the diesel engine can start the glow plug preheat period and the delay glow period are necessary. A warning light on the dash goes out when the preheat period has ended. At the end of this preheat period the glow plug continues to receive voltage (delay glow period) for 10 to 25 seconds. In order to check the glow plug system current supply do the following.

1. Connect a test light between No. 4 cylinder glow plug and ground.
2. Turn the ignition key to the preheat position, the light should come on.
3. If the light does not light, check the glow plug relay, ignition switch or the fuse box relay plate.
4. Replace the defective component.

In order to check the glow plugs do the following.

1. Remove the wire and bus-bar for the glow plugs.
2. Connect a test light to the positive battery terminal and touch the test light probe to each glow plug.
3. If the test light lights then the glow plug is okay.
4. If the light does not light then the plug is defective and should be replaced.

Checking the Injector Opening Pressure

1. Remove the injector from the engine and install in the injector test stand.
2. Pump the tester pump several times to remove any air from the injector and line.
3. Press the tester pump lever down slowly and note the injector opening spray pressure.
4. The opening pressure should be 120 to 130 BAR (1706 to 1849 psi).
5. If the opening pressure is not to specifications, the injector can be adjusted by the changing of selective shims, located within the injector.

DIESEL INJECTOR PUMP

Removal and Installation

NOTE: *All fuel injection systems are sensitive to dirt. When working on the injection system, everything must be kept clean. Make it a practice to wipe every pipe connector before removing it.*

1. Crank the engine until the TDC mark on the flywheel is aligned with the boss on the bell housing.
2. Disconnect the battery ground cable.
3. Lock the camshaft into position using the setting bar (VW tool #2065 or 2065A) as outlined in the section covering Injection Pump Timing.
4. Remove the drive belt.
5. Loosen the injector pump sprocket slightly.
    A special puller is used for the sprocket (VW tool #3032 or 2036).

NOTE: *If a suitable puller is used the repair technician must satisfy himself that the puller will not damage the sprocket. The puller is not used to pull the sprocket off the pump. The purpose is to apply tension with the puller, then tap the center bolt (spindle) of the puller with light hammer taps until the sprocket loosens from the injection pump tapered shaft.*

6. Once the sprocket is loose, remove the puller, the sprocket retainer nut and the sprocket.
7. Clean the pipe unions and then remove the fuel pipes from the pump. Cover the connections with clean cloths to keep out the dirt. Remove the fuel feed and the return lines by removing the hex head pipe union screws.

NOTE: *Mark them so that they will not be interchanged at assembly.*

8. Disconnect the cold start cable, the accelerator cable and the wire from the fuel shut-off solenoid.
9. Examine the injection pump from the fuel distribution end. Note that there are four bolts in the corners of the fuel distribution head. Do not remove or loosen these bolts or the distributor plunger will be damaged. Locate the mounting bolt at the 5 o'clock position of the pump and remove it.
10. Remove the bolts from the front injection pump mounting plate, as well as the support. Remove the injection pump from the vehicle.

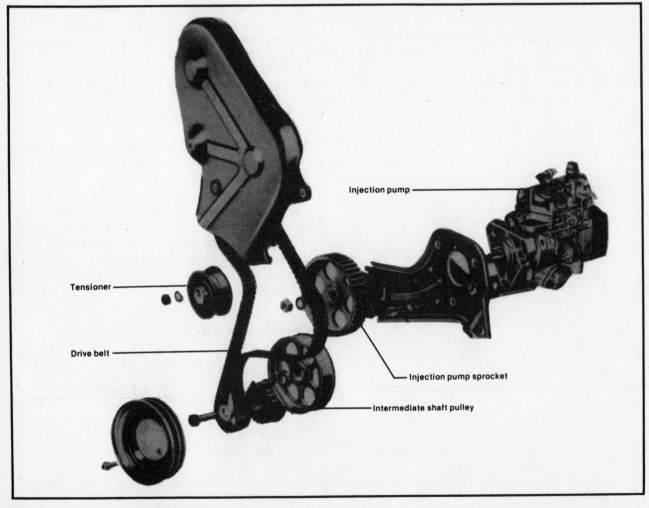

Injection pump and related components

11. To install, reverse the removal procedures. Take note of the alignment marks on the pump and the mounting plate. When installing the pump align these marks with each other.

12. Torque the pump bolts to 18 ft-lbs, the fuel pipes to 18 ft-lbs and the pump sprocket to 33 ft-lbs.

13. Attach the fuel pipes and the hoses as required. Do not interchange the fuel supply and the fuel return pipe attaching screws. The fuel return pipe union screw is marked "OUT" on the hex head.

Overhaul

Volkswagen does not recommend that the injection pump be disassembled. If this unit is found to be defective it should be replaced with either a new unit or a rebuilt one.

DIESEL FUEL INJECTORS

Diagnosis

The first sign of an injector problem may appear as any one of the following:

1. Knocking in one or more cylinders
2. Engine overheating
3. Loss of power
4. Black exhaust smoke
5. Increased fuel consumption

A faulty injector may be located by loosening the pipe union at each injector in turn, with the engine at fast idle. If the engine speed does not drop when the pipe union is loosened then the injector at that union is faulty.

NOTE: *Always keep injection parts clean when working on them.*

Removal

1. Clean all pipe fittings and remove the injector pipes.
2. Disconnect the fuel return hoses.
3. Remove the injectors using Volkswagen tool #2775 or equivalent.
4. Take off the old heat shields and install new ones before installation.

Cleaning

1. Clamp the upper part of the injector in a vise and loosen the lower part.
2. Turn the injector over and clamp it lightly in the vise for disassembly.
3. Clean the parts of the injector in diesel fuel. If carbon deposits won't clean, gasoline may be used, but all parts must immediately be rinsed in diesel fuel.
4. Check all injector parts for wear or damage.

5. Reassemble the injector and tighten halves to 70 Nm (51 ft-lbs).

Testing

SPRAY TEST

1. Using a test stand or an equivalent, fill the container with clean fuel and attach the injector to the tester.
2. Pump the tester a few times to clear any air bubbles and turn the valve so the pressure gauge on the tester is off.
3. Pump the tester with rapid short strokes, 4 to 6 times per second.
4. The spray should be even, well atomized, stop cleanly and the injector must not drip after it stops spraying.

OPENING PRESSURE TEST

1. Turn the valve on the tester so the pressure gauge is on.
2. Press the pump lever down slowly and note the opening spray pressure. The opening pressure should be 120–130 bar (1706–1849 psi).
3. If the opening pressure is not within specifications, remove the injector and disassemble it.
4. Remove and measure the injector shim.
5. Select a shim of the proper thickness to correct the pressure.
6. A thicker shim will increase the pressure.
7. A change of 0.05 mm (0.0019 in.) will change the pressure approximately 5 bar (71 psi).
8. Shims are available from 1 to 1.95 mm (0.039 in.) in steps of 0.05 mm (0.0019 in.).
9. Reassemble the injector and retest until the proper pressure is reached.

LEAKAGE TEST

1. Leave the pressure gauge on and press the pump lever down slowly.
2. Hold the pressure at approximately 110 bar (1564 psi) for 10 seconds.
3. The fuel should not drop from the injector. If needed replace the injector.

Installation

1. Make sure the injectors have new heat shields.
2. Intall the injectors in the head and torque them to 70 Nm (51 ft-lbs).
3. Install and torque the injector pipes to 25 Nm (18 ft-lbs).
4. Reconnect the fuel return hoses.
5. Start the engine and accelerate a few times to clean the air bubbles.
6. Check for fuel leaks.

CYLINDER HEAD

Removal

The head is retained by Allen bolts. The engine should be cold when the head is removed. The word TOP or OBEN on the new gasket should face up.

1. Disconnect the battery ground cable.
2. Drain the cooling system.
3. Remove the air cleaner.
4. Disconnect the fuel lines. Disconnect and tag all electrical wires and leads.
5. Separate the exhaust manifold from the pipe. Disconnect the radiator and heater hoses.

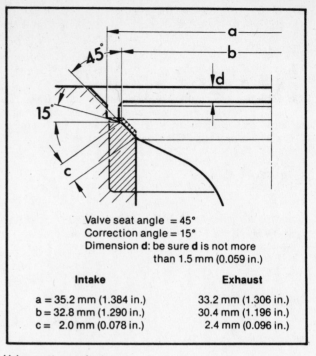

Valve seat angle = 45°
Correction angle = 15°
Dimension **d**: be sure **d** is not more
              than 1.5 mm (0.059 in.)

	Intake	Exhaust
a =	35.2 mm (1.384 in.)	33.2 mm (1.306 in.)
b =	32.8 mm (1.290 in.)	30.4 mm (1.196 in.)
c =	2.0 mm (0.078 in.)	2.4 mm (0.096 in.)

Valve seat resurfacings

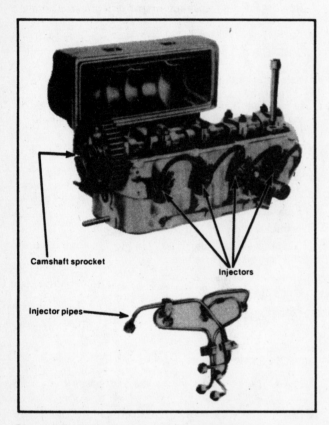

Diesel cylinder head and related components

6. Remove the timing cover and belt.
7. Loosen the cylinder head bolts in the reverse order of the tightening sequence.
8. Remove the head. Do not lay the head on the gasket surface with the injectors installed. Support it at the ends on strips of wood.

Overhaul

NOTE: *Diesel cylinder heads should not be machined.*

1. Check the cylinder head for distortion. The maximum allowable is 0.1 mm.
2. Remove the combustion chamber inserts by placing a

drift through the injector hole and knocking the inserts out.

3. Check the valve guides by inserting a new valve. Rock the valve back and forth against a dial indicator. The dial indicator reading will show valve guide wear. The maximum reading is 1.3 mm for both the exhaust and intake valves.
4. If the valve guides require replacement, press out the old guides from the valve face side. Coat the new valve guides with oil and press them into the cold cylinder head from the camshaft side. Press the valve guides in as far as they will go.

NOTE: *Once the guide shoulder is seated, do not use more than one ton of pressure or the guide shoulder may break. The valve guides may be reamed using the proper hand tool and a suitable lubricant.*

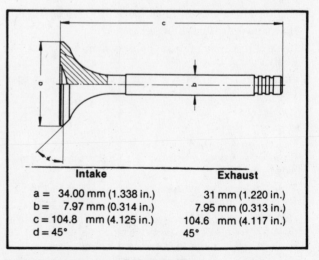

	Intake	Exhaust
a =	34.00 mm (1.338 in.)	31 mm (1.220 in.)
b =	7.97 mm (0.314 in.)	7.95 mm (0.313 in.)
c =	104.8 mm (4.125 in.)	104.6 mm (4.117 in.)
d =	45°	45°

Intake/exhaust valve refacing angles

5. Valve seats that are worn or burned can be refaced provided the proper angle and seat are maintained. If not, the cylinder head will have to be replaced.

NOTE: *When resurfacing the valve seats, be sure to follow the equipment manufacturer's instructions so that you do not damage the aluminum head. Do not use excess pressure on the valve seat cutter and be sure that the seat refacing pilot is properly installed.*

6. If necessary both the intake and the exhaust valves may be refaced. Do not rework exhaust valves, grind them in only.

NOTE: *Before installing new valves, be sure to replace the valve stem seal. Use a seal protector from the gasket set to prevent the valve keeper grooves from cutting the seal.*

7. Check the end-play of the camshaft. Measure it with the cam followers removed and caps #1 and #5 installed. The end-play should not be more than 0.15 mm. The camshaft run-out should not be more than 0.01 mm.

Installation

1. Install the cylinder head to the engine block. Be sure the new gasket has the same number of notches and the same identifying number as the old one, unless the pistons were also replaced.
2. Insert bolts #8 and #10 first, to center the cylinder head on the block. Tighten the rest of the head bolts in the order shown in the cylinder head torque sequence picture.

NOTE: *Cylinder head bolts may be torqued with the engine either cold or warm. With the engine cold, torque the bolts to 60 ft-lbs. With the engine warm torque the bolts to 70 ft-lbs. After 1000 miles loosen all the bolts 1/3 turn and retorque them to specification.*

3. Check and adjust valve clearance as required.
4. Continue the installation in the reverse order of the removal procedure.

INTAKE MANIFOLD

Removal and Installation

1. Remove the flexible hose from the air cleaner to the intake manifold.
2. Remove the intake and exhaust manifold supports.
3. Remove the intake manifold retaining bolts. Remove the assembly from the vehicle.
4. Installation is the reverse of removal. Torque the manifold retaining bolts to 25 Nm (18 ft-lbs).

EXHAUST MANIFOLD

Removal and Installation

1. Disconnect the front exhaust pipe at the flange.

2. Remove the intake and the exhaust manifold supports.
3. Remove the exhaust manifold attaching bolts. Remove the assembly from the vehicle.
4. Installation is the reverse of removal. Torque the manifold retaining bolts to 25 Nm (18 ft-lbs).

OIL PAN

Removal and Installation

1. Raise the vehicle on a hoist and support it safely.
2. Drain the engine oil. Remove the engine cover plate, if equipped.
3. Support the engine with a suitable engine support bar.
4. Remove the subframe bolts and engine mount nuts where required, and remove the subframe.
5. Remove the oil pan retaining bolts. Remove the oil pan from the vehicle.
6. Installation is the reverse of the removal procedure. Torque the oil pan bolts to 25 Nm (18 ft-lbs).
7. Install the proper grade and type engine oil. Start the engine and check for leaks.

PISTONS AND CONNECTING RODS

Removal and Installation

For information on piston and connecting rod installation procedures refer to the Volkswagen Rabbit/Dasher/Scirocco section of this manual under the heading Pistons and Connecting Rods. However, whenever new pistons or a short block are installed, the piston projection must be checked.

A spacer (VW 385/17) and bar with a micrometer are necessary, and must be set up to measure the maximum amount of piston projection above the deck height. The following chart should be used to select a head gasket of the correct thickness to match piston projection.

Piston Projection (mm)	Gasket Identification No. of Notches	Part Number
0.43–0.63	2	068 103 383
0.63–0.82	3	068 103 383C
0.82–0.92	4	068 103 383G
0.92–1.02	5	068 103 383H

NOTE: *1978 and later models (beginning with engine CK 024 944) have pistons with a new piston height and a thicker cylinder head gasket. These pistons are marked with a "9" next to installation direction arrow. New pistons can be used in earlier cars, but only in sets of 4.*

CRANKSHAFT

For the proper procedures regarding crankshaft information refer to the respective section in this manual.

CAMSHAFT

Removal and Installation

1. Remove the timing belt.
2. Remove the camshaft sprocket.
3. Remove the air cleaner.
4. Remove the camshaft cover.
5. Unscrew and remove the No. 1, 3, and 5 bearing caps (No. 1 is at the front).
6. Unscrew the No. 2 and 4 bearing caps, diagonally and in increments.
7. Lift the camshaft out of the cylinder head.
8. Lubricate the camshaft journals and lobes with assembly lube or gear oil before installing it in the cylinder head.
9. Replace the camshaft oil seal with a new one whenever the cam is removed.
10. Install the No. 1, 3, and 5 bearing caps and tighten the nuts to 14 ft-lbs. Note that the bores are offset, and the numbers are not always on the same side.
11. Install the No. 2 and 4 bearing caps and diagonally tighten the nuts to 14 ft-lbs.

NOTE: *If checking end-play, install a dial indicator so that the feeler touches the camshaft snout. End-play should be no more than 0.006 in. (0.15 mm).*

12. Replace the seal in the No. 1 bearing cap. If necessary, replace the end plug in the cylinder head.
13. Install the camshaft cover.
14. Install the camshaft pulley and the timing belt.
15. Check the valve clearance.

OIL PUMP

Removal and Installation

1. Remove the oil pan.
2. Remove the two mounting bolts.
3. Pull the oil pump down and out of the engine.
4. Unscrew the two bolts and separate the pump halves.
5. Remove the driveshaft and gear from the upper body.
6. Clean the bottom half in solvent. Pry up the metal edges to remove the filter screen for cleaning.
7. Examine the gears and driveshaft for wear or damage. Replace them if necessary.
8. Reassemble the pump halves.
9. Prime the pump with oil and install in the reverse order of removal.

WATER PUMP

The diesel engine is water cooled by a belt driven water pump. The system uses a main radiator plus an auxiliary radiator to cool the engine. The cooling fan is run by a thermostatically controlled electric fan.

Removal and Installation

1. Drain the cooling system.
2. Remove the alternator and drive belt.
3. Remove the timing belt cover.
4. Disconnect the lower radiator hose, engine hose, and heater hose from the water pump.
5. Remove the four pump retaining bolts.
6. Turn the pump slightly and lift it out of the engine block.
7. Installation is the reverse of removal. Use a new seal on the mating surface with the engine.

GM 350 V-8 DIESEL ENGINE

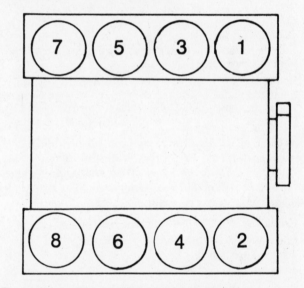

Engine firing order: 1-8-4-3-6-5-7-2 (© G.M. Corp.)

DESCRIPTION

The 5.7 liter, 350 cu. in. V8, 4 cycle diesel is the first factory-built diesel engine to be installed in a G.M. truck. The base of the engine (short block) is very similar in design to a V8 gasoline engine; the major differences being the cylinder heads, combustion chamber, fuel distribution system, air intake manifold and the method of ignition. The cylinder block, crankshaft, main bearings, connecting rods and pistons look much the same as their gasoline engine counterparts, although they are of much heavier construction due to the higher compression ratio required to ignite diesel fuel. The cylinder heads are also designed for much higher compression. The intake and exhaust valves are of special design and construction.

TUNE-UP

Compression Test

When checking the compression, always make sure that the batteries are at or near full charge. The total reading for any given cylinder is not as important as the difference between all cylinders. The cylinder with the lowest reading should not be less than 70% of the one with the highest reading and no cylinder should be less than 275 p.s.i.

1. Remove the air cleaner and cover the air crossover.
2. Disconnect the wire from the fuel solenoid terminal on the injection pump.
3. Tag and disconnect all glow plug wiring and then remove the glow plugs.
4. Screw a compression gauge into the hole of the cylinder that is being checked.
5. Crank the engine. Six "puffs" per cylinder should be enough for an accurate reading. Normal compression will build up quickly and evenly if the cylinder is OK.

NOTE: *Never add oil to any cylinder during a compression test, as extensive damage may result.*

6. Installation is in the reverse order.

VALVE ADJUSTMENT

This engine uses hydraulic valve lifters; no adjustment is necessary or possible.

Injection Timing Adjustment

For the engine to be properly timed, the marks on the top of the injection pump adapter and the flange of the injection pump must be in alignment. This is done with the engine turned off.

1. Loosen the three pump retaining nuts with the proper tool.

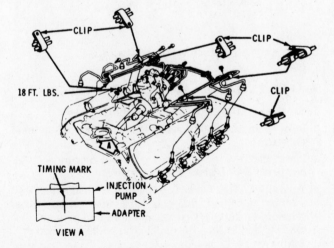

Injection pump timing marks (© G.M. Corp.)

2. Use a ¾ in. open end wrench on the boss at the front of the injection pump and rotate the pump until the two timing marks align.
3. Tighten the retaining nuts to 35 ft lbs and then adjust the throttle rod.

ESTABLISHING A NEW TIMING MARK

When a new injection pump adapter has been installed you will need to make a new timing mark also.

1. File off the original mark on the adapter. DO NOT file off the mark on the pump flange.

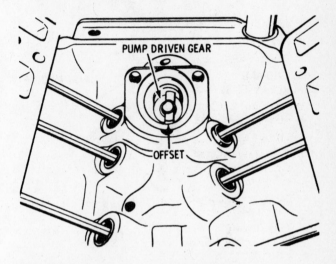

Offset on the pump driven gear (© G.M. Corp.)

2. Position the No. 1 cylinder at TDC of the compression stroke.
3. Align the mark on the vibration balancer with the zero mark on the indicator. The position of the injection pump driven gear should be offset to the right when the No. 1 cylinder is at TDC.
4. Install a special timing tool into the pump adapter. Torque the tool, toward the No. 1 cylinder, to 50 ft lbs.
5. Mark the pump adapter, remove the special tool and install the injection pump.

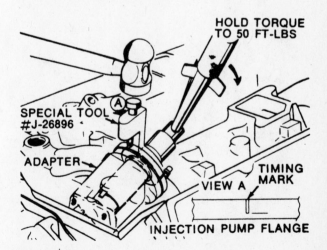

Marking the injection pump adapter (© G.M. Corp.)

Throttle Rod Adjustment

1. Check timing.
2. Remove the clip from the cruise control rod (if so equipped) and disconnect the rod from the throttle lever assembly.
3. Disconnect the detent cable from the throttle assembly.

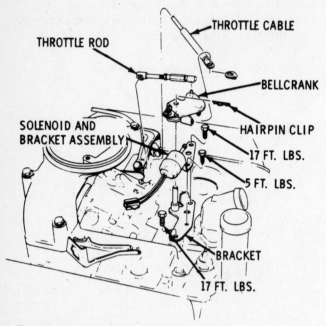

Throttle linkage (© G.M. Corp.)

4. Loosen the lock nut on the pump rod and shorten it several turns.
5. Rotate the lever assembly to the full throttle position and hold it there.
6. Lengthen the pump rod until the injection pump lever just contacts the full throttle stop.
7. Release the lever assembly and tighten the pump rod lock nut.
8. Remove the pump rod from the lever assembly and reconnect the detent cable.

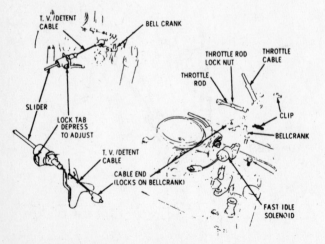

Detent cable adjustment (© G.M. Corp.)

Detent Cable Adjustment

NOTE: *The throttle rod must be adjusted before adjusting the detent cable.*

1. Depress and hold the metal lock tab on the cable upper end.
2. Move the slider through the fitting, away from the lever assembly, until it stops against the metal fitting.
3. Release the metal tab, rotate the lever assembly to the full throttle stop and then release it.
4. Reconnect the pump rod and the cruise control rod if necessary.

Idle Speed

SLOW IDLE ADJUSTMENT

1. Run the engine until it reaches normal operating temperature.
2. Insert the probe of a magnetic pickup tachometer into the timing indicator hole.
3. Set the parking brake and block the drive wheels.
4. Place the transmission in Drive and turn the A/C off (if so equipped).
5. Turn the slow idle adjustment screw on the injection pump to obtain the idle speed specified on the emission control label.

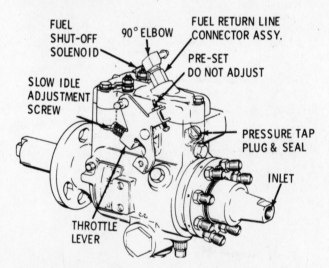

Slow idle adjustment screw (© G.M. Corp.)

FAST IDLE SOLENOID ADJUSTMENT—1978-79

1. Set the parking brake and block the drive wheels.
2. Run the engine until it reaches normal operating temperature.
3. Place the transmission in Drive and disconnect the compressor clutch wire.
4. Turn the A/C on. On cars without A/C, disconnect the solenoid wire and then connect jumper wires to the solenoid terminals. Ground one wire and connect the other to the battery, this will activate the solenoid.
5. Adjust the fast idle solenoid plunger to obtain 650 rpm.

FAST IDLE SOLENOID ADJUSTMENT—1980-81

1. With the ignition off, disconnect the single green wire from the fast idle relay located on the firewall.
2. Set the parking brake and block the drive wheels.
3. Start the engine and adjust the solenoid (energized) to the specifications on the underhood emission control label.
4. Turn off the engine and reconnect the green wire.

Glow Plugs

Eight glow plugs are used to heat the prechamber to aid in starting. They are essentially small heaters that turn on when the ignition switch is turned to the "RUN" position prior to starting the engine. They remain on for a short time after starting and then automatically shut off.

There are two types of glow plugs used on G.M. diesels; the "fast-glow" type and the "slow-glow" type. The fast-glow type use pulsing current applied to 6 volt glow plugs, while the slow-glow type use a continuous current applied to 12 volt glow plugs.

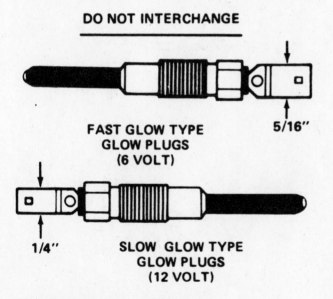

DO NOT INTERCHANGE

FAST GLOW TYPE GLOW PLUGS (6 VOLT) 5/16"

1/4" **SLOW GLOW TYPE GLOW PLUGS (12 VOLT)**

Glow plug identification (© G.M. Corp.)

An easy way to tell the plugs apart is that the fast-glow (6V) plugs have a 5/16 in. wide electrical connector plug, while the slow glow (12V) connector is 1/4 in. wide. Do not attempt to interchange any parts of these two glow plug systems.

REMOVAL AND INSTALLATION

NOTE: *Use extreme care when removing a glow plug as the tip may break off; requiring cylinder head removal.*

1. Tag and disconnect the electrical connectors.
2. Using the large hex nut, loosen the glow plug and carefully lift it out of the cylinder head.
3. Installation is in the reverse order.

FUEL SYSTEM

Fuel Supply Pump

These engines use a small, mechanical fuel pump to deliver fuel from the lines to the injection pump.

REMOVAL

1. Disconnect and plug the two fuel lines. Disconnect the vapor return hose (if so equipped).
2. Remove the two mounting bolts.
3. Remove the pump and gasket.

INSTALLATION

1. Install pump and gasket. Tighten mounting bolts to 27 ft lbs.
2. Install both fuel lines and the vapor return hose.
3. Start engine and check for leaks.

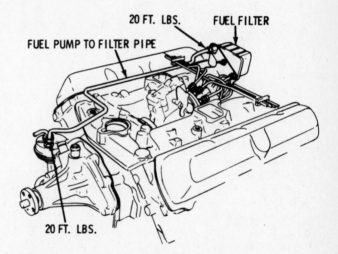

Fuel supply pump, filter and lines (© G.M. Corp.)

Fuel Filter Removal and Installation

The fuel filter is a square assembly located at the back of the engine, above the intake manifold. Disconnect the fuel lines, remove the mounting bolt and remove the filter. Install a new filter in the reverse.

Injection Pump

REMOVAL

1. Remove the air cleaner.
2. Remove the filters and pipes from the valve covers and air crossover.
3. Remove the air crossover and cap the intake manifold with screened covers or tape.
4. Disconnect the throttle rod and return spring.
5. Remove the bellcrank.

6. Remove the throttle and detent cables from the intake manifold brackets.

7. Disconnect the fuel lines from the filter and remove the filter.

8. Disconnect the fuel inlet line at the pump.

9. Remove the rear A/C compressor brace (if so equipped) and remove the fuel line.

10. Disconnect the fuel return line from the injection pump.

11. Remove the clamps and pull the fuel return lines from each injection nozzle.

12. Using two wrenches, disconnect the high pressure lines at the nozzles.

13. Remove the three injection pump retaining nuts.

14. Remove the pump and cap all lines and nozzles.

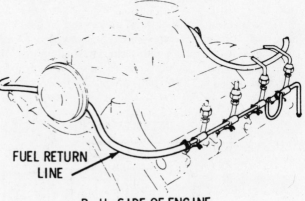

L. H. SIDE OF ENGINE

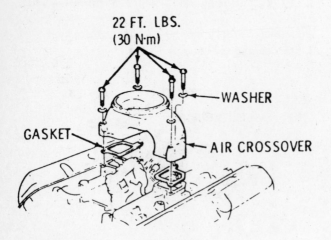

Typical air crossover (© G.M. Corp.)

R. H. SIDE OF ENGINE

Fuel return lines—all but Calif. (© G.M. Corp.)

INSTALLATION

1. Remove the protective caps from all lines and nozzles. Place the engine on TDC for the No. 1 cylinder. The mark on the harmonic balancer on the crankshaft will be aligned with the zero mark on the timing tab, and both valves for No. 1 cylinder will be closed. The index mark on the injection pump driven gear should be offset to the right when No. 1 is at TDC. Check that all of these conditions are met before continuing.

2. Line up the offset tang on the pump driveshaft with the pump driven gear and install the pump.

3. Install, but do not tighten the pump retaining nuts.

4. Connect the high pressure lines at the nozzles.

5. Using two wrenches, torque the high pressure line nuts to 25 ft. lbs.

6. Connect the fuel return lines to the nozzles and pump.

7. Align the timing mark on the injection pump with the line on the pump adaptor and torque the mounting nuts to 35 ft. lbs.

NOTE: *A ³⁄₄ in. open end wrench on the boss at the front of the injection pump will aid in rotating the pump to align the marks.*

8. Adjust the throttle rod.

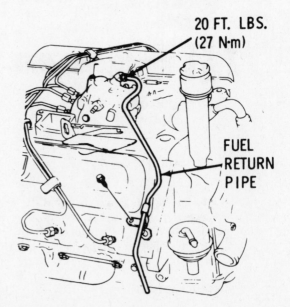

Fuel return pipe—Calif. (© G.M. Corp.)

9. Install the fuel inlet line between the transfer pump and the filter.

10. Install the rear A/C compressor brace (if so equipped).

11. Install the bellcrank and clip.

12. Connect the throttle rod and return spring.

13. Adjust the transmission cable.

14. Start the engine and check for fuel leaks.

15. Remove the screened covers or tape and install the air crossover.

16. Install the tubes in the air flow control valve in the air crossover and install the ventilation filters in the valve covers.

17. Install the air cleaner.

18. Start the engine and allow it to run for two minutes. Stop the engine and let it stand for two minutes, then restart. This permits the air to bleed off within the pump.

INJECTORS

Removal and Installation

1978–79

1. Remove the fuel return line from the nozzle.

2. Remove the injector spring clamp and spacer.

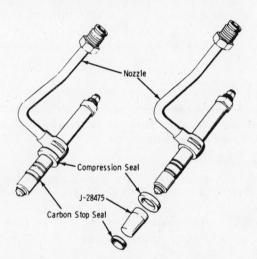

Nozzle seal installation—1978–79 (©G.M. Corp.)

3. Remove the injector using the proper tool.

4. Cap the high pressure line and the injector tip.

NOTE: *The injector tip is highly susceptible to damage and must be protected at all times.*

5. If an old nozzle is being installed, a new compression seal and carbon stop seal must be installed after removal of the used ones.

6. Remove the caps and install the injector, spacer and clamps. Tighten to 25 ft lbs.

7. Replace the return line, start the engine and check for leaks.

1980–81

The injectors on these engines are simply unscrewed from the cylinder head, after the fuel lines have been

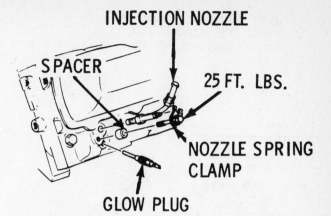

Injector nozzle installation—1978–79 (©G.M. Corp.)

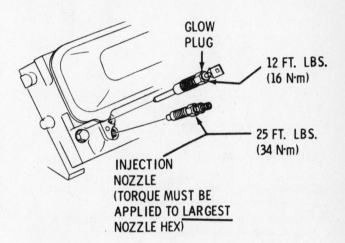

Injector nozzle installation—1980–81 (©G.M. Corp.)

removed, much like a spark plug. Be careful not to damage the injector tip and make sure that the copper gasket is removed from the cylinder head if it does not come off with the injector.

Clean the carbon build-up from the tip of the injector with a soft brass wire brush. Installation is in the reverse.

NOTE: *1981 engines use two types of injectors; CAV Lucas and Diesel Equipment. When installing the inlet fittings, tighten to 45 ft lbs. on the Diesel Equipment injector and to 25 ft lbs. on the CAV injector.*

INJECTION PUMP FUEL LINES

When any fuel lines are to be removed, clean all the fittings before loosening. Immediately cap all lines, nozzles and fittings to maintain system cleanliness.

Removal and Installation

All lines may be removed without removing the injection pump. No back-up wrench is necessary when removing a line from the pump fitting.

1. Remove the air cleaner.

**INLET FITTING TO BODY TORQUE
DIESEL EQUIPMENT – 45 FT. LBS.
C.A.V. LUCAS – 25 FT. LBS.**

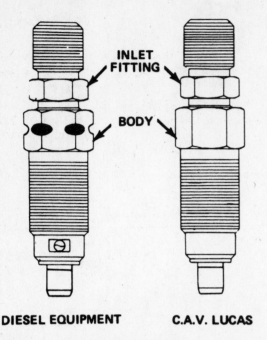

DIESEL EQUIPMENT   **C.A.V. LUCAS**

Injector identification—1981 (© G.M. Corp.)

2. Disconnect and remove all filters and pipes from the valve covers and the air crossover.
3. Remove the air crossover and cap the openings with screened covers or tape.
4. Remove the injection pump line clamps. Cap all open lines, nozzles or fittings. Use a back-up wrench on the upper hex nut of the injector to prevent a fuel leak.
5. Loosely install the new fuel lines. Check that routing is correct and then tighten the pump end to 35 ft lbs and the nozzle end to 25 ft lbs. Use a back-up wrench on the upper hex nut of the injector to prevent nozzle damage.

NOTE: *If more than one line is being replaced, always start with the bottom line.*

6. Install the clamps. Installation of remaining components is the ???
7. Start the engine and check for leaks.

COOLING SYSTEM

Water Pump

REMOVAL

1. Drain the radiator. Disconnect the lower radiator hose at the water pump.
2. Disconnect the heater and by-pass hoses at the water pump.
3. Remove the fan assembly and all accessory drive belts.
4. Remove the water pump pulley.

5. Disconnect the alternator, power steering pump bracket and, if so equipped, the A/C compressor bracket.
6. Unscrew the mounting bolts and remove the water pump.

INSTALLATION

1. Transfer studs from old pump to new one (if pump is being replaced).
2. Clean all old gasket material from the engine block.
3. Apply a thin coat of RTV sealant to the pump housing and then position the new gasket on housing.
4. Remaining installation is in the reverse. Adjust all drive belts and refill the cooling system.

FAN AND HUB

REMOVAL

1. Disconnect the negative battery cable.
2. Remove the radiator fan shroud as necessary.
3. Matchmark the fan clutch hub and the water pump hub and then unscrew the fan clutch hub-to-water pump hub mounting nuts and remove the entire fan clutch assembly.
4. Remove mounting screws and separate fan from fan clutch.

INSTALLATION

NOTE: *No attempt should be made to repair a bent or damaged fan blade. A damaged fan assembly should always be replaced with a new one.*

1. Attach the fan to the fan clutch hub.
2. Install the fan clutch assembly to the water pump hub and tighten the bolts to 20 ft lbs. Be sure to align the matchmarks made earlier.
3. Reinstall the radiator shroud if removed.
4. Reconnect the negative battery cable.

THERMOSTAT

REMOVAL

1. Disconnect the negative battery cable.
2. Drain the cooling system until the coolant level is below that of the thermostat.
3. Remove the water outlet attaching bolts and remove the outlet.
4. Remove the thermostat.

INSTALLATION

1. Make sure the sealing surfaces are clean and then place a 1/8 in. bead of RTV sealant around the coolant outlet sealing surface on the thermostat housing.
2. Place the thermostat in the housing and install the coolant outlet while the RTV sealant is still wet.
3. Connect the battery cable and refill the cooling system.

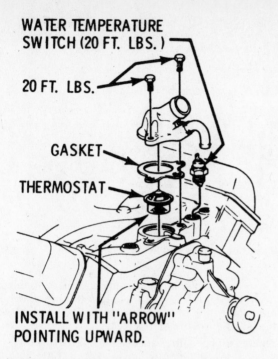

Typical thermostat installation (© G.M. Corp.)

INDUCTION SYSTEM

Intake Manifold

REMOVAL

1. Remove the air cleaner.
2. Drain the radiator. Loosen the upper bypass hose clamp, remove the thermostat housing bolts and remove the housing and thermostat.
3. Remove the breather pipes from the valve covers and the air crossover. Remove the air crossover and cap the holes with screened covers or tape.
4. Disconnect the throttle rod and return spring. If equipped with cruise control, remove the servo.
5. Remove the hairpin clip at the bell crank and disconnect the cables. Disconnect the throttle cable from the bracket on the manifold; position it out of the way. Tag and disconnect any wiring as necessary.
6. Remove the alternator and A/C compressor as necessary.
7. Disconnect the fuel line from the pump and filter. Remove the filter and bracket.
8. Remove the fuel injection pump and lines.
9. Remove the vacuum pump or oil pump drive assembly from the rear of the engine.
10. Remove the intake manifold drain tube.
11. Unscrew the mounting bolts and remove the intake manifold. Remove the adapter seal and the injection pump adapter.

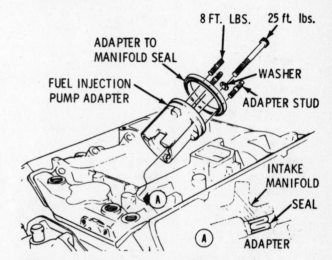

Injection pump adapter and seal (© G.M. Corp.)

INSTALLATION

1. Clean the mating surfaces and coat all with sealer. Position the manifold gasket on the heads and install the end seals; make sure the ends are positioned under the heads.
2. Carefully lower the manifold into position on the engine.
3. Clean the mounting bolts thoroughly and then dip them in clean engine oil. Install the bolts and tighten them in sequence to 15 ft lbs. Next, tighten all bolts to 30 ft lbs, and finally to 40 ft lbs, always in sequence.

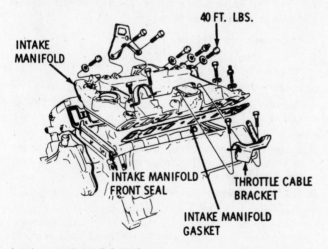

Intake manifold (© G.M. Corp.)

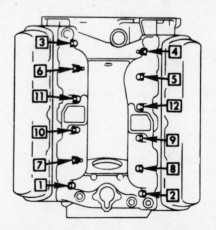

Intake manifold torque sequence (© G.M. Corp.)

4. Install the drain tube and clamp.

5. Apply chassis lube to the adapter and the seal, install the seal on the adapter with the proper tool and then install the adapter.

6. Align the offset tang on the pump drive shaft with the offset in the pump driven gear and install the pump. Connect the fuel lines to the injectors. Align the mark on the injection pump with the one on the adapter. A 3/4 in, open end wrench can be used on the boss at the front of the pump to aid in rotating the pump to align the marks.

7. Installation of the remaining components is in the reverse order.

CYLINDER HEAD AND VALVETRAIN

Cylinder Head

REMOVAL

1. Remove the intake manifold.

2. Remove the rocker arm cover(s), after removing any accessory brackets that are in the way.

3. Tag and disconnect the glow plug wiring.

4. If the right cylinder head is being removed, disconnect the ground strap from the head.

5. Remove the rocker arm bolts, the bridged pivots, the rocker arms and the pushrods. Make sure to keep all parts in order so they can be returned to their original position.

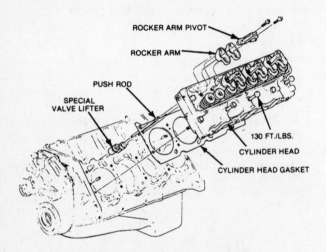

Cylinder head and components (©G.M. Corp.)

6. Remove the fuel return lines from the injectors.

7. Remove the exhaust manifold(s).

8. Remove the engine block drain plug on the side of the engine that the head is being removed from.

9. Unscrew the head bolts and carefully lift off the cylinder head.

INSTALLATION

1. Clean the cylinder head-to-engine block mating surfaces thoroughly. Install new head gaskets on the

engine block. Do NOT coat the gaskets with any kind of sealer. The gaskets have a special coating that eliminates the need for sealer. The use of any additional sealer will interfere with this coating and lead to leakage.

2. Carefully position the cylinder head on the block.

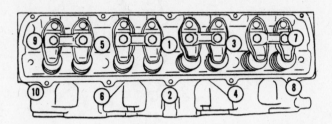

Cylinder head torque sequence (©G.M. Corp.)

3. Clean the head bolts thoroughly and then dip them in clean engine oil. Install them into the cylinder head until the heads of the bolts are in light contact with the top of the cylinder head.

4. Tighten all bolts (in sequence illustrated) to 100 ft lbs. When this is done, retighten all bolts to 130 ft lbs.

5. Installation of the remaining components is in the reverse. Use RTV silicone sealant when installing the rocker arm covers.

NOTE: *Never install the rocker arms without first following the valve lifter bleed down. Procedure detailed later in this section.*

VALVETRAIN

Rocker Arm

REMOVAL AND INSTALLATION

NOTE: *When the rocker arms are loosened or removed, the lifters must be bled down to prevent the buildup of oil pressure inside each lifter. If this pressure is not eliminated, the lifter could raise higher than normal and bring the valves within striking distance of the piston. Valve lifter bleed-down procedures are detailed later in this section.*

1. Remove the air cleaner.

2. Remove the high pressure fuel lines from the injectors.

3. Remove the valve cover.

4. Remove the rocker arm pivot bolts, the bridged pivot and the rocker arms. Each rocker set (one set to a cylinder) is removed as a unit.

5. Lubricate the pivot wear points and position each set of rocker arms in its proper location. Do not tighten the pivot bolts.

6. Bleed the lifters as detailed later in this section

7. Tighten the pivot bolts alternately to 25 ft lbs. Installation of the remaining components is in the reverse. Remember that the valve cover uses RTV sealant, NOT a gasket.

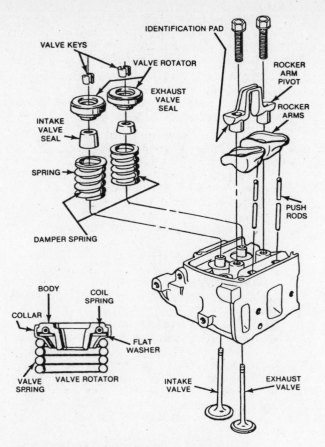

Exploded view of the cylinder head (© G.M. Corp.)

Valve Lifters

REMOVAL

Valve lifters and pushrods should be kept in order so they can be reinstalled in their original position. The pushrods have a "wing" at the upper end so they can only be installed one way. Some engines will have both standard and .010 in. oversize lifters. The oversize lifter will have a '0' etched on the side of the lifter. The cylinder block will also be marked.

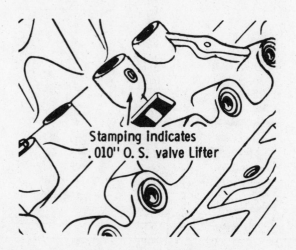

Oversize valve lifters are marked (© G.M. Corp.)

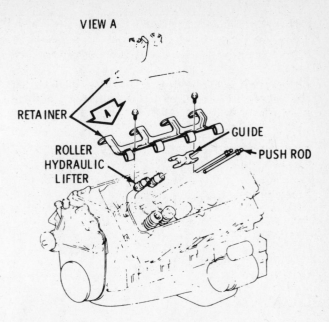

Valve lifter retainer guides (© G.M. Corp.)

1. Remove the intake manifold.
2. Remove the valve covers and the rocker arm assemblies. Lift out the pushrods.
3. Remove the valve lifter guide retainer bolts and then remove the retainer guides.
4. Remove the valve lifters.

DISASSEMBLY

1. Pry out the retainer ring with a small screwdriver.
2. Remove the pushrod seat and the oil metering valve.
3. Remove the plunger and the plunger spring.
4. Remove the check valve retainer from the plunger and then remove the valve and spring.

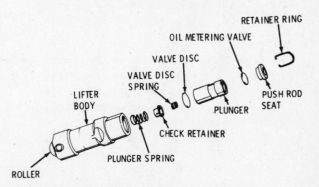

Exploded view of the valve lifter (© G.M. Corp.)

CLEANING AND INSPECTION

After the lifters are disassembled, all parts should be cleaned in solvent. A small particle under the check valve will cause malfunctioning of the lifter. Inspect all parts for nicks, burrs or scoring. If the roller body or the plunger are found to be defective in any way, the entire lifter assembly should be replaced. Whenever the lifters are removed, check as follows:

1. The roller should rotate freely, but without excessive play.
2. Check that the needle bearing is not missing or broken.
3. The roller should be free of pitting or roughness. If either of these conditions are present, check the camshaft for a similar condition. Replace the lifter or the camshaft if necessary.

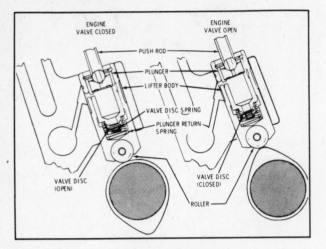

Cross section of a valve lifter (©G.M. Corp.)

ASSEMBLY

1. Coat all parts with a light coating of clean engine oil.
2. Assemble the valve disc spring and retainer into the plunger. Make sure the retainer flange is pressed tight against the bottom of the recess in the plunger.
3. Install the plunger spring over the check retainer.
4. Hold the plunger with the spring facing up and insert it into the lifter body. Hold it vertically to prevent cocking the spring.
5. Install the oil metering valve and the pushrod seat into the lifter. Install the retaining ring.

INSTALLATION

Prime the new lifter by working the lifter plunger while the assembly is submerged in new kerosene or diesel fuel. A dry lifter can be damaged when starting the engine.

1. When a rocker arm is loosened or removed, valve lifter bleed down is required.
2. Install the lifters and pushrods into their original position in the cylinder block.
3. Install the intake manifold.
4. Installation of the remaining components is the reverse.

Valve Lifter Diagnosis

1. Momentarily Noisy When Car Is Started:
   This condition is normal. Oil drains from the lifters which are holding the valves open when the engine is not running. It will take a few seconds for the lifter to fill after the engine is started.
2. Intermittently Noisy On Idle Only, Disappearing When Engine Speed Is Increased:

Intermittent clicking may be an indication of a pitted check valve disk, or it may be caused by dirt.
Correction: Clean the lifter and inspect. If check valve disc is defective, replace lifter.

3. Noisy At Slow Idle Or With Hot Oil, Quiet With Cold Oil Or As Engine Speed Is Increased:
   Leak check the suspected lifters and replace any lifters that do not meet specifications.

4. Noisy At High Car Speeds And Quiet At Low Speeds:
   a. High oil level—Oil level above the "Full" mark allows crankshaft counterweights to churn the oil into foam. When foam is pumped into the lifters, they will become noisy since a solid column of oil is required for proper operation.
   b. Low oil level—Oil level below the "Add" mark allows the pump to pump air at high speeds which results in noisy lifters.
      Correction: Fill until proper oil level is obtained.
   c. Oil pan bent on bottom or pump screen cocked, replace or repair as necessary.

5. Noisy At Idle Becoming Louder As Engine Speed Is Increased To 1500 rmp:
   This noise is not connected with lifter malfunction. it becomes most noticeable in the car at 10 to 15 mph "L" range, or 30 to 35 mph "D" range and is best described as a hashy sound. At slow idle, it may be entirely gone or appear as a light ticking noise in one or more valves. It is caused by one or more of the following:
   a. Badly worn or scuffed valve tip and rocker arm pad.
   b. Excessive valve stem to guide clearance.
   c. Excessive valve seat runout.
   d. Off square valve spring.
   e. Excessive valve face runout.
   f. Valve spring damper clicking on rotator.
      To check valve spring and valve guide clearance remove the valve covers:
   1. Occasionally this noise can be eliminated by rotating the valve spring and valve. Crank engine until noisy valve is off its seat. Rotate spring. This will also rotate valve. Repeat until valve becomes quiet. If correction is obtained, check for an off square valve spring. If spring is off square more than 1/16 in free position, replace spring.

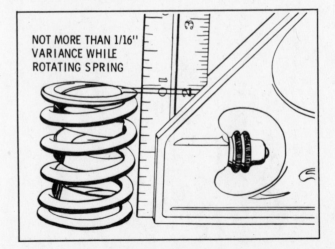

NOT MORE THAN 1/16"
VARIANCE WHILE
ROTATING SPRING

Checking the valve spring (©G.M. Corp.)

2. Check for excessive valve stem to guide clearance. If necessary, correct as required.

6. **Valves Noisy Regardless Of Engine Speed:** This condition can be caused by foreign particles or excessive valve lash.

Check for valve lash by turning engine so the piston in that cylinder is on top dead center of firing stroke. If valve lash is present, the push-rod can be freely moved up and down a certain amount with rocker arm held against valve. If OK, clean suspected valve lifters.

Valve lash indicates one of the following:
 a. Worn push-rod.
 b. Worn rocker arm.
 c. Lifter plunger stuck in down position due to dirt or carbon.
 d. Defective lifter.

Checking of the above four items:
 1. Look at the upper end of push-rod. Excessive wear of the spherical surface indicates one of the following conditions.
    a. Improper hardness of the push-rod ball. The push-rod and rocker arm must be replaced.
    b. Improper lubrication of the pushrod. The pushrod and rocker arm must be replaced. The oiling system to the push-rod should be checked.
 2. If push-rod appears in good condition and has been properly lubricated, replace rocker arm and recheck valve lash.
 3. If valve lash exists and push-rod and rocker arm are okay, trouble is in the lifter. Lifter should be replaced.

Any time the valves are removed for service the tips should be inspected for improper pattern which could indicate valve rotator malfunction.

Valve Lifter Bleed Down

If the intake manifold has been removed and if any rocker arms have been loosened or removed, it will be necessary to remove those valve lifters, disassemble them, drain the oil from them and then reassemble them.

If the intake manifold has not been removed, but the rocker arms have been loosened or removed, the valve lifters must be bled down by the following procedure:

1. Before installing any removed rocker arms, rotate the engine crankshaft so that No. 1 cylinder is 32° before top dead center. This is ½ in. counterclockwise from the 0° pointer. To verify that No. 1 cylinder TDC is coming up, remove the No. 1 cylinder glow plug, then turn the engine: compression pressure will force air out the glow plug hole.

NOTE: *Use only hand wrenches to torque the rocker arm pivot bolts to avoid engine damage.*

2. If removed, install the No. 5 cylinder pivot and rocker arms, then torque the bolts alternately between the intake and exhaust valves until the intake valve begins to open, then stop.

3. Install the remaining rocker arms except No. 3 and No. 8 intake valves (if these rocker arms were removed).

4. If removed, install the No. 3 and No. 8 intake valve pivots, but do not torque beyond the point that the valve would be fully open. This is indicated by strong resistance while still turning the pivot retaining bolts. Going beyond this point will bend the push-rod. Torque the bolts SLOWLY, allowing the lifter to bleed down.

5. Finish torquing No. 5 cylinder rocker arm pivot bolt slowly. Do not go beyond the point that the valve would be fully open, as in step 4.

6. Do not turn the engine for at least 45 minutes.

7. Finish assembling the engine as the lifters are being bled.

CAUTION: *Do not rotate the engine until the valve lifters have been bled down, or metal to metal contact can occur, between piston and valve.*

Valves and Springs—Head Removed

NOTE: *If only the valve/springs are being removed, the cylinder head need not be removed.*

REMOVAL AND INSTALLATION

1. Remove the valve keys by compressing the valve springs with a valve spring compressor.

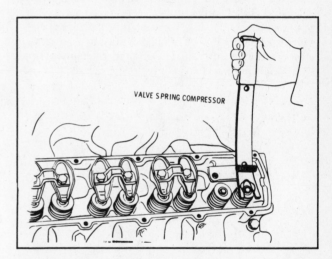

Removing the valve spring (© G.M. Corp.)

2. Remove the valve spring rotators or the retainers and springs.

3. Remove the oil seals from the valve stems.

4. Remove the valves. Keep them separated so they can be installed in their original locations.

5. Install the valves in the respective guides.

6. Install new seals over the valve stem. Position them as far down the stem as possible, they will position themselves correctly when the engine is started.

7. Position the valve springs over the valve stems.

8. Install the valve rotators, compress the springs and install the valve stem keys. Check the springs and keys to make sure they are properly seated.

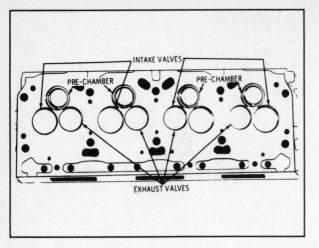

Valve locations (© G.M. Corp.)

MEASURING VALVE STEM HEIGHT

Whenever a new valve is installed, or after grinding valves, it will be necessary to measure valve stem height as follows:

There should be at least .015″ clearance on all valves between gauge surface and end of valve stem. (Valve stem can be gauged with or without the valve rotator on the valve.) If clearance is less than .015″ remove valve and grind tip of valve stems as required on a valve refacing machine, using the "Vee" block attachment to insure a smooth 90° end. Also be certain to break sharp edge on ground valve tip. Ovserve an original valve to determine chamfer.

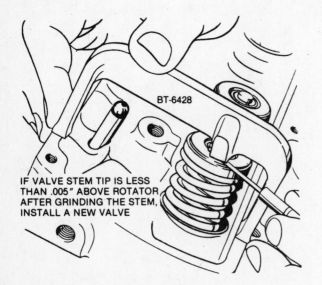

IF VALVE STEM TIP IS LESS THAN .005″ ABOVE ROTATOR AFTER GRINDING THE STEM, INSTALL A NEW VALVE

Checking rotator height (© G.M. Corp.)

After all valve keys have been installed on valves, tap each valve stem end with a mallet to seat valve rotators and keys. Regauge all valves between valve stem and gauge (.015″ minimum) and valve rotator and gauge (.030″ minimum). If any valve stem end is less than .005″ above rotator, the valve is too short and a new valve must be installed.

EXAMPLE:
Valve Rotator to
Gauge Clearance .038″
Minus Valve Stem to
Gauge Clearance —.035″ —.003″

This is less than .005″ and a new valve should be installed.

NOTE: *There must be a minimum of .030″ clearance between valve rotator and gauge. Failure to maintain this clearance will cause rocker arm and valve rotator interference.*

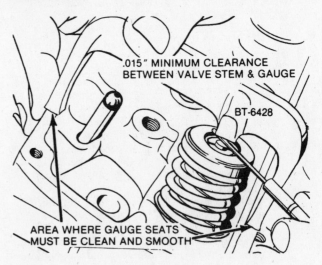

.015″ MINIMUM CLEARANCE BETWEEN VALVE STEM & GAUGE

BT-6428

AREA WHERE GAUGE SEATS MUST BE CLEAN AND SMOOTH

Checking valve height (© G.M. Corp.)

ENGINE

REMOVAL AND INSTALLATION

1. Drain the cooling system.
2. Remove the air cleaner.
3. Mark the hood-to-hinge position and remove the hood.
4. Disconnect the ground cables from the batteries.
5. Disconnect the ground wires at the fender panels and the ground strap at the cowl.
6. Disconnect the radiator hoses, cooler lines, heater hoses, vacuum hoses, power steering pump hoses, air conditioning compressor (hoses attached), fuel inlet hose and all attached wiring.
7. Remove the bellcrank clip.
8. Disconnect the throttle and transmission cables.
9. Remove the radiator.
10. Raise and support the car.
11. Disconnect the exhaust pipes at the manifold.
12. Remove the torque converter cover and the three bolts holding the converter to the flywheel.
13. Remove the engine mount bolts.
14. Remove the three right side transmission-to-engine bolts. Remove the starter.
15. Lower the car and attach a hoist to the engine.
16. Slightly raise the transmission with a jack.

17. Remove the three left side transmission-to-engine bolts and remove the engine.

18. Installation is the reverse of removal. Converter cover bolts are torqued to 40 ft. lbs.

Front Cover

REMOVAL

1. Drain the cooling system and disconnect the radiator hoses.

2. Remove all belts, fan and pulley, crankshaft pulley and balancer, using a balancer puller.

CAUTION: *The use of any other type of puller, such as a universal claw type which pulls on the outside of the hub, can destroy the balancer. The outside ring of the balancer is bonded in rubber to the hub. Pulling on the outside will break the bond. The timing mark is on the outside ring. If it is suspected that the bond is broken, check that the center of the keyway is 16° from the center of the timing slot. In addition, there are chiseled aligning marks between the weight and the hub.*

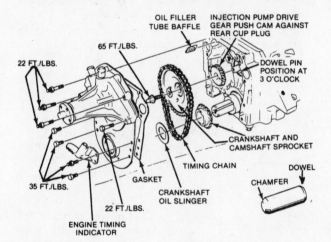

Front cover, timing chain and sprockets (©G.M. Corp.)

3. Unbolt and remove the cover, timing indicator and water pump.

4. It may be necessary to grind a flat on the cover for gripping purposes.

INSTALLATION

1. Grind a chamfer on one end of each dowel pin.

2. Cut the excess material from the front end of the oil pan gasket on each side of the block.

3. Clean the block, oil pan and front cover mating surfaces with solvent.

4. Trim about ⅛ in. off each end of a new front pan seal.

5. Install a new front cover gasket on the block and a new seal in the front cover.

6. Apply sealer to the gasket around the coolant holes.

7. Apply RTV sealer to the block at the junction of the pan and front cover.

8. Place the cover on the block and press down to compress the seal. Rotate the cover left and right and guide the pan seal into the cavity using a small screwdriver. Oil the bolt threads and heads, install two to hold the cover in place, then install both dowel pins (chamfered end first). Install remaining front coverbolts.

9. Apply a lubricant, compatible with rubber, on the balancer seal surface.

10. Install the balancer and bolt. Torque the bolt to 200-300 ft. lbs.

11. Install all other parts in reverse of removal.

Timing Chain and Sprockets

REMOVAL AND INSTALLATION

1. Remove the timing case cover and take off the camshaft gear.

2. Remove the oil slinger, timing chain, and the camshaft sprocket. If the crankshaft sprocket is to be replaced, remove it also at this time. Remove the crankshaft key before using the puller. If the key can not be removed, align the puller so it does not overlap the end of the key, as the keyway is only machined part of the way into the crankshaft gear.

3. Reinstall the crankshaft sprocket being careful to start it with the keyway in perfect alignment since it is rather difficult to correct for misalignment after the gear has been started on the shaft. Turn the timing mark on the crankshaft gear until it points directly toward the center of the camshaft. Mount the timing chain over the camshaft gear and start the camshaft gear up on to its shaft with the timing marks as close as possible to each other and in line between the shaft centers. Rotate the camshaft to align the shaft with the new gear.

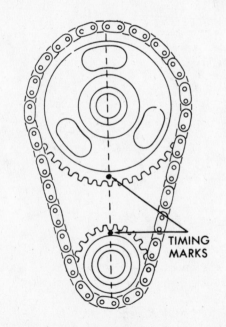

Align timing marks (©G.M. Corp.)

4. Install the fuel pump eccentric with the flat side toward the rear.

5. Drive the key in with a hammer until it bottoms.

6. Install the oil slinger.

NOTE: *Any time the timing chain and gears are replaced, it will be necessary to retime the engine.*

Camshaft

REMOVAL

NOTE: *If camshaft is to be removed, the air conditioning, if equipped, must be discharged by a professional and the condenser removed.*

Removal of the camshaft also requires removal of the injection pump drive and driven gears, removal of the intake manifold, disassembly of the valve lifters, and re-timing of the injection pump.

1. Disconnect the negative battery cables. Drain the coolant. Remove the radiator.

2. Remove the intake manifold and gasket and the front and rear intake manifold seals.

3. Remove the balancer pulley and the balancer. See "Caution" under "Front Cover Removal and Installation." Remove the engine front cover using the appropriate procedure.

4. Remove the valve covers. Remove the rocker arms, pushrods and valve lifters; see the procedure earlier in this section. Be sure to keep the parts in order so that they may be returned to their original positions.

5. If equipped with air conditioning, the condenser must be discharged and removed from the car.

WARNING: *Compressed refrigerant expands (boils) into the atmosphere at a temperature of -21°F or less. It will freeze any surface it contacts, including your skin or eyes.*

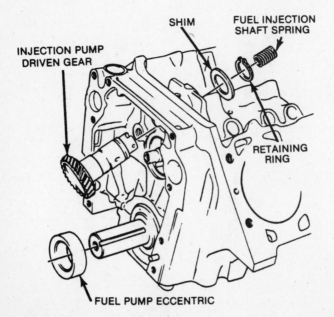

Injection pump driven gear (©G.M. Corp.)

6. Remove the camshaft sprocket retaining bolt, and remove the timing chain and sprockets, using the procedure outlined earlier.

7. Position the camshaft dowel pin at the 3 o'clock position.

8. Push the camshaft rearward and hold it there, being careful not to dislodge the oil gallery plug at the rear of the engine. Remove the injection pump drive gear by sliding it from the camshaft while rocking the pump driven gear.

9. To remove the fuel injection pump driven gear, remove the pump adapter, remove the snap ring, and remove the selective washer. Remove the driven gear and spring.

10. Remove the camshaft by sliding it out the front of the engine. Be extremely careful not to allow the cam lobes to contact any of the bearings, or the journals to dislodge the bearings during camshaft removal. Do not force the camshaft, or bearing damage will result.

INSTALLATION

1. If either the injection pump drive or driven gears are to be replaced, replace both gears.

2. Coat the camshaft and the cam bearings with GM lubricant #1052365 or the equivalent.

3. Carefully slide the camshaft into position in the engine.

4. Fit the crankshaft and camshaft sprockets, aligning the timing marks as shown in the timing chain removal and installation procedure. Remove the sprockets without disturbing the timing.

5. Install the injection pump driven gear, spring, shim, and snap ring. Check the gear end play. If the end play is not within 0.002–0.006 in., replace the shim to obtain the specified clearance. Shims are available in 0.003 in. increments, from 0.080 to 0.115 in.

6. Position the camshaft dowel pin at the 3 o'clock position. Align the zero marks on the pump drive gear and pump driven gear. Hold the camshaft in the rearward position and slide the pump drive gear onto the camshaft. Install the camshaft bearing retainer.

7. Install the timing chain and sprockets, making sure the timing marks are aligned.

8. Install the lifters, pushrods and rocker arms. Make sure you follow the "Valve Lifter Bleed Down Procedure." Failure to bleed down the lifters could bend valves when the engine is turned over.

9. Install the injection pump adapter and injection pump. See the appropriate sections for procedures.

10. Install the remaining components in the reverse order of removal.

Crankshaft

REMOVAL

1. Remove the oil pan, the oil pump and the front cover.

2. Rotate the crankshaft to a position where the connecting rod nuts are most accessible. Unscrew the

nuts and remove the connecting rod caps. Install thread protectors.

3. Remove the fuel pump eccentric from the crankshaft.

4. Remove the main bearing caps.

5. Note the position of the keyway in the crankshaft so it can be installed in the same position.

6. Lift the crankshaft out of the block. The connecting rods will pivot to the center of the engine during removal. Do not allow them to move in their bore any more than that.

INSTALLATION

1. Install enough oil pan bolts into the pan rails so that rubber bands can be stretched between them and the connecting rods. Align the rods so that the inner thread protectors of adjacent rods overlap approximately one inch. Connecting rod alignment can be adjusted by increasing the tension on a rubber band with additional turns around the pan bolts.

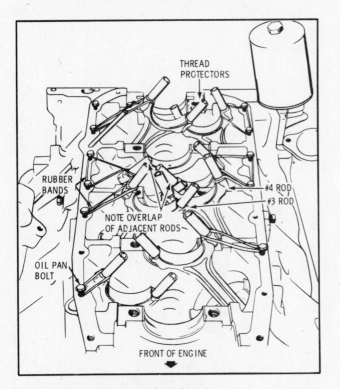

Crankshaft installation (©G.M. Corp.)

2. Measure the crankshaft journals and crankpins with a micrometer to determine the correct size rod and main bearings to be used.

NOTE: *Whenever a new or reconditioned crankshaft is installed, new connecting rod bearings and main bearings should be used.*

3. Position the crankshaft keyway in the same position as removed and lower the crankshaft into the block. The connecting rods will follow the crankpins into the correct position as the crankshaft is lowered.

4. Remove the rubber bands, thread protectors and pan bolts and assemble the remaining components in the reverse order of removal.

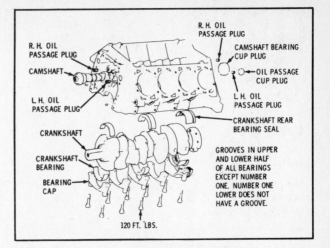

Exploded view of the short block (©G.M. Corp.)

NOTE: *In order to prevent the possibility of cylinder block and/or main bearing cap damage, the main bearing caps should be tapped into their cylinder cavity using a brass or leather mallet before the attaching bolts are installed. Never use the attaching bolts to pull the main bearing caps into their seats.*

Main Bearings

REMOVAL AND INSTALLATION

1. Loosen all main bearing caps.

2. Remove the bearing cap and remove the lower shell.

3. Insert a flattened cotter pin in the oil passage hole in the crankshaft and then rotate the crankshaft in the direction opposite of cranking rotation. The pin will contact the upper shell and roll it out.

4. Check the main bearing journals for roughness or wear. Slight roughness may be removed with a fine grit polishing cloth dipped in oil. Burrs may be removed with a fine oil stone. If the journals are scored or ridged, the crankshaft must be replaced.

5. Clean the crankshaft journals and bearing caps thoroughly.

6. Place the new upper shell on the crankshaft journal with the locating tang in the correct position and rotate the shaft to turn it into position using a cotter pin.

7. Place a new shell in the bearing cap and install the cap. Lubricate the bolt-threads with engine oil and tighten to 120 ft lbs.

NOTE: *Always install new rear main oil seal when replacing the #5 bearing.*

Rear Main Bearing Oil Seal

UPPER OIL SEAL

Tools have been released to provide a means of correcting upper seal leaks without the necessity of removing the crankshaft. The procedure of seal leak correction is detailed below.

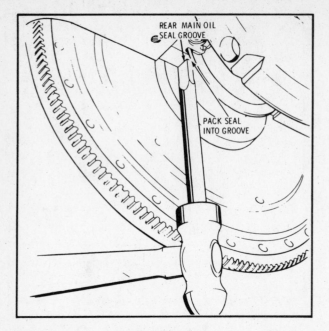

Packing the upper oil seal (©G.M. Corp.)

1. Drain the oil, remove the oil pan and then remove the rear main bearing cap.
2. Insert a packing tool against one end of the upper seal and drive the old seal gently into the groove until it is packed tight. This usually varies between ¹/₂–³/₄ of an inch. Repeat the procedure on the other side.
3. Measure the amount the seal was driven up on one side and add ¹/₁₆ in. Cut this amount from the old seal removed from the main bearing cap. Repeat procedure for other side.
4. Place a drop of sealer on each end of the seal and cap.
5. Using two screwdrivers, work these two pieces of seal into the cylinder block. Use the packing tool and pack each piece up into the block.
6. Replace the lower seal and replace the cap.
7. Installation of the remaining components is in the reverse order.

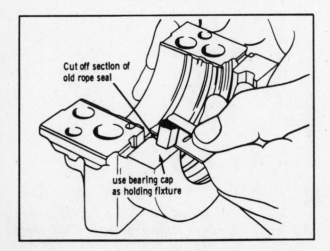

Cutting off the lower seal ends (©G.M. Corp.)

Lower Oil Seal

REMOVAL

1. Drain the oil and remove the oil pan.
2. Remove the rear main bearing cap.
3. Remove the rear main bearing insert and oil seal.
4. Clean the bearing cap and seal grooves. Check for cracks.

INSTALLATION

1. Install the seal into the bearing cap by hand.
2. Use a seal installer and hammer the seal into the groove. To check if the seal is fully seated in the cap, slide the tool away from the seal. With the tool fully seated in the cap, slide the tool against the seal. If the tool butts against the seal, it must be driven further into the groove. If the undercut area of the tool slides over the seal, it's fully seated.

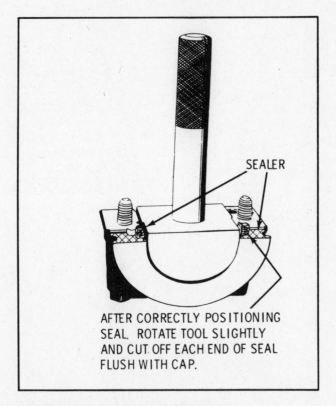

Installing the lower oil seal (©G.M. Corp.)

3. With the tool slightly rotated, cut the seal flush with the mating surface of the cap. Use a small screwdriver and pack the seal and fibers toward the center, away from the edges.
4. Clean and install the bearing insert.
5. Install the bearing caps, lubricate the bolt threads with oil and tighten to 120 ft lbs.
6. Installation of remaining components is the reverse.

Connecting Rods and Pistons

REMOVAL

1. Remove the intake manifold and cylinder head(s).
2. Remove the oil pan and oil pump assembly.
3. Stamp the cylinder number on the machined surfaces of the bolt bosses of the connecting rod and cap to aid in installation.
4. Examine the cylinder bore. If a ridge exists, remove it with a ridge reamer before attempting to remove the piston and rod assembly.
5. Remove the connecting rod bearing cap and bearing. Use a short piece of ⅜ in. hose to cover the bolt threads. This will prevent damage to the threads themselves and to the bearing journal.
6. Remove the rod and piston assembly through the top of the cylinder bore. Repeat this procedure on the other cylinders.

INSTALLATION

1. Make sure that the thread covers are still on all of the rod bolts.
2. Coat the rings and piston with clean engine oil and then install a ring compressing tool onto the piston.
3. Install each rod and piston into its respective cylinder bore so that the curved edge of the valve depression in top of the piston is toward the inner side of the engine.

NOTE: *When installing a piston in the forward two cylinders on either side of the engine, the larger valve depression goes toward the front. On the rear half of the engine, the large depression faces toward the rear.*

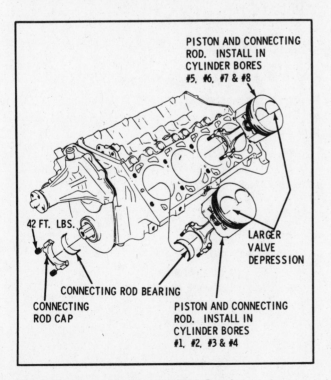

Piston locations in the block (© G.M. Corp.)

4. Lubricate the crankpin with clean engine oil and install the connecting rod bearing and cap, with the bearing index tang in the rod and cap on the same side.
5. When all pistons have been correctly installed in their cylinders, tighten the connecting rod bolt nuts to 42 ft lbs.

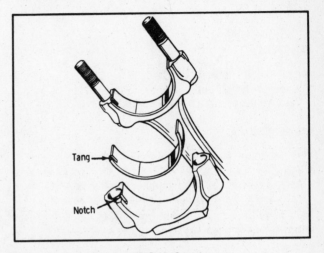

Connecting rod bearing (© G.M. Corp.)

LUBRICATION SYSTEM

Oil Pan

REMOVAL AND INSTALLATION

1. Remove the oil pump drive and the vacuum pump (A/C only).
2. Disconnect the battery cables. Remove the dipstick.
3. Remove the upper radiator support and the fan shroud attaching screws.
4. Raise and support the car. Drain the oil.
5. Remove the flywheel cover.
6. Disconnect the exhaust and crossover pipes.
7. Remove the oil cooler lines at the oil filter base.

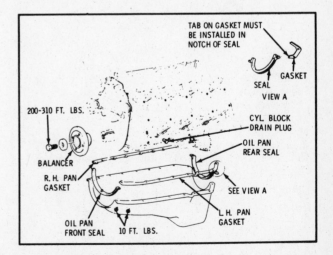

Oil pan installation (© G.M. Corp.)

8. Remove the starter assembly.

9. Remove the engine mounts from the engine block and then jack the front of the engine up.

10. Remove the oil pan.

11. Installation is the reverse of removal.

Oil Pump

REMOVAL

1. Remove the oil pan.

2. Remove the oil pump-to-rear main bearing bolts and remove the pump and drive shaft extension.

DISASSEMBLY

1. Remove the oil pump drive shaft extension.

2. Remove the cotter pin, spring and the pressure regulator valve. Place your thumb over the pressure regulator bore as the spring is under pressure.

3. Remove the oil pump cover and gasket.

4. Remove the drive gear and idler gear from the pump body.

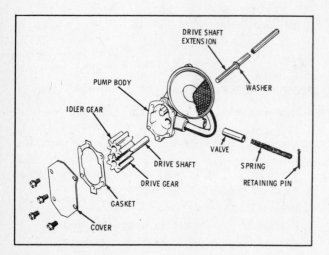

Exploded view of the oil pump (©G.M. Corp.)

ASSEMBLY

1. Install the gear and shaft in the pump body and check the gear end clearance. Place a straight edge over the gears and measure the clearance between the straight edge and the gasket surface. Clearance should be between 0.0005 and 0.0075 in. If the end clearance is near the upper limit, check for scores in the cover that would bring the total clearance over the limit.

2. Install the cover screws and tighten alternately and evenly.

3. Position the pressure regulator valve in the pump cover, closed end first, then install the spring and the retaining pin.

4. Connect the drive shaft extension to the driveshaft.

INSTALLATION

1. Insert the drive shaft extension through the opening in the main bearing cap and block until the shaft mates with the vacuum pump driven gear.

2. Position the pump in the rear main bearing cap and tighten the mounting bolts to 35 ft lbs.

3. Install the oil pan.

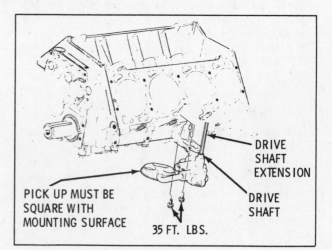

Oil pump installation (©G.M. Corp.)

EXHAUST SYSTEM

Exhaust Manifold

REMOVAL AND INSTALLATION—LEFT SIDE

1. Remove the air cleaner.

2. Remove the alternator lower bracket.

3. Raise and support the car.

4. Remove the crossover pipe.

5. Lower the car and remove the manifold from above.

6. Installation is in the reverse order.

REMOVAL AND INSTALLATION—RIGHT SIDE

1. Raise and support the car.

2. Remove the crossover pipe.

3. Disconnect the exhaust pipe.

4. Remove the right front wheel.

5. Remove the manifold from under the car.

6. Installation is in the reverse order.

12

ROTARY ENGINE OVERHAUL

ROTARY ENGINE OVERHAUL

DISASSEMBLY 1975 AND LATER

NOTE: *Because of the design of the rotary engine, it is not practical to attempt component removal and installation. It is best to disassemble and assemble the entire engine, or, go as far as necessary with the disassembly procedure. Refer to the specification charts for measurements of the components.*

1. Mount the engine on a stand.
2. Remove the oil hose support bracket from the front housing.
3. Disconnect the vacuum hoses, air hoses and remove the decel valve.
4. Remove the air pump and drive belt. Remove the air pump adjusting bar.
5. Remove the alternator and drive belt.
6. Disconnect the metering oil pump connecting rod, oil tubes and vacuum sensing tube from the carburetor.
7. Remove the carburetor and intake manifold as an assembly.
8. Remove the gasket and two rubber rings.
9. Remove the thermal reactor and gaskets.
10. Remove the distributor.
11. Remove the water pump.
12. Invert the engine.
13. Remove the oil pan.
14. Remove the oil pump.

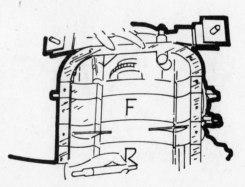

Mark the front and rear rotor housings to prevent confusion during assembly (© Toyo Kogyo Co. Ltd.)

15. Identify the front and rear rotor housings with a felt tip pen. These are common parts and must be identified to be reassembled in their respective locations.
16. Turn the engine on the stand so that the top of the engine is up.
17. Remove the engine mounting bracket from the front cover.
18. Remove the eccentric shaft pulley.
19. Turn the engine on a stand so that the front end of the engine is up.
20. Remove the front cover.

21. Remove the O-ring from the oil passage on the front housing.
22. Remove the oil slinger and distributor drive gear from the shaft.
23. Unbolt and remove the chain adjuster.
24. Remove the locknut and washer from the oil pump driven sprocket.
25. Slide the oil pump drive sprocket and driven sprocket together with the drive chain off the eccentric shaft and oil pump simultaneously.
26. Remove the keys from the eccentric and oil pump shafts.
27. Slide the balance weight, thrust washer and needle bearing from the shaft.
28. Unbolt the bearing housing and slide the bearing housing, needle bearing, spacer and thrust plate off the shaft.
29. Turn the engine on the stand so that the top of the engine is up.
30. If equipped with a manual transmission, remove the clutch pressure plate and clutch disc. Remove the flywheel with a puller.
31. If equipped with an automatic transmission, remove the drive plate. Remove the counterweight.
32. Working at the rear of the engine, loosen the tension bolts.

NOTE: *Do not loosen the tension bolts one at a time. Loosen the bolts evenly in small stages to prevent distortion. Mark tension bolts to replace in original holes during reassembly.*

33. Lift the rear housing off the shaft.

Remove any side seals adhering to the front housing surfaces (© Toyo Kogyo Co. Ltd.)

34. Remove any seals that are stuck to the rotor sliding surface of the rear housing and reinstall them in their original locations.
35. Remove all the corner seals, corner seal springs, side seal and side seal springs from the rear side of the rotor. Mazda has a special tray which holds all the seals and keeps them segregated to prevent mistakes during reassembly. Each seal groove is marked to prevent confusion.
36. Remove the two rubber seals and two O-rings from the rear rotor housing.

Use a felt-tipped pen to mark the bottom of each apex seal (© Toyo Kogyo Co. Ltd.)

37. Remove the dowels from the rear rotor housing.
38. Life the rear rotor housing away from the rear rotor, being very careful not to drop the apex seals on the rear rotor.
39. Remove each apex seal, side piece and spring from the rear rotor and segregate them.
40. Remove the rear rotor from the eccentric shaft and place it upside down on a clean rag.
41. Remove each seal and spring from the other side of the rotor and segregate these.
42. If some of the seals fall off the rotor, be careful not to change the original position of each seal.
43. Identify the rear rotor with a felt tip pen.
44. Remove the oil seals and the springs. Do not exert heavy pressure at only one place on the seal, since it could be deformed. Replace the O-rings in the oil seal when the engine is overhauled.

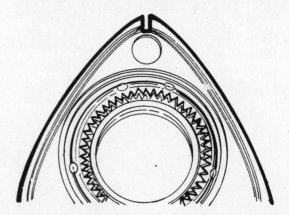

The front rotor is marked with an "F" on its internal gear side; the rear rotor is marked with an "R" in a similar manner (© Toyo Kogyo Co. Ltd.)

45. Hold the intermediate housing down and remove the dowels from it.
46. Lift off the intermediate housing being careful not to damage the eccentric shaft. It should be removed by sliding it beyond the rear rotor journal on the eccentric shaft while holding the intermediate housing up and, at the same time, pushing the eccentric shaft up.
47. Lift out the eccentric shaft.
48. Repeat the above procedures to remove the front rotor housing and front rotor.

Inspection and Replacement

FRONT, INTERMEDIATE AND REAR HOUSINGS

1. Check the housing for signs of gas or water leakage.
2. Remove the carbon deposits from the front housing with extra fine emery cloth.
3. Remove any of the old sealer which is adhering to the housing, using a brush or a cloth soaked in Ke-tone.
4. Check for distortion by placing a straightedge on the surface of the housing. Measure the clearance between the straightedge and the housing with a feeler gauge. If the clearance is greater than 0.002 in. at any point, replace the housing.

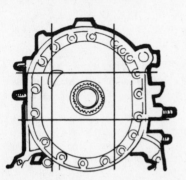

Measure the housing distortion along the axes indicated (© Toyo Kogyo Co. Ltd.)

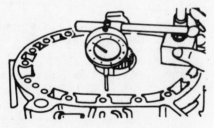

Measuring housing wear with a dial indicator

Most of the front and rear housing wear occurs at the end of the minor axis as shown (© Toyo Kogyo Co. Ltd.)

5. Use a dial indicator to check for wear on the rotor contact surfaces of the housing. If the wear is greater than 0.004 in., replace the housing.

NOTE: *The wear at either end of the minor axis is greater than at any other point on the housing. However, this is normal and should be no cause for concern.*

FRONT STATIONARY GEAR AND MAIN BEARING

1. Examine the teeth of the stationary gear for wear or damage.
2. Be sure that the main bearing shows no signs of excessive wear, scoring, or flaking.
3. Check the main bearing-to-eccentric journal clearance by measuring the journal with a vernier caliper and the bearing with a pair of inside calipers.

MAIN BEARING REPLACEMENT

1. Unfasten the securing bolts, if used. Drive the stationary gear and main bearing assembly out of the housing with a brass drift.
2. Press the main bearing out of the stationary gear.
3. Press a new main bearing into the stationary gear so that it is in the same position that the old bearing was.
4. Align the slot in the stationary gear flange with the dowel pin in the housing and press the gear into place. Install the securing bolts, if required.

NOTE: *To aid in stationary gear and main bearing removal and installation, Mazda manufactures a special tool, part number 49 0813 235.*

REAR STATIONARY GEAR AND MAIN BEARING

Inspect the rear stationary gear and main bearing in a similar manner to the front. In addition, examine the O-ring, which is located in the stationary gear, for signs of wear or damage. Replace the O-ring, if necessary.

To replace the stationary gear, use the following procedure.

1. Remove the rear stationary gear securing bolts.
2. Drive the stationary gear out of the rear housing with a brass drift.

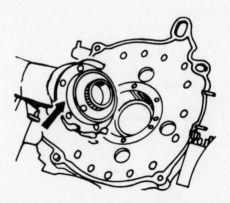

Position the O-ring in the groove on the stationary gear (arrow)

3. Apply a light coating of grease to a new O-ring and fit it into the groove on the stationary gear.

4. Apply sealer to the flange of the stationary gear.

5. Install the stationary gear on the housing so that the slot on its flange aligns with the pin on the rear housing.

CAUTION: *Use care not to damage the O-ring during installation.*

6. Tighten the stationary gear bolts evenly, and in several stages, to 15 ft-lbs.

ROTOR HOUSINGS

1. Examine the inner margin of both housings for signs of gas or water leakage.

2. Wipe the inner surface of each housing with a clean cloth to remove the carbon deposits.

NOTE: *If the carbon deposits are stubborn, soak the cloth in a solution of Ke-tone. Do not scrape or sand the chrome plated surfaces of the rotor chamber.*

3. Clean all of the rust deposits out of the cooling passages of each rotor housing.

4. Remove the old sealer with a cloth soaked in Ke-tone.

5. Examine the chromium plated inner surfaces for scoring, flaking, or other signs of damage. If any are present, the housing must be replaced.

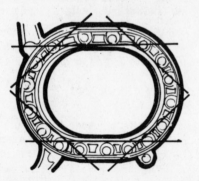

Measure the rotor housing distortion along the axes indicated (© Toyo Kogyo Co. Ltd.)

6. Check the rotor housings for distortion by placing a straightedge on the axes.

7. If distortion exceeds 0.002 in., replace the rotor housing.

8. Check the widths of both rotor housings, at a minimum of eight points near the trochoid surfaces of each housing, using a vernier caliper.

If the difference between the maximum and minimum values obtained is greater than 0.0031 in. (RX-3) or 0.0024 in. (RX-4, RX-7), replace the housing. A housing in this condition will be prone to gas and coolant leakage.

ROTORS

1. Check the rotor for signs of blow-by around the side and corner seal areas.

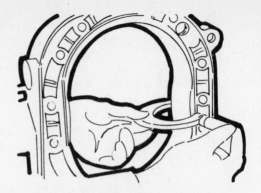

Check the rotor housing width at eight points near the trochoid surface (© Toyo Kogyo Co. Ltd.)

2. The color of the carbon deposits on the rotor should be brown, just as in a piston engine.

NOTE: *Usually the carbon deposits on the leading side of the rotor are brown, while those on the trailing side tend toward black, as viewed from the direction of rotation.*

3. Remove the carbon on the rotor with a scraper or extra fine emery paper. Use the scraper carefully, when doing the seal grooves, so that no damage is done to them.

4. Wash the rotor in solvent and blow it dry with compressed air.

5. Examine the internal gear for cracks or damaged teeth.

NOTE: *If the internal gear is damaged, the rotor and gear must be replaced as a single assembly.*

6. With the oil seal removed, check the land protrusions by placing a straightedge over the lands. Measure the gap between the rotor surface and the straightedge with a feeler gauge.

7. Check the gaps between the housings and the rotor on both of its sides.
   a. Measure the rotor width with a vernier caliper.
   b. Compare the rotor width against the width of the rotor housing which was measured above.
   c. Replace the rotor, if the difference between the two measurements is not within 0.0051–0.0067 in.

8. Check the rotor bearing for flaking, wearing, or scoring and proceed as indicated in the next section, if any of these are present.

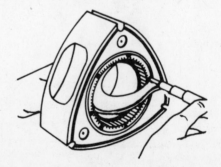

Measure the rotor width at the point indicated

The rotors are classified into five lettered grades, according to their weight. A letter between A and E is stamped on the internal gear side of the rotor. If it becomes necessary to replace a rotor, use one marked with a "C" because this is the standard replacement rotor, and it can be used in most balancing combinations.

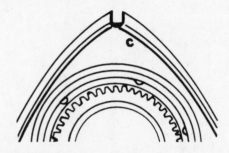

Weight classification letter placement (arrow)

ROTOR BEARING REPLACEMENT

CAUTION: *The use of the special service tools, as indicated in the text, is mandatory, if damage to the rotor is to be avoided.*

Check the clearance between the rotor bearing and the rotor journal on the eccentric shaft. Measure the inner diameter of the rotor bearing and the outer diameter of the journal; The wear limit is 0.0039 in.; replace the bearing if it exceeds this.

1. Install the bearing expander (Mazda part number 49 0813 245) in the rotor bearing. If the expander is not used, bearing deformation will result when the holes are drilled.

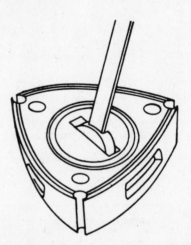

Insert the special bearing expander into the rotor

2. Drill a 0.14 in. diameter hole, roughly 0.028 in. deep, into each of the lockscrews which secure the bearings to the rotor. Use a #28 drill.
3. Remove the bearing expander.
4. Support the rotor with the internal gear facing upward.
5. Using the rotor bearing remover (Mazda part number 49 0813 240), less the adaptor ring, press the bearing out of the rotor.

CAUTION: *Be extremely careful not to damage the internal gear. It cannot be replaced separately from the rotor.*

6. If the bore in which the bearing is installed is damaged, dress it with emery paper and blow it clean with compressed air.
7. With the rotor internal gear facing upward, press-fit a new bearing into the bore. Use the bearing replacer with the adaptor screws removed.

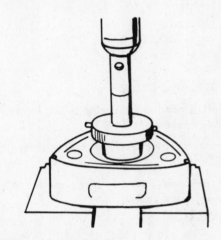

Installing a new rotor bearing

NOTE: *Be sure that the oil hole in the bearing is aligned with the hole in the apex side of the rotor. Once the bearing is installed, it should be flush with the rotor boss.*

8. Insert the rotor bearing expander into the new bearing, as in Step 1.
9. Drill 0.14 in. holes, about 0.28 in. deep, within 0.28 in. of the original lockscrew holes (either to the left or right of them) with a #28 drill. The center of the holes must be 0.02 in. from the rotor bore.

NOTE: *The new holes should all be in the same direction from the original holes; e.g., if the first hole is drilled to the left of the original hole, drill the remaining holes to the left of the other lockscrew holes.*

10. Thread the holes with an M4, P–0.70 mm metric tap.
11. Install the bearing lockscrews and stake them with a punch so that they cannot work loose.
12. Wash the rotor and blow it dry with compressed air.

OIL SEAL INSPECTION

NOTE: *Inspect the oil seal while it is mounted in the rotor.*

1. Examine the oil seal.
2. If the width of the oil seal lip is greater than 0.031 in., replace the oil seal.
3. If the protrusion of the oil seal is greater than 0.020 in., replace the seal.

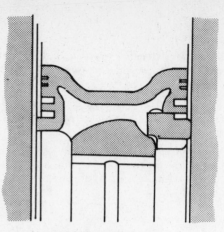

Oil seal protrusion (© Toyo Kogyo Co. Ltd.)

OIL SEAL REPLACEMENT

NOTE: *Replace the rubber O-ring in the oil seal as a normal part of engine overhaul.*

1. Pry the seal out by inserting a screw-driver into the slots on the rotor.

CAUTION: *Be careful not to deform the lip of the oil seal if it is to be reinstalled.*

2. Fit both of the oil seal springs into their respective grooves so that their ends are facing upward and their gaps are opposite each other on the rotor.

3. Insert a new O-ring into each of the oil seals.

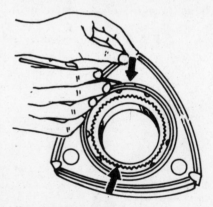

Position the oil seal spring gaps at arrows

NOTE: *Before installing the O-rings into the oil seals, fit each of the seals into its proper groove on the rotor. Check to see that all of the seals move smoothly and freely.*

4. Coat the oil seal groove and the oil seal with engine oil.

5. Gently press the oil seal into the groove with your fingers. Be careful not to distort the seal.

NOTE: *Be sure that the white mark is on the bottom side of each seal when it is installed.*

6. Repeat the installation procedure for the oil seals on both sides of each rotor.

APEX SEALS

CAUTION: *Although the apex seals are extremely durable when in service, they are easily broken when they are being handled. Be careful never to drop them.*

1. Remove the carbon deposits from the apex seals and their springs. Do not use emery cloth on the seals as it will damage their finish.

2. Wash the seals and the springs in cleaning solution.

3. Check the apex seals for cracks.

4. Test the seals springs for weakness.

5. Use a micrometer to check the seal height. Refer to specifications chart.

6. With a feeler gauge, check the side clearance between the apex seal and the groove in the rotor. Insert the gauge until its tip contacts the bottom of the groove. If the gap is greater than 0.005 in., replace the seal.

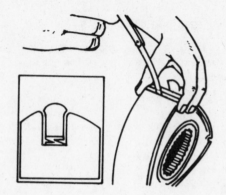

Check the gap between the apex seal and groove with a feeler gauge

7. Check the gap between the apex seals and the side housing in the following manner:
   a. Use a vernier caliper to measure the length of each apex seal.
   b. Compare this measurement to the *minimum* figure obtained when the rotor housing width was being measured.
   c. If the seal is too long, sand the ends of the seal with emery cloth until the proper length is reached.

CAUTION: *Do not use the emery cloth on the faces of the seal.*

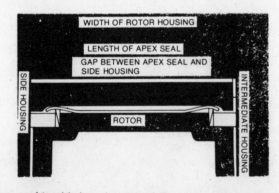

Apex seal-to-side housing gap (© Toyo Kogyo Co. Ltd.)

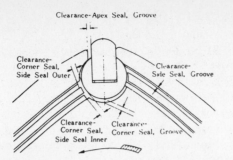

Check the clearance of the seals at the points indicated (© Toyo Kogyo Co. Ltd.)

Corner seal installations

SIDE SEALS

1. Remove the carbon deposits from the side seals and their springs.
2. Check the side seals for cracks.
3. Check the clearance between the side seals and their grooves with a feeler gauge. Replace any side seals with a clearance of more than 0.0039 in.
4. Check the clearance between the side seals and the corner seals with both installed in the rotor.
   a. Insert a feeler gauge between the end of the side seal and the corner seal.

NOTE: *Insert the gauge against the direction of the rotor's rotation.*

   b. Replace the side seal if the clearance is greater than 0.016 in.
5. If the side seal is replaced, adjust the clearance between it and the corner seal as follows:
   a. File the side seal on its reverse side, in the same rotational direction of the rotor, along the outline made by the corner seal.
   b. The clearance obtained should be 0.002–0.006 in. If it exceeds this, the performance of the seals wil deteriorate.

CAUTION: *There are four different types of side seals, depending upon location. Do not mix the seals up and be sure to use the proper type of seal for replacement.*

CORNER SEALS

1. Clean the carbon deposits.
2. Examine each of the seals.
3. Measure the clearance between the corner seal and its groove. The clearance should be 0.008–0.0019 in. The wear limit of the gap is 0.0031 in.

4. If the wear between the corner seal and the groove is uneven, check the clearance with the special "bar limit gauge" (Mazda part number 49 0839 165). The gauge has a "go" end and a "no go" end.
   a. If neither end of the gauge goes into the groove, the clearance is within specifications.
   b. If the "go" end of the gauge fits into the groove, but the "no go" end does not, replace the corner seal with one that is 0.0012 in. oversize.
   c. If both ends of the gauge fit into the groove, then the groove must be reamed out. Replace the corner seal with one which is 0.0072 in. oversize, after reaming.

NOTE: *Take the measurement of the groove in the direction of maximum wear, i.e., that of rotation.*

SEAL SPRINGS

Check the seal springs for damage or weakness. Be exceptionally careful when checking the spring areas which contact either the rotor or the seal.

ECCENTRIC SHAFT

1. Wash the eccentric shaft in solvent and blow the oil passages dry with compressed air.
2. Check the shaft for wear, cracks, or other signs of damage. Make sure that none of the oil passages are clogged.
3. Measure the shaft journals.
   Replace the shaft if any of its journals shows excessive wear.
4. Check eccentric shaft runout. Rotate the shaft slowly and note the dial indicator reading. If runout is more than specifications, replace the eccentric shaft.
5. Check the blind plug at the end of the shaft. If it is loose or leaking, remove it with an Allen wrench and replace the O-ring.

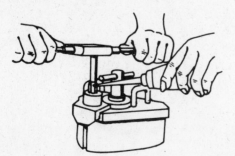

Reaming the corner seal groove

Position the dial indicator as shown to measure shaft run-out

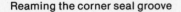

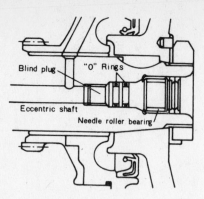

Eccentric shaft blind plug assembly (© Toyo Kogyo Co. Ltd.)

6. Check the operation of the needle roller bearing for smoothness by inserting a mainshaft into the bearing and rotating it. Examine the bearing for signs of wear or damage.

7. Replace the bearings, if necessary, with the special bearing replacer (Mazda part numbers 49 0823 073 and 49 0823 072).

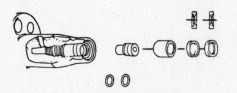

Needle bearing components (© Toyo Kogyo Co. Ltd.)

ASSEMBLY 1975 AND LATER

1. Place the rotor on a rubber pad or cloth.

2. Install the oil seal rings in their respective grooves in the rotors with the edge of the spring in the stopper hole. The oil seal springs are painted cream or blue in color. The cream colored springs must be installed on the front faces of both rotors. The blue colored springs must be installed on the rear faces of both rotors. When installing each oil seal spring, the painted side (square side) of the spring must face upward (toward the oil seal).

3. Install a new O-ring in each groove. Place each oil seal in the groove so that the square edge of the spring fits in the stopper hole of the oil seal. Push the head of the oil seal slowly with the fingers, being careful that the seal is not deformed. Be sure that the oil seal moves smoothly in the groove before installing the O-ring.

4. Lubricate each oil seal and groove with engine oil and check the movement of the seal. It should move freely when the head of the seal is pressed.

5. Check the oil seal protrusion and install the seals on the other side of each rotor.

6. Install the apex seals without springs and side pieces into their respective grooves so that each side piece positions on the side of each rotor.

7. Install the corner seal springs and corner seals into their respective grooves.

8. Install the side seal springs and side seals into their respective grooves.

9. Apply engine oil to each spring and check each spring for smooth movement.

10. Check each seal protrusion.

11. Invert the rotor being careful that the seals do not fall out, and install the oil seals on the other side in the same manner.

12. Mount the front housing on a workstand so that the top of the housing is up.

13. Lubricate the internal gear of the rotor with engine oil.

14. Hold the apex seals with used O-rings to keep the apex seals installed and place the rotor on the front housing. Be careful not to drop the seals. Turn the front housing so that the sliding surface faces upward.

15. Mesh the internal and stationary gears so that one of the rotor apexes is at any one of the four places shown and remove the old O-ring which is holding the apex seals in position.

16. Lubricate the front rotor journal of the eccentric shaft with engine oil and lubricate the eccentric shaft main journal.

17. Insert the eccentric shaft. Be careful that you do not damage the rotor bearing and main bearing.

18. Apply sealing agent to the front side of the front rotor housing.

19. Apply a light coat of petroleum jelly onto new O-rings and rubber seals (to prevent them from coming off) and install the O-rings and rubber seals on the front side of the rotor housing.

NOTE: *The inner rubber seal is of the square type. The wider white line of the rubber seal should face the combustion chamber and the seam of the rubber seal should be positioned as shown. Do not stretch the rubber seal.*

20. If the engine is being overhauled, install the seal protector to only the inner rubber seal to improve durability.

21. Invert the front rotor housing, being careful not to let the rubber seals and O-rings fall from their grooves, and mount it on the front housing.

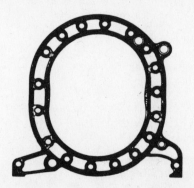

Apply sealer to the grey shadowed areas of the rotor housing (© Toyo Kogyo Co. Ltd.)

22. Lubricate the dowels with engine oil and insert them through the front rotor housing holes and into the front housing.

23. Apply sealer to the front side of the rotor housing.

24. Install new O-rings and rubber seals on the front rotor housing in the same manner as for the other side.

25. Insert each apex spring seal, making sure that the seal is installed in the proper direction.

26. Install each side piece in its original position and be sure that the springs seat on the side piece.

27. Lubricate the side pieces with engine oil. Make sure that the front rotor housing is free of foreign matter and lubricate the sliding surface of the front housing with engine oil.

28. Turn the front housing assembly with the rotor, so that the top of the housing is up. Pull the eccentric shaft about 1 in.

29. Position the eccentric portion of the eccentric shaft diagonally, to the upper right.

Intermediate housing installation

30. Install the intermediate housing over the eccentric shaft onto the front rotor housing. Turn the engine so that the rear of the engine is up.

31. Install the rear rotor and rear rotor housing following the same steps as for the front rotor and the front housing.

32. Turn the engine so that the rear of the engine is up.

33. Lubricate the stationary gear and main bearing.

34. Install the rear housing onto the rear rotor housing. If necessary, turn the rear rotor slightly to mesh the rear housing stationary gear with the rear rotor internal gear.

35. Install a new washer on each tension bolt, and lubricate each bolt with engine oil.

36. Install the tension bolts and tighten them evenly, in several stages following the sequence shown. The specified torque is 23–27 ft/lbs.

NOTE: *Be sure bolts are installed in their original positions. Longer bolts are used in later engines and are not interchangeable.*

37. After tightening the bolts, turn the eccentric shaft to be sure that the shaft and rotors turn smoothly and easily.

38. Lubricate the oil seal in the rear housing.

39. On vehicles with manual transmission, install the

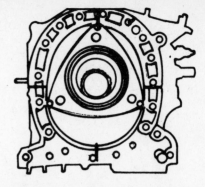

The rear rotor must be positioned as shown during engine assembly

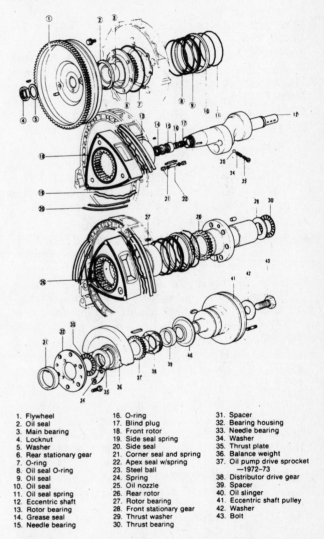

1. Flywheel	16. O-ring	31. Spacer
2. Oil seal	17. Blind plug	32. Bearing housing
3. Main bearing	18. Front rotor	33. Needle bearing
4. Locknut	19. Side seal spring	34. Washer
5. Washer	20. Side seal	35. Thrust plate
6. Rear stationary gear	21. Corner seal and spring	36. Balance weight
7. O-ring	22. Apex seal w/spring	37. Oil pump drive sprocket
8. Oil seal O-ring	23. Steel ball	—1972–73
9. Oil seal	24. Spring	38. Distributor drive gear
10. Oil seal	25. Oil nozzle	39. Spacer
11. Oil seal spring	26. Rear rotor	40. Oil slinger
12. Eccentric shaft	27. Rotor bearing	41. Eccentric shaft pulley
13. Rotor bearing	28. Front stationary gear	42. Washer
14. Grease seal	29. Thrust washer	43. Bolt
15. Needle bearing	30. Thrust bearing	

Rotor and eccentric shaft components (© Toyo Kogyo Co. Ltd.)

flywheel on the rear of the eccentric shaft so that the keyway of the flywheel fits the key on the shaft.

40. Apply sealer to both sides of the flywheel lockwasher and install the lockwasher.

41. Install the flywheel locknut. Hold the flywheel SECURELY and tighten the nut to THREE HUNDRED AND FIFTY FT/LBS (350 ft/lbs) of torque.

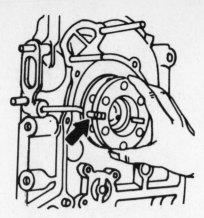

Align the slot in the stationary gear flange with the pin in the housing (arrow)

NOTE: *350 ft/lbs is a great deal of torque. In actual practice, it is practically impossible to accurately measure that much torque on the nut. At least a 3 ft. bar will be required to generate sufficient torque. Tighten it as tight as possible, with no longer than 3 ft. of leverage. Be sure the engine is held SECURELY.*

42. On vehicles with automatic transmission, install the key, counterweight, lockwasher and nut. Tighten the nut to 350 ft. lbs. SEE STEP 41 AND THE NOTE FOLLOWING STEP 41. Install the drive plate on the counterweight and tighten the attaching nuts.

43. Turn the engine so that the front faces up.

44. Install the thrust plate with the tapered face down, and install the needle bearing on the eccentric shaft. Lubricate with engine oil.

45. Install the bearing housing on the front housing. Tighten the bolts and bend up the lockwasher tabs.

   The spacer should be installed so that the center of the needle bearing comes to the center of the eccentric shaft and the spacer should be seated on the thrust plate.

46. Install the needle bearing on the shaft and lubricate it with engine oil.

47. Install the balancer and thrust washer on the eccentric shaft.

48. Install the oil pump drive chain over both of the sprockets. Install the sprocket and chain assembly over the eccentric shaft and oil pump shafts simultaneously. Install the key on the eccentric shaft.

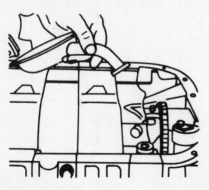

Installing oil pump

NOTE: *Be sure that both of the sprockets are engaged with the chain before installing them over the shafts.*

49. Install the distributor drive gear onto the eccentric shaft with the "F" mark on the gear facing the front of the engine. Slide the spacer and oil slinger onto the eccentric shaft.

50. Align the keyway and install the eccentric shaft pulley. Tighten the pulley bolt to 60 ft/lbs.

51. Turn the engine top so the engine faces up.

52. Check eccentric shaft end-play in the following manner.
   a. Attach a dial indicator to the flywheel. Move the flywheel forward and backward.

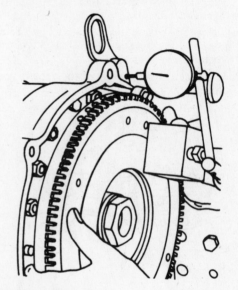

Use a dial indicator attached to the flywheel to measure eccentric shaft end-play

   b. Note the reading on the dial indicator; it should be 0.0016–0.0028 in.
   c. If the end-play is not within specifications, adjust it by replacing the front spacer. Spacers come in four sizes, ranging from 0.3150–0.3181 in. If necessary, a spacer can be ground on a surface plate with emery paper.
   d. Check the end-play again and, if it is now within specifications, proceed with the next step.

53. Remove the pulley from the front of the eccentric shaft. Tighten the oil pump drive sprocket nut and bend the locktabs on the lockwasher.

54. Fit a new O-ring over the front cover oil passage.

55. Install the chain tensioner and tighten its securing bolts.

56. Position the front cover gasket and the front cover on the front housing, then secure the front cover with its attachment bolts.

57. Install the eccentric shaft pulley again. Tighten its bolt to 60 ft/lbs.

58. Turn the engine so that the bottom faces up.

59. Cut off the excess gasket on the front cover along the mounting surface of the oil pan.

60. Install the oil strainer gasket and strainer on the front housing and tighten the attaching bolts.

61. Apply sealer to the joint surfaces of each housing.

62. Install the oil pan.

63. Turn the engine so that the top is up.

64. Install the water pump.

65. Rotate the eccentric shaft until the yellow mark (leading side mark) aligns with the pointer on the front cover.

66. Align the marks on the distributor gear and housing and install the distributor so that the lockbolt is in the center of the slot.

67. Rotate the distributor until the leading points start to separate and tighten the distributor locknut.

68. Install the gaskets and thermal reactor.

69. Install the hot air duct.

70. Install the carburetor and intake manifold assembly.

71. Connect the oil tubes, vacuum tube and metering oil pump connecting rod to the carburetor.

72. Install the decel valve and connect the vacuum lines, air hoses and wires.

73. Install the alternator bracket, alternator and bolt and check the clearance. If the clearance is more than 0.006 in., adjust the clearance using a shim. Shims are available in three sizes: 0.0059 in., 0.0118 in., and 0.0197 in.

ECCENTRIC SHAFT SPACER THICKNESS CHART

Mark-ing	THICKNESS	
	mm	in.
X	8.08 ± 0.01	0.3181 ± 0.0004
Y	8.04 ± 0.01	0.3165 ± 0.0004
V	8.02 ± 0.01	0.3158 ± 0.0004
Z	8.00 ± 0.01	0.3150 ± 0.0004

74. Install the alternator drive belt.

75. Install the air pump.

76. Install the engine hanger bracket.

77. Remove the engine from the stand.

78. Install the engine in the vehicle.

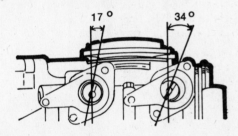

Position the slots in the distributor drive as shown (© Toyo Kogyo Co. Ltd.)

INDEX

Air conditioning, 46
Air-cooled engines, 15
Alignment, main bearings, 78
Alternator, 94
Audi diesel engine, 142

Battery, 93
Battery cables, 94
Bearings, engine, 6
  Design, 6
  Installation, 112
  Materials, 6
  Requirements, 6
Block, engine, 3
  Inspection, 74
  Reconditioning, 74
Boring, cylinders, 76
Break-in, engine, 121

Camshaft, 8
  Bearings, 68
  Checking, OHC engines, 68
  Installation, 110
  Removal, 55
Carburetor
  Adjustments, 120
  Rebuilding, 103
Charging system, 94
Clutch
  Installation, 117
Cleaning, methods, 56, 60
Compression testing, 25
Compressor, piston ring, 41
Connecting rods
  Inspection, 84
  Installation, 86, 115
  Removal, 55
Construction, engine, 1
Cooling system, 12, 91
Cracks, testing for, 61
  Repair, 61
Crankshaft
  Installation, 111
  Removal, 55
Cylinder block (see engine)
Cylinder heads
  Assembly, 73, 108
  Cleaning, 59
  Disassembly, 57
  Inspection, 61
  Reconditioning, 57
  Removal, 47

Damaged threads, 36
Deck flatness, 78
Design, engine, 1
Detonation, 21
Diagnosis, engine, 19
Diesel engines, 15, 135

Audi, 142
  General information, 15, 135
  General Motors, 194
  Mercedes-Benz, 156
  Peugeot, 165
  Volkswagen, 187
  Volvo, 176
Distributor
  Installation, 117
  Rebuilding, 106
  Removal, 48
Dynamometer, 31

Endplay, crankshaft, 113
Engine
  Assembly, 108
  Condition, 19
  Disassembly, 53
  Installation, 118
  Removal, front wheel drive, 52
  Removal, rear wheel drive, 50

Failure
  Bearings, 86
  Camshaft and lifters, 79
  Oil pump, 87
  Piston, 24, 82
  Piston ring, 83
  Timing gear/chain, 89
  Valves, 69
  Valve springs, 69
  Water pump, 91
Fan blades, 93
Fan clutch, 93
Fasteners, 33
  Bolts and screws, 33
  Lockwashers, 34
  Nuts, 33
  Studs, 34
Feeler gauges, 43
Flywheel/flexplate, 4, 117
Four-stroke cycle, 13, 135

Gasket sealers, 108
Gasket sets, 108
General Motors diesel engine, 194
Glaze breaking, cylinders, 41
Groove cleaning, pistons, 40

Hammers, 39
Hand tools, 37
Heads (see Cylinder heads)
Hoisting, engine removal, 44, 52
Hone, cylinder, 41
Honing, cylinder walls, 76

In car, engine services, 47
Inspection
  Cracks, Repairing, 61

Cracks, testing for, 61
  Cylinder head, 61
  Engine block, 74

Knurling
  Pistons, 85
  Valve guides, 64

Lifters, valve, 8, 81
Lubrication, engine, 11

Machine shop, 62
Main bearing, installation, 112, 114
Measuring
  Camshaft, 80
  Crankshaft, 78
  Cylinder bore, 75
  Pistons, 84
Mercedes diesel engine, 156
Micrometers, 42

Noises, 22
  Crankshaft, 20
  Piston, 20
  Valve train, 21

Oil consumption, 19
Oil clearance, 84, 111
Oil pan
  Installation, 116
  Removal, 50
Oil pump, 12, 116
Oversize
  Bearings, 78
  Cylinder, boring, 76
  Pistons, 84
  Valve stems, 64

Performance, loss, 25
Peugeot diesel engine, 165
Pistons, 4
  Changing, 86
  Installation, 115
  Removal, 55
Plastigage, 44, 111
Pliers, 39
Porsche engine (air-cooled), 122
Power tools, 40
Preignition, 21
Pullers, 40
Pushrods, 8

Radiator, 12
Reaming
  Ridge, cylinder, 54
  Valve guides, 64
  Valve seats, 66
Reconditioning
  Alternator, 94

Carburetor, 103
Cylinder head, 57
Distributor, 106
Engine, 74
Starter, 96
Repair
Cracks, 61
Stripped threads, 36
Valve guides, 62
Replacement, valve guides, 63
Resizing, cylinder bore, 76
Rings, piston, 4
Clearance, 84
Grooves, 40, 84
Replacing, 114
Ridge Reamer, 41
Using, 54
Types, 54
Rocker arms, 69, 72
Shaft, 72
Rotary engine rebuilding, 213
Rotators, valve, 11

Safety, v, 44
Screwdrivers, 39

Seals
Main bearing, 111
Valves, 73
Sealer, gasket, 108
Sets, gasket, 108
Shafts,
Camshaft, 8, 55, 68, 110
Crankshaft, 3, 55, 111
Rocker arm, 72
Sleeves, cylinder, 77
Sockets/ratchets, 38
Spark plug, checking, 27, 28
Starters motors, 96
Starting system, 95
Supplies, 33

Telescoping gauges, 43
Theory, engine operation, 1
Thermostat, 12, 92
Timing
Belts, 11, 115
Gears, 11, 115
Ignition, 119
Tools, 33
Torque wrenches, 40

Tune-up, 119
Turbocharging, 139
Two stroke cycle, 18

Vacuum gauge readings, 25, 26
Valves, 10, 65
Adjustment, 117, 121
Guides, 60
Retainers, 11, 68
Rotators, 11
Seals, 11, 73
Seats, 10, 65
Sodium filled, 65
Springs, 11, 68, 109
Valve train failure, 69
Volkswagen diesel engine, 187
Volkswagen engine (air-cooled), 122
Volvo diesel engine, 176

Walls, cylinder, 74
Wankel engine, 15
Rebuilding, 213
Water pump, 12, 91
Installation, 116
Wrenches, 37

Mechanics' Data

SI METRIC TABLES

The following tables are given in SI (International System) metric units. SI units replace both customary (English) and the older gavimetric units. The use of SI units as a new worldwide standard was set by the International Committee of Weights and Measures in 1960. SI has since been adopted by most countries as their national standard.

These tables are general conversion tables which will allow you to convert customary units, which appear in the text, into SI units.

The following are a list of SI units and the customary units, used in this book, which they replace:

To measure:	Use SI units:	Which replace (customary units):
mass	kilograms (kg)	pounds (lbs)
temperature	Celsius (°C)	Fahrenheit (°F)
length	millimeters (mm)	inches (in.)
force	newtons (N)	pounds force (lbs)
capacities	liters (l)	pints/quarts/gallons (pts/qts/gals)
torque	newton-meters (N·m)	foot pounds (ft lbs)
pressure	kilopascals (kPa)	pounds per square inch (psi)
volume	cubic centimeters (cm³)	cubic inches (cu in.)
power	kilowatts (kW)	horsepower (hp)

If you have had any prior experience with the metric system, you may have noticed units in this chart which are not familiar to you. This is because, in some cases, SI units differ from the older gravimetric units which they replace. For example, newtons (N) replace kilograms (kg) as a force unit, kilopascals (kPa) replace atmospheres or bars as a unit of pressure, and, although the units are the same, the name Celsius replaces centigrade for temperature measurement.

If you are not using the SI tables, have a look at them anyway; you will be seeing a lot more of them in the future.

ENGLISH TO METRIC CONVERSION: MASS (WEIGHT)

Current **mass** measurement is expressed in pounds and ounces (lbs. & ozs.). The metric unit of mass (or weight) is the kilogram (kg). Even although this table does not show conversion of masses (weights) larger than 15 lbs, it is easy to calculate larger units by following the data immediately below.

To convert ounces (oz.) to grams (g): multiply th number of ozs. by 28
To convert grams (g) to ounces (oz.): multiply the number of grams by .035

To convert pounds (lbs.) to kilograms (kg): multiply the number of lbs. by .45
To convert kilograms (kg) to pounds (lbs.): multiply the number of kilograms by 2.2

lbs	kg	lbs	kg	oz	kg	oz	kg
0.1	0.04	0.9	0.41	0.1	0.003	0.9	0.024
0.2	0.09	1	0.4	0.2	0.005	1	0.03
0.3	0.14	2	0.9	0.3	0.008	2	0.06
0.4	0.18	3	1.4	0.4	0.011	3	0.08
0.5	0.23	4	1.8	0.5	0.014	4	0.11
0.6	0.27	5	2.3	0.6	0.017	5	0.14
0.7	0.32	10	4.5	0.7	0.020	10	0.28
0.8	0.36	15	6.8	0.8	0.023	15	0.42

ENGLISH TO METRIC CONVERSION: TEMPERATURE

To convert Fahrenheit (°F) to Celsius (°C): take number of °F and subtract 32; multiply result by 5; divide result by 9

To convert Celsius (°C) to Fahrenheit (°F): take number of °C and multiply by 9; divide result by 5; add 32 to total

Fahrenheit (F)	Celsius (C)	Celsius (C)	Fahrenheit (F)	Fahrenheit (F)	Celsius (C)	Celsius (C)	Fahrenheit (F)	Fahrenheit (F)	Celsius (C)	Celsius (C)	Fahrenheit (F)
°F	°C	°C	°F	°F	°C	°C	°F	°F	°C	°C	°F
−40	−40	−38	−36.4	80	26.7	18	64.4	215	101.7	80	176
−35	−37.2	−36	−32.8	85	29.4	20	68	220	104.4	85	185
−30	−34.4	−34	−29.2	90	32.2	22	71.6	225	107.2	90	194
−25	−31.7	−32	−25.6	95	35.0	24	75.2	230	110.0	95	202
−20	−28.9	−30	−22	100	37.8	26	78.8	235	112.8	100	212
−15	−26.1	−28	−18.4	105	40.6	28	82.4	240	115.6	105	221
−10	−23.3	−26	−14.8	110	43.3	30	86	245	118.3	110	230
−5	−20.6	−24	−11.2	115	46.1	32	89.6	250	121.1	115	239
0	−17.8	−22	−7.6	120	48.9	34	93.2	255	123.9	120	248
1	−17.2	−20	−4	125	51.7	36	96.8	260	126.6	125	257
2	−16.7	−18	−0.4	130	54.4	38	100.4	265	129.4	130	266
3	−16.1	−16	3.2	135	57.2	40	104	270	132.2	135	275
4	−15.6	−14	6.8	140	60.0	42	107.6	275	135.0	140	284
5	−15.0	−12	10.4	145	62.8	44	112.2	280	137.8	145	293
10	−12.2	−10	14	150	65.6	46	114.8	285	140.6	150	302
15	−9.4	−8	17.6	155	68.3	48	118.4	290	143.3	155	311
20	−6.7	−6	21.2	160	71.1	50	122	295	146.1	160	320
25	−3.9	−4	24.8	165	73.9	52	125.6	300	148.9	165	329
30	−1.1	−2	28.4	170	76.7	54	129.2	305	151.7	170	338
35	1.7	0	32	175	79.4	56	132.8	310	154.4	175	347
40	4.4	2	35.6	180	82.2	58	136.4	315	157.2	180	356
45	7.2	4	39.2	185	85.0	60	140	320	160.0	185	365
50	10.0	6	42.8	190	87.8	62	143.6	325	162.8	190	374
55	12.8	8	46.4	195	90.6	64	147.2	330	165.6	195	383
60	15.6	10	50	200	93.3	66	150.8	335	168.3	200	392
65	18.3	12	53.6	205	96.1	68	154.4	340	171.1	205	401
70	21.1	14	57.2	210	98.9	70	158	345	173.9	210	410
75	23.9	16	60.8	212	100.0	75	167	350	176.7	215	414

Mechanics Data

ENGLISH TO METRIC CONVERSION: LENGTH

To convert inches (ins.) to millimeters (mm): multiply number of inches by 25.4

To convert millimeters (mm) to inches (ins.): multiply number of millimeters by .04

Inches	Decimals	Milli-meters	Inches to millimeters inches	mm		Inches	Decimals	Milli-meters	Inches to millimeters inches	mm
1/64	0.051625	0.3969	0.0001	0.00254		33/64	0.515625	13.0969	0.6	15.24
1/32	0.03125	0.7937	0.0002	0.00508		17/32	0.53125	13.4937	0.7	17.78
3/64	0.046875	1.1906	0.0003	0.00762		35/64	0.546875	13.8906	0.8	20.32
1/16	0.0625	1.5875	0.0004	0.01016		9/16	0.5625	14.2875	0.9	22.86
5/64	0.078125	1.9844	0.0005	0.01270		37/64	0.578125	14.6844	1	25.4
3/32	0.09375	2.3812	0.0006	0.01524		19/32	0.59375	15.0812	2	50.8
7/64	0.109375	2.7781	0.0007	0.01778		39/64	0.609375	15.4781	3	76.2
1/8	0.125	3.1750	0.0008	0.02032		5/8	0.625	15.8750	4	101.6
9/64	0.140625	3.5719	0.0009	0.02286		41/64	0.640625	16.2719	5	127.0
5/32	0.15625	3.9687	0.001	0.0254		21/32	0.65625	16.6687	6	152.4
11/64	0.171875	4.3656	0.002	0.0508		43/64	0.671875	17.0656	7	177.8
3/16	0.1875	4.7625	0.003	0.0762		11/16	0.6875	17.4625	8	203.2
13/64	0.203125	5.1594	0.004	0.1016		45/64	0.703125	17.8594	9	228.6
7/32	0.21875	5.5562	0.005	0.1270		23/32	0.71875	18.2562	10	254.0
15/64	0.234375	5.9531	0.006	0.1524		47/64	0.734375	18.6531	11	279.4
1/4	0.25	6.3500	0.007	0.1778		3/4	0.75	19.0500	12	304.8
17/64	0.265625	6.7469	0.008	0.2032		49/64	0.765625	19.4469	13	330.2
9/32	0.28125	7.1437	0.009	0.2286		25/32	0.78125	19.8437	14	355.6
19/64	0.296875	7.5406	0.01	0.254		51/64	0.796875	20.2406	15	381.0
5/16	0.3125	7.9375	0.02	0.508		13/16	0.8125	20.6375	16	406.4
21/64	0.328125	8.3344	0.03	0.762		53/64	0.828125	21.0344	17	431.8
11/32	0.34375	8.7312	0.04	1.016		27/32	0.84375	21.4312	18	457.2
23/64	0.359375	9.1281	0.05	1.270		55/64	0.859375	21.8281	19	482.6
3/8	0.375	9.5250	0.06	1.524		7/8	0.875	22.2250	20	508.0
25/64	0.390625	9.9219	0.07	1.778		57/64	0.890625	22.6219	21	533.4
13/32	0.40625	10.3187	0.08	2.032		29/32	0.90625	23.0187	22	558.8
27/64	0.421875	10.7156	0.09	2.286		59/64	0.921875	23.4156	23	584.2
7/16	0.4375	11.1125	0.1	2.54		15/16	0.9375	23.8125	24	609.6
29/64	0.453125	11.5094	0.2	5.08		61/64	0.953125	24.2094	25	635.0
15/32	0.46875	11.9062	0.3	7.62		31/32	0.96875	24.6062	26	660.4
31/64	0.484375	12.3031	0.4	10.16		63/64	0.984375	25.0031	27	690.6
1/2	0.5	12.7000	0.5	12.70						

ENGLISH TO METRIC CONVERSION: TORQUE

To convert foot-pounds (ft. lbs.) to Newton-meters: multiply the number of ft. lbs. by 1.3

To convert inch-pounds (in. lbs.) to Newton-meters: multiply the number of in. lbs. by .11

in lbs	N-m	in lbs	N-m	in lbs	N-m	in lbs	N-m	in lbs	N-m
0.1	0.01	1	0.11	10	1.13	19	2.15	28	3.16
0.2	0.02	2	0.23	11	1.24	20	2.26	29	3.28
0.3	0.03	3	0.34	12	1.36	21	2.37	30	3.39
0.4	0.04	4	0.45	13	1.47	22	2.49	31	3.50
0.5	0.06	5	0.56	14	1.58	23	2.60	32	3.62
0.6	0.07	6	0.68	15	1.70	24	2.71	33	3.73
0.7	0.08	7	0.78	16	1.81	25	2.82	34	3.84
0.8	0.09	8	0.90	17	1.92	26	2.94	35	3.95
0.9	0.10	9	1.02	18	2.03	27	3.05	36	4.0/

ENGLISH TO METRIC CONVERSION: TORQUE

Torque is now expressed as either foot-pounds (ft./lbs.) or inch-pounds (in./lbs.). The metric measurement unit for torque is the Newton-meter (Nm). This unit—the Nm—will be used for all SI metric torque references, both the present ft./lbs. and in./lbs.

ft lbs	N-m	ft lbs	N-m	ft lbs	N-m	ft lbs	N-m
0.1	0.1	33	44.7	74	100.3	115	155.9
0.2	0.3	34	46.1	75	101.7	116	157.3
0.3	0.4	35	47.4	76	103.0	117	158.6
0.4	0.5	36	48.8	77	104.4	118	160.0
0.5	0.7	37	50.7	78	105.8	119	161.3
0.6	0.8	38	51.5	79	107.1	120	162.7
0.7	1.0	39	52.9	80	108.5	121	164.0
0.8	1.1	40	54.2	81	109.8	122	165.4
0.9	1.2	41	55.6	82	111.2	123	166.8
1	1.3	42	56.9	83	112.5	124	168.1
2	2.7	43	58.3	84	113.9	125	169.5
3	4.1	44	59.7	85	115.2	126	170.8
4	5.4	45	61.0	86	116.6	127	172.2
5	6.8	46	62.4	87	118.0	128	173.5
6	8.1	47	63.7	88	119.3	129	174.9
7	9.5	48	65.1	89	120.7	130	176.2
8	10.8	49	66.4	90	122.0	131	177.6
9	12.2	50	67.8	91	123.4	132	179.0
10	13.6	51	69.2	92	124.7	133	180.3
11	14.9	52	70.5	93	126.1	134	181.7
12	16.3	53	71.9	94	127.4	135	183.0
13	17.6	54	73.2	95	128.8	136	184.4
14	18.9	55	74.6	96	130.2	137	185.7
15	20.3	56	75.9	97	131.5	138	187.1
16	21.7	57	77.3	98	132.9	139	188.5
17	23.0	58	78.6	99	134.2	140	189.8
18	24.4	59	80.0	100	135.6	141	191.2
19	25.8	60	81.4	101	136.9	142	192.5
20	27.1	61	82.7	102	138.3	143	193.9
21	28.5	62	84.1	103	139.6	144	195.2
22	29.8	63	85.4	104	141.0	145	196.6
23	31.2	64	86.8	105	142.4	146	198.0
24	32.5	65	88.1	106	143.7	147	199.3
25	33.9	66	89.5	107	145.1	148	200.7
26	35.2	67	90.8	108	146.4	149	202.0
27	36.6	68	92.2	109	147.8	150	203.4
28	38.0	69	93.6	110	149.1	151	204.7
29	39.3	70	94.9	111	150.5	152	206.1
30	40.7	71	96.3	112	151.8	153	207.4
31	42.0	72	97.6	113	153.2	154	208.8
32	43.4	73	99.0	114	154.6	155	210.2

Mechanics Data

ENGLISH TO METRIC CONVERSION: FORCE

Force is presently measured in pounds (lbs.). This type of measurement is used to measure spring pressure, specifically how many pounds it takes to compress a spring. Our present force unit (the pound) will be replaced in SI metric measurements by the Newton (N). This term will eventually see use in specifications for electric motor brush spring pressures, valve spring pressures, etc.

To convert pounds (lbs.) to Newton (N): multiply the number of lbs. by 4.45

lbs	N	lbs	N	lbs	N	oz	N
0.01	0.04	21	93.4	59	262.4	1	0.3
0.02	0.09	22	97.9	60	266.9	2	0.6
0.03	0.13	23	102.3	61	271.3	3	0.8
0.04	0.18	24	106.8	62	275.8	4	1.1
0.05	0.22	25	111.2	63	280.2	5	1.4
0.06	0.27	26	115.6	64	284.6	6	1.7
0.07	0.31	27	120.1	65	289.1	7	2.0
0.08	0.36	28	124.6	66	293.6	8	2.2
0.09	0.40	29	129.0	67	298.0	9	2.5
0.1	0.4	30	133.4	68	302.5	10	2.8
0.2	0.9	31	137.9	69	306.9	11	3.1
0.3	1.3	32	142.3	70	311.4	12	3.3
0.4	1.8	33	146.8	71	315.8	13	3.6
0.5	2.2	34	151.2	72	320.3	14	3.9
0.6	2.7	35	155.7	73	324.7	15	4.2
0.7	3.1	36	160.1	74	329.2	16	4.4
0.8	3.6	37	164.6	75	333.6	17	4.7
0.9	4.0	38	169.0	76	338.1	18	5.0
1	4.4	39	173.5	77	342.5	19	5.3
2	8.9	40	177.9	78	347.0	20	5.6
3	13.4	41	182.4	79	351.4	21	5.8
4	17.8	42	186.8	80	355.9	22	6.1
5	22.2	43	191.3	81	360.3	23	6.4
6	26.7	44	195.7	82	364.8	24	6.7
7	31.1	45	200.2	83	369.2	25	7.0
8	35.6	46	204.6	84	373.6	26	7.2
9	40.0	47	209.1	85	378.1	27	7.5
10	44.5	48	213.5	86	382.6	28	7.8
11	48.9	49	218.0	87	387.0	29	8.1
12	53.4	50	224.4	88	391.4	30	8.3
13	57.8	51	226.9	89	395.9	31	8.6
14	62.3	52	231.3	90	400.3	32	8.9
15	66.7	53	235.8	91	404.8	33	9.2
16	71.2	54	240.2	92	409.2	34	9.4
17	75.6	55	244.6	93	413.7	35	9.7
18	80.1	56	249.1	94	418.1	36	10.0
19	84.5	57	253.6	95	422.6	37	10.3
20	89.0	58	258.0	96	427.0	38	10.6

ENGLISH TO METRIC CONVERSION: LIQUID CAPACITY

Liquid or fluid capacity is presently expressed as pints, quarts or gallons, or a combination of all of these. In the metric system the liter (l) will become the basic unit. Fractions of a liter would be expressed as deciliters, centiliters, or most frequently (and commonly) as milliliters.

To convert pints (pts.) to liters (l): multiply the number of pints by .47
To convert liters (l) to pints (pts.): multiply the number of liters by 2.1
To convert quarts (qts.) to liters (l): multiply the number of quarts by .95

To convert liters (l) to quarts (qts.): multiply the number of liters by 1.06
To convert gallons (gals.) to liters (l): multiply the number of gallons by 3.8
To convert liters (l) to gallons (gals.): multiply the number of liters by .26

gals	liters	qts	liters	pts	liters
0.1	0.38	0.1	0.10	0.1	0.05
0.2	0.76	0.2	0.19	0.2	0.10
0.3	1.1	0.3	0.28	0.3	0.14
0.4	1.5	0.4	0.38	0.4	0.19
0.5	1.9	0.5	0.47	0.5	0.24
0.6	2.3	0.6	0.57	0.6	0.28
0.7	2.6	0.7	0.66	0.7	0.33
0.8	3.0	0.8	0.76	0.8	0.38
0.9	3.4	0.9	0.85	0.9	0.43
1	3.8	1	1.0	1	0.5
2	7.6	2	1.9	2	1.0
3	11.4	3	2.8	3	1.4
4	15.1	4	3.8	4	1.9
5	18.9	5	4.7	5	2.4
6	22.7	6	5.7	6	2.8
7	26.5	7	6.6	7	3.3
8	30.3	8	7.6	8	3.8
9	34.1	9	8.5	9	4.3
10	37.8	10	9.5	10	4.7
11	41.6	11	10.4	11	5.2
12	45.4	12	11.4	12	5.7
13	49.2	13	12.3	13	6.2
14	53.0	14	13.2	14	6.6
15	56.8	15	14.2	15	7.1
16	60.6	16	15.1	16	7.6
17	64.3	17	16.1	17	8.0
18	68.1	18	17.0	18	8.5
19	71.9	19	18.0	19	9.0
20	75.7	20	18.9	20	9.5
21	79.5	21	19.9	21	9.9
22	83.2	22	20.8	22	10.4
23	87.0	23	21.8	23	10.9
24	90.8	24	22.7	24	11.4
25	94.6	25	23.6	25	11.8
26	98.4	26	24.6	26	12.3
27	102.2	27	25.5	27	12.8
28	106.0	28	26.5	28	13.2
29	110.0	29	27.4	29	13.7
30	113.5	30	28.4	30	14.2

Mechanics Data

ENGLISH TO METRIC CONVERSION: PRESSURE

The basic unit of pressure measurement used today is expressed as pounds per square inch (psi). The metric unit for psi will be the kilopascal (kPa). This will apply to either fluid pressure or air pressure, and will be frequently seen in tire pressure readings, oil pressure specifications, fuel pump pressure, etc.

To convert pounds per square inch (psi) to kilopascals (kPa): multiply the number of psi by 6.89

Psi	kPa	Psi	kPa	Psi	kPa	Psi	kPa
0.1	0.7	37	255.1	82	565.4	127	875.6
0.2	1.4	38	262.0	83	572.3	128	882.5
0.3	2.1	39	268.9	84	579.2	129	889.4
0.4	2.8	40	275.8	85	586.0	130	896.3
0.5	3.4	41	282.7	86	592.9	131	903.2
0.6	4.1	42	289.6	87	599.8	132	910.1
0.7	4.8	43	296.5	88	606.7	133	917.0
0.8	5.5	44	303.4	89	613.6	134	923.9
0.9	6.2	45	310.3	90	620.5	135	930.8
1	6.9	46	317.2	91	627.4	136	937.7
2	13.8	47	324.0	92	634.3	137	944.6
3	20.7	48	331.0	93	641.2	138	951.5
4	27.6	49	337.8	94	648.1	139	958.4
5	34.5	50	344.7	95	655.0	140	965.2
6	41.4	51	351.6	96	661.9	141	972.2
7	48.3	52	358.5	97	668.8	142	979.0
8	55.2	53	365.4	98	675.7	143	985.9
9	62.1	54	372.3	99	682.6	144	992.8
10	69.0	55	379.2	100	689.5	145	999.7
11	75.8	56	386.1	101	696.4	146	1006.6
12	82.7	57	393.0	102	703.3	147	1013.5
13	89.6	58	399.9	103	710.2	148	1020.4
14	96.5	59	406.8	104	717.0	149	1027.3
15	103.4	60	413.7	105	723.9	150	1034.2
16	110.3	61	420.6	106	730.8	151	1041.1
17	117.2	62	427.5	107	737.7	152	1048.0
18	124.1	63	434.4	108	744.6	153	1054.9
19	131.0	64	441.3	109	751.5	154	1061.8
20	137.9	65	448.2	110	758.4	155	1068.7
21	144.8	66	455.0	111	765.3	156	1075.6
22	151.7	67	461.9	112	772.2	157	1082.5
23	158.6	68	468.8	113	779.1	158	1089.4
24	165.5	69	475.7	114	786.0	159	1096.3
25	172.4	70	482.6	115	792.9	160	1103.2
26	179.3	71	489.5	116	799.8	161	1110.0
27	186.2	72	496.4	117	806.7	162	1116.9
28	193.0	73	503.3	118	813.6	163	1123.8
29	200.0	74	510.2	119	820.5	164	1130.7
30	206.8	75	517.1	120	827.4	165	1137.6
31	213.7	76	524.0	121	834.3	166	1144.5
32	220.6	77	530.9	122	841.2	167	1151.4
33	227.5	78	537.8	123	848.0	168	1158.3
34	234.4	79	544.7	124	854.9	169	1165.2
35	241.3	80	551.6	125	861.8	170	1172.1
36	248.2	81	558.5	126	868.7	171	1179.0

ENGLISH TO METRIC CONVERSION: PRESSURE

The basic unit of pressure measurement used today is expressed as pounds per square inch (psi). The metric unit for psi will be the kilopascal (kPa). This will apply to either fluid pressure or air pressure, and will be frequently seen in tire pressure readings, oil pressure specifications, fuel pump pressure, etc.

To convert pounds per square inch (psi) to kilopascals (kPa): multiply the number of psi by 6.89

Psi	kPa	Psi	kPa	Psi	kPa	Psi	kPa
172	1185.9	216	1489.3	260	1792.6	304	2096.0
173	1192.8	217	1496.2	261	1799.5	305	2102.9
174	1199.7	218	1503.1	262	1806.4	306	2109.8
175	1206.6	219	1510.0	263	1813.3	307	2116.7
176	1213.5	220	1516.8	264	1820.2	308	2123.6
177	1220.4	221	1523.7	265	1827.1	309	2130.5
178	1227.3	222	1530.6	266	1834.0	310	2137.4
179	1234.2	223	1537.5	267	1840.9	311	2144.3
180	1241.0	224	1544.4	268	1847.8	312	2151.2
181	1247.9	225	1551.3	269	1854.7	313	2158.1
182	1254.8	226	1558.2	270	1861.6	314	2164.9
183	1261.7	227	1565.1	271	1868.5	315	2171.8
184	1268.6	228	1572.0	272	1875.4	316	2178.7
185	1275.5	229	1578.9	273	1882.3	317	2185.6
186	1282.4	230	1585.8	274	1889.2	318	2192.5
187	1289.3	231	1592.7	275	1896.1	319	2199.4
188	1296.2	232	1599.6	276	1903.0	320	2206.3
189	1303.1	233	1606.5	277	1909.8	321	2213.2
190	1310.0	234	1613.4	278	1916.7	322	2220.1
191	1316.9	235	1620.3	279	1923.6	323	2227.0
192	1323.8	236	1627.2	280	1930.5	324	2233.9
193	1330.7	237	1634.1	281	1937.4	325	2240.8
194	1337.6	238	1641.0	282	1944.3	326	2247.7
195	1344.5	239	1647.8	283	1951.2	327	2254.6
196	1351.4	240	1654.7	284	1958.1	328	2261.5
197	1358.3	241	1661.6	285	1965.0	329	2268.4
198	1365.2	242	1668.5	286	1971.9	330	2275.3
199	1372.0	243	1675.4	287	1978.8	331	2282.2
200	1378.9	244	1682.3	288	1985.7	332	2289.1
201	1385.8	245	1689.2	289	1992.6	333	2295.9
202	1392.7	246	1696.1	290	1999.5	334	2302.8
203	1399.6	247	1703.0	291	2006.4	335	2309.7
204	1406.5	248	1709.9	292	2013.3	336	2316.6
205	1413.4	249	1716.8	293	2020.2	337	2323.5
206	1420.3	250	1723.7	294	2027.1	338	2330.4
207	1427.2	251	1730.6	295	2034.0	339	2337.3
208	1434.1	252	1737.5	296	2040.8	240	2344.2
209	1441.0	253	1744.4	297	2047.7	341	2351.1
210	1447.9	254	1751.3	298	2054.6	342	2358.0
211	1454.8	255	1758.2	299	2061.5	343	2364.9
212	1461.7	256	1765.1	300	2068.4	344	2371.8
213	1468.7	257	1772.0	301	2075.3	345	2378.7
214	1475.5	258	1778.8	302	2082.2	346	2385.6
215	1482.4	259	1785.7	303	2089.1	347	2392.5